BASIC STATISTICS

FOR PSYCHOLOGISTS

palgrave
macmillan

First published 2011 by
PALGRAVE MACMILLAN

Palgrave Macmillan in the UK is an imprint of Macmillan Publishers Limited,
registered in England, company number 785998, of Houndmills, Basingstoke,
Hampshire RG21 6XS.

Palgrave Macmillan in the US is a division of St Martin's Press LLC,
175 Fifth Avenue, New York, NY 10010.

Palgrave Macmillan is the global academic imprint of the above companies
and has companies and representatives throughout the world.

Palgrave® and Macmillan® are registered trademarks in the United States,
the United Kingdom, Europe and other countries

ISBN 978-0-230-27542-3

This book is printed on paper suitable for recycling and made from fully
managed and sustained forest sources. Logging, pulping and manufacturing
processes are expected to conform to the environmental regulations of the
country of origin.

A catalogue record for this book is available from the British Library.

A catalog record for this book is available from the Library of Congress.

10   9   8   7   6   5   4   3   2   1
20   19   18   17   16   15   14   13   12   11

Printed in China

Table of contents

Detailed table of contents

Preface

In his book, *The Lady Tasting Tea*, David Salsburg describes a tea party in Cambridge in the late 1920s. The sun was shining and a group of university dons, their wives, and some guests were sitting around a table in the garden. During the conversation, one of the women remarked that tea tasted different depending upon whether the tea was poured into the milk or whether the milk was poured into the tea. A lively discussion followed. The men in particular couldn't believe the idea. After all, there was no difference in the chemistry of the mixture that could explain the effect. Still, the lady insisted she could tell the difference. The discussion went on for some time, until a thin, short man with thick glasses and a Van Dyke beard suddenly said, 'Why don't we test it?' And so they did. Preparations were made to present the lady with a sequence of cups of tea. In some the milk had been poured into the tea and in others the tea had been poured into the milk. The lady would simply be asked which type each cup of tea belonged to. If she could do so correctly, her point was proven. If not, the men were right. The first cup was brought. The lady sipped for a minute and declared that the milk had been poured into the tea. The man with the Van Dyke beard noted her response without comment and asked for the second cup to be given...

This anecdote illustrates why scientific psychology became so successful in the 20th century. Although most people think of themselves as experts in human behaviour, every time you ask them a question about psychology, you get different answers. In addition, quite often upon further testing the dominant opinion turns out to be wrong. So, we cannot rely on people's intuitions alone when we want to build a science of human behaviour. We need to confirm, and sometimes correct, these intuitions by careful observation and testing. The only way to know for sure whether tea tastes different depending on whether it is poured into the cup before or after the milk is to test many cups of tea. It is not to ask 'experts' what they think. Similarly, the only way to know whether violent video games increase aggressive behaviour, or whether people befriend or try to avoid colleagues who are doing better than them, is to place a number of people in the relevant conditions and to carefully observe their behaviour.

At the same time, the anecdote of the lady tasting tea illustrates another aspect of scientific psychology. It is not enough to observe and test, you must also know how to do it properly. How many cups does the lady have to identify correctly before we believe her? One cup would certainly not be enough, because then the chances are too high (one out of two) that the lady simply guessed and got it right. But how many cups of tea: two? three? four? five? ten? And what would we do if the lady made one single mistake? Would we then stop the experiment and conclude that there is no difference in taste at all? Or would we continue for some time, to see whether errors occur repeatedly, or whether it was just a one-off? Also, how will we make sure that the person who brings the tea does not betray the nature of the tea in a subtle – and often unconscious – way?

I do not want to spoil the story of the Cambridge lady by going into too much detail. (According to the witness who passed down the story, the lady tasted every single cup correctly.) The only point I want to make is that when psychologists set up a study to test one or another idea, they introduce much more knowledge and insight than most people imagine. It is not difficult to air opinions and to run badly designed studies; anybody can do that. However, when it comes to really furthering our understanding of the human mind, there is a clear difference between craftsmen and hobbyists, just as in any other profession.

You have the ambition to contribute to this science and to acquire the skills needed for good research (and to be able to distinguish good research from bad when it has been done by others). One of the first things you need to know then is how to analyse your data, so that you get an answer to the question you are asking. Inferior research usually betrays itself when, after the hard labour of data collection, the investigator discovers that the data cannot be analysed easily or can be explained in another, much less interesting, way. Good researchers know how they will process the data well before they start collecting them; and they have a clear idea of which traps they must avoid in the design of their study.

This book primarily deals with data analysis. I assume you have another course (book) on research methods, and I will only include as much as is necessary to understand statistics. I am well aware that very different people start psychology degrees. Some students have tried to avoid mathematically oriented courses ever since they finished primary school and they dread a statistics course, seeing it as the main obstacle to their degree. Other students have taken mathematical courses in their secondary education and don't like the idea of having to repeat everything they have learned (in a slightly different way). In between are the students for whom statistics is a new subject, but who look forward to it in confidence, and see it as another potentially interesting challenge in their quest for knowledge.

Because of the heterogeneity of students, I have divided the chapters of this book into three layers. In the first layer, I explain the basics of each statistical test and ask you to calculate elementary examples by hand. Even if you hate statistics (or think you do at this moment), this is the part you must know. I have tried to make it easy for you by keeping the formulas simple, by constantly referring to the intuitions you have and by giving the bones as much flesh as possible. In the second layer, I tell you how you can implement the topics we've covered on your own computer using the SPSS computer program, even if you have no prior experience of using this program. In this age of widespread access to computers, I always find it amazing that many textbooks still talk about statistics as if everything has to be calculated by hand. Though SPSS is most widely used by psychologists and other social scientists dealing with statistics, it is by no means the only option and if you are keen to explore further, I would recommend writing your own Excel file for drawing a histogram, or for calculating a t-test. The companion website to this book (www.palgrave.com/psychology/brysbaert) has a detailed guide on how to do statistical tests using Excel. Finally, in the last layer, I give some more demanding formulas, just in case you are one of these people who love a challenge of this type!

Before we embark, there is but one last piece of advice I can give you. Learning statistics is a bit like learning to swim. You will never acquire the necessary statistical skills by simply reading this (or any other) book. The only way to acquire those skills is to exercise them repeatedly, until you have them in your fingers. In the beginning, this will involve some effort (and it can be a bit tedious at times), but once you master the skills, they are quite easy and even fun to use. Think of this when you're a bit tired or afraid of the deep waters you find yourself in.

At present, we are seeing a major shift in the way statistics is taught in psychology. Up to a few years ago, students had to learn how to *calculate* the different test results, but nowadays they learn how to *use* a statistical computer package. Critics of the this approach sometimes call this the 'cookbook approach' ('Now do this, then click there, add a few variables, wait a few seconds, and …'). On the other hand, if you have a computer next to you, it is much more efficient to know how to use it properly than to know how to calculate a bunch of tests by hand. There is nothing wrong with learning to work with a widely used computer package such as SPSS, as long as you know what you are doing and you understand the meaning of the different numbers and terms. The purpose of this book is to give you this information. We will always start from simple, practical problems and then see step-by-step how they are solved. This will give you a firm basis to embark on the more complex designs and analyses that will be covered in more advanced courses.

The organisation of the book comprises three main areas. First, there is a short review of the different types of research we do in psychology and the statistics we are likely to calculate for them (Chapter 1). Then, we examine how the raw data of a study can be presented so that they are easy to understand. This involves plotting the data in a frequency distribution (Chapter 2), calculating a single value of central tendency that is representative for the entire distribution (Chapter 3), and calculating a measure that gives us an idea of the variability in the data (Chapter 4).

In the next eight chapters we go beyond our observed sample, and start to draw conclusions about the wider group to which the individuals belong (the population). First, we will discuss how knowledge of the central tendency and variability allows us to estimate the position of an individual within the population if we can assume that the population is normally distributed (Chapter 5). Then, we will see when we are allowed to assume a reliable difference between two groups of individuals, whether or not the distribution is normal (Chapters 6, 7 and 8), and when we can postulate a trustworthy difference between two scores from the same group of individuals (Chapters 9 and 10). In the two last chapters of this part (Chapters 11 and 12), we discuss how we can determine whether two variables are correlated.

The book ends with two chapters introducing designs that compare more than two conditions. First, we have a look at analysis of variance (ANOVA) (Chapter 13). We see how the different statistics are obtained and how they relate to the simpler tests discussed before. Then we describe how you can use post-hoc tests to get deeper insight into ANOVAs involving more than two conditions, and how you can use multiple regression analysis to analyse correlations between three and more variables (Chapter 14).

This book should provide you with a strong basis for statistical understanding, so that you can confidently run your own tests for simple designs with two different conditions, and that you have enough background knowledge to interpret the computer output of more complex designs. Finally, this book is accompanied by a website, www.palgrave.com/psychology/brysbaert, which includes a tour of the book, a number of exercises, and further information on using computer programs to carry out statistical tests.

Tour of book

Chapter questions and answers

Chapter questions lay out the structure of the chapter, and help you identify your learning goals.

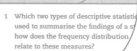

1 Which two types of descriptive statistic used to summarise the findings of a s how does the frequency distribution relate to these measures?

2 What is a frequency distribution How do you make a frequency at does the expression

At the end of each chapter, answers to these questions are provided for you to test your understanding.

The situation is show
This example shows
value of the median. Notice t
to calculate the exact mean be
sizes of 6 and more.

3.9 Answers to chapter qu

1 What is a measure of central t
A measure of central ten
a single score as represe
It is a value somewher
value and it represe
unimodal and sy

2 What is the mea

Performance checks and learning checks

Performance checks let you consolidate your understanding of a topic by running your own test.

Performance checks f

Does your frequency distribution

1 Does the table contain two co observed (X) and one for the f (f)?

2 For ordinal and interval/ratio s from the smallest value of X (to

3 For nominal scales: is the freq arbitraryl way for the different

4 For ordinal and interval/ratio all values of X between the zero frequency?

5 For nominal scales: d categories obtaine participants

Learning checks are short questions or exercises to help you revise key statistical concepts and theories: answers are provided at the end of the chapter.

7 Does the su

8 Does the group what the table is

Learning check for a grouped frequency distribution ta
To make sure that you fully understand grouped frequency distribution tables, make a table for the study in which we asked a sample of 20 students how many cups of coffee th drank the day before.

2.3 Frequency di

2.3.1 Making a f
ratio

Tips and 'Be careful'

Tips include tricks of the trade and useful reminders to make statistical tests as painless as possible.

samp
difference
be meaningfu

Tip When you are asked to interpret a t-statistic, remember that its meaning is similar to that of a z-score. A t-statistic close to 0 means that there is no evidence for a difference between the two groups. A t-statistic smaller than -2 or larger than $+2$ indicates that the evidence for a difference between the groups is becoming more reliable, certainly when the group sizes are reasonably large (N_1 and $N_2 \geq 30$).

enough, thou
Before w

Common pitfalls and problems – and how to avoid them – are highlighted in the 'Be careful' feature.

section, whe
the sum of posit
be zero ($\Sigma R_- = 0$). In
So, just like the Mann
test
great
in min
Ho
before
partic
F
the

Be careful! As for the Mann-Whitney U-statistic, you must remember that the smaller the Wilcoxon signed-rank statistic, the smaller is p. A statistic of $W = 0$ means significance (unless N is smaller than 6). This differs from the interpretation of the t-statistic and the χ^2 statistic!

Step by Step and Recap

The step by step sections provide a quick 'how to' for you to work through, and follow more detailed explanations of theories and tests.

gree with a
Because we have cove
section is a cookbook summ
the standard normal distributi

5.7.5 Step by step: determining p associated with a normal dis

Mr Wilcock obtained a score of 26 tion 12 (scores are normally distribu obtaining a lower score, the probab tile rank, and the percentile this sc

Step 1 Sketch the distribution
Mr Wilcock's score. Us
estimate of the diff

The recap sections offer short summaries of the material covered.

number of dots. Nou
a normal distribution. If
approximation to the norma

Recap | **The central limit theorem**
We have covered quite a bit of gro
summary. Thus far we have seen t

1 When we have a sample of size
standard error of $SD/\sqrt{N}$. This
the mean of the sample than i
the smaller the SE of the mea

2 Theoretically, we can expec
bution. This will always be
distribution (for example
distributed normally f
the approximation

In statistics, th

Using SPSS

Each chapter includes a detailed guide to using the SPSS software package in analysing your findings.

References to *SPSS for Psychologists* (4th edn) by Nicola Brace, Richard Kemp and Rosemary Snelgar (Palgrave Macmillan, 2009) are provided where more complex statistical tests are discussed.

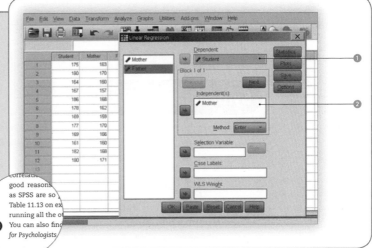

Going further

The **Going further** section at the end of most chapters provides a brief guide to more complex tests or a deeper explanation of some of the concepts covered.

Companion website

The website for this book contains a mine of information and material to help you get to grips with statistics.

There are multiple choice questions, additional SPSS exercises, and links to interesting and useful websites.

In addition, there is a detailed guide to carrying out statistical tests using Microsoft Excel instead of SPSS.

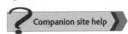

Symbols and abbreviations

α	alpha level of significance
η^2	percentage of variance explained in ANOVA
μ	population mean
ρ	Spearman rank correlation
σ	population standard deviation
χ^2	chi-square
Σ	sum
Σf	sum of frequencies
ANOVA	analysis of variance
d	effect size
df	degrees of freedom
f	frequency
F	F-statistic or F-test
M	sample mean
Mdn	median
MS	mean square (ANOVA)
MSe	mean square of error
N	sample size
p	probability
Q1	first quartile
Q3	third quartile
r	Pearson correlation coefficient
R^2	percentage of variance explained
SD	standard deviation
SE	standard error
SS	sum of squares (ANOVA)
t	t-statistic or t-test
U	Mann Whitney U-test
W	Wilcoxon signed-rank test
X	variable
z	standardised score

Using statistics in psychology research

1

?

1 What is a reliable study?
2 What is a valid study?
3 What is a case study?
4 What is the distinction between a population and a sample?
5 When is a sample representative?
6 What is a convenience sample?
7 What are the three types of descriptive research and what are their subdivisions?
8 What is correlational research?
9 What is the difference between a positive and a negative correlation?
10 What can we conclude from a correlation?
11 Why do psychologists run experiments?
12 What is the difference between an independent variable and a dependent variable?
13 Why is it important to control for confounding variables?
14 What are the three important limitations of experimental research in psychology?
15 What are descriptive statistics, and which ones do we need to calculate for each study?
16 What are inferential statistics, and why do we calculate them?
17 Why is the sampling error important?
18 Why is the scale of measurement important?
19 What are the different types of measurement scales?

Q

1.1 The need for reliable and valid empirical studies
1.2 The population and the sample
1.3 Different types of research in psychology
1.4 Which statistics should we calculate?
1.5 Answers to chapter questions

1.1   The need for reliable and valid empirical studies

Scientific research is based on careful observations. This statement may seem a platitude to you, but it is worth mentioning at the beginning of a chapter on research in psychology. All too often people are convinced that they do not need to see the empirical evidence before they can make up their mind about a phenomenon. They already 'know' the answer. Indeed, as a psychologist one cannot help but be amazed at how willing people are to make claims about issues of which they have very limited knowledge. Just ask a few people around you what they think of inclusive education (whether children with special educational needs should go to a regular school or would benefit more from a specialised school), about the prevalence of suicide among teenagers, about marriage between 70-year olds, about people living abroad, about abortion, or indeed about any other topic related to human behaviour. How many will tell you that they have no first-hand experience with any of these questions, that they would need to see the figures and the available empirical evidence before they can give you an answer? How many will spontaneously refer to such evidence?

As a matter of fact, nearly all writings about human psychology before the 20th century were based on the intuitions of the authors – either novelists or philosophers – without any empirical research. Indeed, the first psychologists had a hard time convincing their contemporaries that there was anything to be gained from the systematic observation of humans. Now, more than a century later, people are much more open to the various findings of psychologists (just look at the number of articles in newspapers and magazines), but they are still convinced that, if a psychologist's findings do not agree with their own intuitions, it is more likely that the psychologist is wrong than that they are. Again, surprisingly, very few feel the need to have a look at the actual evidence before they reach this conclusion. They just 'know'.

To some extent, it is inevitable that people are willing to express opinions about matters of which they have less than full knowledge. Just imagine trying to have a chat with somebody who is unwilling to say anything until they have scrutinised all the available evidence! This book is not meant to convince you that as a psychologist you must never make a statement without proper scientific foundation in your everyday life. However, it is good to keep in mind that not all our current convictions will stand the test of reality, and that a properly conducted scientific study based on careful, unbiased observations is the best way we have to discriminate right from wrong. At the same time, we must not forget that a badly run scientific study can also send out a powerful, but wrong, message if it gets into the media. Therefore, we need to be able to judge for ourselves whether or not we can rely on the evidence that has been gathered.

Two characteristics determine the quality of a study: reliability and validity. **Reliability** is the degree to which the same finding will be observed in a replication of the study. If, in a certain study, a difference in performance was found between males and females, then we expect the same gender difference to appear in the next study on that topic. Otherwise, the data are not reliable.

A good analogy for experimental reliability comes from bathroom scales. If you step on the scales and get a certain weight, you expect to obtain more or less the same weight if you step off and back on again. If the new weight were 2 kg higher or lower than the first one, you would be quite annoyed, and most likely conclude that your scales are useless (unreliable). Because of the need for reliability, researchers often repeat their experiments, or those of others when the data have major consequences, to make sure that the finding is reliable.

The **validity** of a study is the degree to which the study accurately addresses the topic it claims to measure; that is, whether there could be an explanation of the finding other than the one that the authors of the study propose. This is often a matter of hot debate among researchers. Many findings can have multiple origins, with some authors defending one interpretation and other authors defending another. For instance, in a large-scale study on army recruits in the Netherlands, Belmont and Marolla (1973) found that first-born children had higher intelligence scores, as measured with an IQ test, than second-born children, who in turn had higher intelligence scores than third-born children, and so on. Ever since the publication of this study, researchers have addressed the reliability of the finding and the validity of the birth-order explanation. Is birth-order the determining factor, or is the effect due to some other factor associated with birth-order, such as the socio-economic status of the parents?

1.2 The population and the sample

Sometimes researchers are interested in a single person, for instance when someone presents interesting characteristics or when he or she needs a full assessment for further treatment. Then, researchers will run a so-called **case study**. A very famous example of a case study is that of H.M. He was a young man who suffered from untreatable epilepsy and underwent an operation in 1953 to remove the source of the uncontrolled discharges of electricity in his brain. This included the hippocampus on both sides of the brain. Although the operation was successful in terms of the epilepsy treatment, it left H.M. with an unexpected and severely debilitating side-effect: he could no longer remember new material. He could retain new information for a few seconds, but then forgot it. Apparently, he was no longer able to transfer information from a short-term memory store to a more permanent memory system. This finding has been extremely important in psychologists' theorising about the functioning of the human memory and, consequently, H.M. was studied by an estimated total of 100 investigators in the 55 years between the operation and his death in 2008. (See Corkin, 2002, for a review.) Similar well-known case studies exist for many other disorders in the neuropsychological literature.

Most of the time, however, psychologists want to make statements about 'humans in general' or at least about larger groups of people. For such research, they need to study more than one person because many human characteristics show rather large differences between individuals. Suppose, for instance, we want to know how tall university students are. It is not a good idea to base this estimate on the height of a single student, who was picked out at random from the university enrolment lists. In that case, our estimate could be anything between less than 150 cm to more than 200 cm, which would give us a very crude idea of the real situation. A better strategy is to measure a large group of students, so that we get a more complete picture, both of the average height and of the inter-individual differences that exist.

In the best of all worlds, we would have access to the height of each and every student so that our information is complete. However, such full knowledge is rarely necessary. Although it is clear that our estimate should not be based on a single observation, intuitively we feel that very little extra information would be gained from measuring one million students rather than one thousand. The distribution of heights based on one thousand students would look very similar to the distribution of heights based on one million students. In both cases, we would find few observations below 150 cm and above 195 cm, and many observations in the range from 160 to 185 cm. So, it is not necessary to measure the entire group of students whose height we wish to know; a sufficiently large subgroup will suffice. We call the entire group of people about whom we want to make a statement (that is, all university students in our example) the **population**. The subgroup of persons, who actually take part in the research, is called the **sample**.

In psychology we study a sample of people in order to make claims about the population. Two issues are important in the selection of an adequate sample:

- ☐ How large must the sample be?
- ☐ How can we be sure that the sample gives us an adequate picture of the population?

For the **size** of the sample, the basic rule of thumb is that, the more detailed the answer has to be, the larger the sample must be. For instance, suppose a Martian wants to know whether humans are fully-grown at the age of 3 years. To find out, it comes to Earth and starts to measure 3-year-old humans and 21-year-olds. It would probably take only two or three observations in each group before the Martian realised that humans are not yet fully grown at the age of 3. So, for this question – where the difference between the groups is very large in relation to the variability within each group – very small sample sizes will do. However, suppose the Martian wants to know whether humans are fully-grown at the age of 16. Answering this question requires considerably larger samples. (What do you think? Do humans still grow after the age of 16? How could you find out?[1]) Similarly, if we wanted to have a rough idea of what professors do at a university, observation of a few specimens would be enough. Even a case study would provide us with a lot of information. However, if we wanted a very precise estimate of the time that professors spend on various activities (such as lecturing, doing research, talking to colleagues and so on) and the variability in those measures, we would need many observations of many different professors. In the following chapters you will learn the smallest sample that is needed for

---

1 According to American growth charts, on average, boys grow 3.5 cm after the age of 16, and girls 1 cm.

different types of research and different types of questions. This will be called the power of the design and we will see that it is a function of the expected effect size (that is, the magnitude of the effect you are looking for).

Because a sample is smaller than the population, there is always a risk that the sample does not give an adequate picture of the population. This risk depends to some extent on the size of the sample, but also on the way in which the sample has been drawn. Suppose we want to know the average height of a university student in Europe. It is not a good idea to test only students from one country, not even if we measure thousands of them. People in the Netherlands, for example, are among the tallest in the world. Their average height is some 7 cm greater than that of people in the UK, Germany, or France. Similarly, if we want to know the height of students, we must include both males and females, as boys grow some 14 cm taller than girls. In other words, if we want to gener-alise from the sample we test to a population, we must ensure that the sample is **representative** of the population. That is, we must ensure that the sample is approximately the same as the population in every important respect. There are several techniques to achieve this, which will not be discussed here as they should be part of your research methods course.

However, you should always be aware that a fully representative sample is rarely achieved. Most of the time practical considerations lead to a less-than-optimal sample, because the individuals that are easiest to reach have the highest chances of being included in the sample. The vast majority of psychol-ogy research is done by scientists at universities in Europe and America, which means that Western psychology undergraduates have the highest chance of being participants in a psychological study. These samples are not representative of the population of humans in general, but are **convenience samples** that are, at best, representative of highly-educated people in the Western world. Generalisa-tion to all humans then requires the assumption that highly-educated people in the Western world behave in the same way as all other humans. (It is, perhaps, unfair to suggest that many researchers don't care whether their findings have any bearing beyond the group of Western university students to which they have easy access – and to which they themselves belong.)

1.3 Different types of research in psychology

1.3.1 Systematic observation

The first way to collect information about a phenomenon is to observe it care-fully and to take notes about these observations. For instance, much of what we know about the life of animals has been gathered by watching their behaviour over long periods of time, preferentially in their natural habitat, but occasionally also in captivity. Similarly, much has been learnt about the social life of isolated groups of people – whether these be illiterate tribes in forests or university students on campuses – by systematic observation.

Observations can take place in real life, when the observer watches the daily behaviour of the participants. This is called naturalistic observation.

Alternatively, they can be based on some sort of end product, when the observer goes through the records on a particular topic. This is called archive research.

There are two things that can go wrong with naturalistic observations if researchers are not careful. First, humans (and animals) have a tendency to behave differently when they are being watched, even if they are told that the observer will never interfere. Many people will increase the behaviour they perceive as socially desirable, and decrease the behaviour they see as undesirable. Many are also more stressed in the presence of an observer than when they are on their own, which may show up in their behaviour. This problem of reactivity can be reduced either by hidden observations or by staying with the participants for a prolonged period of time. In the first case, precautions are taken to ensure that the study object is not aware of the presence of the observer (for example, through the use of hidden cameras). This is a particularly useful solution for the observation of animals, but with humans it is usually unacceptable on ethical grounds. The other solution is to continue the observations for a long period of time (for example, the observer lives on the campus for a year). Reactive behaviours are most common in the beginning of the observation. After a period of time, the subjects tend to forget that they are being watched and have an increased tendency to show their habitual behaviours (although this tendency may not be complete).

A second problem with naturalistic observations is that usually much more happens than the observer can record. So, there is a danger of biased observations (and notes taken afterwards). Possible solutions are:

1 to work with a predetermined coding scheme which is followed strictly, and
2 to videotape the most important occasions, or at least to take pictures, so that others can confirm the observations.

The early anthropological studies on emotion (see Ekman, 1998) provide a nice example of how wrong things can go without such safeguards. In 1872, Darwin published a book in which he claimed that the expression of emotions was the same in all of the then-known human cultures. For instance, happiness was communicated everywhere with a smile. On the basis of information from an extended network of correspondents, Darwin concluded that the expression of basic emotions such as happiness was innate, the product of an evolutionary selection process. This nativistic view, however, was strongly attacked by the behaviourists of the first half of the 20th century. In their view, all behaviour was learned through social interactions. They referred to a book by Birdwhistell, in which he stated that, on the basis of his research with isolated tribes, he had come to the conclusion that the expression of emotions was culture-specific rather than universal. In the 1950s, the young clinical psychologist Ekman became interested in this topic. He was studying the non-verbal behaviour of clients taking part in psychotherapy, and he wanted to know the range of individual differences in this behaviour. Ekman asked Birdwhistell for a meeting. Being trained as an experimental psychologist, Ekman hoped he would be shown files full of detailed notes, drawings, pictures and possibly films of expressions in the different tribes. However, when Ekman asked to see these documents, Birdwhistell was very surprised. There were no such documents. Everything Birdwhistell had seen and heard was safely stored in his brain! This was the beginning of Ekman's quest for a scientific investigation of the cross-cultural expression of emotions (in which he largely confirmed Darwin's original findings).

It is not always necessary to observe humans in their everyday life. Many questions can be answered by analysing the traces people leave behind in the many files and records – **archives** – that are kept nowadays. For instance, the research by Belmont and Marolla (1973) was based on the detailed records the Dutch army kept about its recruits. Similarly, we can study a language by analysing large collections of written and spoken text. Or we can examine how people interact on the internet by going through the records of their chat sessions. (Psychologists also sometimes take part in these sessions as part of a naturalistic observation.) Such searches are particularly interesting if you have a precise idea of what you are looking for. Otherwise, there is a high chance that you will drown in the vast amounts of data. A big advantage of archive research is that your conclusions can easily be verified by other people.

1.3.2 Interviews

Another way of collecting information about people is to speak to them. Many people are willing to answer questions, even on rather sensitive issues (although their answers may not always be complete or accurate). Interviews are usually quicker than naturalistic observations, and are not limited to overt (that is, perceptible) behaviours. We can ask people questions about their thoughts, attitudes, opinions or feelings.

There are two types of interview: structured and unstructured. In a structured interview all participants answer the same list of questions to ensure that comparable data are obtained from everyone. In an unstructured interview, interviewees are asked to respond to broad, open-ended questions that partly depend on the course of the conversation. Many inexperienced psychologists prefer unstructured interviews because these seem to offer more freedom to the interviewer. However, research (for example, on job interviews) has shown that unstructured interviews usually result in less valid data than structured interviews. For instance, it has repeatedly been found that participants who make a positive first impression on the interviewer get more sympathetic questions, to which they can answer positively, than participants who make a negative first impression (for example, Dougherty et al., 1994). There is, therefore, a risk that an unstructured interview does nothing more than confirm the bias created by the interviewee's initial impression on the interviewer. This is less of a problem with structured interviews in which all candidates have to respond to the same list of questions.

1.3.3 Surveys

A survey is a reasonably large-scale series of self-report measures (usually questionnaires, sometimes interviews) which is designed to give an accurate estimate of the behaviours, attitudes, beliefs, opinions or intentions of a large group of people (for example, all the inhabitants of a country or a continent). The quality of survey data is a function of many factors. One factor is the quality of the questions that are asked. When the questions are not clear, or stated in ambiguous terms, it is difficult to interpret the answers. Quite often this aspect of design is underestimated in survey research, certainly when a comparison is made between different groups of individuals. For instance, in a worldwide survey of car drivers (Leaseplan, 2002), respondents were asked: 'Have you ever behaved aggressively to other drivers?' The answers to this question were quite surprising – the top country on the aggressiveness score was Norway (62% Yes) and the bottom country was India (40% Yes). This was unexpected because the roads in Norway are generally considered to be among the safest in the world. (The mortality rate for road traffic accidents in Norway is 7/100,000, compared with 29/100,000 in India.) The most likely interpretation of this finding (as admitted in the survey report) was that the Norwegian respondents used a more sensitive criterion for 'aggressive behaviour' than the Indian respondents: The same behaviour was perceived as aggressive by more Norwegians than Indians.

Another factor that is likely to have an impact on the results of a survey is the group of people questioned. Surveys are usually presented (certainly in newspapers and magazines) as if they were based on a sample of respondents that is completely representative of the population. However, a closer look at the survey report often reveals that the selection criteria favoured some groups more than others. For example, most answers in the Leaseplan 2002 survey were provided by users of leased company cars. The same is true for many other surveys. This need not be a bad thing, except when the media start to cite the study and forget to mention this limitation.

Box 1.1 is an example of how the ambiguous nature of survey questions and the characteristics of the sample can lead to quite divergent answers to a simple and straightforward question.

Box 1.1   How often do couples have sex? Three times a week or twice a month?

An interesting aspect of surveys is that, if participants are guaranteed anonymity, they are willing to give answers to questions that are rarely touched upon in every-day conversations. One of these topics is human sexuality. Information about sexual behaviour is difficult to obtain because sex usually happens in private, and many people do not like to talk about it, even to their friends. So, for a long time very little was known about even the simplest sexual issues, such as how often married couples make love. The first real answer to this question came from a survey conducted by Alfred Kinsey and his associates at Indiana University in the 1940s. Its results constituted the two-volume Kinsey report, *Sexual Behavior in the Human Male* (Kinsey et al., 1948) and *Sexual Behavior in the Human Female* (Kinsey et al., 1953), for which more than 5300 white American males and 5900 white American females had been interviewed.

The Kinsey report caused quite a stir, mainly because participants reported much greater frequency and variety of sex than had been expected. When Kinsey asked married couples how often they had sexual intercourse, they reported an average of

▷

about three times a week if they were in their 20s. This number dropped steadily to about once a week for participants of 50 years and older. Later surveys found slightly higher frequencies, which were attributed to the availability of the birth control pill and greater openness toward sexual behaviour in the 1960s.

A recent survey on the topic again seemed to confirm these numbers. The *2003 Global Survey* by Durex, based on 'more than 150,000 lovers worldwide' revealed that 'people have sex an average of 127 times a year', going from 135 times a year for the 25–34-year old age group to 122 times a year for the 35–44-year old group.

However, a completely different number emerged from a survey at the University of Brussels (Glorieux et al., 2002). In this study, 1500 participants were asked to keep a detailed and anonymous diary of everything they did in a period of one week. When the researchers analysed the diaries for the frequency of intercourse, they obtained averages of a mere .43 per week for the 16–34-year old age group, .51 for the 35–54-year old age group, and .12 for the age group of more than 55 years. [The Durex (2003) average for Belgium was 136 per year or 2.6 per week.] In particular, for families with children and for double-income couples, intercourse was largely confined to two weekends per month.

A closer look at both studies may give us some clues about why the estimates are so different. For a start, the Durex (2003) survey appears to be based on internet surfers who visited the Durex website. As this website predominantly provides information about condoms, it may have attracted a sample that is more interested in sex than the population in general. A second difference is that the Durex survey asked about the frequency of sex, without further detailing what was meant. For many respondents, this will have included masturbation and paid or unpaid extra-marital sex. Also, the respondents may have overlooked the days of menstruation, during which intercourse is more limited. On the other hand, the diary survey of the University of Brussels may have underestimated the actual number, because participants may have failed to mention short episodes immediately before sleeping (on weekdays making love was limited to episodes of some 17 minutes, whereas these episodes lasted 45 minutes on average at the weekend). Participants may also have changed their behaviour in the week they were monitoring themselves, and they may have been reluctant to mention taboo episodes such as extramarital sex.

For these reasons, the Durex survey is likely to provide us with the upper limit of the 'true' number and the University of Brussels survey probably gives us the lower limit. A cynic might conclude from these findings that, although the estimates do not cover the whole range of theoretical possibilities (which can vary from many times a day to a few times in the entire fertile age), they do not restrict the range of common sense estimates a great deal. This certainly seems to be a modest conclusion after 50 years of survey research on the frequency of sexual intercourse in married couples, and it falls a long way short of the promised insight into the dark corners of human sexuality. Maybe the next survey will provide us with a more decisive answer.

1.3.4 Calculating correlations between variables

The main aim of psychology research is to get an accurate description of what is going on in humans. Although this is an essential step in the scientific study of people (and, as shown, by no means a simple task), it is not the most creative or challenging part of research. Data collection only returns a static picture of the reality, a pure description of what is there. Each condition or characteristic is described in isolation, without considering the possible relationships between the different observations or measurements. This falls short of a true understanding of the phenomena we are examining because it is not enough to know what is there. We also need to know why it is the way it is. Why are some people taller than others? Why is each generation in Western society on average 4 cm taller than the previous generation? Why are people behaving aggressively on the road? Why do couples have more sex than is necessary for procreation?

For a long time it was thought that we could find the answers to these questions simply by relying on the researcher's intuitions or by asking the participants why they performed the actions we observed. However, it has become clear that people do not always know the origins of their actions and, when they are pressed to give us answers, they often come up with invalid reasons.

An alternative approach is to look for correlations in the data we have collected. A **correlation** refers to the extent to which two conditions or characteristics are associated. Correlations (and all other statistics) can only be calculated for conditions and characteristics that change and, thus, assume different values (which is the case for the vast majority of conditions and characteristics in the world). Such conditions or characteristics are called **variables**. For example, many forms of aggressive behaviour – antisocial behaviour towards spouses, parents or colleagues; vandalism; stealing; threatening neighbours; fines and convictions related to aggressive behaviour; traffic accidents; a preference for watching violent movies – can assume different values for different individuals (from totally absent to strongly present). These are all variables describing characteristics of aggressive behaviour.

Suppose now that we had a database with many different aggression measurements for a large group of people. In that case, it might be extremely informative to know whether people who are aggressive car drivers also score high on the other measures of aggression, and whether people who are not aggressive drivers have low scores on the other measures as well. If such a correlation existed, then we could (i) use the other scores to predict road rage, and (ii) try to find an explanation for why people who score high on other types of aggressive behaviour also score high on road rage. Alternatively, if we found no relationship between aggressiveness as a car driver and the other measures of aggression, then (i) we would know that we cannot use a general measure of aggressiveness to predict aggression on the road, and (ii) we would have to find an explanation for why individuals who are aggressive car drivers are not more aggressive in other situations than individuals who are less aggressive drivers. We might also want to consider whether car drivers tend to be less aggressive in countries with heavy penalties for traffic offences than in countries with less severe penalties. This correlation could give us another clue about what determines aggressiveness on the road.

Two important things must be said about correlations. First, there exist positive and negative correlations. A positive correlation occurs when two variables change together in the same direction. For example, height and weight are positively correlated (in general, taller people are heavier), as are the height of the parents and the height of the offspring (short parents tend to have short children; tall parents tend to have tall children), and the height of children and their intelligence score (tall children tend to be more intelligent than small children). A negative correlation means that as one variable increases the other decreases. There is a negative correlation between the number of cigarettes smoked and the life span in years (the more cigarettes smoked, the less years on average to live), between marital satisfaction and the number of children (adults who score high on marital satisfaction tend to have fewer children than those who score low), and between depression and quality of life ratings (the more depressed people are, the less highly they rate the quality of their life). In everyday life, people perceive positive correlations more easily than negative correlations. Positive correlation seems to agree more with our intuitions that two correlated variables should change in the same direction: if one increases the other must increase as well, if one decreases the other is also expected to decrease. For instance, if you ask people to list the variables that predict rainfall the next day, most of these variables will be based on positive correlations ('If X is present, then the chances of rain are higher'). Very few, if any, will refer to negative correlations ('It is more likely to rain, when X is absent').

The second caveat about correlations is that, without further information, a correlation between two variables cannot be interpreted as a causal relationship. This is one of the biggest fallacies in human reasoning. As soon as we perceive a correlation between two variables, we feel the urge to see one variable as the cause of the other. So, if we are told that there is a negative correlation between the severity of penalties and the degree of aggressiveness on the road, we almost automatically translate this into a statement like: 'When a country introduces high fines and long jail sentences, people will drive less aggressively.' In this sentence the penalties are the *cause* of the decrease in traffic aggression. (Think back. Did you do this spontaneously for the examples of positive and negative correlations given above? And did some of these examples cause you problems?) However, an alternative – and equally valid – interpretation could be that 'In countries where people are less aggressive in traffic, they impose heavy penalties on those who do drive aggressively.' In this sentence, the degree of aggressiveness is the cause of the heaviness of penalties. Or the negative correlation between aggressive driving and the severity of penalties could be interpreted in a third way – namely that some underlying psychological trait (for example, carefulness or compassion for pedestrians) is the origin of both courteous driving and high penalties for traffic offences. If the second or the third interpretation is right, then increasing penalties in an attempt to curb traffic offences will be of no help, because the penalties are not the factor that determine aggression on the road.

To further remedy your bias to automatically interpret a correlation as a cause–consequence pair, here are some more examples of correlations that have a less straightforward interpretation. First, there is a strong positive correlation between the number of churches in a town and the number of crimes committed in that town (the more churches, the more crimes). Second, there is a positive correlation between the weight and the average income of female employees (the heavier the woman, the higher her income). And third, there is a very strong correlation between the number of ice creams sold at the beach in one day and the number of people that must be saved from drowning (the more people must be saved, the more ice creams are sold). Can you come up with a sensible explanation for each of these situations?[2]

In summary, a correlation tells us something about the coherence of variables. This allows us to better predict phenomena (for example, you can make a better prediction of the height of a person if you know the height of his/her father and mother than if you do not know these heights) and it gives us a clue to the next stage of the investigation. However, the correlation itself does not provide us with information about how to interpret the association. So, although we know that studies consistently show a negative correlation between marital satisfaction and the number of children (Twenge et al., 2003), we do not know the cause of this correlation. Although many of us may be tempted to interpret it as meaning that having children decreases (is the cause of) marital satisfaction, other possible interpretations are:

1 couples with less marital satisfaction have a higher need for children;
2 couples without children need a high degree of marital satisfaction to stay together, otherwise they divorce (and are not included in the samples tested);
3 couples without children rate their marital satisfaction higher than couples with children, although in reality there is no perceptible difference; or
4 people who have an interesting job are more satisfied with their marriage and feel less need for children.

Nothing in the correlation itself allows us to make a choice among these (and many other) possible explanations. That information has to come from other sources, if possible from an experimental study.

1.3.5 Running experiments

The surest way to find out whether a variable is the cause of a phenomenon is to run an experiment in which this variable is manipulated and the effects of the manipulation are examined. If the variable is the cause we are looking for, then changing it should have an effect. So, the best way to find out whether the severity of penalties has an effect on traffic aggression is to increase or decrease the penalties and to look at the consequences. If an increase in the fine has no effect on the aggression, then this is quite strong evidence that the severity of the penalties has nothing to do with the degree of road rage. In contrast, if an increase in the fine is followed immediately by a decrease of aggression, then we have good reason to argue that the severity of penalties is a determining factor of people's behaviour on the road. And we would be even more sure about our interpretation if after a year we decreased the penalties and saw the aggression bounce back to its original level.

2 The bigger the town, the more churches it is likely to have and the more inhabitants who might commit crimes (London has more churches than Camberley, and it also has a higher number of crimes). Junior employees usually earn less than more experienced employees; most women gain over 10 kilograms between the age of 20 and the age of 60; hence the positive correlation between weight and income. Finally, on hot days a lot of people go to the sea; they are likely to eat ice creams and bathe in the sea. On cold days, very few people eat ice cream at the beach or go into the sea.

Non-scientists often underestimate the charm and the power of a good experiment. Basically a researcher is saying, 'If I am right and I do this, then that will happen. If it does not happen, then I am wrong.' This is nothing less than a contest between brain and reality (which explains the joy and pride researchers feel when they are proven right, and their frustration when the experiment does not work out the way they had hoped). In my career I've seen many examples of how powerful experiments can be. One in particular stands out, because it involved someone who did not really believe in the need to test his ideas. For one of my studies on sentence reading, I needed filler sentences to obscure the manipulation. Instead of taking uninformative sentences, I asked colleagues from the Department of Linguistics whether they wanted to have some of their ideas tested. (Normally, linguists do not test their ideas empirically; they only look at the coherence and the persuasiveness of their theories of language processing.) One of the linguists decided to take up the challenge and gave me some sentences. They were of two types and he was 100% sure that one type would be more difficult to understand than the other. (I asked not to be told which sentences would be more difficult, so that I would not be biased in my experimenting.) I presented these sentences, together with many others, to a group of students and monitored their eye movements while they were reading so that I had a precise measure of how long they needed to read each sentence, and where in the sentence they experienced difficulties. When I analysed the data, I observed that the first type of sentence required more time to read than the second type, and so I told the linguist, who had already started to nod: 'Yes, yes, I told you so, didn't I?' Then suddenly he froze: 'Wait a minute', he said, 'did you say that the FIRST type of sentences was more difficult than the second? I had predicted that they would be EASIER!' Slowly but surely I saw the self-confidence (which had been very close to arrogance) shrink. This was no longer a game. In fact, this was the end of his theory. He had to start all over again.

Although experiments are the strongest technique we have for finding out whether a variable is the cause of a phenomenon, it is important to appreciate their limitations as well, certainly in psychological research. For a start, we cannot manipulate each and every independent variable at our own discretion. The **independent variable** is the variable which we suspect is an underlying causal factor, and which we would like to manipulate in our experiment. Some independent variables are easy to manipulate. Suppose, for instance, that on the basis of previous research, I have come to think that students study statistics better in pairs than alone. It is not difficult to design an experiment in which students have to learn some statistical test alone or with someone else. In addition, I can assign each participant randomly to one or the other condition. However, suppose I think that having children is the cause of decreased marital satisfaction in couples. In this case, I cannot force some couples to have children and deny others in order to see whether that manipulation has the expected effect. For this type of question, I cannot really manipulate my independent variable. The only thing I can do is compare two existing groups of couples (those with and without children) and make sure that there are no other variables correlated with this selection (for example, years of marriage, work satisfaction and so on) that could explain the difference between the groups. The latter, however, is extremely difficult to achieve (see 'confounding variables' below).

A second limitation of experiments is that each involves choices. First, we have to decide how to manipulate the independent variable (How will the severity of the penalties for traffic offences be manipulated? Extra fines? Jail sentences? For which offences? And how will these penalties be imposed?). Then, we have to decide how we will measure the effect of the manipulation. It is not enough to say that it will decrease aggressiveness on the roads; we have to decide how we will measure 'aggressiveness on the roads' (Number of accidents registered? A survey among the population about their road rage? Independent observers taking notes at a number of black spots?). In other words, we have to define our dependent variable(s). The **dependent variable** is the variable that we measure in our research to see whether the manipulation of the independent variable has an effect. If you are not sure which is the dependent variable of an experiment, ask yourself: 'At the end of the experiment, the participant left some numbers for the experimenter to analyse. What were they measuring?'

For many new researchers, the need to select the independent and dependent variables is a frustrating experience. They want to answer the big questions and each selection seems to limit the scope of their experiment. By the time they have defined their independent variables and their dependent variables, the experiment looks much less impressive than the study they initially had in mind. Suppose they began with the question: 'Does watching violence on television cause an increase in aggressive behaviour in society?' They then find themselves confronted with the questions: 'How do I manipulate the exposure to violence on television in my experiment?' and 'How will I measure the degree of aggressive behaviour in my experiment?' The solutions to these problems seriously reduce the initial range of possibilities. For example, 'exposure to violence' may be translated into asking one group of youngsters to watch a particular violent movie and asking another group to watch another non-violent movie, and 'degree of aggressive behaviour' might be the number of offences committed by each participant in a subsequent game of football. In making these initial decisions, the researchers have already limited the age range of interest and, possibly, the gender and/or fitness levels of the participants. New researchers soon start to realise that their selection can be criticised because they may not have chosen the best possible alternatives. The fact that each experiment involves choices is also the reason why a single experiment rarely settles an issue. What is needed is a whole series of experiments manipulating and measuring different aspects of the same phenomenon, and all yielding converging evidence about the processes involved.

A final limitation of experiments is that they never provide us with 100% certain conclusions. This is an inherent limitation of behavioural research. Even when our manipulation of the independent variable induces a large change in our dependent variable as predicted, there is still a small possibility that in reality our finding was due to chance fluctuations, or that our effect was caused by a variable that correlated with the independent variable and that we failed to control. In experiments, we always try to keep everything constant, except for the independent variable that we manipulate (and whose effect interests us). However, in many psychological designs it is impossible (and undesirable) to achieve full control over 'everything else'. There is always a risk that the effect we obtained was not due to the independent variable we manipulated but to a **confounding variable** – a variable that correlated with the independent variable. Alternatively, not finding an effect of our manipulation does not necessarily imply that our independent variable is without influence on our dependent variable. Maybe our manipulation of the independent variable was poor? Or we selected the wrong dependent variable? Or the effect was too small to be perceived in our experiment? The last factor is the main reason why many psychology students fail to find an effect in their first experiments. They all believe that the effects they are investigating are so large that a significant effect will be found in each and every study. More formally, they seriously overestimate the power of their experiment. We will return to this topic in all the chapters where we describe the statistical procedures for the different types of research.

1.4 Which statistics should we calculate?

1.4.1 Descriptive statistics

For each study we run – whether it is an observation, an interview, a survey, a correlational study or an experiment – we will want to have an adequate description of the main findings we obtained. For the general public, this 'adequate description' consists of some average value ('How many car drivers say they have behaved aggressively towards other drivers in the last year?', 'How often do couples have intercourse?').

However, for you as a scientist, the average value is not enough. You must insist on having additional information about the variability in the data, because knowledge about the variability, in addition to knowledge about the average value, allows you to have a very precise idea of what each and every observation means. If you have access to the average value only, your conclusions are limited to assessing whether an individual is above or below the average. Knowledge of the variability allows you to conclude whether the individual is within the normal range (where a lot of other individuals are) or whether her/his value is so extreme that it falls beyond the usual range.

For instance, the information that a child has achieved 20/40 on a certain test does not tell you much. You know more when you hear that the average score on the test was 28/40, because now you know that the child did worse than average. However, the average does not yet allow you to assess whether the child did much worse than the other children, or only slightly worse. To do so, you need access to the variability in the data. For instance, the situation if 95% of the children performed between 24/40 and 34/40 is very different from the situation if 95% of the children performed between 12/40 and 40/40. In the former case, you know that this particular child performed very badly (and hence may require extra support), whereas in the latter case you know that the child did not perform brilliantly, but still was within the range of his/her peers.

More formally, for all the studies we run, we need to organise and summarise our data. To do so, we will use **descriptive statistics** – statistical procedures to summarise, organise, and simplify the data. Descriptive statistics comprise a measure of central tendency to get an idea of the average, typical value and a measure of variability to indicate how strong the deviation from the central tendency is (for example, from which values do we have to start to worry?). A typical example of the use of descriptive statistics is presented in Box 1.2.

1.4.2 Inferential statistics

For many studies, we want more than just a summary of what was found – more than the descriptive statistics of central tendency and variability. We want to draw conclusions that go beyond the specific sample tested. Specifically, we want to know to what extent we can generalise our findings to the population from which the sample was drawn. For instance, in Box 1.2, we see that health-care professionals use growth charts to check whether a child is growing well. How can they be sure that these charts represent an adequate picture of reality – the population of all babies that are born? Would you as a doctor trust such a growth chart if it were based on a sample of 10 children? Probably not, because you cannot get a complete picture of all possible weights on the basis of 10 observations only. In addition, one slightly deviating score – one girl with a birth weight of 2.5 kg – would seriously distort the estimates. How many babies would you need to give an adequate picture? 100? 1000? 100,000? Several millions?

We use **inferential statistics** to assess the reliability of our sample data. These are techniques that allow us to generalise the results from our study sample to the population. Inferential statistics are needed because the descriptive statistics we obtain in a study are likely to vary to some extent from sample to sample. This is called the sampling error, the amount of error that exists between a sample estimate (the descriptive *statistic*) and the corresponding population *parameter*. As we will see in Chapter 6, the variability of the sample statistics (the sampling error) is larger for small samples than for large samples. Therefore, doctors feel safer about growth charts based on 10,000 babies than about growth charts based on 100 children. They consider that, if another sample of 10,000 babies were taken, the resulting growth chart would not really differ from the chart based on the original 10,000 babies. This would probably not be the case if a new sample of 100 babies were taken and compared to the original group of 100 babies. (Sometimes growth charts are based on 100 babies, for instance when we are dealing with a rare condition, such as dwarfism. Doctors know that these growth charts only give a rough picture, but they are better than nothing.)

Inferential statistics serve two purposes. First, they allow us to draw confidence intervals around the sample estimates. They tell us the range of uncertainty around a sample statistic such as the average value. This information is sometimes included when the results of a survey are communicated. After a survey about voting intentions, we get information as follows: 'According to our survey, 32% of the voters intend to vote for the Conservative party, with an uncertainty margin of 2%.' This statement means that, if there were a general

Box 1.2   Is my baby growing well? The use of descriptive statistics

When a child is born, one of the first questions parents and doctors ask is: 'Is everything okay with the baby?' So a newborn is virtually immediately submitted to a series of measurements. In large parts of the world, it has to pass its first 'test' within minutes after birth. In particular, the APGAR score is calculated – Activity, Pulse, Grimace, Appearance, and Respiration – to know whether resuscitation measures are needed. The two other body measures everyone wants to know are the length and the weight of the baby. For these measures (as well as the head circumference), there is even close follow-up in the first months after birth. Is the baby growing well?

To answer this question, doctors need to know two figures: the typical development pattern and the degree of deviation that is acceptable. For instance, they need to know that the average birth weight of a girl at 1 month is 4.2 kg (see Figure 1.1) and that all weights between 3.2 kg and 5.5 kg are 'acceptable'.[3] Thus, every parent with a female child between 3.2 kg and 5.5 kg will be told that everything is fine. Babies with a higher or lower weight will get a number of extra screenings, to find out whether something is wrong. Past records show that only 2% of girls weigh less than 3.2 kg at 1 month and only 2% of girls weigh more than 5.5 kg. The records also show that babies with extremely high or low weights often have health problems which need special attention.

The weight of the baby will be monitored throughout childhood, not to check whether the weight exactly follows the average value but to check whether it stays 'within reasonable limits'. Notice that 'within reasonable limits' includes both the central tendency (the average value) and the variability observed in the data. Also notice in Figure 1.1 that as the weight increases so does the variability. The range of acceptable weights is considerably larger for 1-year olds (7.0 kg–11.4 kg) than for 1-month olds (3.2 kg–5.5 kg).

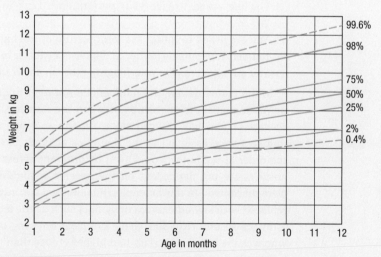

Figure 1.1 An application of descriptive statistics: growth curves for baby girls. Copyright © 2009 Department of Health.

3 At these extreme values doctors may question the parents about their own birth weight. Notice that by doing so the doctors assume a positive correlation between the birth weight of the parents and that of the offspring: parents with a low birth weight are expected to have babies with a low birth weight, and parents with a high birth weight are expected to have babies with a high birth weight.

election now and if people voted in the same way as they said they would in the survey, the poll for the Conservative party would lie between 30% and 34%. It also means that, if the same survey were repeated on a new, random sample of the population, we would expect to find a percentage between 30% and 34%.

The second purpose of inferential statistics is to help us decide whether a difference between two conditions is big enough to be reliable. Suppose that we tested a group of 100 male first-year psychology students and a group of 100 female first-year psychology students on their feeling of well-being at the beginning of term, and that we obtained a score of 35/50 for the males and 38/50 for the females. In such a situation, we may want to know whether this gender difference is reliable; that is, whether we would find it again with two new random groups of 100 males and 100 females from the same population. Again, inferential statistics will help us to make this decision. They will form the second half of this book (Chapters 6 to 14).

1.4.3   Measurement scales

Something else you must know as a scientist is that not all numbers have the same meaning and, therefore, cannot be analysed in the same way. Thus far I have discussed numbers as if they all referred to quantities (height, weight, frequency of intercourse, amount of aggression, scores on a maths test and so on). This, however, is not always the case. Consider the following four situations:

☐ In a questionnaire you are faced with 4 different scenarios and you have to indicate which one you prefer: 1, 2, 3, or 4.
☐ You are asked to give your performance rank in the class last year: 1st, 2nd, …
☐ You are asked to report the temperature of the building you are in, and the temperature outside (either in degrees Celsius or in Fahrenheit).
☐ You are asked to give your height (either in cm or in inches).

In the first situation, the numbers do not refer to quantities at all. There are no mathematical relationships between the numbers: scenario 2 is not double scenario 1 and half of scenario 4. On the contrary, it is very likely that the numbers were assigned to the scenarios at random. (In a well-designed study the order of scenarios would even be different across participants, so that the answers are not dependent on the specific sequence in which the scenarios were presented.) In this example, the numbers are only labels and they could be replaced with any other word or symbol such as the letters of the alphabet.

In the second situation, there is a clear ordering of the numbers. Someone who was the best in the class had higher grades than the second best, the third best, and so on. However, two people who were the best in their class may have very different grades (depending on the level of the class). Similarly, in some classes the difference between the best and the second best may have been very small, in others it may have been much larger. Finally, the numbers cannot be treated mathematically: the person who came second is not half as intelligent as the first and twice as intelligent as the fourth. The numbers just indicate a rank, nothing more.

At first sight, the third situation seems pretty close to the 'normal' use of numbers as references to quantities. If it is 24 degrees Celsius inside and 3 degrees Celsius outside, then we know that this difference of 21 degrees means that outside we will need a warm coat, while inside we do not even require a jumper. The difference between 24 and 3 degrees has the same meaning as a difference between 30 degrees inside and 9 degrees outside. However, there is one subtle difference between this situation and true quantities. When it is 24 degrees inside and 3 degrees outside, we cannot say that inside it is 8 times warmer than outside. To illustrate this, it simply suffices to change degrees Celsius into degrees Fahrenheit: 3 degrees Celsius equals 37 degrees Fahrenheit, and 24 degrees Celsius equals 75 degrees Fahrenheit. So, on the Fahrenheit scale inside it would only be 'twice' as warm as outside, rather than 8 times. What is happening here?

The reason why the Celsius and the Fahrenheit scale result in different ratios of temperatures is that the scales use different zero-points. Celsius defined the zero-point of his scale as the temperature at which water freezes. Fahrenheit, however, defined zero as the temperature at which an equal mixture of water and salt freezes. The same situation occurs when we try to measure two lines of length 4 and 8 cm with two different, broken rulers. According to the first ruler, which starts at 10 cm, the lengths would be 14 and 18; according to the second, which starts at 20 cm, they would be 24 and 28. Although both rulers inform us correctly that the second length is 4 units longer than the first, neither allows us to draw the conclusion that the length of the second line is double that of the first line. Similarly, we do not know which temperature is double another, because there is no obvious situation of no temperature (no quantity). The zero-point of a temperature scale is arbitrary.

The fourth situation depicts a situation that we spontaneously associate with numbers. An adult who is 180 cm tall, is not only 90 cm taller than a child of 90 cm, but is also twice as tall. Nobody will misunderstand us when we use the latter expression. And our statement is true both in cm and in inches (180 cm = 70.86 in; 90 cm = 35.43 in; 180/90 = 70.86/35.43 = 2). The reason for this is that there is an obvious zero-point of no height (no quantity).

These four situations refer to four different *scales of measurement*. When the numbers are merely labels of categories and do not refer to any inherent ordering (as in situation 1), the measurement scale is a **nominal scale**. As we will see in the next section, the calculations that can be done on this type of number are very limited (not more than would be possible if the labels were letters). When the numbers only refer to ranks and do not provide any other magnitude information (as in situation 2), then the measurement scale is an **ordinal scale**. This type of scale, too, requires specific statistics. Finally, if the numbers do provide magnitude information in addition to rank information (as in situations 3 and 4), we have an **interval scale** or a **ratio scale**. The ratio scale is the scale we intuitively associate with numbers. In this scale, the differences between all numbers have the same meaning (the difference between 2 and 3 is the same as the difference between 202 and 203) and the numbers convey information about ratios (4 is twice as much as 2 and half as much as 8). However, for the latter

condition to be met, we need an absolute zero-point of no quantity that coincides with the number 0. Many believe that in psychology we rarely achieve such
a situation, so we cannot make statements about the ratios between numbers.
For instance, it is very unlikely that the absolute zero point of intelligence is an
IQ of 0. Therefore, we cannot say that a person with an IQ of 120 is 20% more
intelligent than a person with an IQ of 100. If there is no absolute zero-point for
the scale but the intervals between the numbers are constant, then we have an
interval scale. Although the distinction between an interval and a ratio scale is
important for the interpretation of the data, it does not matter for statistical
analysis. Therefore in the remainder of this book I will group them and refer to
them as the **interval/ratio scale**.

1.4.4   Which statistics for which scale of measurement?

The scale of measurement is important because it determines the type of statistics we can calculate on our data and the kind of conclusions we can draw. In this
section, I will run ahead of topics covered in later chapters, so don't worry if you
do not understand everything yet. It will become clearer as you continue reading
this book. However, for later reference, you will find this introduction more helpful at the beginning of the book than if it had been placed nearer the end.

Because the numbers on a **nominal scale** do not refer to quantities, we cannot
add or average them. The only thing we can do is count the frequency of each
number (how many 1s there are, how many 2s, and so on), in the same way as
we could count the frequencies of other labels. Subsequently, we can organise
and summarise the frequencies by making a frequency distribution table or a
bar graph (not a histogram!). If a measure of central tendency is required, we will
give the mode (the most frequent category). A measure of variability is meaningless, except for an enumeration of the total number of different categories that
are present. In this book, the only inferential statistics with nominal scales are
the chi-square tests.

The numbers on an **ordinal scale** only refer to ranks and do not provide
magnitude information. So, we cannot sum or average them. However, we can
count the frequencies of the ranks and tabulate these in a frequency distribution table and a bar graph (not a histogram!). Because the ranks are ordered,
we can calculate the median as a measure of central tendency, and the range
as a measure of variability. The inferential statistics have to be non-parametric
tests such as the Mann-Whitney test, the Wilcoxon test or the Spearman rank
correlation.

Because the numbers of an **interval/ratio scale** include magnitude information, they can be added and subtracted. So, for these numbers not only can we
count the frequencies of the different values and plot them in a frequency distribution table or a histogram (not a bar graph!). We can also calculate the mean
as a measure of central tendency (in addition to the median), and the standard
deviation as a measure of variability. For these numbers, we will normally use
parametric tests (t-tests, Pearson correlations), although we can also use non-
parametric tests if we want.

1.5　Answers to chapter questions

The chapter started with a list of questions which you should be able to answer now. Try them! For revision purposes, you will find the answers here. Every chapter opens with a list of questions and closes with the answers to them.

1　What is a reliable study?

> A study is reliable when the findings of the study are the same in a replication of the study. It is not reliable if the findings differ when the study is repeated.

2　What is a valid study?

> A study is valid when it effectively assesses the issue it claims to measure. It is not valid if the findings can be explained in another way (see confounding variables in Answer 13).

3　What is a case study?

> A case study is the intensive study of one particular individual's experiences and behaviour.

4　What is the distinction between the population and a sample?

> The population is the entire group of people about whom we want to draw conclusions on the basis of our study; the sample is the subgroup of the population that actually takes part in our study.

5　When is a sample representative?

> A sample is representative when it has the same features as the population in every important respect. When a sample is representative of the population, we are allowed to generalise the findings from the sample to the whole population using inferential statistics.

6　What is a convenience sample?

> A convenience sample is a sample of the most readily available individuals. This sample is only representative for a particular subgroup of the population (for example, university students) unless it can be assumed that, for the topic under investigation, the subgroup is representative of the entire population.

7　What are the three types of descriptive research, and what are their subdivisions?

> The three types of descriptive research are systematic observations, interviews and surveys. Systematic observations can be divided into naturalistic observations (in which the observer watches the behaviours of the participants while they are happening) and archive research (when the observer analyses the records of someone else's observations). Interviews can be either structured or unstructured, depending on whether all interviewees get the same list of questions. Surveys are usually short, self-report measures which are administered to a large, representative group of people in order to gauge the population's opinion.

8 **What is correlational research?**

Correlational research involves the measurement of a number of variables and the assessment of the relationships between those variables to find out which variables are associated (correlated) with each other, and which are independent of one another. Variables are the conditions/characteristics that can assume different values.

9 **What is the difference between a positive and a negative correlation?**

A positive correlation occurs when two variables change in the same direction: when one increases, the other increases; when one decreases, the other decreases as well. A negative correlation occurs when two variables change in opposite directions: when one increases, the other decreases; when one decreases, the other increases.

10 **What can we conclude from a correlation?**

Correlations tell us which variables are associated. This allows us to better predict outcomes and gives us clues for further interpretation. Correlations, however, do not provide us with information about how to interpret them. In particular, we must be careful not to follow our tendency to translate correlations into statements that one variable is the cause of the other.

11 **Why do psychologists run experiments?**

Experiments are the best way we have to assess whether one event is caused by another event – whether a variable is affected by the cause we suspect. This is done by changing (manipulating) the suspected cause, and measuring the consequences of this change.

12 **What is the difference between an independent variable and a dependent variable?**

The independent variable is the variable that we suspect is an underlying causal factor. This is the variable that we are going to manipulate in our experiment to find out whether it has the predicted effect. The dependent variable is the variable that we measure in our experiment to find out whether the manipulation of the independent variable has any effect. Identify the independent variable of an experiment by asking: 'What change (manipulation) did the experimenter introduce in the experiment?' To find the dependent variable, ask: 'At the end of the experiment the participant left one or more numbers for the experimenter to analyse. What do they refer to?'

13 **Why is it important to control for confounding variables?**

A study is valid when the conclusions drawn by the researchers are correct. One reason why studies can lack validity is that the observed difference in the dependent variable was not due to the independent variable that was manipulated, but to another variable that correlated with the independent variable and that was not controlled. In an experiment, the experimenter must try to keep everything constant except for the independent variable, so that only the manipulation of the independent variable can be responsible for the observed difference. However, all too often one or more variables that should have been controlled are overlooked, and then the experimenter can no longer conclude with certainty that the difference was due to the independent variable. It could have been caused by the uncontrolled variable – the confounding variable.

14 **What are the three important limitations of experimental research in psychology?**

The first limitation of psychological experiments is that the independent variable cannot always be manipulated at the experimenter's discretion, for instance because it is a person-related variable such as the gender or the age of the participants. All the experimenter can do then is to compare two groups of people that differ on the independent variable and that are controlled for *all possible confounding variables*. However, this is extremely difficult to achieve. The second limitation is that the selection of the independent and the dependent variables usually induces a serious narrowing of the original, wide-ranging research question, so that a single study rarely settles an issue. Finally, a third limitation is that the technicalities of an experiment make it impossible to reach 100% firm conclusions. This limitation will be discussed extensively in the rest of the book.

15 **What are descriptive statistics, and which ones do we need to calculate for each study?**

Descriptive statistics are statistical procedures to summarise, organise and simplify the data (the data are the measurements or observations made in the study). A good researcher always calculates (and requires others to calculate!) a measure of central tendency to get an idea of the average, typical value and a measure of variability to get an idea of how strong the deviation from the central tendency is.

16 **What are inferential statistics, and why do we calculate them?**

Inferential statistics are statistical techniques that allow us to generalise from our study sample to the population. They allow us to calculate the region of uncertainty around the sample statistics (see the next answer on sampling error), and they help us to decide whether a difference between two conditions is big enough to be reliable.

17 **Why is the sampling error important?**

Because a sample is smaller than the population, there is a high chance that the descriptive statistic based on a sample deviates to some extent from the statistic we would get if we could measure the whole population (the population parameter). If we calculate the same statistic (for example, the mean value) for two different samples from the same population, we are likely to find some difference between them. The sampling error is the discrepancy between the sample statistic and the population parameter. This is the reason why there is always a region of uncertainty (or a confidence interval) around sample statistics. The larger the sample, the smaller the sampling error (and the confidence interval). The means of two random samples of one million observations each will be very much the same; the same need not be true for the means of two random samples of ten observations each. The sampling error will be discussed extensively in Chapter 5.

18 **Why is the scale of measurement important?**

The scale of measurement is important because numbers do not always refer to quantities that can be added, subtracted or multiplied. When numbers do not refer to quantities (or magnitudes), a whole range of statistics become meaningless and, therefore, must not be calculated. This is becoming more and more of a problem, because computer programs always return the requested statistic (for example, the average colour or gender), regardless of whether it makes sense or not.

19 **What are the different types of measurement scales?**

There are four scales of measurement: the nominal scale (when the numbers are just labels), the ordinal scale (when the numbers must be interpreted as ranks, not as magnitudes), the interval scale (when the numbers refer to magnitudes, but when there is no clear zero-point of 'no quantity'), and the ratio scale (when numbers truly refer to magnitudes and all possible mathematical operations are allowed). For statistics, it is important to keep in mind that no averaging of numbers is allowed with nominal and ordinal scales. For these scales, other statistics will have to be used.

Summarising data using the frequency distribution

2

?

1 Which two types of descriptive statistics can be used to summarise the findings of a study and how does the frequency distribution of the data relate to these measures?
2 What is a frequency distribution table?
3 How do you make a frequency distribution table?
4 What does the expression Σf mean?
5 How do you make a grouped frequency distribution table?
6 What is a frequency distribution graph?
7 What is a histogram?
8 How do you make a histogram?
9 What is a histogram with relative frequencies?
10 What is a bar graph?
11 How do you make a bar graph?
12 What is a symmetrical frequency distribution?
13 What is a positively skewed frequency distribution?
14 What is a negatively skewed frequency distribution?

Q

2.1 Introduction

In Chapter 1 we learnt that descriptive statistics are statistical procedures to summarise, organise and simplify the data of a study so that we can interpret them more easily. Two measures are important in this respect: the central tendency and the variability. The former gives us an idea of the average, typical value; the latter tells us how much scatter there is in the data. They will be discussed in the next two chapters. However, before we calculate these measures, we can already learn a lot from our data by simply looking at them in a sensible way. In particular, by grouping the data according to the different response categories and by ordering the response categories from small to large (this is not possible for nominal scales of measurement), we get a pretty good estimate of both the central tendency and the variability of the data.

Suppose you run a variant of a classic short-term memory experiment on 12 friends or fellow students. (By the way, it may be a good idea to do this experiment yourself and to use your own data as you learn the material in this chapter!) You test each friend individually and ask them to repeat sequences of letters in the correct order. The first two sequences are three letters long, the next two consist of four letters, followed by five letters, and so on. You read aloud the letters at a rate of one per second and give a sign when your friend can start repeating. You simply note whether or not your friend could repeat each sequence correctly. These are the sequences:

```
Z  B  V
S  V  Q

D  B  S  L
G  J  L  Q

Z  N  S  B  L
B  Z  N  Q  N

Q  Z  G  L  B  S
D  V  Z  B  Q  G

G  S  V  G  D  N  L
V  J  Z  V  G  L  J

J  N  D  Z  J  S  Q  G
G  B  G  Z  N  L  Z  B

Z  Q  V  Z  G  J  N  Q  J
J  D  G  S  L  D  L  N  B

G  B  N  Q  Z  G  S  N  Q  J
D  J  S  N  J  Z  N  Z  G  D

Q  B  G  J  L  V  Z  G  Z  Q  V
J  S  B  G  N  V  D  G  J  N  D

D  J  G  N  B  J  Z  Q  B  Z  Q  V
Z  L  V  D  Q  B  S  Z  V  J  L  J

J  D  B  G  J  D  J  V  S  B  Z  S  G
S  B  Z  Q  V  D  L  S  Z  L  Z  N  D
```

There are several measures you can take as an estimate of your friend's letter span. To keep things simple, take the length below the trial where they made their first mistake. For example, if your friend makes their first mistake on one of the two trials with length 8, you define the short-term memory letter span as 7; if your friend made their first mistake on one of the 3-letter trials, you define the letter span as 2.

Suppose your first friend makes a mistake on the first series of length 9 so you define her span score as 8. Your second friend makes a mistake on the second series of length 8, and you define his score as 7. These are the data of all 12 participants:

8, 7, 5, 6, 4, 5, 7, 10, 7, 6, 10, 7

With such a limited set of simple numbers, it is not difficult to see that the short-term memory digit span falls somewhere between 4 (the minimum value) and 10 (the maximum value). Already, this gives us a fairly good estimate of the typical span and the variability we can expect. Below, we discuss how we organise our data more formally, so that our procedure remains useful when the number of observations (the sample size) increases and/or when the data consist of more complex numbers. Remember, however, that it is always a good strategy to make a rough estimate before you start organising your data. If, afterwards, you find that there is a big difference between this initial hunch and the carefully calculated statistic, you will know that there is something wrong, either an error in your initial estimate or an error in your calculations. In the long run, it will help you to get a better feeling for the data you are working with, and your guesses will become more and more accurate. It will also help you to avoid accepting the results of outrageous calculation errors. Just as we intuitively feel that 5 + 9 can never be 104, a quick look at the data above tell us the realistic ranges for our statistics. No observation falls outside the range 4–10, so no measure of central tendency for this sample can be smaller than 4 or larger than 10. Similarly, no measure of variability can be larger than 6 because it must be smaller than the difference between the maximum and the minimum value.

Tip Before starting a statistical analysis, always have a look at the raw data (even when they are numerous and frightening). Look for the smallest and the largest value. No observations in your frequency distribution tables and graphs must fall outside these two extreme values. Similarly, all measures of central tendency must lie between these values, and the measures of variability cannot be larger than the difference between them.

2.2 Frequency distribution tables

2.2.1 Making a frequency distribution table for data from an ordinal and an interval/ratio scale

In the preceding section, we discussed a small study that gave us data about the short-term memory letter span of 12 participants. These were the data:

8, 7, 5, 6, 4, 5, 7, 10, 7, 6, 10, 7

A first step to improve the organisation of these data is to order them. If the observations come from an ordinal scale or an interval/ratio scale, the ordering is straightforward and happens from the smallest value to the largest value. If the data come from a nominal scale, then there is no inherent ordering in the scale, and we can use whatever ordering of the categories we want (alphabetical, for example; see Section 2.2.2). In our example of the short-term memory span we have data from an interval/ratio scale. So, we will order the values from smallest to largest. The smallest memory span is 4, which we put at the beginning. Next, we have two values of 5, two of 6 and so on. The reordered series is:

4, 5, 5, 6, 6, 7, 7, 7, 7, 8, 10, 10

Our second simplification is to group the observations with the same values. There is only one letter span of 4, but there are two of 5, two of 6, four of 7 and two of 10. The grouping of observations with the same values gives us a frequency distribution table. A **frequency distribution table** is an ordered table of the values of a variable from low to high,[1] together with the numbers of times the values have been observed. The values of the variable are indicated by the symbol X, the frequencies by the symbol f. Table 2.1 shows the frequency distribution table of our study. Notice that if we take the sum of all frequencies, we must obtain the same number as the original sample size. In the remainder of this book we represent a sum of numbers with the Greek capital letter sigma Σ. So, the sum of the frequencies is written as Σf. In addition, we will use the capital letter N to indicate the sample size. Thus,

$$\Sigma f = N$$

Summary of symbols
X = values of a variable
f = frequency of a value
Σf = the sum of all observed frequencies
N = the sample size

Table 2.1 The frequency distribution table for the study on the short-term memory span for letters.

X	f
4	1
5	2
6	2
7	4
8	1
9	0
10	2
	$\Sigma f = 12 = N$

Be careful! Notice that when the data come from an ordinal or an interval/ratio scale, we will list *all* values between the minimum and the maximum, including those that have a zero frequency (that is, those that were not observed in the sample). So, in the example of the short-term memory span, even though there was no span of 9, this value is still included in the frequency distribution table of Table 2.1, and given a frequency of 0.

1 Note that American researchers sometimes order the frequency tables from high to low, with the highest values at the top of the table and the lowest at the bottom. Both orderings are, of course, acceptable.

2.2.2 Making a frequency distribution table for data from a nominal scale

The situation is very much the same when we make a frequency distribution table for data from a nominal measurement scale, except that there is no inherent ordering in the data. So, there is no default way of ordering the rows in the table (unlike data from an ordinal or interval/ratio scale, when the values have to be ordered from small to large). In principle, we can choose any ordering we want. However, in practice, researchers will order the rows in some 'sensible way', either by ranking the response labels alphabetically or by using some theoretically motivated grouping.

Suppose we ask a sample of 12 participants to indicate their favourite colour (red, green, yellow, or blue). The first participant says she prefers green, the second prefers yellow, the third yellow as well and so on. Suppose in the end we get the following raw (unordered) data:

green, yellow, yellow, blue, red, green, green, yellow, green, blue, red, blue

In this study, the ordering of the different response categories is arbitrary. However, two obvious candidates are an alphabetical ranking or a ranking according to the complementary colours: red and green, blue and yellow. If we use alphabetical order, we get the frequency distribution table shown in Table 2.2. Because three participants said they preferred blue, the frequency of the response category 'blue' [f(blue)] equals 3. Four people said green was their favourite colour so f(green) = 4. Similarly, f(red) = 2 and f(yellow) = 3. Notice that the sum of all frequencies again equals the sample size, the number of participants tested: $\Sigma f = 3 + 4 + 2 + 3 = 12 = N$.

In general, a frequency distribution table for nominal data will not contain rows with zero frequencies. There is no inherent order in the values of the observations and, hence, there can be no 'missing' values (as was the case for the memory span of 9 letters in Table 2.1). An exception occurs when the participants have a choice from a limited set of possible responses, and never select one of the proposed response categories. For instance, if nobody in the study on colour preferences had indicated red as their favourite colour, we would still have included this response in Table 2.2 and given it a frequency of 0, because it is important to know that nobody chose red, *even though it was among the response alternatives*.

Table 2.2 Frequency distribution table for the study on colour preferences.

X	f
blue	3
green	4
red	2
yellow	3
	$\Sigma f = 12 = N$

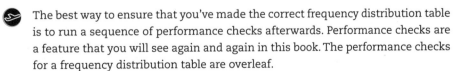

The best way to ensure that you've made the correct frequency distribution table is to run a sequence of performance checks afterwards. Performance checks are a feature that you will see again and again in this book. The performance checks for a frequency distribution table are overleaf.

Many topics close with a set of learning checks. You will find the answers to the learning checks at the ends of the chapters.

Performance checks for a frequency distribution table

Does your frequency distribution table have all the following characteristics?
1 Does the table contain two columns: one for the different values that could be observed (X) and one for the frequencies with which these values were observed (f)?
2 For ordinal and interval/ratio scales: is the frequency distribution table ordered from the smallest value of X (top) to the largest value (bottom)?
3 For nominal scales: is the frequency distribution table ordered in a sensible (albeit arbitrary) way for the different values of X?
4 For ordinal and interval/ratio scales: does the frequency distribution table contain all values of X between the minimum and the maximum, including values with a zero frequency?
5 For nominal scales: does the frequency distribution table contain all the response categories obtained in the study (or all the response alternatives given to the participants)?
6 Does each row in the frequency distribution table refer to a different value of X (that is, there are no two rows with the same value of X)?
7 Does the sum of the frequencies (Σf) equal the size of the sample tested (N)?
8 Does the frequency distribution table have a title which tells the reader what the table is about?

Learning check for a frequency distribution table

To check whether you have understood everything covered thus far, it is a good idea now to make a frequency distribution table yourself.

Suppose we asked a sample of 20 students how many cups of coffee they drank the day before.

Here are the data in the order in which they were collected:

5, 1, 0, 2, 2, 2, 2, 4, 8, 2, 4, 1, 4, 1, 1, 4, 5, 2, 2, 1

Make a frequency distribution table of the data, using the performance checks.

2.2.3 Grouped frequency distribution tables

In our previous examples, the situation was fairly simple because the observations we made (memory spans, preferred colours, cups of coffee drunk in a day) were limited in the range of possible values. Suppose, however, we administered an intelligence test to a sample of 12 participants. Then, in theory we could get IQ scores going from less than 50 to more than 150. However, given that our sample is likely to be a convenience sample consisting of fellow students, it is more realistic to expect that our IQ scores will lie in the upper half of all possible intelligence scores, that is, between 100 and about 150. Still, this range is too wide to give every possibility in a frequency distribution table. (Remember that all the values between the minimum and the maximum must be included in the table, so we would end up with many rows of zero frequencies.)

Suppose these were the IQ scores we obtained:

124, 103, 152, 111, 106, 137, 118, 129, 131, 127, 125, 113

If every possible score was listed, this sample would require a frequency distribution table of 50 rows (going from 103 to 152) with 12 frequencies of 1 and 38 frequencies of 0, as can easily be seen when we reorder the data from small to large:

103, 106, 111, 113, 118, 124, 125, 127, 129, 131, 137, 152

In such a case, when the range of values is too wide, we group the scores into intervals and list these intervals in the frequency distribution table. Grouping will usually occur for variables from an interval/ratio scale. Data from a nominal or an ordinal scale rarely have to be grouped so our discussion will be limited to variables from an interval/ratio scale. To group these data into intervals, we use four rules of thumb:

1 Ideally, a grouped frequency distribution table has no more than 10 intervals (depending on the sample size).
2 We use simple numbers for the width of the interval: 2, 5, 10, 20, 50, 100, …
3 The bottom score in each class interval is a multiple of the interval width. So, if we have a width of 2, we use the intervals 0–1, 2–3, 4–5, 6–7, and so on. For a width of 5, we use the intervals 0–4, 5–9, 10–14, 15–19, …
4 All intervals have the same width.

Applying these rules to our example of IQ scores, an interval width of 10 would seem ideal. This results in 6 intervals for a total of 12 observations. An interval width of 5 would give too many intervals relative to the number of observations; and an interval width of 20 would result in too much compression (only 3 intervals). For an interval width of 10, the bottom scores of the intervals are 100, 110, 120, 130, 140, and 150 (that is, multiples of 10). The top scores of the intervals are the values just below the lower limit of the next interval. Thus, the top score of the first interval is 109 (the value just below 110), the top score of the second interval is 119, etc. This gives us the following intervals: 100–109, 110–119, 120–129, 130–139, 140–149, 150–159.

In the interval going from 100 to 109 we find two observations: 103 and 106. In the interval 110–119 we have three observations: 111, 113, and 118. There are four observations in the interval 120–129 (124, 125, 127, 129), two in the interval 130–139 (131 and 137), none in the interval 140–149 and one in the interval 150–159 (152). This gives us the grouped frequency distribution table shown in Table 2.3. Notice again that $\Sigma f = N$.

Table 2.3 The grouped frequency distribution table for the study on IQ scores.

X	f
100–109	2
110–119	3
120–129	4
130–139	2
140–149	0
150–159	1
	$\Sigma f = 12 = N$

At first sight, many students find it confusing that an interval of width 10 has limits like 100 and 109, because this seems to indicate that there are only 9 values in the interval 109 minus 100). However, if you tabulate all the values, you see that this is not true. The interval 100–109 contains the required 10 values: 100, 101, 102, 103, 104, 105, 106, 107, 108, and 109. This is because both the lower limit and the upper limit are included in the interval. (When you take away 100 from 109, then the lower limit of 100 is taken away as well.) A simple way to avoid confusion is always to start with the lower limits of all the intervals in the table (100, 110, 120, ...) and then insert the upper limits, which will always be one unit less than the lower limit of the next interval.

Thus far, things have been simple because we have only looked at observations that were expressed as integers (numbers without decimal places). However, the approach is exactly the same for real numbers with decimal points. Suppose we ran a word identification study with words presented for 30 milliseconds (30 thousandths of a second), and we looked at the proportion of words that were recognised. These are the data of 12 participants:

0.52, 0.46, 0.89, 0.17, 0.22, 0.65, 0.78, 0.55, 0.24, 0.56, 0.28, 0.69

> **Tip** Always start a grouped frequency distribution table by listing the lower limits of all the intervals. These have to be multiples of the interval width. Once you have entered all the lower limits, then insert the upper limits of the intervals. The upper limit of an interval is the value just below the lower limit of the next interval.

A reasonable interval width here would be 0.10. In theory, this will result in 11 intervals, with the lower limits 0.00, 0.10, 0.20, 0.30, 0.40, 0.50, 0.60, 0.70, 0.80, 0.90 and 1.00.[2] The upper limit of each interval is the value just below the lower limit of the next interval. So, the upper limit of the first interval is 0.09 (i.e., the value just below 0.10), the upper limit of the second interval is 0.19, and so on. Similarly, if we had numbers with three decimal places, we would define the intervals as 0.000–0.099, 0.100–0.199, 0.200–0.299, 0.300–0.399, and so on. (A more mathematically grounded discussion of the margins of intervals is given in Section 2.6 (Going further), where we discuss the distinction between the apparent limits and the real limits of an interval.) Table 2.4 displays the grouped frequency distribution table with interval width 0.10 for the word recognition experiment.

Table 2.4 The grouped frequency distribution table for the study on tachistoscopic visual word recognition (proportion of words recognised).

X	f
0.10–0.19	1
0.20–0.29	3
0.30–0.39	0
0.40–0.49	1
0.50–0.59	3
0.60–0.69	2
0.70–0.79	1
0.80–0.89	1
	$\Sigma f = 12 = N$

 Performance checks for a grouped frequency distribution table

To ensure that your grouped frequency distribution table is correct, run the following checks after you have finished it. Remember that a grouped frequency distribution table is usually restricted to data from an interval/ratio scale.

1 Does the table contain two columns: one for the different intervals of X that could be observed, and one for the frequencies with which values in these intervals were observed (f)?

2 Is the frequency distribution table ordered from the interval to which the smallest value of X belongs (at the top), to the interval to which the largest value of X belongs (at the bottom)?

2 In practice, this theoretical number of 11 intervals (with one only very partial interval, because there are no observations possible between 1.01 and 1.10) will rarely be used, either because there are no values of 1.00 (100% correct) or because the few values of 1.00 will be added to the interval starting at 0.90.

3	Is the lower limit of each interval a multiple of the interval width?
4	Is the upper limit of each interval the value just below the lower limit of the next interval?
5	Does the grouped frequency distribution table contain all the intervals of X between the minimum and the maximum, also those intervals with a zero frequency?
6	Does each row in the frequency distribution table refer to a *different* interval of X (that is, there are no two rows with the same interval of X)?
7	Does the sum of the frequencies (Σf) equal the size of the sample tested (N)?
8	Does the grouped frequency distribution table have a title which tells the reader what the table is about?

Learning check for a grouped frequency distribution table

To make sure that you fully understand grouped frequency distribution tables, make a table for the study in which we asked a sample of 20 students how many cups of coffee they drank the day before.

For your convenience, here are the data again:

5, 1, 0, 2, 2, 2, 2, 4, 8, 2, 4, 1, 4, 1, 1, 4, 5, 2, 2, 1

Make a grouped frequency distribution table, using the performance checks..

2.3 Frequency distribution graphs

2.3.1 Making a frequency distribution graph for data from an interval/ratio scale – the histogram

A picture sometimes says more than a thousand words and it certainly does when many different values are involved. Therefore, it is a good idea to represent a frequency distribution table graphically as well as presenting the figures. A **frequency distribution graph** is a picture of the information available in a frequency distribution table.

The frequency distribution graph, used mostly for data from an interval/ratio scale, is called a histogram. A **histogram** comprises a series of vertical bars that indicate how often each value was observed (that is, the height of the vertical bar corresponds to the frequency of the value). The bars are drawn so that adjacent bars touch each other, to emphasise the continuity of the variable. We will illustrate the making of a histogram with the short-term memory (STM) letter spans, presented in Section 2.1 and summarised in the frequency distribution table (Table 2.1).

We start a histogram by drawing two perpendicular lines, called axes. The horizontal line is the X-axis (or abscissa) and represents the measurement values. In the example of the STM letter span, these are the memory spans and they vary from 4 to 10. In a histogram, the smallest value is always placed to the left and the largest value to the right. The vertical line of a histogram is the Y-axis (or the ordinate) and indicates the frequencies with which the different values on the X-axis were observed. In the STM example, the frequencies ranged from 0 (for span 9) to 4 (for span 7). The height of the Y-axis of a histogram should be about 2/3 of the X-axis.

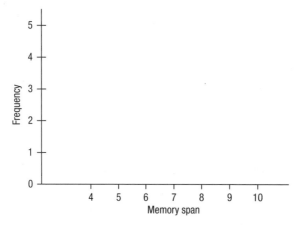

Figure 2.1 Drawing the axes for a histogram of the short-term memory letter spans

Figure 2.1 shows the result of the steps taken thus far. First, we have a horizontal X-axis, showing memory spans going from a minimum value of 4 (left) to a maximum value of 10 (right). Second, we have a vertical Y-axis, indicating frequencies and labelled from a minimum of 0 (bottom) to a maximum of 5 (top). Notice that each axis has a legend indicating what the axis represents (memory span for the X-axis, frequency for the Y-axis).

Next, we have to add our vertical bars to the histogram. Each bar represents the frequency of each observation. One participant had a memory span of 4 (see Table 2.1) so we will draw a vertical bar on top of the X-value 4, indicating that this value was observed with a frequency of 1. This is shown in Figure 2.2. Notice that the width of the bar corresponds to the width of the interval between numbers of the X-axis. In this way, adjacent vertical bars will touch each other and create the impression of continuity across the X-axis.

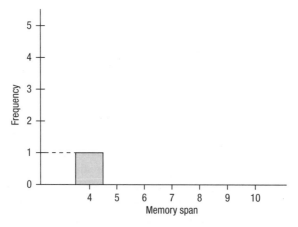

Figure 2.2 Drawing a vertical bar on top of the X-value 4, to indicate that this value was observed with a frequency of 1

Once we have drawn the first vertical bar, the same principle is used to draw the other bars. The frequency of memory span 5 was 2, so that this bar will have to reach up to frequency 2 (twice as high as the bar for memory span 4). The same is true for memory span 6. Memory span 7 was observed with a frequency of 4 so the height of this vertical bar will have to reach up to 4. Memory span 8 had a frequency of 1 (like memory span 2), and memory span 10 had a frequency of 2 (like spans 5 and 6). Finally, there were no observations of memory span 9 so we don't need to draw a bar (or, more correctly, the height of the bar is 0). Bringing everything together, we get the histogram shown in Figure 2.3.

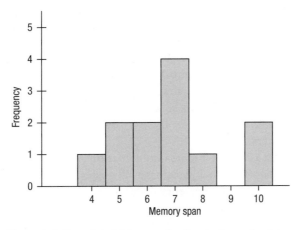

Figure 2.3 Complete histogram for the study on short-term memory span for letters

The procedure for a grouped frequency distribution graph is exactly the same except that, on the X-axis, we write the intervals rather than the individual X-values. Figure 2.4 gives the histogram for the study on IQ scores, which corresponds to the frequency distribution table in Table 2.3.

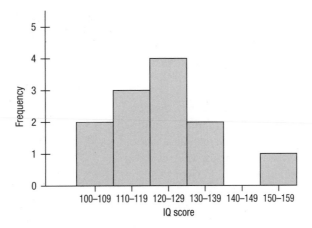

Figure 2.4 Histogram for the study on IQ scores (grouped frequency data)

2.3.2   Histograms with relative frequencies

When the study involves a large number of participants, the **relative frequencies** are often of more interest than the observed frequencies. Relative frequencies are the observed frequencies expressed as percentages. For instance, an American organisation ran a survey on the number of computers per household at the beginning of the 21st century (MRI subscriber study, February 2002). In total, 177,135 people were questioned and Table 2.5 shows the frequency distribution table of the data. (Notice that the observations of 4, 5, 6, … computers per household were grouped under '4 or more', because so few households owned more than 3 computers.)

Table 2.5 Frequency distribution table of the number of computers per household according to a survey of 177,135 participants.

Number of computers (X)	f
0	28,873
1	75,460
2	49,598
3	15,588
4 or more	7,616
	Σf = 177,135 = N

In such a study, it is more informative to have the percentages rather than the raw frequencies. What percentage of households has 0, 1, 2, 3, or 4+ computers? So, rather than the frequency distribution table of Table 2.5, we would prefer a frequency distribution table with percentages. These percentages are obtained by dividing each frequency (f) by the total number of participants (N), and multiplying the result by 100. So,

$$\text{Percentage} = \frac{\text{Frequency}}{\text{Sample size}} \times 100 = \frac{f}{N} \times 100$$

For instance, 28,873 participants of the sample of 177,135 said they had no computer at home. This equals 16% of the sample ((28,873/177,135) * 100 = 0.16 * 100 = 16). Table 2.6 shows the frequency distribution table with percentages. A useful calculation check for such a frequency table is to verify that all the percentages in the table add up to 100.

Similarly, the frequency distribution graph will be more informative when it displays percentages rather than raw frequencies. The resulting histogram is shown in Figure 2.5.[3]

Table 2.6 Frequency distribution table of the number of computers per household (percentages based on a survey of 177,135 participants).

Number of computers (X)	Percentage
0	16%
1	43%
2	28%
3	9%
4 or more	4%
	ΣPercentage = 100%

3 Notice that, for this particular example, a bar graph could also be used, because it might be argued that the 4+ category violates the basic requirement of an interval/ratio scale (equal intervals). In such a strict interpretation, the number of computers per household would be an ordinal variable rather than an interval/ratio variable.

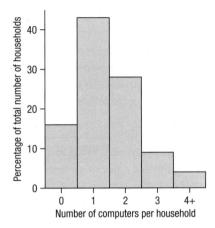

Figure 2.5 Histogram of the number of computers per household (percentages based on a survey of 177,135 participants)

 Performance checks for histograms

Because mistakes and omissions are so easily overlooked when you are drawing a frequency distribution graph, it is always good at the end of the process to run the following performance checks.

1 Are the data from an interval/ratio scale? (If not, you have to draw a bar graph.)

2 Does the X-axis contain all the values (intervals) between the smallest X-value observed and the largest X-value observed, including those with a frequency of 0?

3 Does the X-axis go from small (left) to large (right)?

4 Does the X-axis contain a legend explaining what the values on this axis mean?

5 Does the Y-axis span all the frequencies (or percentages) from 0 at the bottom to the maximum frequency (percentage) observed for the X-values (intervals)?

6 Does the Y-axis contain a legend explaining what the values on this axis mean (frequencies or percentages)?

7 Is the Y-axis approximately 2/3 of the X-axis?

8 Does each bar indicate the correct frequency (percentage) for each X-value? To answer this question, you will have to consult the data of your frequency distribution table. Be especially careful when some rows of the frequency distribution table contain 0 frequencies (percentages), because for these values your histogram must show a gap (that is, no bar on top of this value).

9 Does the frequency distribution table have a title which tells the reader what the table is about?

10 Do adjacent bars touch each other?

Learning check for histograms

Draw a histogram summarising the results of the study on the number of cups of coffee drunk on an average day by 20 participants. Do this for the individual data and for the grouped data.

These were the data:
5, 1, 0, 2, 2, 2, 2, 4, 8, 2, 4, 1, 4, 1, 1, 4, 5, 2, 2, 1
Check that your solutions are correct by applying the performance checks. See Section 2.5 on SPSS for the solution.

2.3.3 Making a frequency distribution graph for data from an ordinal or nominal scale – the bar graph

Virtually all the knowledge we have gathered about histograms for data from interval/ratio scales can be applied to data from ordinal and nominal scales as well. There is only one difference. Because ordinal and nominal data do not refer to magnitudes, they do not form continuous variables. Therefore, we cannot use histograms with adjoining vertical bars. Instead, there have to be clear spaces between the bars to emphasise that the scale consists of separate, distinct categories. The resulting graph is called a **bar graph**.

Figure 2.6 shows an example of a bar graph for ordinal data. It displays the BSc grades obtained by the psychology students from Royal Holloway in 2002. The grades in the British university system range from a failure (indicated by the number 4), a simple pass (indicated by the number 3), a lower second (indicated by 2.2), an upper second (indicated by 2.1), to a first degree (indicated by the number 1) for the top performers. These numbers do not form an interval scale (or a ratio scale), because each degree covers a different range of performances (a first requires marks of 70+, a 2.1 ranges from 60% to 69.9%, etc.). Therefore, these university degrees are merely a ranking of the students. A further peculiarity is that, for this particular scale, larger numbers even indicate worse performance! For all the above reasons, the numbers referring to degrees form an ordinal scale, going from bad to good performance. As you can see in Figure 2.6, in 2002 none of the students failed or had a simple pass. Most of them (60/82) obtained an upper second; the others gained either a lower second or a first. We could also use a graph with the relative frequencies rather than the raw frequencies. Then, the frequency of the 2.1s would be $60/82 \times 100 = 73\%$.

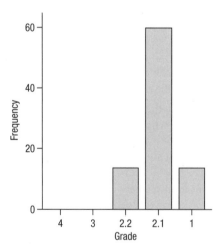

Figure 2.6 Grades obtained at the psychology department of a British university – an example of a bar graph for ordinal data

Performance checks for bar graphs

Does your bar graph have the following characteristics?
1 Are the data from an ordinal or nominal scale? (If not, you have to draw a histogram.)
2 Does the *X*-axis contain all the values observed (or asked for)?
3 Does the *X*-axis contain a legend explaining what the values on this axis mean?
4 Does the *Y*-axis contain all the frequencies (or percentages) from 0 to the maximum frequency (percentage) observed for the *X*-values?
5 Does the *Y*-axis contain a legend explaining what the values on this axis mean (frequencies or percentages)?
6 Is the *X*-axis approximately 2/3 of the *Y*-axis?
7 Does each bar indicate the correct frequency (percentage) for each *X*-value? To answer this question, you will have to consult the data in your frequency distribution table.
8 Do adjacent bars have empty spaces between them?

Learning check for bar graphs

Draw a bar graph summarising the results of the study on colour preference (Section 2.2.2, Table 2.2). These were the data:

green, yellow, yellow, blue, red, green, green, yellow, green, blue, red, blue

Check that your solution is correct by applying the performance checks. See Section 2.5 on SPSS for the solution.

2.4 The shape of a frequency distribution

More can be learned from frequency distributions by looking at their shapes. As we will discuss more extensively in Chapter 5, psychologists usually assume that the distribution of their data has a single peak and is symmetrical. Figure 2.7 shows an example of such a distribution.

A distribution with a single peak (or a single mode; see Chapter 3) is a distribution grouped around a value with maximum frequency. This is an indication that the distribution comes from a single population. A distribution with two (or more) obvious peaks usually indicates that the scores come from two (or more) distinct populations with different performance levels. For instance, suppose we administer a large-scale maths test to all the children in the top year of a primary school. In that case, it may be useful to look at the distribution of the scores: Does it contain a single peak (indicating that all children come from a single population) or is there evidence for two separate peaks, one at the high end and one at the low end? Two peaks could indicate that there are two separate populations of children, one with high mathematical intelligence and one with low mathematical intelligence, which might arise because some children were taught by a better teacher than others.

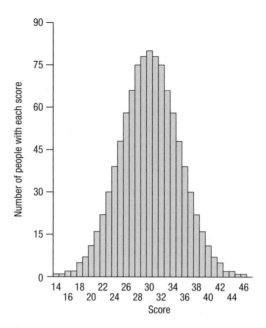

Figure 2.7 An example of a symmetrical distribution with a single peak (mode)

A distribution is symmetrical when it is possible to draw a vertical line through the middle so that one side of the distribution is a mirror image of the other (see Figure 2.7). As indicated above, psychologists generally assume that distributions will be symmetrical. There are, however, many well-known exceptions. A typical example of an asymmetrical distribution is that of household sizes. The most frequent household size in the UK is 2 (35% of all households consist of 2 people). These include households of two friends or partners living together (for example, couples without children and couples whose children have left home) and households of one parent living with one child. There are also many single-person households (28%). This is the only household size to the left of the peak of the distribution. On the right hand side of the peak there are several more observations, which occur with decreasing frequency. There are quite a few households of 3 persons (16%), 4 persons (14%), and – to a lesser extent – 5 persons (5%). However, the percentages of households with 6, 7, 8, ... people become so low that all households of 6 and more (2%) are usually grouped in government and other official statistics. For this reason, it is very difficult to find information about the maximum household size in the UK. A reasonable estimate is probably 14 persons (either a couple with 12 children at home, or two families living together, possibly with the grandparents). Whatever the exact maximum value, it is clear that the distribution is not symmetrical (see Figure 2.8). The part of the distribution to the right of the peak (also called the right tail) is substantially more stretched than the part to the left of the peak (the left tail). Such a distribution with a long tail to the right (that is, towards the high values of X) is called a **positively skewed** distribution.

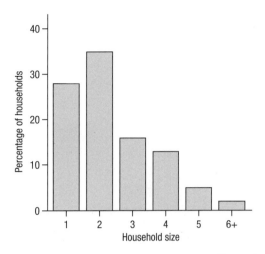

Figure 2.8 Frequency distribution graph of household sizes in the UK (Census, 2001). Notice that the distribution is positively skewed (that is, it has a longer tail to the right than to the left). Also notice that the right tail has been truncated, because the percentages of size 6 and more have been grouped. Had they been plotted as individual observations, the bars would have become too small to see.

Other examples of positively skewed distributions are the number of computers per household (see Figure 2.5) and the earnings of people in a country. For instance, in the UK in 2003, the average disposable household income was around £450 a week (Craggs, 2004). The tail of incomes higher than this average is much bigger than the tail of lower incomes because on the high end a tiny percentage of households have access to as much as £30,000 a week, whereas on the low end the government claims to guarantee a minimum income of some £100 per week for a single-person household. (In fact, the average disposable weekly income for the lowest 20% was £120, and that for the highest 20% was £980.)

In psychological research, the most common example of a positively skewed distribution is the distribution of reaction times. Figure 2.9 displays the distribution of a single person's grouped reaction times from 120 measurements in a test which required them to press a response button as quickly as possible on seeing a small light flash on a computer screen. Even in this very simple situation, the distribution of reaction times is clearly positively skewed.

The reverse pattern to a positively skewed distribution is a **negatively skewed** distribution (see Figure 2.10). Such a distribution has a longer tail to the left (the small values) than to the right (the large values). Unlike positively skewed distributions, negatively skewed distributions are very rare in normal life. The distribution of marks for an easy exam is the only example I am familiar with. If the most frequent score on an exam is 17/20, it is not uncommon to see a gradual decrease of marks to as low as 0/20 (certainly when the group examined was quite large, say a few hundred students).

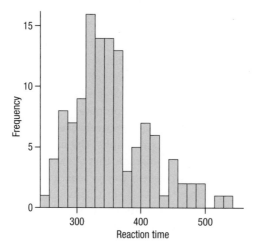

Figure 2.9 The frequency distribution graph of 120 reaction times
Notice that the distribution is positively skewed (it has
a longer tail to the right than to the left).

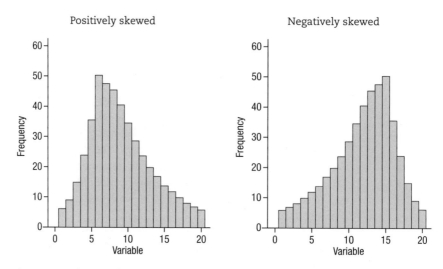

Figure 2.10 Shapes of positively and negatively skewed distributions

2.5 Making a frequency distribution table and a frequency distribution graph in SPSS

Knowing how to make a frequency distribution table and a frequency distribution graph by hand may be satisfying (and necessary if you want to become a good psychologist), but the process is rather cumbersome and is certainly unnecessary if you have access to a computer.

There are three ways in which you can use computers to help you make frequency distribution tables and graphs. The first is to search on the internet for freely available software programs that allow you to make frequency distribution tables and graphs. The best way to search for these websites is to use a search engine to look for 'frequency distribution table', 'frequency distribution graph', 'applet', and 'java program'. The latter two terms are important because without them you get lots of websites that refer to class notes without any software attached to them. Alternatively, you can visit the companion website for this book www.palgrave.com/psychology/brysbaert, where we will provide you with links to useful sites. (One problem with internet sites is that they are extremely dynamic, with regularly changing addresses and websites that come and go within a few months. There is, therefore, little point in providing the addresses in this book because they may quickly become outdated.)

A second possibility is to make use of the facilities on your personal computer. All operating systems supply a spreadsheet, which will provide many helpful functions for the basic analyses presented here (but not for the non-parametric statistics). For instance, Microsoft Excel allows you to draw history graphs. Again, see the companion website for a number of examples.

Finally, there are commercially available statistical software packages, which offer elegant solutions for all the analyses discussed in this book (and many more). Most psychology departments use SPSS to run the analyses taught in statistics courses (going from the simplest to the most complicated). This is the package you are most likely to work with and, for that reason, it has been included here. The main limitation of learning a commercially available software package is that you may not have access to it once you leave university. In that case, this book and the website should be able to guide you to one of the two other options.

2.5.1 Opening SPSS

One of the clearest books available on using the SPSS program is by Nicola Brace, Richard Kemp and Rosemary Snelgar: *SPSS for Psychologists* (4th edition, 2009). Throughout this book, but particularly as we look at more advanced material in the later chapters, you will find references to chapters in Brace, which will help you to carry out more advanced tests using SPSS.

In addition, the companion website for *SPSS for Psychologists* has a number of data sets and exercises, which provide additional guidance and revision material: www.palgrave.com/psychology/brace.

Once you have opened SPSS, you should have something similar to this on your screen. There are small differences between different versions of SPSS, but these will not matter for the analyses discussed in this book.

2.5.2 Making a frequency distribution table for ordinal and interval/ratio data

We will illustrate the making of a frequency distribution table with the example on the number of cups of coffee drunk by students on the previous day (see Section 2.3.2):

5, 1, 0, 2, 2, 2, 2, 4, 8, 2, 4, 1, 4, 1, 1, 4, 5, 2, 2, 1

First, we enter the data in the first column:

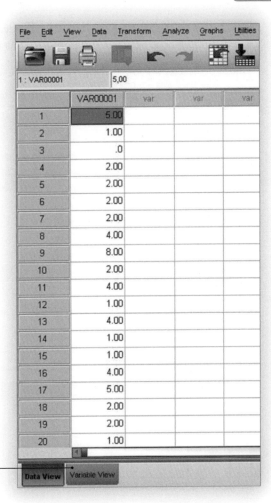

As you can see, SPSS automatically assumes that variables are numeric and have two decimal places. You can change this (or change the type of variable to nominal) by clicking on the *Variable View* box ❶.

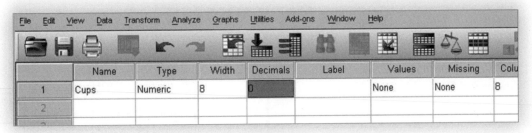

This gives you the following screen, in which you can change the number of *Decimals*. At the same time, we can change the *Name* of the variable to Cups.

To make a frequency table, we click on *Analyze*, *Descriptive Statistics* and *Frequencies*.

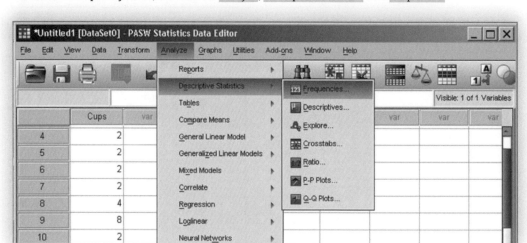

This gives the following dialogue box, in which we put Cups into the Variable(s) section by clicking on the central arrow.

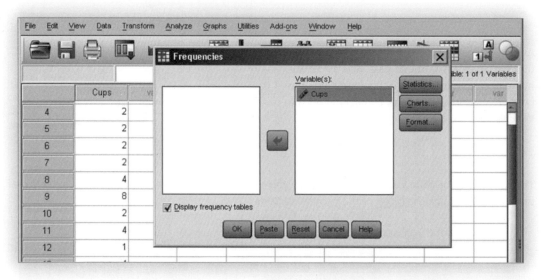

Then click on OK. This will give you the following table:

Notice that this table contains everything you need, but does not contain the empty rows with 3, 6, and 7 cups. **Be careful** about this when you use your SPSS output to make a frequency table!

Cups				
		Frequency	Percent	Valid Percent	Cumulative Percent
Valid	0	1	5.0	5.0	5.0
	1	5	25.0	25.0	30.0
	2	7	35.0	35.0	65.0
	4	4	20.0	20.0	85.0
	5	2	10.0	10.0	95.0
	8	1	5.0	5.0	100.0
	Total	20	100.0	100.0	

2.5.3   Making a frequency distribution graph for ordinal and interval/ratio data

To make a frequency distribution graph, click on the *Charts* button of the Frequencies screen. This will open a new box in which you click on *Histograms*.

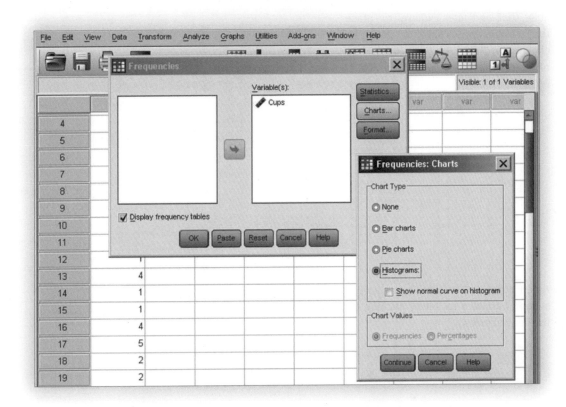

Then click on *Continue* and *OK*, to get the following output:

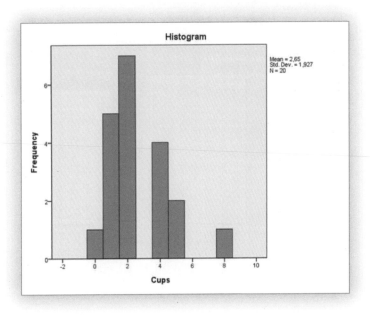

By double-clicking on the graph, you can change its appearance in any way you want.

2.5.4 Making a grouped frequency distribution table and graph for ordinal and interval/ratio data

To make a grouped frequency table in SPSS, you must define a new variable that indicates where to place the observations. This is done by clicking on *Transform* in the upper line of commands. Then click on *Visual Binning*.

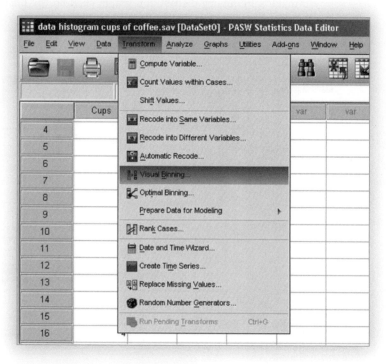

Again bring the variable Cups into the section Variables to Bin by clicking on the central arrow.

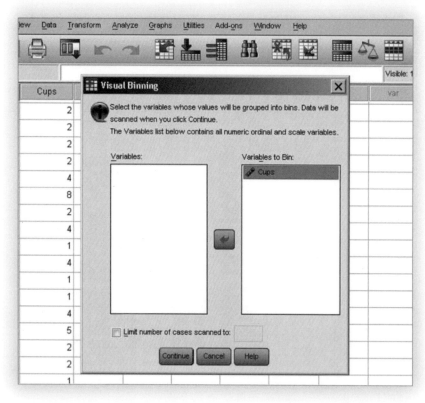

Then click on *Continue*.

Now, give a name to the new variable, such as Cups_grouped 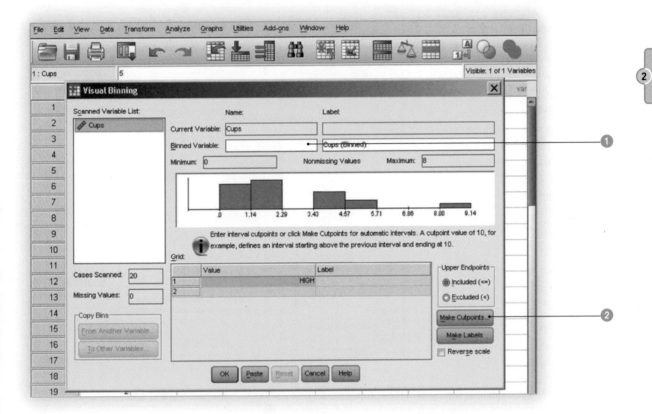, and then click on *Make Cutpoints* ❷.

You will be required to enter the first cutpoint location, the number of cutpoints and the width of the bin. The first cutpoint is the upper limit of the first interval (1 in our example). The number of cutpoints is one less than the number of bins we want. Say we want 5 bars in our grouped table, then we will set the number of cutpoints to $5-1=4$. Because we want to include two values of number of cups, we define the width as 2.

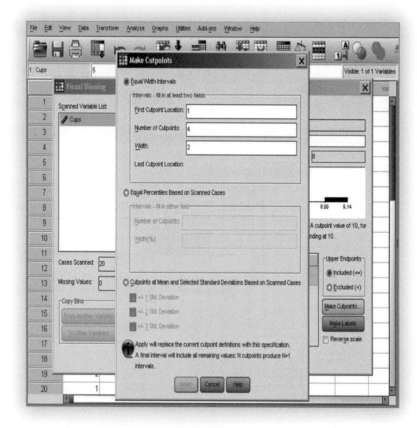

Click on Apply to go back to the panel Visual Binning. In this panel click on *Make Labels* ❶. You can also change the label of the first bin from <=1 into 0-1, as shown ❷.

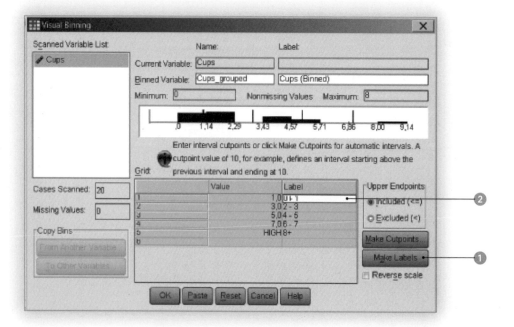

Click on OK to take you back to your data sheet, you will see that a new column has been added: Cups_grouped.

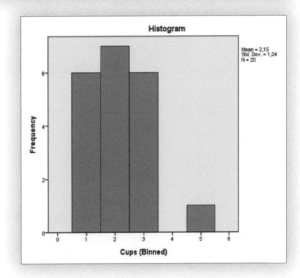

Now you can make a frequency table and frequency graph for the Cups_grouped variable. The outcome will look as follows.

Cups (Binned)					
		Frequency	Percent	Valid Percent	Cumulative Percent
Valid	0 - 1	6	30.0	30.0	30.0
	2 - 3	7	35.0	35.0	65.0
	4 - 5	6	30.0	30.0	95.0
	8+	1	5.0	5.0	100.0
	Total	20	100.0	100.0	

An annoying aspect of SPSS is that the X-axis displays the values of the bins rather than meaningful labels. One way around this problem is to work with *Graphs*, *Chart Builder*.

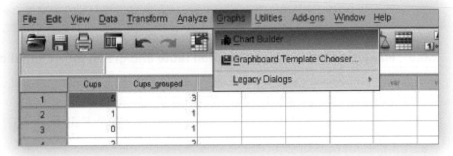

Select the Bar option in the *Choose from* panel and drag Cups (Binned) onto the X-axis:

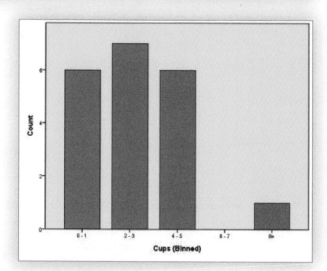

Click on OK to get the following graph.

If you double-click on the bars in this figure, you can adjust their width so that you have a histogram rather than a bar graph.

2.5.5 Making a frequency distribution table and graph for nominal data

To illustrate the frequency distribution table and graph for nominal data, we will use the data from the study on colour preferences in which 12 participants chose their favourite primary colour:

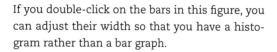

green, yellow, yellow, blue, red, green, green, yellow, green, blue, red, blue

We begin by entering these data in SPSS. First, we define our variable by clicking on *Variable View* ❶.

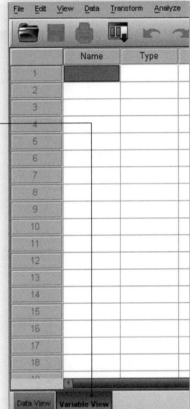

We enter the name in the first column, define the variable as a string variable (that is, a sequence of characters), and click on OK.

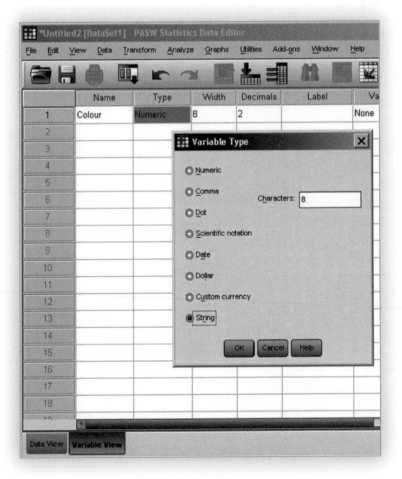

Now we go to _Data View_ and enter the values. Next we click on _Analyze_, _Descriptive Statistics_ and _Frequencies_.

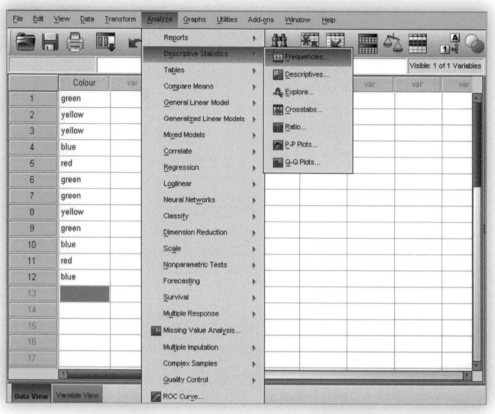

Under the _Charts_ button we select _Bar charts_.

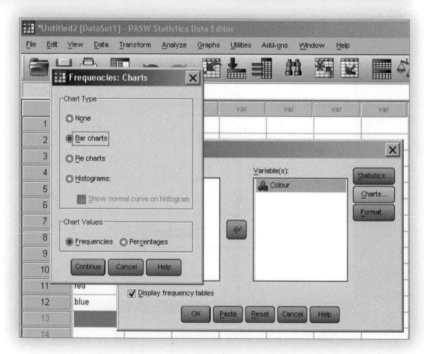

After some clicks on Continue and OK, we get the desired output:

		Frequency	Percent	Valid Percent	Cumulative Percent
Valid	blue	3	25.0	25.0	25.0
	green	4	33.3	33.3	58.3
	red	2	16.7	16.7	75.0
	yellow	3	25.0	25.0	100.0
	Total	12	100.0	100.0	

Colour

By clicking on the graph and then on selected parts, you can again change whatever aspect you are unhappy with.

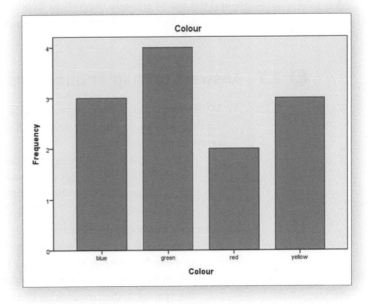

2.6 Going further: continuous variables, real limits and theoretical distributions

You have probably noticed that we have only worked with discrete variables – variables that can be divided into separate, indivisible categories. This was particularly clear when we worked with integer values such as the number of cups of coffee. In our examples, there were no values between 0 and 1, 1 and 2, and so on. The examples were chosen on purpose, partly because they are easier to grasp intuitively and partly because they constitute the type of data that researchers come across in their studies. Even when an analogue continuum is measured with decimal precision (for example, the weight of a person: 62.251 kg), the measurements still form a set of discrete variables because of measurement limitations. However, working with discrete variables has its limitations and it may have been obvious to you that it would be better to define the intervals as: lower limit $\leq X <$ upper limit. Examples might be intervals of $0 \leq X < 10$, $10 \leq X < 20$, ...; or $-0.5 \leq X < 9.5$, $9.5 \leq X < 19.5$, ...

The discussion in this chapter has been limited to discrete variables because the majority of psychology students struggle with continuous variables and do not find them helpful at all. However, if you are mathematically oriented, nothing prevents you from reading and studying this chapter within the framework of continuous variables and seeing the examples as a limited representation of the more general principle. In this view, each discrete value refers to an *interval* rather than a single point on the number line. So, rather than talking about the values 0, 1, 2, … cups of coffee, we can think of the intervals $-0.5 \leq X < 0.5$, $0.5 \leq X < 1.5$, $1.5 \leq X < 2.5$, … cups of coffee. The boundaries of these intervals are called the real limits of the interval. Understanding the notion of real limits will help you to better understand the calculation of the range, discussed in Chapter 5, and the use of smooth, theoretical frequency distribution graphs, such as the normal distribution in Chapter 3, rather than the histograms based on discrete variables, discussed here.

❷ 2.7 Answers to chapter questions

1 Which two types of descriptive statistics can be used to summarise the findings of a study and how does the frequency distribution of the data relate to these measures?

These statistics are a measure of central tendency and a measure of variability. Before you calculate them it is a good idea to have a look at the frequency distribution of the data so that you can avoid gross calculation errors.

2 What is a frequency distribution table?

A frequency distribution table is an ordered table of the values of a variable from low to high, together with the numbers of times the values have been observed. The values of the variable are indicated by the symbol X, the frequencies by the symbol f.

3 How do you make a frequency distribution table?

See pp. 27–30.

4 What does the expression Σf mean?

The expression Σf refers to the sum of the frequencies of the observations. It equals the sample size N.

5 How do you make a grouped frequency distribution table?

See pp. 30–33.

6 What is a frequency distribution graph?

A frequency distribution graph is a picture of the information available in a frequency distribution table. There is a difference between a histogram (interval/ratio scale) and a bar graph (ordinal scale and nominal scale).

7 What is a histogram?

A histogram is a graph comprising a series of vertical bars that indicate for each value how often it was observed. It is used for data from an interval/ratio scale. The bars touch each other to indicate that the variable is continuous.

8 **How do you make a histogram?**

See pp. 33–37.

9 **What is a histogram with relative frequencies?**

A histogram with relative frequencies is a histogram in which the vertical bars do not represent the raw frequencies but the relative frequencies, expressed either as a proportion of all the observations or as a percentage.

10 **What is a bar graph?**

A bar graph comprises a series of vertical bars that indicate for each value on the X-axis how often it was observed. It is used for data from an ordinal or a nominal scale. The bars do not touch each other, because an ordinal or a nominal variable is not a continuous variable.

11 **How do you make a bar graph?**

See pp. 38–39.

12 **What is a symmetrical frequency distribution?**

This is a frequency distribution in which the left half is a mirror image of the right half.

13 **What is a positively skewed frequency distribution?**

This is an asymmetrical distribution that has a longer tail on the right side than on the left side. A typical example is the distribution of household sizes. The highest frequency consists of households of 2 people, but there are households of up to 14 members.

14 **What is a negatively skewed frequency distribution?**

This is an asymmetrical distribution that has a longer tail on the left side than on the right side. An example is the scores in an easy exam.

☑ 2.8 Learning check solutions

Make your own frequency distribution table

Frequency distribution table for the number of cups of coffee drunk in a day

X	f
0	1
1	5
2	7
3	0
4	4
5	2
6	0
7	0
8	1
	$\Sigma f = 20 = N$

Notes: Number of cups is a measure from an interval/ratio scale. So, all the values must be ordered from the minimum value observed (0 cups) to the maximum number observed (8 cups), including those with zero frequency (3, 6 and 7 cups). The sum of the frequencies equals the sample size (20).

Make your own grouped frequency distribution table

Grouped frequency distribution table for the number of cups of coffee drunk in a day

X	f
0–1	6
2–3	7
4–5	6
6–7	0
8–9	1
	$\Sigma f = 20 = N$

Notes: An interval width of 2 is the best choice because this gives us 5 intervals for a total of 20 observations. Intervals are ordered from the interval containing the minimum value observed (0 cups) to the interval containing the maximum number observed (8 cups). The ordering includes an interval with zero frequency (the interval of 6–7 cups). The sum of the frequencies equals the sample size (20).

Make a histogram

Histogram – individual data

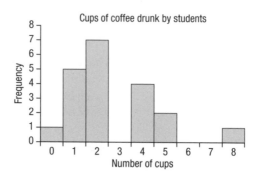

Histogram – grouped data

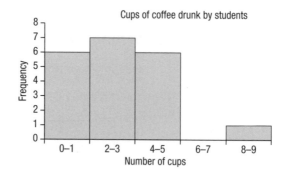

Make a bar graph

See also the histograms made in the SPSS section.

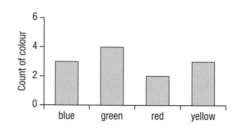

3

Summarising data using measures of central tendency

?

1 What is a measure of central tendency?
2 What is the mean and how is it calculated?
3 What is the median and how is it calculated?
4 What is the mode and how is it calculated?
5 Which measure of central tendency is to be preferred?

3.1   The need for summary data and the danger of them

When we read 'the dog was eating a bone', we automatically create an image of some typical dog and some typical bone. Otherwise, we would not be able to communicate with one another. In addition, if we could not generalise beyond isolated experiences, our thinking would be seriously limited. Suppose we could not think of 'dogs' in general, but only of each individual dog we happen to have seen (for example, 'Sam', 'Max', and 'Trixie').[1] Then, we would not be able to appreciate the similarities in dogs, and we would not be able to recognise new 'things' as dogs (or even as 'things' for that matter). All we would have would be a huge collection of unrelated memory images.

The capacity to generalise beyond individual experiences – the capacity to categorise – involves the extraction of typical, average features. How exactly humans achieve this is not yet fully understood, but there is no doubt that we do it all the time and that it involves us ignoring small individual differences and capitalising on what is common, typical to all instances. Very much the same happens when statisticians calculate a measure of central tendency. A measure of **central tendency** is a statistical measure that identifies a single score as representative of an entire frequency distribution. This score will always be a value somewhere between the minimum and the maximum of the distribution. With this measure of central tendency we subsequently refer to the entire distribution in the same way as we assume a typical weight, height, speed and colour when we hear someone talking about 'a dog'. The major difference between a statistical measure and a human-defined category is that in statistics everyone must come up with the same value for a given input. Human definitions often differ between individuals who receive the same input – what image comes to mind when you hear the word 'dog'? Write down the features and compare them to a friend's description. Are they the same?

The central tendency captures the essence of a distribution best when the distribution has a single peak and is symmetrical, as shown in Figure 3.1a. In that case, we intuitively see that the measure of central tendency must coincide with the X-value in the middle of the distribution. This value also happens to be the value with the highest frequency. The situation is slightly less obvious when we have a positively skewed distribution, as shown in Figure 3.1b. Remember from Chapter 2 that, in psychology, nearly all skewed distributions are positively skewed. Where do we define the central tendency here? Finally, calculating a single measure of central tendency may be misleading if the distribution has more than one peak, as shown in Figure 3.1c, because then the distribution is a combination of two or more subdistributions.

Tip When you are working with a variable of which the distribution is not known from previous research, it is always a good idea to make a frequency distribution graph of the data before calculating the measures of central tendency, just to make sure that the distribution has only one clear peak.

1 In the past, people tended to name their pets after a physical or personality trait, hence Spot or Rover. A look at the databases of currently registered dogs, however, reveals that human names are all the rage. The 10 most popular names for male dogs in the UK are Sam, Spot, Pip, Duke, Piper, Max, Charlie, Rocky, Zak, and Tiny. Those for female dogs are Trixie, Polly, Jessie, Lucy, Bonnie, Cassie, Daisy, Heidi, Susie, and Holly.

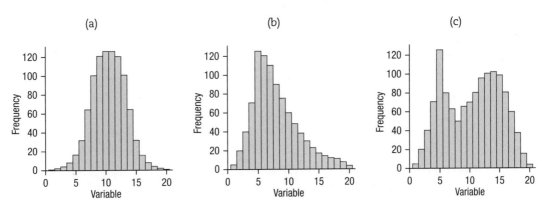

Figure 3.1 Three distributions demonstrating the difficulty of calculating one single measure of central tendency as representative of the entire distribution

Suppose the distribution in Figure 3.1c represented the exam marks of two classes taught by two different teachers. Should we conclude that the average value is 10/20 and thus that everything is well? Similarly, researchers may miss the most important feature of their data when they blindly calculate measures of central tendency without first having a look at the distribution of the data.

In statistics, there are three commonly used measures of central tendency: the mean, the median and the mode. We will discuss them separately in the sections below. In Section 3.5, we will then see which measure is appropriate for which situation.

3.2 The mean

The **mean** of a sample is calculated by adding all the scores in the distribution and dividing the sum of scores by the number of scores. The symbol used to represent the mean of a sample is **M**. Suppose we asked 9 participants how many pints of beer they drank last weekend and we got the following responses:

5, 4, 3, 5, 4, 2, 4, 3, 6

Then, the mean of these 9 observations would be calculated as:

$M = (5 + 4 + 3 + 5 + 4 + 2 + 4 + 3 + 6)/9$
$\quad = 36/9$
$\quad = 4$

So, we would conclude that the mean number of pints drunk by the participants in the preceding weekend was 4. The sum of the scores is represented by the symbol ΣX, and the number of observations in the sample by **N**, so that the mean is formally defined as

$$M = \frac{\Sigma X}{N}$$

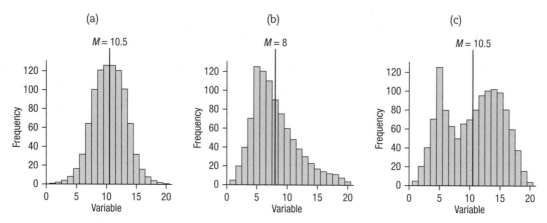

Figure 3.2 The mean as a measure of central tendency

To give you an idea of what the mean represents, Figure 3.2 displays the means of the three distributions in Figure 3.1: (a) a symmetric distribution with one peak, (b) a positively skewed distribution with one peak and (c) a distribution with two peaks.

The interpretation of the mean is very easy to grasp when the frequency distribution is unimodal and symmetric, because then the mean corresponds to the X-value in the centre of the distribution. If you draw a vertical line through this value, you split the distribution in two mirror halves.

When the distribution is skewed or has more than one peak, an appropriate analogy is that of a seesaw. Suppose the bars of the frequency distribution represent boxes placed on a seesaw, where would you put the pivot so that the seesaw stays in balance? This balance point coincides with the mean, as shown in Figure 3.3 for all three distributions.

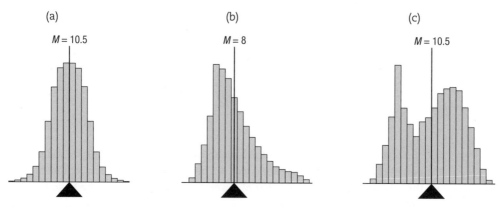

Figure 3.3 The interpretation of the mean as the pivot of a seesaw

When the data of a sample have been summarised in a frequency distribution table, researchers use a different approach to calculate the mean. Let's illustrate this with our beer drinking example in which 9 participants indicated how many pints they drank the previous weekend:

5, 4, 3, 5, 4, 2, 4, 3, 6

Above, we calculated the mean as:

$$M = (5 + 4 + 3 + 5 + 4 + 2 + 4 + 3 + 6)/9$$
$$= 36/9$$
$$= 4$$

Another way to calculate the mean is to group all observations with the same values and then calculate the sum of the scores on the basis of these groups, as shown below:

$$M = (2 + 3 + 3 + 4 + 4 + 4 + 5 + 5 + 6)/(1 + 1 + 1 + 1 + 1 + 1 + 1 + 1 + 1)$$
$$= [(1 \times 2) + (2 \times 3) + (3 \times 4) + (2 \times 5) + (1 \times 6)]/(1 + 2 + 3 + 2 + 1)$$

In this equation all observations with the same values are grouped. This is particularly useful when there are many observations. It is much easier to calculate 1115×5 than to do 1115 additions of $+5$. Grouped frequency data are exactly the type of data that make up a frequency distribution table. Table 3.1 is the frequency distribution table for our example (see Chapter 2).

By adding a single column to this frequency distribution table in which we multiply each value of X by its frequency (that is, $1 \times 2, 2 \times 3, ...$), we have a quick and easy way to calculate the sum of scores. This is shown in Table 3.2.

So, when we have a frequency distribution table, instead of using the equation

$$M = \frac{\Sigma X}{N}$$

we will use the equation

$$M = \frac{\Sigma fX}{\Sigma f} = \frac{36}{9} = 4$$

This provides us with a much faster and easier way to calculate the mean when there are many observations.

Table 3.1 The frequency distribution table of the example of the number of pints drunk in a weekend.

X	f
2	1
3	2
4	3
5	2
6	1
	$\Sigma f = 9 = N$

Table 3.2 The frequency distribution table of the example of the number of pints drunk in a weekend, with a column added to easily calculate the sum of scores.

X	f	f*X
2	1	2
3	2	6
4	3	12
5	2	10
6	1	6
	$\Sigma f = 9 = N$	$\Sigma f^*X = 36$

The mean is reported in a manuscript either in the main text or between brackets as $M =$. So, we would write something like 'A sample of 9 students reported that they had drunk an average of 4 pints of beer the previous weekend.' or 'Students reported the number of pints of beer drunk the previous weekend ($M = 4$), and ...'

Learning check
Calculate the mean number of letters remembered in the short-term memory experiment of Chapter 2 (summarised in Table 2.1).

3.3 The median

The second measure of central tendency that is often used is the median. The **median** is the score that divides the frequency distribution exactly in half. The same number of observations have a value below the median as the number of observations with a value above the median. To calculate the median, we first rank the scores from small to large. So, for the example of the number of pints drunk, we would reorder the original data:

5, 4, 3, 5, 4, 2, 4, 3, 6

into:

2, 3, 3, 4, 4, 4, 5, 5, 6.

When there is an *odd* number of scores, the median corresponds to the middle score in the list. So, in our example with 9 observations, the median equals 4 (the fifth number in the row).

With an *even* number of scores in the distribution, the median corresponds to the mean of the middle two scores. Thus, a series of 8 scores:

5, 3, 2, 5, 3, 5, 10, 1

is first ordered into:

1, 2, 3, 3, 5, 5, 5, 10

and then the median is defined as the mean of the two middle values: $(3 + 5)/2 = 4$.

To give you a better idea of what the median stands for, Figure 3.4 shows the median values for the three distributions in Figure 3.1. You can easily see from Figure 3.4a that the median is the same as the mean for the symmetric distribution with the single peak. The mean and median are also nearly the same for the distribution with the two peaks (Figure 3.4c), because this distribution is reasonably symmetric as well. Whenever a distribution is symmetric, mean and median will coincide, and will be equal to the X-value that splits the distribution in two mirror images.

The mean and median differ from one another when the distribution is not symmetric. So, for the positively skewed distribution in Figure 3.1b, there is a difference between the mean and the median. For a positively skewed distribution, the median will be lower than the mean (that is, the median is shifted

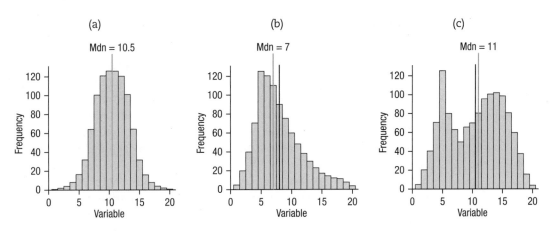

Figure 3.4 The median as a measure of central tendency

more towards the short tail). For a negatively skewed distribution, the median will be higher than the mean (that is, also shifted more towards the short tail). Given that many distributions in psychology are positively skewed (for example, reaction times, incomes), the median in a study will quite often be lower than the mean.

Another characteristic of the median is that it is less influenced by extreme values than the mean. Sometimes in a study we observe values that are difficult to bring into line with the other observations. These are called **outliers**. For instance, in reaction time (RT) experiments it is quite common to observe a few very long RTs. So, in an experiment where participants have to press a button as soon as they detect a light flash on the computer screen, it is possible to get the following set of data (in milliseconds):

220, 214, 185, 863, 192, 211, 199

If we calculate the mean and the median of these data, we get the following values:

$$M = (220 + 214 + 185 + 863 + 192 + 211 + 199)/7$$
$$= 298 \text{ ms}$$
$$Mdn = 185, 192, 199, 211, 214, 220, 863$$
$$= 211 \text{ ms}$$

In this example, the mean seems to summarise the distribution of reaction times less well than the median, because six of the seven data fall well below the mean, whereas all data lie nicely around the median. The mean is inflated by the presence of the one reaction time of 863 ms. Suppose this value had been 221 ms, then the data would have looked as follows:

$$M = (220 + 214 + 185 + 221 + 192 + 211 + 199)/7$$
$$= 206 \text{ ms}$$
$$Mdn = 185, 192, 199, 211, 214, 220, 221$$
$$= 211 \text{ ms}$$

The 'outrageously' long RT of 863 ms shifts the mean by some 90 ms, whereas it has no more impact on the median than the 'more reasonable value' of 221 ms. Confronted with such data, the researcher has to decide on the importance of the deviating value of 863 ms for the question under investigation. Is it caused by factors inherent to the process being measured (manual responses to light detection), or is it caused by extraneous factors (for example, a lack of attention, or cramp in the finger)? In the former case, the mean captures something important in the data (namely that from time to time very long RTs are observed). When the latter is the case, the median captures the frequency distribution better.

The symbol for reporting the median in the literature is **Mdn**. However, most of the time you will not see this symbol, because the median is simply integrated into the narrative text. So, for the examples above, we are likely to see something like: 'The median number of pints drunk in a weekend is 4' and 'The median manual response time to light flashes is 211 ms.' However, we could also write something like: 'The median number of pints drunk in a weekend was higher for male students (Mdn = 5) than for female students (Mdn = 4).'

Learning check

Calculate the median number of letters remembered in the short-term memory experiment of Chapter 2 (summarised in Table 2.1). Does it differ much from the mean you calculated earlier? Why?

3.4 The mode

The **mode** of a distribution refers to the X value with the highest frequency. So, for the example of the number of pints drunk (5, 4, 3, 5, 4, 2, 4, 3, 6), the mode is 4, because this score was observed with the highest frequency (3 occurrences). The mode can be spotted easily in a frequency distribution table (see Table 3.1) or in a frequency distribution graph (Figures 3.5 and 3.6). When a distribution contains one clear peak, it is called *unimodal*; when it has two distinct peaks, it is *bimodal*; and when it has more peaks, it is called *multimodal*.

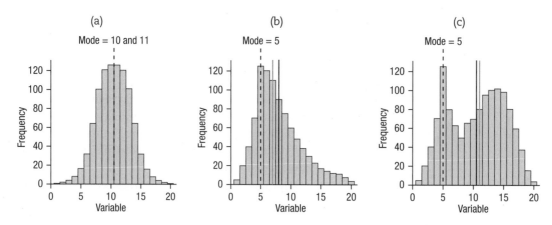

Figure 3.5 The mode as a measure of central tendency

The interpretation of the mode is easy when the distribution is unimodal and symmetric, as shown in Figure 3.5a. Then, the mode coincides with the mean and the median. When the distribution is unimodal and positively skewed, the mode is also easy to understand. Its value will be lower than the median, which in turn is lower than the mean (see Figure 3.5b).

The interpretation of the mode becomes more contentious when the distribution does not have a simple shape. (This is often the case when the number of observations is limited relative to the number of X-values observed.) Figure 3.5c shows a situation where a mindless selection of the mode is likely to misrepresent the frequency distribution. Because the mode only captures the value observed with the *highest* frequency, it misses the second, lower peak. Therefore, you should always have a look at the frequency distribution when you use the mode as a measure of central tendency. Keep in mind that a frequency difference of 1 unit can make a huge difference in the value of the mode, as illustrated in Figure 3.6. The only difference between the distributions in Figures 3.6a and 3.6b is that one variable in the (b) has a value of 8 instead of 7. As you can see, this has had profound consequences for the mode.

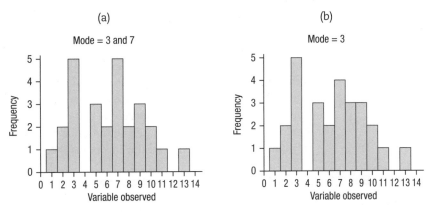

Figure 3.6 Susceptibility of the mode to minute differences in frequency when the frequency distribution is based on a small number of observations

There is no special symbol or convention for reporting the mode in a text. Usually, the measure is reported in full, as in 'The number of pints drunk in a weekend has a mode of 4, with 3 of the 9 participants reporting this value.'

Learning check

What is the mode of the number of letters remembered in the short-term memory experiment of Chapter 2 (summarised in Table 2.1). Does it differ much from the mean and the median you calculated earlier? Why?

3.5 Which measure of central tendency to use?

With a few exceptions reported below, the **mean** is the preferred measure of central tendency because it reflects the position of each score in the distribution.

This measure is also used to calculate the variability in the data (see Chapter 4). However, because the mean is influenced by values that may not be representative for the bulk of the distribution – the outliers – it is good practice always to check how strongly the mean is influenced by such unrepresentative observations. This is particularly important when the number of observations is rather small. The larger the number of observations, the smaller the impact of one outlying value. Another way to limit the impact of unrepresentative values is to restrict the range of values included in the mean. For instance, in studies of word naming, in which participants are asked to read aloud a word as soon as they perceive it, it is customary to exclude all naming latencies smaller than 200 ms and larger than 1,500 ms. We know that no word can be read rapidly enough for the participant to start its pronunciation in less than 200 ms. Also, naming latencies of words rarely require more than 1.5 seconds to initiate, so that longer reaction times are likely to be the result of a temporary lack of attention.

In a number of cases, the **median** is the preferred alternative to the mean. This arises when the distribution is skewed and it is felt that the mean becomes unrepresentative of the majority of the distribution. A good example of such a situation is the average disposable household income. The bulk of weekly household incomes in the UK lie between £250 and £750. However, a small percentage of households make much more money, so the mean income is considerably higher than the median income. This raises the question of which measure of central tendency best captures the impact of a new tax, as is nicely illustrated in the boxed excerpt from a debate in the House of Commons on the impact of an increase in local tax (House of Commons Daily Debates, 10 February 2004, Column 1357). In order to fully appreciate this exchange, it is important to know that local taxes in the UK are based on the value of the house and are, therefore, only indirectly related to the weekly income of the household.

Box 3.1 **Excerpt from a debate in the House of Commons on the impact of an increase in local tax**

> **Mr. Eric Pickles** (Con): I shall just give the hon. Gentleman the figures; then he can dispute them. In England, the couple would pay an extra £547 a year, in Scotland an extra £510 a year and in Wales an extra £471 a year. Were there a third or fourth person earning in the household, there would be a heavy extra burden. A son or daughter still at home with their parents and just starting out at work would find the tax very heavy.
>
> **Matthew Green** (LD): It would be helpful if the hon. Gentleman confirmed that the median household income in the UK is £21,700, and not the £48,000 that the Conservative briefings quoted in the Sunday Express suggested is the average household income. I would love to know where all those people earning that amount are.
>
> **Mr. Pickles:** I am sorry that the hon. Gentleman disputes our figures, because they stand the test of scrutiny. We are talking about average male earnings—I do not think anyone would dispute that that figure is £525 a week—and average female earnings, which are £396 a week. Those are the facts—[Interruption.] The hon. Gentleman should face reality. People on average earnings will lose out under his proposals, and the Liberal Democrats' blindness to that fact is leaving them looking utterly foolish.

▷

▷

> **David Taylor** (Lab/Co-op): I am reluctant to rise to the defence of the Liberals, but will not the hon. Gentleman accept that there can be an enormous difference between median income and mean income because of the distorting effect of the many huge household incomes at the upper end of the spectrum? It is therefore fair of the hon. Member for Ludlow (Matthew Green) to quote the figure of £21,700.
>
> **Mr. Pickles:** I am not disputing what the hon. Gentleman says about the difference between median and mean incomes. I choose my figures carefully—[Laughter.] They are based on income, because we are debating a local income tax. It is right to take into account the level of people's incomes in such a debate.
>
> © Crown copyright.

3

When an extra tax of £500 is discussed, the difference between an alleged median income of £21,700 and an alleged mean income of £48,000 becomes much more than an academic subtlety.[2]

The median will also be preferred to the mean when the data come from an ordinal scale. Remember from Chapter 1 that not all numbers refer to magnitudes. Some numbers only refer to ranks, with unequal distances between the different ranks (for example, the difference between the first and the second of a class need not be the same as the difference between the second and the third). For such numbers, there are fewer disputes when the median value is reported than the mean, because the mean requires the data to be added and divided, which is not really possible for data with unequal intervals between them. However, in practice there will rarely be a big difference between the mean and the median value and, therefore, many authors still report the mean rather than the median.

Finally, the median is more appropriate than the mean when the values at the end of distribution cannot be determined with precision. In many surveys – in particular those dealing with positively skewed distributions – individual frequencies are not given above a certain cut-off score because these frequencies become too low. For instance, many surveys on household sizes group all sizes of six or more people (see Figure 2.8). Given such data, it is not possible to calculate the exact mean. However, it is possible to calculate the median – see also Section 3.8 (Going further) for the exact calculation of the median for this example. Similar situations may arise if an experimenter cannot measure variables outside a given range, for example, times longer than a minute or shorter than a second because of the stopwatch that is used.

In general, the use of the mode is limited to data from a nominal scale. Remember from Chapter 1 that these data are not really numbers (even when they are represented in numerical form), but labels. Because these labels (for example, the preferred colour) cannot be summed, it is impossible to calculate their mean value. Similarly, because these data are not part of an ascending

---

2 The 'average household income' of £48,000 (which Mr. Pickles takes to be the mean income) is based on the assumption that each household consists of a working male and a working female (£525 × 52 + £396 × 52 = £47,892). This is another example of how careful one must be, even with correct measures of central tendency.

(ordered) scale, it is impossible to determine a median score that would split the lower half from the upper half of the distribution. All we can do is indicate which category was observed most. This is the exact definition of the mode. So, whenever the data come from a nominal scale, the measure of central tendency to use is the mode. This measure will be particularly informative when the number of categories is not too high (for example, a few colour categories to choose from, a limited number of political parties for which to vote) and/or when the frequency of the modal value clearly exceeds that of the other categories.

3.6 Comparing the different measures of central tendency

Because nowadays measures of central tendency are so easy to calculate with a computer, it is always a good idea to compute all three measures, even if you do not report them (unless you are working with data from a nominal scale). A comparison of the different values can provide you with valuable information about your data. When the median is much lower than the mean, this implies that the distribution is likely to be positively skewed and/or that there are one or more extreme values (outliers) at the high end. Conversely, when the median is much higher than the mean you are dealing with a negatively skewed distribution or, more likely, with extreme values (outliers) at the lower end of the distribution. Differences between the mean (or the median) and the mode are again informative when they are large. Suppose, for instance, that you ran a word naming study and you find a mean naming latency of 350 ms and a mode of 0 ms. A very likely explanation of this finding is that the microphone was often triggered by noise before the participant started to speak. Doing this type of elementary performance check can help you to better understand the data you are dealing with and protect you from publishing embarrassing summary data.

3.7 Calculating measures of central tendency in SPSS

Once you know the basics of SPSS (see Section 2.5.1) it is very straightforward to calculate the measures of central tendency with this software package. As an example, we will make a file that calculates the mean, the median and the mode of an input column of observed values.

For a more detailed guide to calculating the measures of central tendency using SPSS, see Brace, Kemp and Snalgar, *SPSS for Psychologists*, Chapter 3, section 5.

First, we open the SPSS spreadsheet and enter, in the first column, the data from our example of the pints of beer drunk (use the *Variable View* to give this column a name and to get rid of the decimal places).

Then click on *Analyze*, *Descriptive Statistics* and *Frequencies*, as we did in Chapter 2 for the frequency distribution.

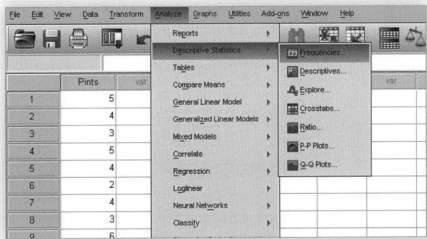

At the top right of the Frequencies panel, you find a button *Statistics*.

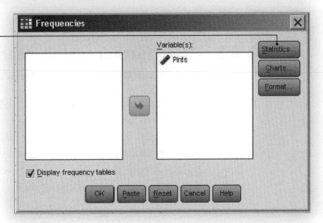

Click on it and indicate you want the *Mean*, the *Median* and the *Mode*.

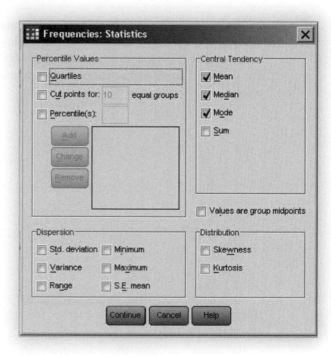

Then click on Continue and OK to get the table with the values of central tendency.

Statistics		
Pints		
N	Valid	9
	Missing	0
Mean		4.00
Median		4.00
Mode		4

And that's all there is to it!

Learning check

Using SPSS, enter the data of the number of letters remembered in the short-term memory experiment of Chapter 2 (summarised in Table 2.1). Calculate the measures of central tendency. Do they agree with what you found?

 3.8 Going further: using interpolation to find a more exact value of the median

In Section 3.3 we saw how to calculate the median. In general, this procedure works very well, except when we have many observations and a limited number of X-values. Then, it is possible that the median value calculated as the midpoint of the ordered observations is not precise enough. A typical example is the household size in the UK, reported in Chapter 2 (Figure 2.8) and repeated in Table 3.3 as a frequency distribution table.

To calculate the median as described in Section 3.3, we could rewrite the frequency distribution table of Table 3.3 as a hypothetical sample of 100 observations as follows:

1111111111111111111111111111
2222222222222222222222222222222222
3333333333333333
44444444444444
55555
66

Table 3.3 A frequency distribution table of the household sizes in the UK (Census, 2001).

Size	Relative frequency
1	28%
2	35%
3	16%
4	14%
5	5%
6+	2%

The median of this sample is the average of the 50th and the 51st observation (that is, the two observations in the middle of the sample), as shown below:

1111111111111111111111111112222222222222222222222
2222222222223333333333333333334444444444444445555566

Given that the values of the 50th and the 51st observation are both 2, the median of the sample is (2 + 2)/2 = 2. So, according to this analysis, the median household size in the UK is 2.

Although this value will do for most purposes, sometimes we may want to have more precision, say to one decimal place. To find this value, we will make use of the fact that each value in Table 3.3 represents a theoretical interval (see Section 2.6) going from X – 0.5 to X + 0.5. So, we can rewrite Table 3.3 as Table 3.4.

Table 3.4 The theoretical frequency distribution table of the household sizes in the UK.

Size	Relative frequency
$0.5 \leq X < 1.5$	28%
$1.5 \leq X < 2.5$	35%
$2.5 \leq X < 3.5$	16%
$3.5 \leq X < 4.5$	14%
$4.5 \leq X < 5.5$	5%
$5.5 \leq X$	2%

The median value is the value that splits the frequency distribution in half, so it has to fall somewhere in the interval between 1.5 and 2.5 because 28% of the household sizes are smaller than 1.5 and 28% + 35% = 63% of the household sizes are smaller than 2.5. More precisely, it has to be located at the value that splits the interval 1.5–2.5 into a portion of 22% (needed to get 28% + 22% = 50%) and the remainder. The median value is calculated as: the lower limit of the interval plus the part of the interval needed to reach the midpoint of the entire distribution.

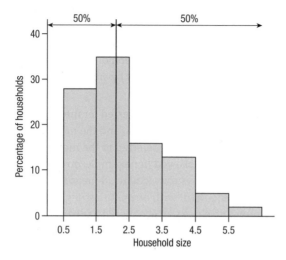

Figure 3.7 Frequency distribution graph of household sizes, showing where to find the median value with one digit precision

Mdn = 1.5 + 22/35

= 1.5 + 0.6 = 2.1, rounded to 1 decimal place

The situation is shown in Figure 3.7.

This example shows how we can use interpolation to find a more precise value of the median. Notice that, for the data given in Table 3.3, it is not possible to calculate the exact mean because we do not have precise data for household sizes of 6 and more.

❓ 3.9 Answers to chapter questions

1 What is a measure of central tendency?

A measure of central tendency is a statistical measure that identifies a single score as representative of the entire frequency distribution. It is a value somewhere between the minimum and the maximum value and it represents the distribution best when the distribution is unimodal and symmetric.

2 What is the mean and how is it calculated?

The mean is a measure of central tendency that can be thought of as the point in the distribution that would balance the distribution if it were placed on a seesaw. It is calculated by taking the sum of the observations divided by the number of observations, that is $M = \Sigma X/N$.

3 What is the median and how is it calculated?

The median is a measure of central tendency that splits the distribution into two equal halves. To calculate it, the observed X-values are ordered from small to large. The median then equals the middle value when N is odd and the mean of the two middle values when N is even.

4 What is the mode and how is it calculated?

The mode is a measure of central tendency that indicates the X-value with the highest frequency. It is advisable always to check whether the mode is a good representation of the underlying distribution because it can be influenced heavily by small changes in frequency.

5 Which measure of central tendency is to be preferred?

In general the mean is preferred for interval/ratio scales. The median is preferred for ordinal data, and the mode must be used for nominal data. The median is preferred to the mean when the underlying distribution is skewed (for example, on household income). It is a good idea always to calculate all measures of central tendency and to compare them with one another. Big deviations in their values are interesting clues to the underlying distribution.

☑ 3.10 Learning check solutions

The mean number of letters remembered in Table 2.1 was 6.83. The median number was 7, and the mode was also 7. The values are close together because the underlying frequency distribution is unimodal and reasonably symmetric.

Summarising data using measures of variability

4

4.1   The underestimated importance of variability

In the previous chapter, we saw that measures of central tendency are used to represent distributions all the time. Nearly all of our concepts are based on average values assembled over many different experiences and because the statistical measures of central tendency are so close to everyday intuitions, they are easy to understand.

However, as a scientist you must know that measures of central tendency hide one important aspect of the world around us: the variability that is present in everything. Not everyone is exactly the same and having knowledge of the differences is essential if you want to truly understand human functioning. Remember from Chapter 1 that when parents and nurses want to check whether a baby is growing well, they need to know more than the average values in the growth charts (that is, the measures of central tendency). They must also know the range of acceptable values. Very few babies follow exactly the middle line of the curve (that is, the central tendency). They are either slightly above or below this line. As long as they stay within a 'reasonable band', there is nothing untoward; only when they get out of this range is further action required. To determine the band of 'reasonable values', we must know the variability of the scores within the population.

Understanding the notion of variability will also help you to avoid typical misunderstandings in everyday communication. For instance, when people read in a newspaper that research in the USA has shown that male university students dream about sex (in 12% of their dreams) more often than female university students (in 4% of their dreams), they all too often reach the conclusion that *all* men dream more about sex than *all* women. They assume that the measure of central tendency applies to the entire population, as if all observations in the frequency distribution were limited to this single score. Reducing an entire distribution to its mean may be economical for our thinking because it reduces the amount of information we have to store. However, it often leads to misunderstandings and to group stereotypes – such as 'all men dream more about sex than all women'. Our understanding would be very different, depending on whether we were told that the percentages of sex-related dreams in men ranged from 0% to 50% or that they ranged from 9% to 15%. In the former case, the higher number of sex-related dreams in men than in women is likely to be due to a small subpopulation of men dreaming about sex nearly every night, while the great majority of men do not dream about sex any more than women do. In the latter case, it is clear that all male university students have regularly occurring sex dreams. Similarly, the mean value of 4% for females has a different meaning if it is based on observations between 0% and 40% than if it is based on observations ranging from 1% to 7%.

To avoid erroneous conclusions on the basis of information about central tendencies alone, your first reaction as a scientist upon hearing a measure of central tendency must be: 'OK, but what about the variability in the data?' Because the interpretation of measures of central tendency depends on the variability in the data, you must insist on getting access to this information.

Only then can you get an accurate picture of the entire frequency distribution, as will be explained in the next chapter.

There are two common measures of variability: the range and the standard deviation. They will be discussed in Sections 4.2 and 4.3. However, before we discuss them, it is good for you to remember that these measures cannot be applied to all measurement scales. The range requires that the measurement scale is ordinal or interval/ratio; the standard deviation can only be used for interval/ratio measurement scales. Measures of variability involve numerical operations that cannot be applied to numbers from nominal scales. The only measure of variability we can calculate for a nominal measurement scale is the number of categories observed. There is more variability in the answers of a colour preference study, for example, when participants use 15 different colour names than when they use 6.

> **Be careful!** The range cannot be calculated on numbers from a nominal scale. The standard deviation cannot be calculated on numbers from a nominal or an ordinal scale.

4.2 The range

The **range** is the distance between the largest and the smallest score of the distribution. The easiest (and the most frequently used) way of communicating the range is to list the minimum and the maximum scores, in addition to the measure of central tendency. So, a researcher investigating how many numbers university students store on their mobile phone may conclude: 'Students have on average 15 telephone numbers programmed into their mobiles (range 2–99).' Notice that such a statement includes much more information than the mean alone. For a start, it informs us that all students have at least two numbers in their phonebook. There are no students with an empty phonebook. Second, we also learn that there is quite some variability in the number of telephone numbers: even though the mean is 15, the observations vary between 2 and 99. Our understanding of telephone use in students would be different if we knew that the range was 11–23. Third, there is a very high chance that we are dealing with a positively skewed distribution because the distance between the mean and the lowest score (15–2) is smaller than the distance between the highest score and the mean (99–15).

A limitation of the range statistic is its vulnerability to outliers. That is, the minimum or the maximum value observed may be due to one or two observations that are not in line with the others. Such an example is shown in Figure 4.1. In this distribution we see that nearly all observations (73/75) are between 10 and 20, and that the minimum and maximum values are distorted by two outliers; one of 2 telephone numbers and one of 99 telephone numbers.

Furthermore, in general, the range statistic is limited in its use because it does not take into account all scores in the distribution. It only considers the two extreme scores, as if nothing in between matters.

A second limitation of the range statistic is that its value varies with the sample size. As a rule, the range tends to be larger for big samples than for small samples. This is because, all other things being equal, the chances of observing extreme values increase when more observations are made. If only one student

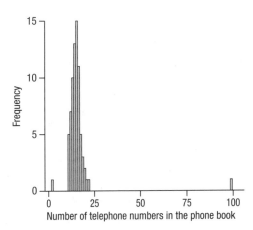

Figure 4.1 The frequency distribution graph of a study on the number of telephone numbers students have in their phonebooks. Notice the outlying values of 2 and 99 which have a strong influence on the range

in 100 has a phonebook with 99 telephone numbers, chances that such a student will be in the sample studied are larger for a sample of 1000 students than for a sample of 10 students.[1]

For these reasons (and some others), the standard deviation discussed below is the preferred measure of variability in psychological research. Still, the range is a useful measure, in particular when researchers want to convey a quick picture about the variability in their data. For instance, in many research articles, the range is used to indicate the variability in the ages of the participants. You often read sentences like: 'The participants were 20 undergraduate students. Their mean age was 19 years (range 18–36 years).' Coincidentally, in this particular example the range conveys quite a lot of information because the text can safely be read as meaning that the age of all but one participant was about 18 years, and that the remaining participant was a mature student of 36 years. The range is also the indicated measure of variability for measurements from an ordinal measurement scale, because the calculations needed for the standard deviation require an interval/ratio scale of measurement.

4.3 Standard deviation and variance

As indicated in the previous section, the range statistic defines the variability in the data as the difference between the lowest and the highest score, and ignores the characteristics of all the observations in between. A better measure of variability would look at the average distance between all the scores and

---

1 The chance that at least one such a person will be present in a sample of 1000 people equals 1 minus the chance that none of the students have the maximum number of 99 telephone numbers. This probability equals $.99^{100}$, which is .00004317. So, the chance of observing at least one person with 99 telephone numbers in a sample of 1000 equals $1 - .00004317 = .99995673$. In contrast, the chance that there will be at least one such a person in a sample of 10 equals $1 - .99^{10} = .095618$ (that is, less than 10%).

the measure of central tendency that is used to represent the distribution as a whole. This, in a nutshell, is what the **standard deviation** stands for: the average distance of each and every observation to the mean of the distribution. Because the standard deviation is based on the *mean* distance (or deviation), it can only be calculated for data that come from an interval/ratio measurement scale.

4.3.1 The reasoning behind the standard deviation

As stated above, the standard deviation is a measure of the average distance between the observed values and the sample mean. Unfortunately, for two reasons, the standard deviation is more complicated than a simple mean deviation.

The first problem is that the average distance between the observations and the mean *by definition* equals 0. This is easily illustrated by looking at the data from the beer-drinking study we introduced in the preceding chapters. In this study, 9 students wrote down how many pints of beer they drank the previous weekend:

5, 4, 3, 5, 4, 2, 4, 3, 6

As we saw in Chapter 3, the mean of this sample is:

$$M = \frac{\Sigma X}{N}$$
$$= \frac{5+4+6+5+4+2+4+3+6}{9} = \frac{36}{9} = 4$$

We now list the differences between all the observations (X) and the mean (M) in an auxiliary table (Table 4.1).

Table 4.1 Auxiliary table to calculate the mean distance between the observations and the mean for the study on the number of pints drunk in the weekend. Mean (M) of the sample is 4 pints.

X	X − M	= X − 4
5	1	= 5 − 4
4	0	= 4 − 4
3	−1	= 3 − 4
5	1	= 5 − 4
4	0	= 4 − 4
2	−2	= 2 − 4
4	0	= 4 − 4
3	−1	= 3 − 4
6	2	= 6 − 4
ΣX = 36	Σ(X − M) = 0	
N = 9	$\overline{(X − M)}$ = 0/9 = 0	
M = 4		

Σ(X − M) is the sum of the difference scores and $\overline{(X − M)}$ is the mean of the difference scores

In the rest of the book, we will make extensive use of auxiliary tables and you are strongly encouraged to do so when you are studying. Be careful, though. Auxiliary tables, like the one shown in Table 4.1, differ in a number of respects from the frequency distribution tables introduced in Chapter 2. These differences are listed in Box 4.1 (overleaf). Take note of them, because confusions between frequency distribution tables and auxiliary tables are a source of many errors in the understanding of statistics (and in exams!).

As can be seen in Table 4.1, the mean distance (deviation) between the observed values and the sample mean equals 0. This is to be expected because of the way the mean is calculated. We can visualise this as follows (at least for a symmetrical distribution). Because the mean of a distribution is the value 'in the middle', half of the deviations between the observed values and the mean will be negative (because the observed values are smaller than the mean) and half will be positive (because the observed values are larger than the mean). The negative and the positive deviations will cancel out each other, leaving us with a mean deviation value of 0.

One solution to this problem could be to work with the absolute values of the deviation scores. These are the deviations between the observed values and the mean, independent of whether the observed values are smaller or larger than the mean. The absolute value of an observation X is indicated by the symbol $|X|$. When the value of X is positive, so is the absolute value of X (that is, $|+4| = +4$); when the value of X is negative, the absolute value of X is positive (that is, $|-4| = +4$). In other words, the absolute value is always positive.

Table 4.2 shows the auxiliary table to calculate the mean absolute deviation between the observed values and the mean. From the table you can see that the mean absolute distance between the observations and the sample mean is .9.

Table 4.2 Auxiliary table to calculate the mean absolute distance between the observations and the mean for the study on the number of pints drunk in the weekend. Mean (M) of the sample is 4 pints.

X	X − M	|X − M|
5	1	1
4	0	0
3	−1	1
5	1	1
4	0	0
2	−2	2
4	0	0
3	−1	1
6	2	2
$\Sigma X = 36$ $N = 9$ $M = 4$	$\Sigma(X - M) = 0$ $\overline{(X - M)} = 0$	$\Sigma\|X - M\| = 8$ $\overline{\|X - M\|} = 8/9 = .9$

$\Sigma(X - M)$ is the sum of the difference scores, $\overline{(X - M)}$ is the mean of the difference scores and $\overline{|X - M|}$ is the mean of the absolute difference scores

Box 4.1   **Differences between frequency distribution tables and auxiliary tables for the calculation of standard deviations, *t*-tests and correlation coefficients**

Frequency distribution tables	Auxiliary tables
1 *X*-values are ordered from small to large.	1 *X*-values are entered in the table in the same order as they were observed in the study.
2 There is only one entry for each *X*-value. The fact that there may be multiple observations of a particular *X*-value is captured in the frequency column.	2 There is one line per observation. Multiple observations of an *X*-value result in multiple entries in the table.
3 *X*-values between the minimum and the maximum value that are not observed in the sample are included in the table and given a frequency of 0.	3 Only *X*-values that are observed in the sample are included in the table.

This makes sense, given that the largest absolute deviation was 2 (between the value 2 and the mean, for example), and that there were several deviation scores of 0 (when the observed values were the same as the mean).

However, for a number of reasons that are too specialised to be explained here, statisticians have opted not to work with absolute deviations but with squared deviations. In other words, rather than taking the absolute value of the deviation scores, they have decided to square the individual deviation scores and to take the square root of the average value. Before I explain how this is done, it may be a good idea for you to check whether your understanding of squares and square roots is still up to date. Solve the problems in the learning check. Extra explanation of squares and square roots is given in the learning check solutions at the end of this chapter if you need it.

Learning check on your understanding of squares and square roots
Solve the following problems. You can use a calculator.

$(2)^2 =$	$(-12)^2 =$	$(1.1)^2 =$	$\sqrt{16} =$	$\sqrt{0.001} =$
$(-2)^2 =$	$(0.1)^2 =$	$(-1.1)^2 =$	$\sqrt{-16} =$	$\sqrt{9.61} =$
$(12)^2 =$	$(-0.1)^2 =$		$\sqrt{0.1} =$	

The auxiliary table (Table 4.3) shows how the average deviation between the observed values and the sample mean is calculated on the basis of squared values.

By squaring the deviation scores, we solve the problem of the positive and negative values that cancelled each other out. The mean squared deviation $\overline{(X - M)^2}$ is called the population variance, which is defined as follows:

$$\text{variance}_{\text{population}} = \frac{\Sigma(X - M)^2}{N}$$

Table 4.3 Auxiliary table to calculate the mean squared distance between the observations and the mean for the study on the number of pints drunk in the weekend. Mean (M) of the sample is 4 pints.

X	X − M	(X − M)²
5	1	1
4	0	0
3	−1	1
5	1	1
4	0	0
2	−2	4
4	0	0
3	−1	1
6	2	4
ΣX = 36 N = 9 M = 4	Σ(X − M) = 0 $\overline{(X - M)}$ = 0	Σ(X − M)² = 12 $\overline{(X - M)^2}$ = 12/9 =1.3

Applied to our example:

$$\text{variance}_{\text{population}} = \frac{12}{9} = 1.3$$

Let us go over the calculation of the population variance again. The population variance is simply the mean squared deviation between the observed values and the mean. First, we calculate the mean M. Then, for each observed value X we calculate X − M. Next, we square the X − M scores and add them together. Finally, we divide the sum of squares by the number of observations to get the mean squared deviation. The easiest way to do this is to make use of an auxiliary table like Table 4.3. First, we have a column with all the observed X-values. On the basis of this column we calculate M. Then we add a column with the deviations between the observed X-values and M, and a column with the squared deviation scores. By adding the values in the last column we get the sum of the squared values, which we then divide by the number of observations.

However, statisticians have discovered that this definition of variance is not completely correct, particularly when the sample size is small. This brings us to the second reason why the calculation of the standard deviation is so complicated. The issue is that, although in our example we have 9 observations, only 8 of them are free to vary. If we have 8 observations and we know the mean value, the last observation is bound to have the value it has (that is, it has no variability). In the equation

$$\frac{5 + 4 + 3 + 5 + 4 + 2 + 4 + 3 + ?}{9} = 4,$$

the ? mark can have only one value, namely the value 6.

For this reason, when we are calculating the **variance of a sample**, we divide the sum of squares by the number of observations that are free to vary, the so-called **degrees of freedom**, abbreviated to **df**.

Because the number of observations that are free to vary in a sample is one less than the total number of observations, the degrees of freedom correspond to N – 1. So, instead of dividing the sum of squares by the sample size N, for empirical sample data we have to divide the sum of squares by the sample size minus one. This does not change much for large samples, but makes a difference when the sample size is small.

Irrespective of the reasons why we have to divide the sum of squares by the degrees of freedom, you must know that the formula to use whenever you are analysing sample data is:

$$\text{variance}_{\text{sample}} = \frac{\Sigma(X - M)^2}{N - 1}$$

Applied to our example this means that:

$$\text{variance}_{\text{sample}} = \frac{12}{8} = 1.5$$

Now that we know how to calculate the variance of sample data, we just need to correct our measure for the fact that we squared the deviations between the observed X-values and M. This is done by taking the square root of the sample variance. The resulting statistic is the **standard deviation of the sample**, abbreviated to SD. The equation to calculate the standard deviation is:

$$SD = \sqrt{\frac{\Sigma(X - M)^2}{N - 1}}$$

Applied to our example:

$$SD = \sqrt{\frac{12}{9 - 1}}$$
$$= \sqrt{1.5} = 1.22$$

When we compare the value of SD (1.22) to the value we obtained by taking the average of the absolute deviations |X – M| (0.9; see Table 4.2), we see that the standard deviation is slightly larger. This is because of the two transformations we made. First, squaring the deviation scores and taking the square root of the sum results in a slightly larger value than simply taking the mean of the absolute deviation scores. Second, the fact that we have to divide by N – 1 rather than by N also increases the value of SD, in particular when the sample size is small. However, the standard deviation still fulfils its purpose: it gives an estimate of the average deviation between all the observed values and the sample mean.

4.3.2 How to interpret the standard deviation?

Because the standard deviation is a measure of the *average* deviation between all the observed values in the sample and the sample mean, its value must fall somewhere between the largest and the smallest deviation. In practice, the smallest deviation between the observed values and the mean will be close to 0 (when the observed value and the sample mean agree). (See the beer-drinking example in which several observed values coincided with the mean, yielding an X – M measure of 0.) So, the standard deviation will roughly coincide with the value halfway between a deviation of 0 (the smallest deviation observed) and the largest deviation observed. Or to phrase it differently: **the value of the standard deviation will be close to half the distance between the sample mean and the extreme scores observed in the sample.**

Because the standard deviation roughly coincides with half of the distance between the sample mean and the extreme values of the sample, **the vast majority of observations in a sample will lie between the mean minus twice the standard deviation and the mean plus twice the standard deviation.** This is a very important insight, because it forms the basis of much of our statistical knowledge. It implies that when you know the mean and the standard deviation of a frequency distribution, you know nearly everything about the distribution. If you know that the mean income of academic staff (before taxes) is £40,000 and that the standard deviation is £7,000, you can infer that the vast majority of academic members of staff earn between £26,000 and £54,000 a year. So, when you encounter an academic member of staff who claims to make £70,000 a year, you know that this person is exceptionally well-paid or has some extra income (or is not telling you the truth). As we shall see in the next chapter, the region between M – 2SD and M + 2SD roughly defines the region of 'reasonable' or 'acceptable' values (for example, to determine whether a child is growing well).

The fact that the value of the standard deviation is roughly half the distance between the sample mean and the extreme scores, also allows you to rapidly check whether your calculations of SD are correct. You simply check whether the majority of measurements fall between the mean plus twice the standard deviation and the mean minus twice the standard deviation. Applied to the beer-drinking example, if the SD value of 1.22 is correct then we should find that nearly all observations are packed in the region between M – 2SD and M + 2SD, or between 1.56 (4 – 2 × 1.22) and 6.44 (4 + 2 × 1.22). This is indeed the case (see Table 4.3). Suppose your calculations had left you with an SD estimate of .5. Then, you can easily see that this value must be wrong, because six of the nine observations fall outside the region 3–5. Similarly, you should know that an SD estimate of 10 is impossible, because then you should find the data scattered all over the region between –16 and +24.

Tip Because the standard deviation, *SD*, is a measure of the average distance between the observed *X*-values and the sample mean *M*, the vast majority of *X*-values must be within the region between *M* – 2*SD* and *M* + 2*SD*. If this is not the case, the calculated value of *SD* is probably wrong. Use this as a quick calculation check.

4.3.3 Step by step: calculating the standard deviation

We have covered quite a lot of new ground in this chapter. As a revision exercise, we will reiterate the different calculation steps with a new example. We will calculate the standard deviation of the sample, 1, 3, 5, 3.

First, we have to remember that the equation to calculate the standard deviation of a sample is:

$$SD = \sqrt{\frac{\Sigma(X - M)^2}{N - 1}}$$

in which M is the mean of the sample and N is the number of observations in the sample.

In the example:

$N = 4$

$M = \dfrac{\Sigma X}{N}$

$= \dfrac{1 + 3 + 5 + 3}{4}$

$= \dfrac{12}{4} = 3$

To calculate the standard deviation, we make use of an auxiliary table with three columns: X, $X - M$, and $(X - M)^2$.

X	X – M	(X – M)²
1	–2	4
3	0	0
5	2	4
3	0	0
$\Sigma X = 12$ $N = 4$ $M = 12/4 = 3$	$\Sigma(X - M) = 0$	$\Sigma(X - M)^2 = 8$

First, we calculate ΣX, N and M on the basis of the first column, which contains all the observations made in the sample. Then, we use the value of M to calculate the values of $X - M$. The sum of these deviations must equal zero [that is, $\Sigma(X - M) = 0$]. Then we square each value of $(X - M)$ and we sum the $(X - M)^2$ values. This sum, $\Sigma(X - M)^2$, gives us the numerator of the equation of SD. The number of observations (that is, the number of lines in the auxiliary table) gives us the denominator of the equation. Inserting them in the appropriate places:

$SD = \sqrt{\dfrac{8}{4 - 1}}$

$= 1.63$

 Performance checks for the standard deviation

Once you have calculated the standard deviation, it is always good to check that your calculations are correct. These are a few of the checks you can do.

1 Are the data distributed over the region between $M - 2SD$ and $M + 2SD$? (Remember that for very small sample sizes, the SD may seem a bit too large because of the denominator $N - 1$.)

2 In the auxiliary table, the sum of the values in the second column $\Sigma(X - M)$ must be equal to 0, because the deviations between the observations and the mean must add up to 0. Is this the case?

3 Are all values in the third column positive? This must be so, because squaring the values in column 2 makes them all positive.

Learning check for the standard deviation
Calculate the standard deviation for the sample, 5, 2, 2, 3, 3, and do the three performance checks

4.3.4 Reporting the standard deviation

The standard deviation of a sample is always reported immediately after the mean, using the symbol *SD*. So, for the beer-drinking example, we would write something like: 'Students reported that the number of pints of beer they drank in the previous weekend was 4 (*SD* = 1.63), and ...'.

4.4 Calculating the range and standard deviation with SPSS

You may have noticed in previous chapters that the commands *Analyze*, *Descriptive Statistics*, *Frequencies*, *Statistics* ① also contained a panel with measures of dispersion (variability). These are the steps to take again:

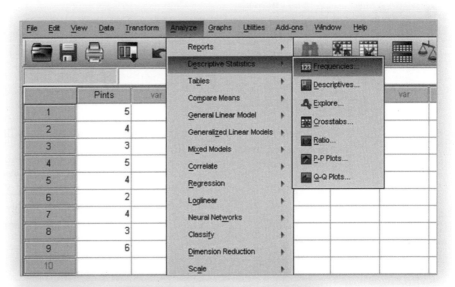

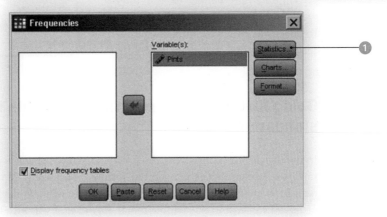

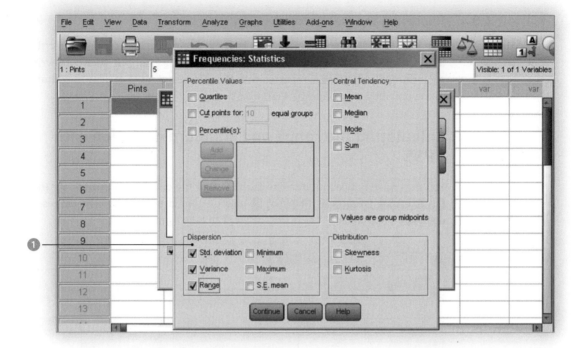

When you check the first column of measures ❶, you will get the following information in your SPSS output:

Statistics		
Pints		
N	Valid	9
	Missing	0
Mean		4.00
Median		4.00
Mode		4
Std. Deviation		1.225
Variance		1.500
Range		4

Compare the values to the ones we calculated above. Now use SPSS to check the other examples we have discussed.

4.5 Going further: a computational formula for the standard deviation

In the days before computers, the formula used to calculate the standard deviation was known as the conceptual formula, because it remained close to the definition of the standard deviation, being the average deviation between the observed values and the sample mean. However, it was also known as a computationally cumbersome formula for reasons that are easy to see. In the above examples, the input data have always been carefully chosen so that the mean was an integer number. However, in reality this is rarely the case. Consider the following example:

0, 5, 2, 2, 1, 0

The mean of this sample is

$$M = \frac{0+5+2+2+1+0}{6}$$

$$= \frac{10}{6} \approx 1.6667$$

This gives us the following auxiliary table.

X	X – M	(X – M)²
0	–1.6667	2.7779
5	3.3333	11.1109
2	0.3333	0.1111
2	0.3333	0.1111
1	–0.6667	0.4445
0	–1.6667	2.7779
ΣX = 10 N = 6 M = 1.6667	Σ(X – M) = –0.0002	Σ(X – M)² = 17.3334

$$SD = \sqrt{\frac{\Sigma(X-M)^2}{N-1}} = \sqrt{\frac{17.3334}{6-1}} = \sqrt{3.466668} = 1.86$$

In this example with a non-integer mean, the calculations become quite cumbersome (even with a calculator) because we have to work with lots of decimals in order to avoid rounding-off errors. A bit of elementary mathematics, however, demonstrates that we do not need to work with the sample mean to calculate the variance or the standard deviation. The reasoning goes as follows:

$$\Sigma(X-M)^2 = \Sigma(X^2 - 2XM + M^2)$$
$$= \Sigma X^2 - 2\Sigma(XM) + \Sigma M^2$$

Because $\Sigma X = N*M$ (the sum of the observations equals N times M) and $\Sigma M = N*M$ (check this in the auxiliary tables we made), we can rewrite the formula as

$$\Sigma(X-M)^2 = \Sigma X^2 - 2(N*M*M) + N*M^2$$
$$= \Sigma X^2 - 2(N*M^2) + N*M^2$$
$$= \Sigma X^2 - N*M^2$$
$$= \Sigma X^2 - N\left(\frac{\Sigma X}{N}\right)^2$$
$$= \Sigma X^2 - N\frac{(\Sigma X)^2}{N^2}$$
$$= \Sigma X^2 - \frac{(\Sigma X)^2}{N}$$

This gives us two new formulas to calculate the standard deviation of a sample without having to calculate the deviation between each observation and the mean. They are:

$$SD = \sqrt{\frac{\Sigma X^2 - N * M^2}{N-1}} \quad \text{and} \quad SD = \sqrt{\frac{\Sigma X^2 - \frac{(\Sigma X)^2}{N}}{N-1}}$$

The attraction of these formulas becomes clear when we construct the auxiliary table. In this table, we no longer need columns for $X - M$ and $(X - M)^2$. We only need a column of X and one of X^2:

X	X²
0	0
5	25
2	4
2	4
1	1
0	0
$\Sigma X = 10$	$\Sigma X^2 = 34$
N = 6	
M = 1.6667	

Using the formula with M^2 first, we get:

$$SD = \sqrt{\frac{34 - 6(1.6667)^2}{6-1}} = \sqrt{3.466} = 1.86$$

Obviously, we should get the same solution if we use the formula with $(\Sigma X)^2$:

$$SD = \sqrt{\frac{34 - \frac{(10)^2}{6}}{6-1}} = \sqrt{3.466} = 1.86$$

Because these two computational formulas are so much easier to calculate by hand and by calculator, they figure prominently in all books of statistics. However, for many students, they cloud the picture because they have to put more effort into computing the standard deviation than understanding it. For this reason, except in the Going further sections ,we only use formulas that stay close to the conceptual equation, even if they are a bit more cumbersome to calculate. In practice, you will use a computer program to calculate the standard deviations so it is more important that you understand the underlying logic than that you are able to calculate the standard deviation by hand. Needless to say, if you feel more comfortable using one of the computational formulas in your hand calculations, you are free to do so. However, in the current age of computers, these formulas are no longer pivotal in an introductory book.

4.6 Answers to chapter questions

1 What is the range and how is it calculated?

The range is the distance between the minimum and the maximum value observed in a sample. The simplest way to report it is simply to give the minimum and the maximum values.

2 Which two limitations does the range have?

The range only takes into account the two extreme values so it is excessively influenced by outliers. The range also depends on the sample size: in general, it will increase as the sample size increases.

3 What is the standard deviation of a sample and how is it calculated?

The standard deviation of a sample (SD) is a measure of the mean deviation between the values observed in a sample and the mean of the sample. Its calculation is slightly more complicated than this simple definition, because we use the squares of the deviations and we have to take into account that one observation of the sample is not free to vary. Taking these two considerations into account, the formula for the standard deviation is fairly straightforward:

$$SD = \sqrt{\frac{\Sigma(X - M)^2}{N - 1}}$$

4 What are auxiliary tables for the calculation of SD and why do we need them?

Auxiliary tables are tables we use to make the calculations easy. For the calculation of SD we will need a table with the X-values (first column), the values $X - M$ (second column), and the values $(X - M)^2$ (third column). Each observation gets one line in an auxiliary table so there will be N rows in the table.

5 What is the critical fact you must remember about the meaning of the standard deviation?

The most important feature of the SD for you to remember is that the vast majority of observations (roughly 95%) fall between $M - 2SD$ and $M + 2SD$. So, if a distribution has M = 100 and SD = 15 (as is the case for IQ scores), the vast majority of scores will be situated between 70 and 130.

☑ 4.7 Learning check solutions

Learning check on your understanding of squares and square roots?

$$(2)^2 = 2 * 2 = 4$$
$$(-2)^2 = (-2) * (-2) = 4$$
$$(12)^2 = 12 * 12 = 144$$
$$(-12)^2 = (-12) * (-12) = 144$$
$$(0.1)^2 = 0.1 * 0.1 = 0.01$$
$$(-0.1)^2 = (-0.1) * (-0.1) = 0.01$$
$$(1.1)^2 = 1.1 * 1.1 = 1.21$$
$$(-1.1)^2 = (-1.1) * (-1.1) = 1.21$$
$$\sqrt{16} = 4 \text{ because } 4 * 4 = 16$$

In algebra $\sqrt{16}$ equals either +4 or –4, because $(+4) * (+4) = 16$ and $(-4) * (-4) = 16$. (You may remember this if you have ever factored quadratic equations.) However, in statistics you only need the positive solution.

$\sqrt{-16} =$ Impossible, because you cannot find a number X so that $X * X$ is a negative number (You can see from the previous answers that all squares are positive)

$$\sqrt{0.1} = 0.3162 \text{ because } 0.3162 * 0.3162 = 0.1$$
$$\sqrt{0.01} = 0.1 \text{ because } 0.1 * 0.1 = 0.01$$
$$\sqrt{9.61} = 3.1 \text{ because } 3.1 * 3.1 = 9.61$$

Learning check on the standard deviation

SD of the sample 5, 2, 2, 3, 3 is 1.225.

Standardised scores, normal distribution and probability

5

?

1 What is a standardised score and why is this helpful?
2 What is a z-score?
3 How do we transform an original score into a z-score?
4 What is the rough interpretation of the value of a z-score? What does a z-score of 0 stand for?
5 How do we transform z-scores into raw scores?
6 What is the normal distribution?
7 What is the probability of an outcome?
8 How do we calculate the probability?
9 What is the standard normal distribution and why do we use it?
10 How do we calculate the probability associated with a z-score?
11 What is a percentile rank and what is a percentile?

Q

5.1   The need for standardised scores

In the previous chapters we have seen that scientists have a pretty accurate picture of a sample when they know the central tendency (typically measured with the mean)[1] and the variability (typically measured with the standard deviation). Therefore, no serious psychologist will be satisfied with a statement like: 'The child had a score of 57 on the literacy test.' The first questions would be: 'What was the mean of the test?' and 'What was the standard deviation?' Only with that knowledge can the psychologist know whether the child performed well.

Because scientists always try to communicate their findings as succinctly as possible, they have looked for a single measure that indicates the position of an individual within a distribution, one that does not depend on the mean and the standard deviation of the specific distribution. This score is known as the **standardised score**, or the z-score. It allows researchers to immediately assess the position of an individual within a distribution because it has the same (standardised) meaning for all distributions. So, whereas you cannot usefully report that a child has a score of 57 on a literacy test, you can tell a psychologist that the child has a z-score of +1.65. This will be enough for them to understand that the child did very well. (As a matter of fact, only about 5% of children are expected to do better.)

In addition, by using standardised scores, psychologists can immediately compare a child's performance on different types of test. So, when they are told that a child has a z-score of +1.65 on a literacy test and a z-score of –0.5 on a reasoning test, they immediately know that the child did much better on the literacy test than on the reasoning test. In this chapter, we will see how z-scores are calculated and interpreted.

5.2   Transforming raw scores into z-scores

The position of an individual within a group is defined in terms of the mean and the standard deviation of the group. We can use these two measures to modify the individual's original score so that all scores have the same, standardised, meaning, which is clear to everyone who has taken a course in statistics. To do so, we calculate the z-score.

The z-score is a transformation of the original score so that the mean is zero and the standard deviation is 1. It is calculated from:

$$z = \frac{X - M}{SD}$$

in which X is the original score, M is the mean, and SD is the standard deviation.

For example, suppose Ms Brewer obtained a score of 26 on her psychology exam, and Ms Davidson obtained a score of 50. Knowing that the mean score

---

[1] This only applies to data from an interval/ratio measurement scale. Note that in the remainder of this chapter, we assume that the data are from such a scale.

for the exam was 44 and the standard deviation was 20, we can calculate the z-scores as follows:

for Ms Brewer: $z = \dfrac{26 - 44}{20} = \dfrac{-18}{20} = -0.9$

for Ms Davidson: $z = \dfrac{50 - 44}{20} = \dfrac{6}{20} = +0.3$

Learning check 1
Calculate the *z*-score of Mr Parkhurst who obtained a raw score of 35 on a driving test that has a mean of 40 and a standard deviation of 10.

5.3 Interpreting *z*-scores

The interpretation of a z-score involves two parts. First, the sign of the z-score tells us whether the score is located above (+) or below (–) the mean. A positive z-score means that the individual did better than average; a negative z-score means that the individual did worse. A z-score of 0 means that the individual's performance was right on the mean of the population. Applied to our example of the psychology exam, Ms Brewer did worse than average, whereas Ms Davidson did better.

The second part of the interpretation involves the numerical value of the z-score. This value tells us how far the score is from the mean in terms of the number of standard deviations. The bigger the value, the more extreme the score. As you may remember from the previous chapter, a z-score of –2 is pretty bad. It indicates an individual whose performance is two standard deviations below the mean. (This is among the worst performances you would expect in the sample.) Conversely, a z-score of +2 is very good, because few people are expected to do better than the mean plus twice the standard deviation. Applied to the example of the psychology exam, it is clear that the scores of both Ms Brewer and Ms Davidson were much less extreme. Whereas Ms Brewer was nearly one standard deviation below the mean (z = –0.9), Ms Davidson's score was less than half a standard deviation above the mean (z = +0.3). As a rule of thumb, psychologists consider z-scores between –1.0 and +1.0 as 'around the average'. They are fairly typical of what can be expected – not much better or worse than would be expected. This usually implies that no further action is required.

In summary, when we interpret a z-score, we first look at the sign, to see whether the individual belongs to the upper half of the group (+ score) or to the lower half (– score). Then we look at the magnitude of the score. As a rule of thumb, the following broad categories can be used:

z-score lower than –2 :   very bad performance (much worse than expected)

z-score between –2 and –1:   quite bad performance (certainly when the z-score approaches –2) z-score between −1 and +1 :   typical performance (as expected)

z-score between +1 and +2 :   quite good performance (the better as the
                                    score comes closer to +2)

z-score above +2 :   very good performance

You can also use these categories to check whether your calculation of a z-score is correct. A negative z-score means that the performance of the individual is worse than the mean performance; a positive z-value means that the individual's score is higher than the mean performance. The more extreme the z-score, the bigger the deviation from the mean (relative to the standard deviation). As a rule, when you obtain a z-score outside the region between −2 and +2, you should check it carefully because these scores should not occur very often. (You may find large z-scores if you are working with special groups; for instance, a group of children with special educational needs taking an intelligence test.)

> **Tip** When you have calculated a z-score, always check whether a negative z-score agrees with performance worse than the mean, and a positive z-score with performance better than the mean. This will help to ensure that you do not communicate wrong conclusions to your colleagues. Also, use the five bands to check whether your calculated z-score agrees with your intuitions on the basis of the test you have given.

Because all z-scores have the same meaning, they allow us to rapidly compare scores on different tests. For example, suppose Mr Camp scored 24 on a test of emotional intelligence (which has a mean of 30 and a SD of 5) and 12 on a test of academic intelligence (which has a mean of 10 and a SD of 1). Are the performances of Mr Camp comparable over the two tests? To answer this question, we calculate the z-scores:

Emotional intelligence: $z = \dfrac{24 - 30}{5} = \dfrac{-6}{5} = -1.2$

Academic intelligence: $z = \dfrac{12 - 10}{1} = \dfrac{2}{1} = +2.0$

On the basis of this information, we immediately see that Mr Camp scored very high on the test of academic intelligence (+2.0 is the start of the exceptional range), whereas he scored quite low on the test of emotional intelligence. Notice that Mr Camp's raw scores went in the opposite direction: The raw score on the test of emotional intelligence (24) was higher than the raw score on the test of academic intelligence (12). However, a comparison of these raw scores makes little sense, as the means and the standard deviations of both tests vary widely. In contrast, the means and standard deviations of the z-scores are, by definition, the same and can be compared.

5.4 Transforming z-scores into raw scores

When we know the z-score of an individual, together with the mean (M) and the standard deviation (SD) of the distribution, we can calculate the individual's raw X-score. For this, we will use the equation:

$X = M + z * SD$

For example, suppose Ms Innis had a z-score of −1.2 on a test with M = 30 and SD = 5. Then, we can calculate Ms Innis's original, raw, score as follows:

$X = 30 + (-1.2 * 5) = 30 + (-6) = 24$

As a calculation check, we use our knowledge that a negative z-score must result in a raw score below the mean and a positive z-score in a raw score above the mean. Given that Ms Innis's z-score was negative (–1.2), her raw score (24) must be lower than the mean (30). In addition, her raw score must be more than one standard deviation below the mean, thus lower than 30 – 5 = 25. Doing this type of elementary calculation checks will ensure that you never come up with solutions that are completely unacceptable.

Thus far, we have talked about z-scores in broad, intuitive terms as scores that refer to very bad results, acceptable results, or very good results. However, as we shall see, z-scores can provide us with much more detailed information about the position of an individual within the population if we can assume that the distribution of the scores is a normal distribution. Therefore, we now turn to a discussion of the normal distribution.

5.5 The normal distribution

5.5.1 Many variables form a normal distribution

In the 19th century, scientists discovered that many biological and behavioural characteristics follow a similar frequency distribution. For many phenomena, there are a lot of observations in a restricted range of values and outside this range the frequencies drop in a consistent and more or less symmetrical way. For instance, when we look at the heights of 50-year old men, we see that many of them are between 170 cm and 180 cm (see Figure 5.1). The numbers

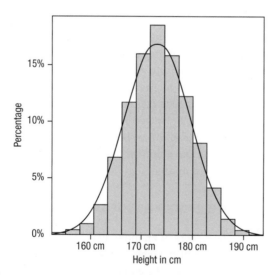

Figure 5.1 Empirical frequency distribution of the height of American men in the 1970s, based on a sample of over 10,000 men. Notice that the frequencies are given in percentages rather than in raw numbers. This is typical for a relative frequency distribution. Also notice the theoretical, normal distribution, assumed to be the distribution of the heights of the population of all American adult men at that age.

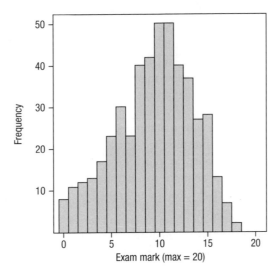

Figure 5.2 Empirical frequency distribution of the marks on an exam with 40 multiple-choice questions (4 alternatives). Notice the similarity of this distribution to the distribution of body heights shown in Figure 5.1.

of men smaller than 170 cm gradually decrease until there are virtually none smaller than 150 cm. Similarly, the numbers of men taller than 180 cm gradually decrease, and there are virtually none taller than 200 cm.[2]

A similar distribution is found when a group of students take an exam (see Figure 5.2). Only a few students do not manage to solve a single problem. Similarly, no students have all answers correct (at least not when the test is well constructed, so that it is not too easy). Instead, there is a mode at a certain performance level and the frequencies of results around this mode quite closely follow the bell-shaped distribution shown in Figure 5.1.

5.5.2 The shape of a normal distribution

Mathematicians discovered that this type of distribution will be observed each time a phenomenon is the result of several independent influences.[3] The mathematical definition of the underlying, theoretical distribution is known as the normal distribution.

The **normal distribution** is a theoretical frequency distribution that has a bell shape, as shown in Figure 5.3. Note that this theoretical frequency distribution

2 The same need not be true for their sons as there has been an average increase of 3–4 cm per generation over recent decades.
3 For those who are interested, the contribution of several independent variables can be approximated by a situation in which a number of independent binary decisions are made (e.g., choose at random left or right). On the internet you find several website applets that simulate this aspect (see the website for this book – www.palgrave.com/psychology/brysbaert – for links). Notice how closely the end result resembles a normal distribution, certainly when the number of choices is large enough.

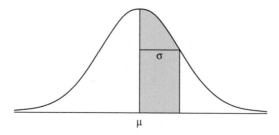

Figure 5.3 The normal distribution. The shaded part shows the width of 1 standard deviation (σ).

no longer consists of the rectangular bars we have come to expect for empirical frequency distribution graphs (as in Figures 5.1 and 5.2). This is because we assume the bars to be so small that they are no longer 'perceivable'. It is the distribution you would expect to find if you were able to examine the entire population from which the observed sample was drawn (see Chapter 1) and if you were able to measure the X-scores with very high (infinite) precision (see Chapter 2).

It is customary in statistics to use Greek symbols to refer to population measures. So, we will use the Greek letter mu, μ (pronounced 'myoo') to refer to the population mean, and the Greek letter sigma, σ, to refer to the population standard deviation.

When a variable is assumed to be normally distributed at the population level,[4] we expect the variable to show the following characteristics:

☐ The frequency distribution of the values is symmetrical. The left side is a mirror image of the right side.
☐ The frequency distribution is unimodal and bell-shaped.
☐ Fifty per cent of the scores fall below the mean, and 50 per cent above the mean (that is, mean = median).
☐ Most of the scores pile up around the mean (i.e., mode = mean = median), and extreme scores (high or low) become increasingly rare (that is, have low frequencies).
☐ In theory, the left and right hand tails of the distribution touch the X-axis (that is, reach 0%) only at infinity. In practice, the frequencies of extreme values become so low that we expect to find less than 1 observation out of 10,000 with a value below the mean minus 4 times the standard deviation or with a value above the mean plus 4 times the standard deviation.

As soon as we know the mean and the standard deviation of a normal distribution, we know the complete distribution. (See Section 5.9 – Going further – for the formula to calculate the distribution on the basis of the mean and the standard deviation.) In addition, the interpretation of the mean and the standard deviation is quite straightforward, as shown in the next section.

4 See Chapter 3 for some notable exceptions – variables that are not normally distributed – such as household sizes and the distribution of reaction times.

5.5.3   Two normal distributions with different means

A difference in means between two normal distributions implies that one distribution is shifted along the X-axis relative to the other distribution, as shown in Figure 5.4.

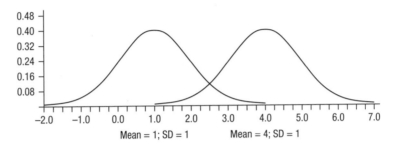

Figure 5.4 Two normal distributions with the same standard deviation but different means (relative frequency distributions).

A typical example of such a difference in means is the difference in height between 10-year old boys and 20-year old men. Both groups show more or less the same variability (that is, they have the same standard deviation), but the 10-year olds are some 38 cm smaller than the 20-year olds. According to the most recent American growth charts, this would translate into two normal distributions: one with a mean of 139 cm and a standard deviation of 6.5 cm for the 10-year olds, and the other with a mean of 177 cm and a standard deviation of 6.5 cm for the 20-year olds. This situation is shown in Figure 5.5. As you can see, the distance between both distributions is so big, that there is virtually no overlap of them. This agrees with our casual observations that 'all' 10-year old boys are smaller than 'all' 20-year old men.

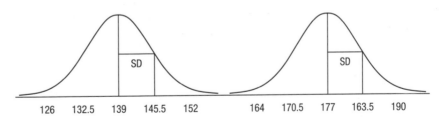

Figure 5.5 The theoretical distributions of the heights of 10-year old boys ($\mu = 139$, $\sigma = 6.5$) and 20-year old men ($\mu = 177$, $\sigma = 6.5$).

5.5.4   Two normal distributions with different standard deviations

A change in the standard deviation alters the spread of the distribution (see Figure 5.6). A small standard deviation means that the data is more tightly clustered around the mean. A large standard deviation increases the spread of the data. Notice in Figure 5.6 that the narrower the bell shape, the higher it

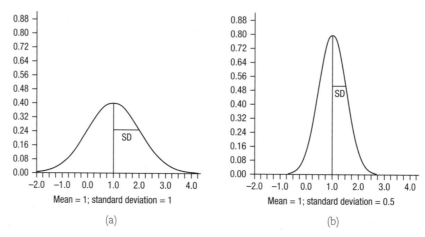

Figure 5.6 Two normal distributions with different standard deviations (relative frequency distributions).

becomes. This is because more observations are squeezed into a narrow range of observations.

A typical example of narrowing the standard deviation happens in the processing of fruit and vegetables. Have you ever wondered why all the tomatoes in your local supermarket are the same size – there is a small standard deviation of sizes? When the harvest was originally collected, there was a much bigger variation in the sizes and shapes of the crop. However, one of the first steps after the initial collection was to separate the fruits into different categories. The small and large tomatoes, together with the funny shaped ones, were discarded, for use in processed food. The remaining, medium-sized, well-shaped tomatoes were divided into separate classes with diameter differences of 1 cm at most, and only one size-range ended up in your supermarket.

The whole selection process was one of reducing the original, quite large range of sizes (going from tomatoes with a diameter of less than 2 cm to those with a diameter of more than 10 cm) to a very small range (of less than 1 cm). Whereas the tomatoes with a diameter between 5.5 cm and 6.5 cm might constitute only one-quarter of the original harvest, they may end up making the totality of the tomatoes you find in your grocery shop. As a result of the selection process a distribution with a large standard deviation (Figure 5.6(a)) has been reduced to a distribution with a small standard deviation (Figure 5.6(b)).

As an alternative, the difference in standard deviations between two normal distributions may be represented by changing the scale of the X-axis instead of the shape of the distribution. Figure 5.7 shows exactly the same situation as Figure 5.6, but this time the shapes of the two distributions have been kept constant and the scale of the X-axis has been altered.[5]

---

5 The fact that two different ways of representation can be used to show a change in standard deviation indicates that the height of the distribution is not important (i.e. the precise values on the Y-axis). What is important is the size of different areas under the curve (see the section on probability).

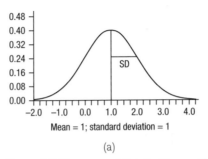

Mean = 1; standard deviation = 1

(a)

Mean = 1; standard deviation = 0.5

(b)

Figure 5.7 Two normal distributions with different standard deviations when the scale of the X-axis changes. Notice that the X-values in (a) vary from –2 to +4, whereas those in (b) vary from –0.5 to +2.5 only.

If Figure 5.7 were applied to the tomato example, the distribution in Figure 5.7(a) (unselected fruits) would range from less than 2 cm to more than 10 cm, whereas the scale in Figure 5.7(b) (for the selected fruits in your store) would range from 5.5 cm to 6.5 cm.

The first way of representing a change in the standard deviation (with the thinner graph, as in Figure 5.6) shows us how the data become more piled around the mean when the standard deviation is smaller. (This will be important when we talk about the distribution of the means of samples in Chapter 7.)

The second way of representing a change in standard deviation (with the same graph, but a change of scale, as in Figure 5.7) tells us that we can use the same curve for every normal distribution, irrespective of the mean and the standard deviation. The only thing we have to do is adapt the scale of the X-axis. For instance, Figure 5.8 shows the expected distributions of two tests, one with a mean of 100 and a standard deviation of 10, the other with a mean of 60 and a standard deviation of 6.

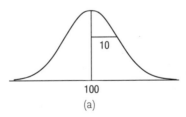

100

(a)

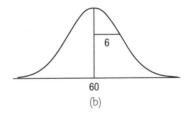

60

(b)

Figure 5.8 Illustrations of two distributions with different means and different standard deviations.

To draw a sketch like the curves in Figure 5.8, all you need to know are three things:

1 the general shape of the normal distribution;
2 where to place the mean of the distribution (at the vertical line that separates the distribution in two mirror halves);
3 where to place the SD (at 60% of the height of the vertical line).

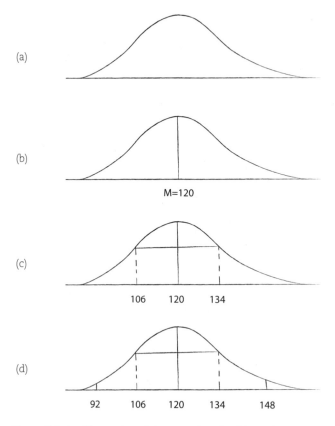

(a)

(b)

M=120

(c)

106   120   134

(d)

92   106   120   134   148

Figure 5.9 An illustration of the steps involved in making a rapid sketch of a normal distribution with M = 120 and SD = 14.

These steps are illustrated in Figure 5.9, which shows a rapid sketch for a normal distribution with M = 120 and SD = 14.

(a) draw the shape of a normal distribution
(b) draw a vertical line through the centre to represent the mean
(c) draw a horizontal line at 60% of the height of the vertical line, then draw vertical lines to the X axis to represent M + 1SD and M – 1SD
(d) add the values of M + 2SD (estimated as twice the SD from the previous step) and M – 2SD (estimated as the mirror position of M + 2SD).

Make a sketch, as outlined in Figure 5.9, every time you are asked to interpret data from a test. This will allow you to rapidly and adequately position a score within the distribution (for example, where a score of 70 lies in a distribution with M = 100, SD = 10, and where it lies in a distribution with M = 65 and SD = 2).

Tip When you are told that the scores on a test follow a normal distribution with a given mean and standard deviation, always make a sketch. This will help you to get a better understanding of the results of the test. It will also help you to check whether your calculations of percentiles and probabilities are correct.

As we will see in Section 5.7, it will also help you to get a fairly good estimate of the chances of observing lower and higher scores. These estimates will help you to avoid gross calculation errors when you are calculating the exact probabilities – a topic we will turn to in Sections 5.6 and 5.7.

5.6 Probability

In Section 5.7 we will see how z-scores and the assumption of a normal frequency distribution can be combined to make precise statements about the chances of observing lower and higher scores. Before we can do so, however, we need to introduce the concept of probability.

5.6.1 The definition of probability

Probability is an important concept in situations where several outcomes are possible. When more than one outcome is possible, we define the probability for any particular outcome as the frequency of that outcome divided by the frequency of all possible outcomes (that is, as the proportion of trials that resulted in the outcome).

For example, when you toss a coin, there are two possible outcomes: heads or tails. You can estimate the probability of the outcome 'heads' by tossing the coin say 100 times and count how many of these trials result in heads. So,

$$\text{Probability of heads} = \frac{\text{Number of outcomes which are heads}}{\text{Total number of trials}}$$

Suppose we find that 60 of the 100 trials result in the outcome 'heads' and 40 result in the outcome 'tails'. Then, the probability of heads is:

$$p(\text{heads}) = \frac{60}{60 + 40} = 0.60$$

and the probability of tails is:

$$p(\text{tails}) = \frac{40}{60 + 40} = 0.40$$

The probabilities add up to 1.00 (or 100%) because there are only two possible outcomes.

5.6.2 How to calculate a probability from a frequency distribution table

The probability of an outcome is easy to calculate when we have a frequency distribution table. In that case, we simply divide the frequency of the outcome by the sum of all the observations. Thus:

$$p(X) = \frac{f(x)}{N}$$

For instance, suppose the frequency distribution table represents the gross annual household incomes in a town with 25,797 households (Table 5.1).

On the basis of Table 5.1, it is not difficult to calculate the probability of a household in the £15,000–20,000 range. This probability is defined as:

$$p(15K \leq X < 20K) = \frac{9541}{25797}$$
$$= 0.37$$

Table 5.2 shows the probabilities of all the income bands.

Table 5.1 Frequency distribution table of gross annual household incomes.

Income band (£)	f
X < 5K	230
5K ≤ X < 10K	890
10K ≤ X < 15K	1620
15K ≤ X < 20K	9541
20K ≤ X < 25K	8954
25K ≤ X < 30K	2543
30K ≤ X < 35K	1166
35K ≤ X < 40K	754
40K ≤ X	99
$\Sigma f = N = 25{,}797$	

Table 5.2 Probabilities of all income bands.

Income band (£)	f	p
X < 5K	230	.009
5K ≤ X < 10K	890	.034
10K ≤ X < 15K	1620	.063
15K ≤ X < 20K	9541	.370
20K ≤ X < 25K	8954	.347
25K ≤ X < 30K	2543	.099
30K ≤ X < 35K	1166	.045
35K ≤ X < 40K	754	.029
40K ≤ X	99	.004
$\Sigma f = N = 25{,}797$		$\Sigma p = 1.000$

On the basis of a frequency table, we can also calculate summed probabilities, such as the probability that a family earns £20,000 or more:

$$p(X \geq 20\text{K}) = \frac{(8954 + 2543 + 1166 + 754 + 99)}{25797}$$
$$= 0.52$$

5.6.3 How to calculate a probability from a frequency distribution graph

Probabilities can also be obtained from a frequency distribution graph. To do this, we calculate the area of the histogram that corresponds to the X-values of interest, and divide this by the total area. Figure 5.10 has been plotted from the

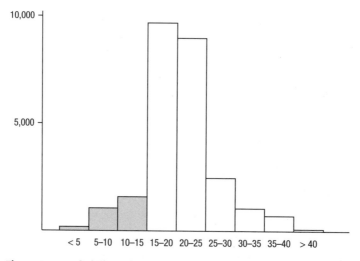

Figure 5.10 Probability calculated on the basis of a frequency distribution graph.

family income data above. So, if we want to know the probability of an annual gross income less than £15,000 on the basis of the frequency distribution graph shown in Figure 5.10, we calculate the area of the first three bars (shaded) and we divide this by the area of all the bars.

To calculate the area of a bar in a frequency distribution graph, measure the height of each bar. In Figure 5.10, the height of the first bar is 1 mm; that of the second bar is 6 mm; that of the third bar is 9 mm and so on until you get the following table:

Income band	Height of the bar in the graph (in mm)
X < 5K	1
5K ≤ X < 10K	6
10K ≤ X < 15K	9
15K ≤ X < 20K	55
20K ≤ X < 25K	51
25K ≤ X < 30K	14
30K ≤ X < 35K	6
35K ≤ X < 40K	4
40K ≤ X	0.5
	Σ = 146.5

Because each bar has the same width, we can use the height of each bar as a measure of its area.[6] The summed area of the first three bars is 1 + 6 + 9 = 16. The area of all the bars is 146.5. So, the probability of observing a gross annual income of less than £15K equals 16/146.5 ≈ 11%. Check this outcome with the exact outcome you would obtain on the basis of the frequency distribution table.

5.6.4 How to calculate a probability from a relative frequency distribution table

Probabilities have a very transparent relationship to relative frequencies expressed as percentages (see Chapter 2): if you multiply a probability by 100, you get the relative frequency. So, in our example of gross annual incomes, a probability of .37 that a household has an income between £15K and £20K means that 37% of the households have an income of this size. Conversely, by dividing the relative frequencies expressed as percentages by 100, we get the associated probabilities. This is shown in Table 5.3, which includes the raw frequencies, as well as the relative frequencies and the probabilities of the household incomes from our example.

So, calculating probabilities on the basis of a frequency distribution table with relative frequencies is very easy. You just divide the percentages by 100,

6 The area of a rectangle is defined by height x width. Assuming that the width equals 1, the area of each bar in the frequency distribution graph corresponds to its height: (area = height × 1).

Table 5.3 Relationship between relative frequency and probability.

Income band	f	Relative frequency (%)	p
$X < 5K$	230	.9%	.009
$5K \leq X < 10K$	890	3.4%	.034
$10K \leq X < 15K$	1620	6.3%	.063
$15K \leq X < 20K$	9541	37.0%	.370
$20K \leq X < 25K$	8954	34.7%	.347
$25K \leq X < 30K$	2543	9.9%	.099
$30K \leq X < 35K$	1166	4.5%	.045
$35K \leq X < 40K$	754	2.9%	.029
$40K \leq X$	99	.4%	.004
$\Sigma = 25{,}797$		100.0%	1.000

and you get the associated probabilities. The relationship between probability and relative frequency is one of the reasons why many researchers present their data as relative frequencies rather than as raw frequencies (see Chapter 2).

5.6.5 How to calculate a probability from a relative frequency distribution graph

There are two ways in which we can calculate probabilities when we have a relative frequency distribution graph. We could calculate the areas of the bars, as discussed in Section 5.6.3, or we could try to estimate the individual relative frequencies from the graph. When we choose for the latter option, we are basically trying to reconstruct the relative frequency distribution table. Figure 5.11

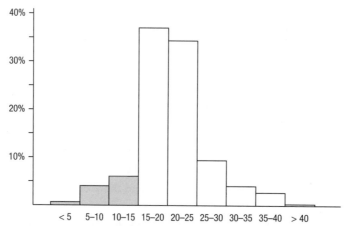

Figure 5.11 Probability calculated on the basis of a relative frequency distribution graph. The probability of an income lower than 15K equals the sum of the estimated probabilities associated with the first three bars (shaded). Roughly, the sum of the relative frequencies in the grey area will agree with 1% (first bar) + 4% (second bar) + 6% (third bar) = 11%, which will give a probability of $p = .11$

illustrates how we can use a relative frequency distribution graph to estimate the probability of an income below £15K. Now, do the same to estimate the probability of a gross annual income between £30K and £40K.

5.7 *Z*-scores, normal distributions, probabilities and percentiles

5.7.1 The standard normal distribution

In this section, we will combine the three concepts we have introduced thus far: z-scores, the normal distribution, and probabilities. We will find out how z-scores can be used to obtain more precise information about the position of an individual within a population. Remember that, in Sections 5.2 to 5.4 on z-scores, we limited ourselves to deciding whether an individual belonged to the upper or the lower half of the distribution (+ or – sign) and to calculating the typical (less than 1 SD from the mean) or the exceptional/ abnormal range (more than 2 SD). Now, we will use our knowledge about the normal distribution to make more precise statements.

First, we need to understand the concept of the **standard normal distribution**. This is a theoretical normal frequency distribution with mean = 0 and standard deviation = 1. Because the mean and the standard deviation fully define a normal distribution, we can draw the standard normal distribution. We just use the sketches from Figure 5.9, and insert a mean value of M = 0, and a standard deviation of SD = 1 (Figure 5.12).

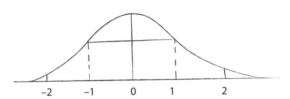

Figure 5.12 A quick sketch of the standard normal distribution.

On the basis of the equation used for the normal distribution, we can calculate exactly how much of the area of the curve is situated in the different parts of the curve. In the same way as we used the frequency distribution graphs in Figures 5.10 and 5.11 to determine how many households had incomes in a certain range, we can use our knowledge about the normal distribution to determine the properties of our data. For example, we might want to know how many observations are expected to be below a standard normal score of –2 (that is, two standard deviations below the mean). This probability is given by dividing the area of the small part of the curve below –2 by the area of the complete distribution. If we do so, we obtain a value of $p = .0228$, meaning that 2.28% of all observations in the standard normal distribution are expected to have a value of less than –2. Similarly, we can calculate the probability of a standard normal

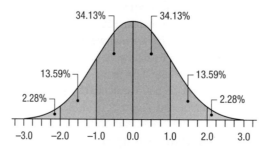

Figure 5.13 Probabilities associated with different parts of the standard normal distribution

score between –2 and –1. This probability equals .1359, meaning that 13.59% of the observed standard normal scores are expected to lie in this range. In fact, we do not need to make any estimates of area because these areas are already known and are shown in Figure 5.13.

Figure 5.13 shows that 34% of the area of the distribution lies between a standard normal score of 0 (the mean) and a score of +1 (one standard deviation above the mean). Similarly, another 34% of the area lies between 0 and –1. This means that scores between –1 and +1 are expected to occur with a probability of 68% (thus, slightly more than two-thirds of the probability of all possible outcomes). This is called the typical range. Similarly, Figure 5.13 shows that X-values larger than +2 are expected to occur in less than 2.5% of the outcomes; the same is true for values less than –2. We have called this the exceptional range, because values more extreme than –2 or +2 are expected in less than 5% of all observations.

Figure 5.13 also shows how we can use the standard normal distribution to extract information about the exact position of an individual relative to all other individuals. Suppose an individual has a standardised score of +1 on a test. Figure 5.13 informs us that the chance of finding a higher score is 2.28% + 13.59% = 15.87%. The chance of finding a lower score is 2.28% + 13.59% + 34.13% + 34.13% = 84.13%. Thus, if this score represented the result of an exam, the individual would belong to the top 20% of students.

5.7.2 The relationship of the standard normal distribution to other normal distributions

You may already have figured out that the standard normal distribution, as depicted in Figure 5.13, is nothing more than a normal distribution of z-scores. This means that we can reduce every possible normal distribution to the standard normal distribution by using z-scores instead of the original raw scores. Similarly, we can replace the standard normal distribution by any other normal distribution by converting the z-scores into raw scores. The only thing we have to do is to change the scale of the X-axis (Figures 5.7 and 5.8).

For instance, many IQ tests yield a normal distribution of scores and have been constructed so that their mean is 100 and their standard deviation is 15. According to these tests, people with an IQ between 85 and 115 have an average intelligence; people with an IQ below 70 and above 130 are called 'exceptional'. About two-thirds of people (68%) are expected to have IQs between 85 and 115; roughly 2.5% are expected to have an IQ lower than 70%, and 2.5% are expected to have an IQ higher than 130. Figure 5.14 shows the application of the normal distribution to IQ scores. Notice that the only thing that has changed from Figure 5.13 (the standard normal distribution) is the values on the X-axis.

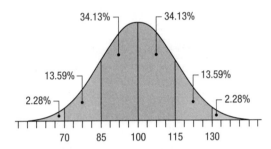

Figure 5.14 Probabilities associated with different parts of the distribution of IQ scores, when the test results in a normal distribution with $M = 100$ and $SD = 15$.

Before we move on to calculate exact probabilities on the basis of the standard normal distribution, there is one cautionary note: the standard normal distribution can only be used to calculate probabilities of data that come from a normal frequency distribution. Changing a raw score into a z-score does not change the shape of the distribution; it only changes the values of the X-axis. Thus, if the original distribution was bimodal or positively skewed, the z-scores will follow the same distribution, and probabilities calculated on the basis of the standard normal distribution will yield bad estimates.

The standard normal distribution is used in many cases because we can assume that most variables follow a normal distribution (see Chapter 6). However, if you have any reason to doubt whether your data are normally distributed, always check the frequency distribution of your raw data (as discussed in Chapter 2) before going any further.

> **Be careful!** You can use the standard normal distribution to calculate probabilities only when the original scores fit a normal frequency distribution. Calculating a z-score changes the values of the X-axis; it does not change the shape of the frequency distribution. You will get incorrect estimates if you use the standard normal distribution to calculate probabilities for other distributions.

5.7.3 Calculating exact probabilities using the standard normal distribution

In the preceding section, we have calculated the probabilities associated with the standard normal distribution on the basis of a crude graph (Figure 5.13) that provided us with the probabilities of the z-scores –2, –1, 0, 1, and 2. We could create a figure that gives us the probabilities for z-scores that are multiples of .5, and that would allow us to make more precise calculations. Unfortunately, such a figure would become quite cluttered and difficult to read. Therefore, rather than keep on using graphs, we will turn to a table. Table 5.4 contains exactly the same information as we would have in our graph of z-scores at intervals of .5. All the information displayed in Figure 5.13 is presented in Table 5.4, as well as the intermediate scores (for example, the probability of observing a z-score lower than –2 is .0228).

Table 5.4 Probabilities of lower and higher scores associated with z-scores that are multiples of 0.5.

z-score	p(lower score)	p(higher score)
–3.0	.0013	.9987
–2.5	.0062	.9938
–2.0	.0228	.9772
–1.5	.0668	.9332
–1.0	.1587	.8413
–0.5	.3085	.6915
0.0	.5000	.5000
+0.5	.6915	.3085
+1.0	.8413	.1587
+1.5	.9332	.0668
+2.0	.9772	.0228
+2.5	.9938	.0062
+3.0	.9987	.0013

Notice that the lower half of Table 5.4 is a mirror image of the upper half. As an example, compare the probabilities of z = –3.0 and z = +3.0. This is to be expected, given that the normal distribution is a symmetrical distribution (see Figure 5.13). Also, notice that the column of p(higher score) always equals 1 – p(lower score). Why is this?

Table 5.4 allows us to calculate exact probabilities associated with z-scores that are multiples of .5. Of course, nothing prevents us from making a larger table with the probabilities of all z-scores between –3.0 and +3.0 with a precision of .01. Indeed, this table is presented in Appendix A. Using Appendix A, therefore, we can calculate the exact probabilities associated with the standard normal distribution.

For reasons that will become clear in the next chapter, two other important z-values are z = –1.96 and z = +1.96. For these values, the chances of observing more extreme data are exactly .025. Thus, p(lower value) of z = –1.96 is .025 and p(higher value) of z = +1.96 is .025 as well. This is shown in Figure 5.15.

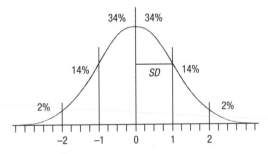

Figure 5.15 The probability of observing lower values than z = –1.96 is .025 and the probability of observing higher values than z = +1.96 is .025 as well. As we will see in the next chapter, these are important values in statistical tests.

Learning check 2
Go to appendix A and find *p*(lower) and *p*(higher) for *z* = +0.23.

It is important for you to understand that Appendix A is just a more detailed version of the data in Figure 5.13. When you are asked to calculate probabilities on the basis of Appendix A, you are strongly advised first to draw a rough sketch of the normal distribution (see Figure 5.16) and to make a rough estimate of the probabilities on the basis of your knowledge of the standard normal distribution. In that way, you will never make gross calculation errors, because you already have a good idea of the values you should obtain. For instance, when you are asked to look up the exact probabilities associated with z = +.23, you know beforehand that this value lies slightly above a z-value of 0. You know that p(lower) = .50 and p(higher) = .50 at a z-value of 0, because this z-value is the median of the standard normal distribution. So, even without consulting Appendix A, you already know that, for z = +.23, p(lower) will be slightly more

Figure 5.16 Using a sketch to find the approximate probabilities associated with a z-score of +0.23. We know that for z = 0.00, p(lower) = 0.50 (or 50%) and p(higher) = .50. In addition, for z = +1.00, we know that p(lower) = 0.84 and p(higher) = .16. So, for z = +.23, p(lower) will lie between .50 and .84 (closer to the former than to the latter), and p(higher) will lie between .50 and .16. A look at Appendix A informs us that the exact probabilities are p(lower) = .5910 and p(higher) = .4090.

than .50, and p(higher) will be slightly less than .50. The only thing to do then is to look up the exact values!

Because we can translate all normal frequency distributions to the standard normal distribution by calculating z-scores, we can use Appendix A to calculate the probabilities for each and every normal distribution. So, we can calculate the probability of observing an IQ score lower than 92 on a test with M = 100 and SD = 15. First, we make an approximate sketch of the situation (Figure 5.17), which informs us that an IQ score of 92 lies nearly half a standard deviation below the mean. Thus the z-score will be roughly −.50, p(lower) will be less than .50, and p(higher) will be more than .50. When we then do the exact calculations using Appendix A, we obtain z = (92 − 100)/15 = −.53; p(lower) = .2981; p(higher) = .7019 (see also Table 5.4).

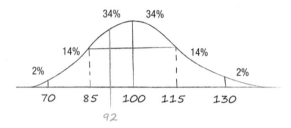

Figure 5.17 Using a sketch to find the approximate probabilities associated with an IQ score of 92 on a test with M = 100 and SD = 15

5.7.4 Percentiles and percentile ranks

In Section 5.7.3, we talked about p(lower) and p(higher) to indicate the probability of observing scores lower and higher than a given X-value. Because these are rather awkward terms for everyday communication, statisticians have invented the term 'percentile rank'. **Percentile rank** is defined as the percentage of individuals in the distribution that have a score below the X-value on which the rank is calculated. So, it is just 100 ∗ p(lower). Applied to our examples above, the percentile rank of the z-score .23 in Figure 5.16 is 100 ∗ .591= 59, indicating that 59% of the individuals are expected to have a z-score below .23. Similarly, the percentile rank of the IQ score of 92 in Figure 5.17 is 100 ∗ .2981 = 30, indicating that 30% of the people are expected to have an IQ score below 92.

Put simply, a person is doing better than average if they have a percentile rank above 50. Similarly, their performance is below average when they have a percentile rank of less than 50. Therefore, it is much easier to tell parents that their child has a percentile rank of 90 on an IQ test than to tell them that their child has a percentile rank of 10.

Learning check 3

Find out, with the help of Appendix A, which IQ scores on a test with M = 100 and SD = 15 correspond to the percentile ranks 10 and 90.

A **percentile** is the *X*-value that corresponds to a particular percentile rank or *p*(lower). So, if we have an IQ test that yields normally distributed scores with *M* = 100 and *SD* = 15, which score is the 95th percentile of this test? To answer this question, it may be good to consider that the 95th percentile is a very high score. It puts the person in the top 5% because 95% of the individuals taking the test will do worse. So, the score will be higher than the mean score. From our knowledge of the normal distribution (Figure 5.13), we know that it will be quite close to the mean plus two standard deviations (which would yield a percentile of 98). A look at Appendix A tells us that percentile 95 agrees with a *z*-score of +1.65 (which has a *p*(lower) of .9505 and a *p*(higher) of .0495). Then we use our knowledge from Section 5.4 to calculate the IQ score that agrees with a *z*-score of +1.65. This score is *M* + 1.65 × *SD* = 100 + 1.65 × 15 = 125.

As was the case for percentile ranks, percentiles above 50 refer to *X*-values above the mean and percentiles below 50 refer to *X*-values below the mean. A percentile of 2 will agree with an *X*-value close to *M* – 2*SD*, and a percentile of 98 will agree with an *X*-value of approximately *M* + 2*SD*.

Because we have covered quite some ground in the preceding pages, the next section is a cookbook summary of how to calculate probabilities on the basis of the standard normal distribution.

5.7.5 Step by step: determining probabilities and percentile ranks associated with a normal distribution

 Mr Wilcock obtained a score of 26 on a test with mean 40 and standard deviation 12 (scores are normally distributed). Calculate his *z*-score, the probability of obtaining a lower score, the probability of obtaining a higher score, the percentile rank, and the percentile this score represents.

Step 1   Sketch the distribution of the test scores and shade the part below Mr Wilcock's score. Use the probabilities from Figure 5.13 to get a rough estimate of the different measures.

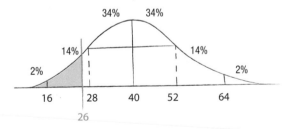

From the sketch we know that Mr Wilcock performed below the mean, even below one standard deviation under the mean. So, the *z*-score will be less than –1.0, *p*(lower) will be less than .16 (2% + 14%), and *p*(higher) will be more than .84. Similarly, the percentile rank will be lower than 16, and Mr Wilcock's score will be lower than percentile 16. Now that we have these rough estimates, we are in a better shape to calculate the exact figures.

Step 2   Transform the X-value into a z-score.

$$z = \frac{X - M}{SD}$$

in which M = the mean of the test and SD = the standard deviation.
   Applied to the example:

$$z = \frac{26 - 40}{12}$$
$$= \frac{-14}{12}$$
$$= -1.17$$

Step 3   Determine the probability of a lower score [p(lower)] and the probability
of a higher score [p(higher)].

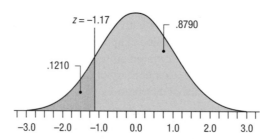

Go to Appendix A. Look under the entry for z = –1.17. There you find
the two values you are looking for: p(lower) = .1210, and p(higher) = .8790.
That is, the proportion of the standard normal distribution lower than
z = –1.17 amounts to .1210; and the proportion of the distribution higher
than z = –1.17 amounts to .8790.

Step 4   The percentile rank is the percentage of the distribution below the
z-score. This is obtained by multiplying p(lower) by 100. So, the percentile rank of Mr Wilcock's score is .1210 x 100 = 12, meaning that only
12% of the population is expected to have a score on the test lower than
Mr Wilcock.

Step 5   Because Mr Wilcock's percentile rank is 12, his score of 26 on the test
corresponds to percentile 12.

 Performance checks

1   Negative z-scores imply that the person performed below the mean; positive
z-scores indicate that the person performed better than average. Is this the case?

2   Percentile ranks of negative z-scores are always lower than 50; those of positive
z-scores are higher than 50 (the percentile rank of z = 0.0 is 50).

3   Look at the sketch you made under Step 1 and check whether the exact numbers
you calculated in Steps 2–5 roughly agree with those initial estimates. If not, try to
find out what caused the difference. This type of performance check will ensure
that you have a good overview of the total situation, and that your calculations are
never grossly wrong.

5.8   Calculating *z*-scores and probabilities in SPSS

To illustrate how we can calculate z-scores in SPSS, we will use the example of the number of pints of beer drunk by people in the previous weekend (Section 3.2):

5, 4, 3, 5, 4, 2, 4, 3, 6

To find the z-scores, we click on *Analyze*, *Descriptive Statistics* and *Descriptives*.

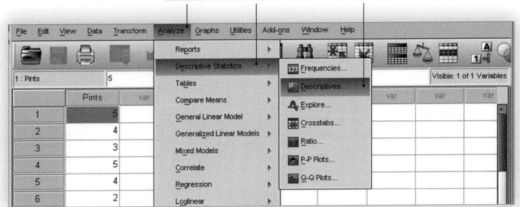

We have to indicate the variable for which we want the descriptives. So, bring Pints from the left panel into the right by clicking on the central arrow ❶.

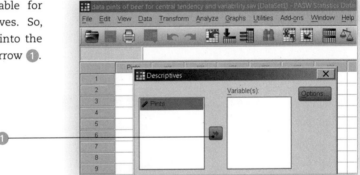

Next check the box *Save standardized values as variables* ❷. By checking this box, a column will be added to your data file with the z-scores. Click on *OK* ❸ and look at your data screen.

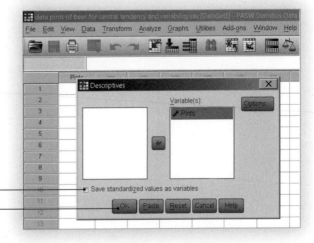

This is what you should get.

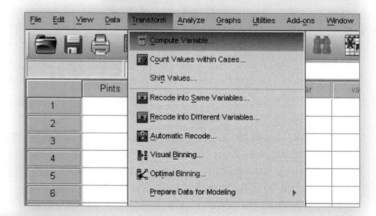

To calculate the probability of lower z-scores (that is, the part of the curve to the left of the observed z-score), click on *Transform*, *Compute Variable*.

This will give you the following dialogue box:

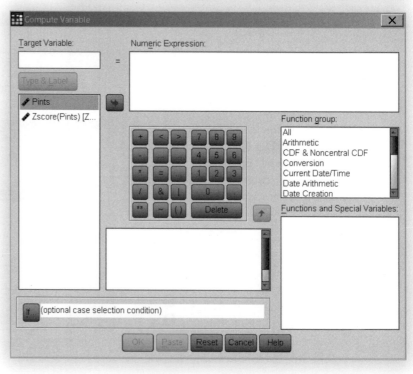

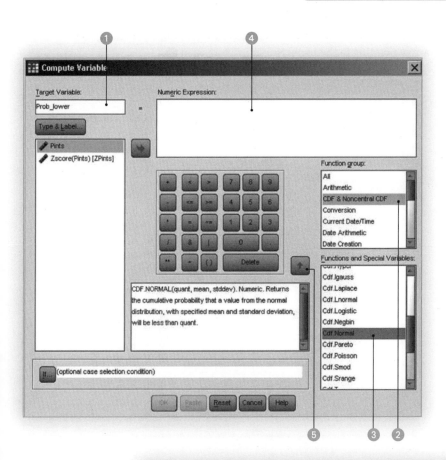

Here you have to do several things.

First, enter a name in the section *Target Variable* (Prob_lower) ❶. Then go to the heading *Function group* and *CDF and Noncentral CDF* ❷ (CDF stands for cumulative density function). Select *Cdf Normal* ❸ from the alphabetical list.

Then put your cursor in the panel Numeric Expression ❹ (position your mouse in this panel and click once). Then click on the upward arrow to bring the Cdf.Normal function to the panel ❺ as shown below.

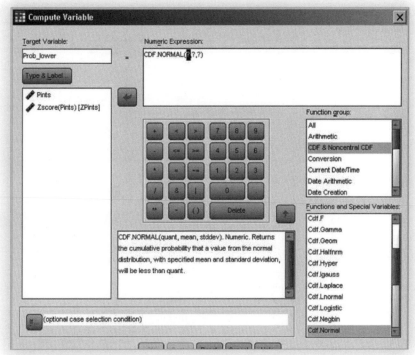

There are three values to be entered now. The first is your z-score. You enter this by clicking on Zscore(Pints) ① and then on the arrow pointing to the panel Numeric Expression ②.

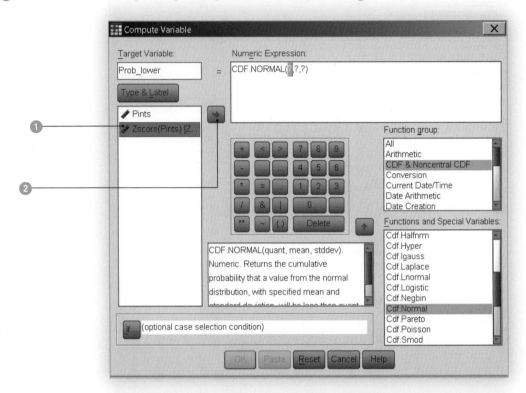

If everything went well, this is what you should have:

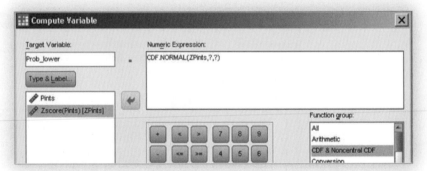

The next two values to enter are the mean ① and the standard deviation ②. Because we are working with z-scores, they are easy: 0 and 1.

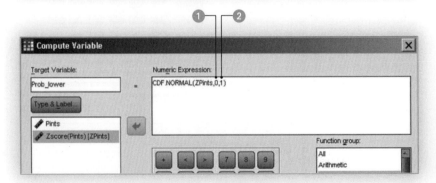

If you click on OK, you will see that a new column has been added to your data called Prob_lower. It gives you p(lower) for each z-value (and, hence, each number of pints). Check a few values with Appendix A!

File	Edit	View	Data	Transform	Analyze	Graphs	Utilities	Add-ons

	Pints	ZPints	Prob_lower
1	5	.81650	.79
2	4	.0	.50
3	3	-.81650	.21
4	5	.81650	.79
5	4	.0	.50
6	2	-1.63299	.05
7	4	.0	.50
8	3	-.81650	.21
9	6	1.63299	.95
10			

This allows you to rapidly calculate the probabilities associated with your values.

5.9 Going further: defining the shape of the normal distribution

Although we could digress onto many interesting topics (such as how the exact values of p(lower) are calculated in SPSS), we will deal with only one of them here – how the shape of the normal distribution is defined. It is based on the equation:

$$f(X) = \frac{1}{\sigma\sqrt{2\pi}}e^{-(X-\mu)^2/2\sigma^2}$$

If you look carefully, you see that this expression is an exponential function of the form $f(X) = a*e^b$. Because the exponent is a negative squared value, $f(X)$ will always be less than 1 unless $X = \mu$. At $X = \mu$, $e^b = e^0 = 1$. So, the function will have its maximum when $X = \mu$ and will tend to 0 when $X << \mu$ or $X >> \mu$. The rest of the equation simply contains variables and constants to make sure the area under the distribution equals 1.

5.10 Answers to chapter questions

1 What is a standardised score and why is this helpful?

A standardised score is a score expressed as the number of standard deviations from the mean. So, a standardised score of 0 means that the raw score coincides with the mean of the distribution (it is 0 standard deviations away from the mean). A standardised score of –1 means that the raw score is 1 standard deviation below the mean. The standardised score is helpful because experts immediately know how to interpret it and because it allows psychologists to directly compare the scores of different tests.

2 What is a z-score?

A z-score is another name for a standardised score.

3 How do we transform an original score into a z-score?

$z = \dfrac{X - M}{SD}$, where M = the mean of the distribution and SD = the standard deviation of the distribution.

4 What is the rough interpretation of the value of a z-score? What does a z-score of 0 stand for?

A z-score lower than –2 represents a very bad performance, a z-score higher than +2 represents a very good performance, and a z-score between –1 and +1 represents an average performance. A z-score of 0 means that the score is exactly in the middle of the distribution.

5 How do we transform z-scores into raw X-scores?

$X = M + z * SD$.

6 What is the normal distribution?

A normal distribution is a distribution that looks as follows:

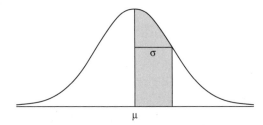

The function is fully defined by the mean (μ) and the standard deviation (σ). Many observations and measurements of real life features are distributed like this. The normal distribution forms the basis of all parametric statistics.

7 What is the probability of an outcome?

The probability of any particular outcome is the frequency of this outcome divided by the sum of the frequencies of all possible outcomes.

8 How do we calculate the probability?

$p(X) = \dfrac{f(X)}{N}$, in which $f(X)$ and N are either obtained from a frequency distribution table or estimated on the basis of a frequency distribution graph.

9 What is the standard normal distribution and why do we use it?

The standard normal distribution is a normal distribution with μ = 0 and σ = 1. It is the distribution of the z-scores, assuming the original X-scores formed a normal distribution. We use the standard normal distribution to calculate the probability values (p-values) associated with X-scores.

10 How do we calculate the probability associated with a z-score?

There are several methods. First, we can get a good idea by making use of a sketch as outlined in Figure 5.13. Second, we can make use of Appendix A if we want to have precise values. Finally, we could write a function in Excel that will give us the probability associated with a z-score. (See the website: www.palgrave.com/psychology/brysbaert.)

11 What is a percentile rank and what is a percentile?

A percentile rank is the percentage of individuals in the distribution that have a score below the X-value on which the rank is calculated. A percentile is the X-value that corresponds to a particular percentile rank or p(lower).

☑ 5.11 Learning check solutions

Learning check 1

z-score Mr Parkhurst: $z = (35 - 40)/10 = -5/10 = -.5$

Learning check 2

p(lower) and p(higher) for $z = +.23$ are p(lower) = .5910 and p(higher) = .4090. Looking at Figure 5.13, you can see that $z = +.23$ lies slightly above $z = .00$, at which point p(lower) = .5 and p(higher) = .50. So, p(lower) should be slightly higher than .50, and p(higher) should be slightly lower.

Learning check 3

A percentile rank of 10 means than p(lower) = .10. Appendix A informs us that we will find this at $z = -1.28$. A z-value of -1.28 corresponds to an IQ score of $100 + (-1.28 \times 5) = 100 - 19 = 81$. Similarly, a percentile rank of 90 means that p(lower) = .90, which we will find at $z = +1.28$, corresponding to IQ $= 100 + (128 \times 15) = 119$.

?

1 Why do psychologists need statistical tests to decide whether there is a difference between two groups?

2 Why is the prediction that smokers die earlier than non-smokers not invalidated when you hear of a 100–year old who still smokes?

3 What are inferential statistics?

4 What is the standard error of the mean? Can we calculate this on the basis of a single sample?

5 Why can we have more confidence in the mean of a large sample than in the mean of a small sample?

6 Why can researchers be reasonably sure that the mean of a sample will be part of a normal distribution? What are the restrictions?

7 What is sampling error and how does it relate to research findings?

8 How do we calculate the t-statistic for independent groups?

9 Which three factors does the t-statistic for independent groups depend upon?

10 How should we interpret a t-statistic?

11 What is hypothesis testing and what does the t-statistic have to do with this?

12 What are the null hypothesis and the alternative hypothesis? And what is their relationship to the courtroom?

13 Why does a t-test depend on the degrees of freedom?

14 What is the level of significance?

15 When do researchers talk of a significant effect?

16 What has the confirmation bias to do with hypothesis testing?

In this chapter, we will see how we can decide whether the difference in performance between two groups is reliable enough to be trustworthy. This will be done with a *t*-test for independent samples. Before we discuss this test, however, we must cover some background information about why we need a statistical test.

6.1 Few differences between groups can be spotted with the naked eye

Psychologists are constantly bombarded with questions about differences between groups of people. Are boys better at maths than girls? Do elderly people learn more slowly? Do left-handers die earlier than right-handers? Are people who are treated for a mental disorder more violent than people who are not being treated? Will premature babies do less well in school than full-term babies? Do blind people hear better than seeing people?

The reason why psychologists are asked these questions is that people do not know the answer or, at least, cannot agree among themselves about the correct answer. (Notice that it is quite common to hear someone claiming that there are no differences in arithmetic performance between boys and girls with many in the audience dissenting.) This, in itself, is an interesting observation, certainly when it involves groups of people that are frequently compared (such as elderly and young people, or males and females). It suggests that, if a difference exists, it cannot be large. Otherwise, people would not ask the question. Nobody ever asks a psychologist whether a 6–year old can write more words correctly than an undergraduate student!

There are two reasons why few differences between groups can be spotted with the naked eye – the overlap of distributions and the limited number of observations – and these will be explained below.

6.1.1 Many distributions overlap with one another

It is worth going into more detail on why so many differences between groups of people are difficult to spot. For example, why is it so difficult to reach a decision about whether girls are better than boys in literacy? And what does that imply? To answer these questions, we will return to an example that we first introduced in Chapter 1: the stature of different groups of people. We are not using this example because an individual's height is such an exciting psychological variable, but because we have very detailed information about people's heights and it is a feature that we can easily relate to. Once you grasp the statistical concepts in the context of people's height, it is easy to extend them to less tangible characteristics, such as intelligence, well-being or work productivity.

Why are psychologists never asked whether 3-year old girls are the same height as 18-year old girls? Before you continue reading, you may want to try to formulate the answer yourself. There are two concepts you will have to take into account: the central tendency of each group (the mean stature) and the variability of heights within the groups.

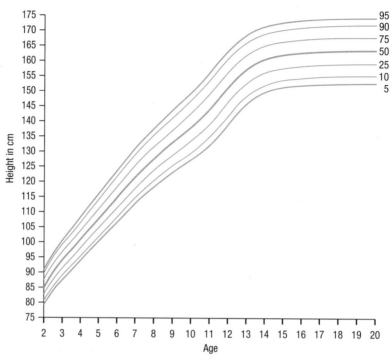

Figure 6.1 US growth chart for girls from 2 to 20 years
© Center for Disease Control and Prevention

If we first look at the stature of 3-year old children, official records (for example, the US growth charts shown in Figure 6.1) tell us that the mean stature of 3-year old girls is 94 cm. There is some variability because not all girls are equally tall, but 90% of the girls have a height between 87 cm and 101 cm. (The upper line of the curve indicates the 95th percentile and the lower line the 5th percentile; see Chapter 5). On the basis of these data, we do not expect to find many girls smaller than 80 cm or taller than 110 cm. When we then look at the data for 18-year olds, we see that their mean height is 163 cm. Again, there is quite some variability between the girls, with 90% of the measures ranging from 153 to 174 cm. However, we do not expect to encounter many 18-year old girls that are smaller than 140 cm (although *Guinness World Records* cites a Brazilian woman of 93 cm who married a man of 90 cm). That means that the smallest 18–year old girl we are likely to meet (140 cm) is much taller than the tallest 3-year girl we are likely to know (110 cm).

Figure 6.2 presents the same information in a different way. If we measured the heights of the complete population of 3-year old girls, we would find that these measures form a normal distribution with $M = 94$ cm and $SD = 4.0$ cm. Similarly, the statures of 18-year old girls are expected to form a normal distribution with $M = 163$ cm and $SD = 6.5$ cm. These two distributions are shown in Figure 6.2. We can see that they are so far apart that there is no discernable overlap between the two of them. The number of 18-year old girls expected to be smaller than a 3-year old girl is negligible. This is why nobody disputes that 3-year old girls are

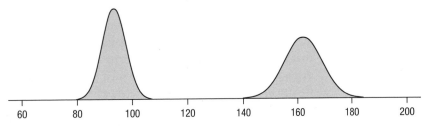

Figure 6.2 Normal distributions representing the heights of 3-year old and 18-year old girls

smaller than 18-year olds. The difference is clear, not to be denied by anyone. However, how many differences between groups of people are as big as this one? Can you find an example of a psychological characteristic that yields a difference of the same size? Can you come up with a psychological difference between two groups of people that is so clear that no-one denies its existence? If you can, you will probably find that you are comparing two extreme groups.

Now, let us see what happens when we compare the heights of 12-year old girls with those of 18-year old girls. Figure 6.1 informs us that 90% of the 12-year olds have a height between 139 cm (5th percentile) and 164 cm (95th percentile), with a mean of 151.5 cm. These numbers agree with a normal distribution that has M = 151.5 cm and SD = 7.6 cm. When we superimpose this distribution on that for the 18-year olds (see Figure 6.3), we see something interesting.

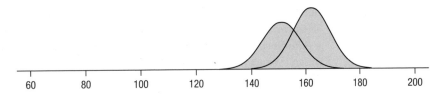

Figure 6.3 Normal distributions representing the heights of 12-year old and 18-year old girls

Although there is a difference of 11.5 cm between the mean stature of 12-year old girls (M = 151.5 cm) and that of 18-year olds (M = 163 cm), there is quite a large overlap of the distributions. Some 6% of the 12-year olds are taller than the average 18-year old, and some 4% of the 18-year olds are smaller than the average 12-year old. Or, to put it differently, if you select at random a 12-year old and an 18-year old, there would be a 12.5% chance that the 12-year old is taller than the 18-year old. This is the reason why people might start to doubt whether 12-year olds are indeed smaller than 18-year olds, and why some may claim that girls are physically grown-up by the age of 12. (These are the people who happen to know some tall 12-year olds.)

This demonstrates why many differences between groups of people are impossible to spot with the naked eye. In each group there is variability, which means that the values of one group partly overlap with those of the other group. Only in extreme cases are the distributions so far apart that there is no perceptible overlap between the two groups.

Probably the best example of how the overlap of the distributions has hindered the general public's perception of a genuine and important difference is the effect of smoking on life expectancy. Although it is now well established that smoking shortens a person's life by an average of 10 years (for example, Doll et al., 2004), some smokers live into their 80s (and some non-smokers die of lung cancer in their 20s). Many people (especially smokers!) react to the statement that smoking kills by pointing to some relative who is well over 80 years old and still smoking, or to some other relative who never smoked but nevertheless died of cancer at the age of 35, as if these single cases give us reason to discard all the other evidence.

On the basis of your knowledge of normal distributions, you should know that both exceptional cases – the healthy aged smoker and the dying non-smoking youngster – are bound to happen because the tails of a normal distribution never really reach 0. Therefore, cases that seem to disprove the overall difference between two normal distributions are expected to exist. (This explains why it is possible, according to *Guinness World Records* to find an adult woman who is smaller than an average 3-year old.) However, these exceptions will be much less frequent than cases that agree with the difference between the distributions.

The percentage of exceptions to the overall pattern depends on the difference between the distributions. The chances of observing a 12-year old girl who is taller than an 18-year old girl are higher than the chances of finding a 3-year old girl who is taller than an 18-year old girl (compare Figures 6.3 and 6.2). The closer the distributions are to one another, the more difficult it is to see the difference, because an increasing number of examples seem to contradict the conclusion. The overlap of distributions is the first reason why it is often impossible to spot a difference between two groups with the naked eye, and why it is sometimes difficult to convince the public to accept a difference you observed in a study. This is particularly so when your finding goes against people's prejudices (or intuitions, as they prefer to call them). The other side of the coin is that some differences between groups, which are reported in the media, are indeed too small to have practical implications. As we will see in the next chapter, if your samples are big enough you can detect reliable differences between two groups that have almost perfectly overlapping distributions!

6.1.2 Decisions often have to be based on a limited number of observations

The second reason why differences between groups are often difficult to spot is that we only have limited evidence at our disposal. Suppose someone claims that girls perform better in primary schools than boys. This may be a rather difficult statement for you to evaluate because you know only a few children of that age (and your recollections of your own performance at that age have become a bit rusty and are likely to be biased because of your gender and the fact that you were probably one of the high-performing individuals of your school).

The lack of data is a problem for researchers as well as the general public. The availability of thousands of measurements, like the ones on which the growth charts are based, is a rare event. Most of the time, comparisons have to be based on a few tens of observations, either because there are no more data (when a particular condition is rare) or because it is too costly to collect the data. So, instead of having population-wide data at their disposal, researchers have to base their conclusions on data from small samples. Figure 6.4 shows the heights of ten 12-year old girls and ten 18-year old female students. Notice how the limited number of observations, together with the overlap of the groups, is a far cry from the situation depicted in Figure 6.3. This is the situation people spontaneously evoke when they hear about a difference between two groups. No wonder they have difficulty making up their minds about many real-life differences between groups!

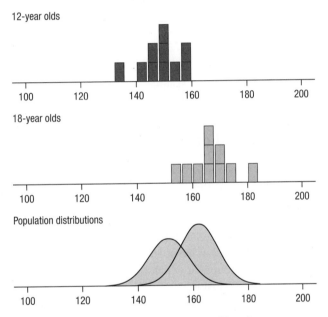

Figure 6.4 Samples of heights of 12-year old and 18-year old girls ($N = 10$ in each sample)

This, then, is the challenge of inferential statistics: to give us the tools to decide whether data are more likely to come from two population distributions with different means or from a single one. This basic question is illustrated in Figure 6.5. If we have a limited set of empirical data from two different groups of people, as shown in Figure 6.4, can we justify our conclusion that there is a genuine difference between the groups? Given the school results of 100 girls and 100 boys, can we justifiably conclude that girls in general (that is, the population of all girls) are doing better or worse than boys in general? This is what the *t*-test will tell us. However, before we introduce this test, there are a few more things you need to know. First, there is less variability in the mean score of a sample than in the individual scores of the sample. This will be illustrated in the next section.

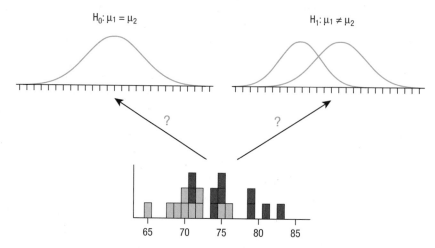

Figure 6.5 The basic question for inferential statistics. Given the observed data from two samples of people (the grey v. the green blocks), are we allowed to conclude that there is a genuine difference between the samples or are the data more in line with the conclusion that both groups perform the same?

6.2 The standard error of the mean

How can we decide whether there is a difference between two groups of people when the scores of the groups overlap? How can we decide that people who smoke die earlier than people who do not smoke, given that some smokers live till they are 100 and some non-smokers die at an early age? The underlying principle turns out to be quite simple: take the mean life span of a group of smokers and the mean life span of a group of non-smokers and compare them. The larger the groups on which the means have been calculated, the surer we are about our conclusion.

This principle probably rings a bell with you. After all, when you hear that an opinion poll was based on 20 interviews, you feel much less secure about its conclusions than when you hear that a poll was based on 2000 interviews. Similarly, when you read about a study which says that people are happier when they have control over the organisation of their work, you would be more convinced if you read that this study was based on two groups of 100 people than if you read that it was based on two groups of 5 participants. So, intuitively you already have a good grasp of the underlying principle. Now we have to make your intuitions more explicit and detailed. Why do we feel more confident about the mean of a large sample than the mean of a small sample? And how exactly is the variability of the mean determined by the size of the sample?

6.2.1 An example of how the variability of the findings depends on the size of the sample

The best way to show why conclusions are more reliable when they are based on large samples than when they are based on small samples is to work on a concrete example. Suppose you want to determine whether adult women are smaller than adult men. You find yourself a busy spot on the university campus and you ask students their height. You ask a woman and a man alternately. The first student says she is 168 cm. The second says he is 169 cm. The third says she is 177 cm. The fourth says he is 168 cm, and so on until you have data of 16 female students and 16 male students. These are your data:

Females		Males	
student 1	168 cm	student 2	169 cm
student 3	177 cm	student 4	168 cm
student 5	165 cm	student 6	170 cm
student 7	154 cm	student 8	181 cm
student 9	161 cm	student 10	179 cm
student 11	159 cm	student 12	186 cm
student 13	162 cm	student 14	191 cm
student 15	163 cm	student 16	178 cm
student 17	159 cm	student 18	174 cm
student 19	168 cm	student 20	168 cm
student 21	169 cm	student 22	177 cm
student 23	163 cm	student 24	182 cm
student 25	164 cm	student 26	173 cm
student 27	158 cm	student 28	185 cm
student 29	172 cm	student 30	169 cm
student 31	151 cm	student 32	184 cm

From these data, you can see that if you had based your conclusions on individual student pairs, you would have concluded in 2 out of 16 cases that women were taller than men (that is, student 3 v. student 4 and student 29 v. student 30) and in 1 out of 16 cases that there was no difference (student 19 v. student 20). For the remaining 'studies' of paired students, the estimates of the difference between male and female stature would have varied from 1 cm (student 1 v. student 2) to 33 cm (student 31 v. student 32). Overall, your findings would have differed greatly from one 'study' to the next, and you would have run a high risk of reaching a conclusion that another researcher would find difficult to replicate.

Now, look at what happens when, instead of taking a sample of one from each group, you take four (N = 4) and you look at the means of these samples. Then your data become:

Females		Males	
students 1–7	M = 166 cm	students 2–8	M = 172 cm
students 9–15	M = 161 cm	students 10–16	M = 183 cm
students 17–23	M = 165 cm	students 18–24	M = 175 cm
students 25–31	M = 161 cm	students 26–32	M = 178 cm

Now each 'study' indicates that male students are taller than female students, and the estimates of the gender difference vary from 6 cm (students 1–7 v. students 2–8) to 22 cm (students 9–15 v. students 10–16). Notice the stability of these findings relative to those from the individual student pairs (for which the differences ranged from –9 cm to +33 cm). The conclusion you would reach on the basis of each study would now be similar to the results another researcher would find (although there is still considerable variability in the estimates of the difference, ranging from 6 cm to 22 cm).

The data become even more stable if we further increase the sample size to $N = 8$. Then we get:

Females		Males	
students 1–15	M = 164 cm	students 2–16	M = 178 cm
students 17–31	M = 163 cm	students 18–32	M = 176 cm

In this case, we see that there are very few differences between the first study and the second. Both indicate a difference between males and females of approximately 14 cm. So, the conclusion reached after the first study is very much the same as the conclusion reached after the second study, and the finding of each study becomes reliable.

What is happening here? Why does the variability of the findings decrease when we average over increasingly large sample sizes? Look again at the data and compare them with Figure 6.1. The first female (student 1) was slightly taller than average. The second female (student 3) happened to be taller as well. (As a matter of fact, she was one of the tallest female students you would expect to encounter on campus because she was more than 2 standard deviations above the mean: 177 cm = 163 cm + 2.15 ∗ 6.5.) By contrast, the fourth female (student 7) was rather small. Now, when you take the mean of tall, small and medium students you end up with a value that is somewhere in between – a value that is closer to the population mean. The more data there are in the sample the closer the sample mean comes to the population mean μ (at least when the sample is representative; see Chapter 1) and the less one sample mean differs from the next. Although you may find a difference up to 26 cm between the smallest and the tallest female student on the campus, I bet my whole income you won't be able to come up with a difference of 26 cm between two groups of 25 randomly sampled female students, no matter how long you try! (Although in theory the probability is not zero.)

An interesting concept to introduce at this moment is the **sampling error**. It refers to the discrepancy between a sample statistic, such as the mean, and the population parameter you are trying to measure. The higher the sampling error, the more difference there can be between the sample statistic and the population parameter. A high sampling error means that there can be quite large differences from one sample to the next. As our example illustrates, an important variable in the sampling error is the sample size: the smaller the size, the larger the sampling error.

So, if we want to compare the performance of two types of people, we must compare the mean performance of two reasonably large samples. Although the scores within each group may show a large variability (and hence a large overlap; see Figures 6.3 and 6.4), there will be much less variability in the means of the groups. In the next section, we will reformulate these insights in mathematical terms, so that we can make more precise statements than the vague words 'quite ', 'much less', and 'reasonably large'.

6.2.2 The straightforward relationship between the standard deviation of a sample, the size of the sample and the standard error of the sample mean

Remember from Chapters 4 and 5 that the standard deviation is a measure of the variability in the sample's data. It indicates the average distance between the individual observations and the mean of the sample. Observations more than two standard deviations away from the mean are rare (less than 5% of the observations).

In the same way as we use the standard deviation to indicate the variability of the data in a sample, we will use the **standard error (SE)** to indicate the variability we expect to observe in the means of the samples if we repeat our study a number of times. Suppose we ask 100 samples of ten 18-year old female students to tell us their heights. This would give us 100 means, as follows:

Sample 1	$N_1 = 10$, $M_1 = 163$ cm
Sample 2	$N_2 = 10$, $M_2 = 166$ cm
Sample 3	$N_3 = 10$, $M_3 = 162$ cm
...	
Sample 99	$N_{99} = 10$, $M_{99} = 160$ cm
Sample 100	$N_{100} = 10$, $M_{100} = 162$ cm

We do not expect all the sample means to be exactly the same because some samples will contain more tall girls and others more small girls. There will be variability in the 100 sample means – variability we can represent by means of the standard error.

From Section 6.2.1 we know that the standard error of the means will be smaller than the standard deviation of the data within the samples. However, how much smaller will SE be, when the sample sizes are $N = 10$? Do we have to calculate the means of several samples with $N = 10$ before we can calculate SE, or is there a way to calculate SE directly on the basis of the standard deviation of the raw X-scores (SD) and the sample size (N)?

Mathematicians have proved that the SE of the sample mean is related to the SD of the sample in the following straightforward way:

$$SE = \frac{SD}{\sqrt{N}}$$

So, if the standard deviation of the statures of 18-year old females is 6.5 cm (Section 6.1.1), we expect the standard error of the means of samples of 10 female students to be:

$$SE = \frac{6.5}{\sqrt{10}} = 2.055$$

In other words, whereas some 95% of the heights of 18-year old females are situated between 150 cm (M – 2SD) and 176 cm (M + 2SD), we expect 95% of the means of samples with size N = 10 to be situated between 159 cm (M – 2SE) and 167 cm (M + 2SE).

Similarly, if we have samples of size N = 100, we expect SE to be equal to

$$SE = \frac{6.5}{\sqrt{100}} = .65$$

and 95% of the means of samples with size N = 100 will fall between 161.7 cm (M – 2SE) and 164.3 (M + 2SE). Notice how small the interval has become!

This shows why the sample size is so important. The larger the value of N, the smaller the standard error and the more stable the sample mean (because the measure will not differ very much from one sample to another).

Learning check 1

What standard error do you expect for the mean height of 18-year old female students when the mean is based on a sample size of N = 10,000? What standard error would you expect in the mean height of 12-year old girls if the mean is based on a sample size of N = 400? (See Section 6.1.1 for the values of M and SD.)

The relationship between SD and SE means that we can estimate SE directly from the standard deviation of the sample and the sample size. We do not have to test several samples to calculate the SE of the means. As we will see below, we can even go further because we have a good idea of how the sample means are distributed.

6.2.3 The distribution of sample means is a normal distribution

There is one more interesting aspect of sample means: they usually form a normal distribution. If you plotted the mean statures of 100 samples of 10 female students in a frequency distribution graph, you would see not only that the standard error is smaller than the standard deviation of the individual observations (as indicated in the previous section), but also that the distribution of the sample means is a normal distribution. This is because each observation in a sample has been taken at random, and the sum of a large number of independent variables always forms a normal distribution. If you do not believe me, take a die and do the following two experiments.

First, throw your die 120 times and note how many times the result is 1, 2, 3, 4, 5 or 6. If you threw well, you should roughly find a rectangular distribution, because each outcome has the same probability of occurrence. So, you'd expect to find about 20 ones, about 20 twos and so on.

Now throw the die 10 times ($N = 10$) and take the mean of your 10 scores. Repeat this 120 times and plot the 120 means in a frequency distribution graph. Look at the shape of your graph. Most of the values will be in the range of 3.0–4.0 and the extreme values become increasingly unlikely. (Did you observe any runs of 10 ones or 10 sixes?) Overall, the shape of your distribution will look much more like a normal distribution than the rectangular distribution you obtained in your first experiment with $N = 1$. The approximation to the normal distribution becomes even better if you take sample sizes of $N = 30$ rather than $N = 10$ (although this involves quite a lot of die throwing!).

Figure 6.6 shows the results I obtained when I did both experiments ($N = 1$ and $N = 10$). How do they compare to yours?

(a) $N = 1$ (120 samples)   (b) $N = 10$ (120 samples)

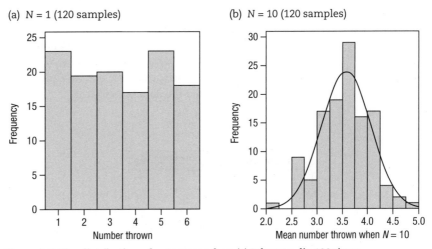

Figure 6.6 The distribution of outcomes when (a) I threw a die 120 times and (b) I threw 120 times a sequence of 10 dice and calculated the mean number of dots. Notice that the distribution in (b) starts to approximate a normal distribution. If I further increased the sample size, the approximation to the normal distribution would be even better.

 Recap

The central limit theorem

We have covered quite a bit of ground in Sections 6.2.1–6.2.3 so it is time for a short summary. Thus far we have seen that:

1 When we have a sample of size N, then the mean of this sample, M, will have a standard error of $SD/\sqrt{N}$. This means that there will be much less variability in the mean of the sample than in the original scores. The larger the sample size, the smaller the SE of the mean.
2 Theoretically, we can expect that the sample mean is part of a normal distribution. This will always be the case if the original scores came from a normal distribution (for example, heights, IQs). For other distributions, the means will be distributed normally from sample sizes of $N = 30$ on. Even for smaller samples, the approximation is quite good (see the dice example in Figure 6.6).

In statistics, these two characteristics of sample means are known as the **central limit theorem**. They form the cornerstone on which the *t*-test and the parametric tests are based.

6.2.4   Step by step: comparing two groups of people

Before we plunge into the *t*-test, let us look at a numerical example on which to do the calculations. The example involves a study in which young and old adults were compared on the likelihood of remembering a mistake they had made (based on Rabbitt, 2002). Participants sat in front of a computer screen that displayed four boxes. Underneath the screen were four response keys. On each trial a light appeared in one of the boxes and the participants had to press the corresponding key as quickly as possible. The trials followed each other rapidly. Occasionally, the computer program stopped and asked the participants whether they had made an error in the previous 3 trials (for example, they had pressed key 3, whereas the light was shown in box 2). The experiment was programmed in such a way that the program often stopped two trials after the participants had made an error. These were the critical trials on which the results were based. There was a group of young participants ($M = 20.1$ years, $SD = 1.1$ years) and a group of old participants ($M = 71.2$ years, $SD = 5.1$ years). Suppose there were 10 participants in each group (the actual study had 40 participants in each group), which generated the data in Table 6.1:

Table 6.1 Percentage of errors noticed by young and old adults.

Young adults	Old adults
71	72
75	65
81	70
79	76
75	72
84	75
74	68
74	69
71	71
79	70

A researcher wants to find out from the 20 scores in Table 6.1 whether young adults in general (that is, the population of young adults) are more or less likely to notice the errors they make than the population of old adults. Notice that we only have a very limited view of the populations (that is, of reality) and that the scores of the two groups overlap to a large extent (with those of the young adults going from 71 to 84 and those of the old adults going from 65 to 76).

As indicated in the previous sections, first calculate the mean and the standard deviation of each group using the auxiliary tables (Tables 6.2 and 6.3).

Table 6.2 Auxiliary table to calculate the mean and the standard deviation of the percentages of errors noticed by the young adults.

X_1	$X_1 - M_1$	$(X_1 - M_1)^2$
71	−5.3	28.09
75	−1.3	1.69
81	4.7	22.09
79	2.7	7.29
75	−1.3	1.69
84	7.7	59.29
74	−2.3	5.29
74	−2.3	5.29
71	−5.3	28.09
79	2.7	7.29
$\Sigma X_1 = 763$ $N_1 = 10$ $M_1 = 76.3$	$\Sigma(X_1 - M_1) = 0.0$	$\Sigma(X_1 - M_1)^2 = 166.10$

$$M_1 = 76.3, \ SD_1 = \sqrt{\frac{\sum(X_1 - M_1)^2}{N_1 - 1}} = \sqrt{\frac{166.10}{10 - 1}} = 4.30$$

Table 6.3 Auxiliary table to calculate the mean and the standard deviation of the percentages of errors noticed by the old adults.

X_2	$X_2 - M_2$	$(X_2 - M_2)^2$
72	1.2	1.44
65	−5.8	33.64
70	−0.8	0.64
76	5.2	27.04
72	1.2	1.44
75	4.2	17.64
68	−2.8	7.84
69	−1.8	3.24
71	0.2	0.04
70	−0.8	0.64
$\Sigma X_2 = 708$ $N_2 = 10$ $M_2 = 70.8$	$\Sigma(X_2 - M_2) = 0.0$	$\Sigma(X_2 - M_2)^2 = 93.60$

$$M_2 = 70.8, \ SD_2 = \sqrt{\frac{\sum(X_2 - M_2)^2}{N_2 - 1}} = \sqrt{\frac{93.60}{10 - 1}} = 3.22$$

If we assume that the means and the standard deviations of the samples are good estimates of the population parameters, then Figure 6.7 shows the two distributions associated with the percentages of error detection by young and old adults. Notice the large overlap of the distributions, which was also clear in the sample data.

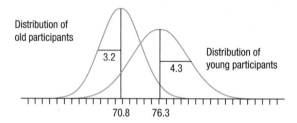

Figure 6.7 The distributions of percentages of error detection by young and old adults. Assume that the data in Table 6.1 provide us with good estimates of the population parameters.

Figure 6.8 shows the same information when we focus, not on the data themselves, but on the means of the samples. Notice that the overlap of the distributions of the means is much smaller, because the standard errors of the means are $\sqrt{10}$ (= 3.16) times smaller than the standard deviations of the raw observations (SE = SD/3.16 in the example). The *t*-test will allow us to decide whether the difference is big enough to be reliable.

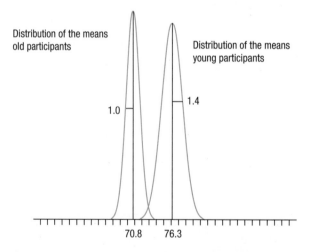

Figure 6.8 The theoretical distributions of the mean percentages of error detection by young and old adults for sample sizes N = 10. Assume that the data in Table 6.1 provide us with good estimates of the population parameters.

Learning check 2

Calculate the distributions of the means if they were based on 1,000 young adults and 1,000 old adults. Would it then be easier to decide whether there is a genuine difference between the performance of the young and the old?

6.3 The *t*-statistic for independent samples

We have reached the point where you have enough background knowledge to understand how a t-test works. As with all other statistical concepts, there is nothing mysterious about the test once you understand the basics of the data analysis.

Let's repeat what we have so far:

1 Many differences between groups are difficult to observe with the naked eye because the differences are hidden by the variability that exists in each group (Figure 6.3).

2 The differences between groups become clearer if we take the mean of a sample rather than the raw X-scores. This is because the standard error of the mean is smaller than the standard deviation of the sample, so the overlap of the (theoretical) distributions is smaller for the means than for the original scores.

3 The standard error of the mean depends on the sample size: the larger the sample size, the smaller the standard error.

These three principles will be used to determine the likelihood that a difference observed between two sample means is also present at the population level. Before researchers start their study, they do not know whether the two groups really differ or not (otherwise they would not run the research). Even worse, when their understanding of a phenomenon is wrong, researchers sometimes erroneously predict a difference that is not there at the population level. They speculate about a difference between two groups that does not exist in reality (that is, at the population level). So, they need a method to determine whether the difference they observe between the two sample means is reliable enough to generalise to the population level or whether the difference could simply be due to chance fluctuations. Such fluctuations, like the height comparison between a woman of 170 cm and a man of 165 cm, are referred to as 'sampling errors'.

6.3.1 Calculating the *t*-statistic for two independent samples

In this section we will calculate the t-statistic for two independent samples. Remember that **independent samples** are samples from two different groups of people, such as boys v. girls, youngsters v. elderly, university students v. workers and so on. Importantly, the members of the two groups have been tested independently from one another and most of the time do not even know each other. (In Chapter 8, we will discuss the t-test for related samples, when the observations in the two different conditions come from the same participants and are, therefore, related to each other.)

The formula to calculate the t-statistic for independent samples is:

$$t = \frac{M_1 - M_2}{\sqrt{\dfrac{SD_1{}^2}{N_1} + \dfrac{SD_2{}^2}{N_2}}}$$

in which M_1 is the mean of the first sample, M_2 is the mean of the second sample, $SD_1{}^2$ is the square of the standard deviation of the first sample, $SD_2{}^2$ is the square of the standard deviation of the second sample, N_1 is the size of the first sample and N_2 is the size of the second sample. For reasons that are made clear in the 'Going further' section, we assume that the sample sizes are the same, unless specified otherwise. Thus, $N_1 = N_2$. This considerably simplifies the discussion. Applied to the data in Table 6.1, the equation gives us:

$$t = \frac{76.3 - 70.8}{\sqrt{\frac{(4.30)^2}{10} + \frac{(3.22)^2}{10}}} = \frac{5.5}{\sqrt{1.8456 + 1.04}} = 3.24$$

The attentive among you will have noticed that we made a needless detour by first taking the square roots of the variances in Tables 6.2 and 6.3 to calculate the standard deviations, and then squaring them again for the t-statistic. In future, we will take the simpler route of calculating the variances in the auxiliary tables and using them for the calculation of the t-statistic. In Table 6.2 we add variance$_1$ = 166.1/9 = 18.456, and in Table 6.3 we add variance$_2$ = 93.6/9 = 10.4. Then the calculation of the t-statistic becomes:

$$t = \frac{M_1 - M_2}{\sqrt{\frac{\text{variance}_1}{N_1} + \frac{\text{variance}_2}{N_2}}} = \frac{76.3 - 70.8}{\sqrt{\frac{18.456}{10} + \frac{10.4}{10}}} = 3.24$$

I included the SDs of the samples rather than the variances in the initial equation of the t-test because this clearly illustrates that the value of the t-statistic depends on three components:

1 *The difference between the means of the samples:* The larger the difference between the samples, the higher the t-statistic. (For example, if the difference between young and old adults in Table 6.1 had been 20% rather than 5.5%, then the t-statistic would have been 11.77.) Furthermore, when there is no difference in the means (that is, when both samples perform at exactly the same level), the t-statistic will be 0 (because the numerator $M_1 - M_2 = 0$).

2 *The variability of the data in the samples, as measured by the standard deviations or the variances:* The larger the variability, the smaller the t-statistic. This again makes sense because larger standard deviations imply more overlap of the distributions.

3 *The sample sizes:* The larger N_1 and N_2, the higher the t-statistic will be (because high values of N_1 and N_2 reduce the value of the denominator in the equation). Again, this makes sense, because a t-statistic is about a comparison of two means and, as indicated above, a comparison of mean values depends on the SEs and not on the SDs.

As a matter of fact, if you look carefully at the equations of the t-statistic and the standard error, you will notice that the equation of the t-statistic can also be written as follows:

$$t = \frac{M_1 - M_2}{\sqrt{SE_1{}^2 + SE_2{}^2}}$$

because

$$\frac{SD^2}{N} = \left(\frac{SD}{\sqrt{N}}\right)^2 = SE^2$$

This new equation of the *t*-statistic illustrates more clearly than the original one that the *t*-statistic actually measures the overlap of the two theoretical distributions of the means; that is, the overlap shown in Figure 6.8 and not the one in Figure 6.7. As a matter of fact, the interpretation of a *t*-statistic very much resembles that of a *z*-score (Chapter 5): a *t*-statistic indicates how many standard errors there are between M_1 and M_2. In the next section we will illustrate how to interpret a *t*-value.

6.3.2 Intuitive interpretation of the *t*-statistic

In the previous section, we saw that a *t*-statistic can be interpreted as the difference between M_1 and M_2 in terms of standard errors. This is very similar to the way we interpret a *z*-score. So, a *t*-value of 0 means there is no difference at all between M_1 and M_2. A *t*-value between 0 and 1 or between 0 and –1 means that there is not much of a difference, either because of a small numerical difference between M_1 and M_2 or because of the large variability in the scores of the samples. Finally, a *t*-value higher than +2 or lower than –2 indicates that the difference between the means of the two samples is becoming large enough to be meaningful. How large the *t*-statistic has to be for us to consider it as sound

evidence against the idea that $M_1 - M_2 = 0$, depends on the sizes of the samples involved. For large samples the values of –2 and +2 can be taken as the critical values, but for small samples we require higher values. The smaller the sample, the more uncertain we are about the correct interpretation and, hence, the larger the *t*-statistic has to be before we trust it.

> **Tip** When you are asked to interpret a *t*-statistic, remember that its meaning is similar to that of a *z*-score. A *t*-statistic close to 0 means that there is no evidence for a difference between the two groups. A *t*-statistic smaller than –2 or larger than +2 indicates that the evidence for a difference between the groups is becoming more reliable, certainly when the group sizes are reasonably large (N_1 and $N_2 \geq 30$).

If we look at the *t*-statistic we obtained for the memory errors of young and old adults, described in Table 6.1, we see that the value of +3.24 is higher than +2. There is, therefore, some evidence for a difference between the groups. Is it enough, though, given that we had rather small sample sizes ($N_1 = N_2 = 10$)? Before we can answer this question, we need to know more about the *t*-statistic.

6.3.3 Interpreting a *t*-statistic as the probability of obtaining more extreme values

Thus far we have again limited the discussion to vague words such as 'reasonably large', 'close to 0' and so on. However, as for *z*-scores (Chapter 5), statisticians can say much more about the probability of *t*-values, because they know the shape of the *t*-value distribution. In the same way as we can say that the probability of a lower score for $z = -1.0$ equals .1587 (Table 5.1), we can compute the probability of finding a score lower than $t = -1.0$.

As a matter of fact, the *t*-distribution looks very much like the normal distribution, in particular when *t*-statistic is based on large sample sizes. For smaller sample sizes, the *t*-distribution still resembles a normal distribution but with thicker tails: The smaller the sample size, the thicker the tails.

Because the distribution of t depends on the number of observations on which it is based, we always have to indicate this number. However, as we saw for the standard deviation, it is not the actual number of observations that is important, but the number of observations that *are free to vary*. You may remember from Chapter 4 that these are called the degrees of freedom (df). For the t-statistic of independent means, df = $N_1 - 1 + N_2 - 1$, because each of the two variances in the equation have N – 1 degrees of freedom (see p. 83). So, the t-statistic of the study on the percentage of mistakes noticed by young and old adults has df = 10 – 1 + 10 – 1 = 18 ($N_1 = N_2 = 10$, given that there were 10 young and 10 old adults).

Figure 6.9 shows the t-distribution for various degrees of freedom. Notice how closely these distributions resemble the standard normal distribution, certainly when df = 200. In Figure 6.9 you can also see the t-values for which the probability of more extreme values is .05 (that is, 2.5% at the low end and 2.5% at the high end). Remember that, for the standard normal distribution, these values were z = –1.96 and z = +1.96 (Figure 5.15).

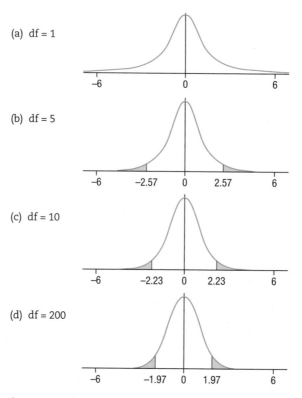

Figure 6.9 Distributions of the *t*-statistic for different degrees of freedom. Like normal distributions, t-distributions are symmetrical and bell-shaped. However, they have more variability, indicated by the flatter and more spread-out shape. The lower the df, the larger the variability. As a consequence, in (a) (df = 1) the areas of the 2.5% most extreme values could not be drawn because they are situated below –12.71 and above +12.71.

Similarly, theoreticians can calculate the exact probability of finding a *t*-value larger than a given value. For our example of the study on the percentage of errors noticed by old and young people, the *t*-value is +3.24. The probability of finding a *t*-value greater than +3.24 is .002272 when the *t*-distribution has 18 degrees of freedom. As we will see below, this probability plays a critical role in hypothesis testing.

6.4 Hypothesis testing on the basis of the *t*-statistic

Remember that the basic question we are trying to answer in this chapter is whether there is a difference between two groups of people. More specifically, we are attempting to make a statement about two groups at the population level on the basis of two samples of empirical data we have gathered. This procedure is called hypothesis testing. A **hypothesis test** is a statistical method that uses sample data to evaluate a hypothesis about population parameters.

In our example, we are trying to establish whether old and young adults are equally likely to notice their mistakes. Using the data in Table 6.1, we noted that the old people's mean detection percentage (70.8%) was 5.5% lower than that of the young adults (76.3%). Is this an indication that old adults are less likely to see that they did something wrong or is it simply a glitch, due to the fact that sample means show some variation around the population mean? If we were to repeat the experiment with 20 other participants, would we again find that the old participants performed less well than the young people (making the difference more reliable) or would we be just as likely to find the opposite?

6.4.1 The null hypothesis and the alternative hypothesis

In order to decide whether there is a reliable difference between two conditions, psychologists always start from the assumption that there is no such difference. Thus, for the data in Table 6.1 the starting point is the hypothesis that old adults perform at exactly the same level as young adults. If we knew the population distribution of the performances of the old adults, we would see that this distribution overlaps entirely with that of the young adults. This does not mean that all old adults perform equally well (their performances form a normal distribution around the population mean μ_1 with a standard deviation of σ_1) but that the distribution of their performances is the same as that of the young adults (that is, $\mu_2 = \mu_1$ and $\sigma_2 = \sigma_1$). This initial assumption is called the **null hypothesis** (H_0).

The null hypothesis is either correct (meaning that the two groups do not really differ in their performance) or incorrect. In the latter case, there is a genuine difference between the two groups. Their population distributions do not overlap entirely. Or to put it more formally: $\mu_2 \neq \mu_1$. (Unless otherwise specified, researchers assume that at the population level $\sigma_2 = \sigma_1$; see the 'Going further' section for further discussion of this assumption.)

The situation of $\mu_2 \neq \mu_1$ is called the **alternative hypothesis** (H_1). Notice that the alternative hypothesis does not state whether the young adults will perform better or worse than the old adults. It just says that their performance will be *different* ($\mu_2 \neq \mu_1$). So, the *t*-value can be positive (when $\mu_2 < \mu_1$) as well as negative (when $\mu_2 > \mu_1$). Such an alternative hypothesis, which does not state the direction of the difference that will be found, is called a *non-directional hypothesis* and will result in a so-called *two-tailed test*. (A two-tailed test takes into account the probabilities in both tails of the *t*-distribution; see Figure 6.9.) Two-tailed tests are by far the commonest tests used in psychology. Only occasionally do researchers make use of a directional or one-tailed test, which is briefly explained in Chapter 7.

To decide which hypothesis applies to the issue under study – the null hypothesis or the alternative hypothesis – psychologists use the *t*-statistic. If the *t*-statistic is close to 0, they conclude that the initial null hypothesis was probably correct and, hence, should be retained. Alternatively, if the *t*-statistic is very high (either very positive or very negative), they will conclude that the initial hypothesis of no difference was wrong and should be replaced by the alternative hypothesis of a genuine difference between the groups. Of course, most of the time, the *t*-values are not zero or very large or small. Therefore, researchers need a critical threshold value to decide whether the *t*-statistic deviates enough from 0 for them no longer to accept the null hypothesis. The determination of the critical value is discussed in the next section.

6.4.2 The level of significance and the degrees of freedom

The next step is to define the critical values that will decide whether the *t*-statistic is close enough to 0 to be in line with the null hypothesis or so extreme that the null hypothesis should be rejected. Statisticians could have used a simple rule of thumb and decided that *t*-values of –2 and +2 were a good choice. However, as we saw before, these values would be too low for small values of df (Figure 6.9). The chances of finding a value lower than –2 or higher than +2 for df = 1 are .295 or 29.5% (14.75% at the low end of distribution and 14.75% at the high end). In other words, if df = 1 (which we would obtain when both sample sizes are 2; $N_1 = N_2 = 2$) the chances of obtaining a *t*-statistic lower than –2 or higher than +2, when, at the population level, there is no difference between M_1 and M_2 are more than 1 in 4 (25%)! This agrees with the large sampling error we discussed for small sample sizes. Similarly, the chances of finding *t*-values lower than –2 or higher than +2 for df = 4 ($N_1 = N_2 = 3$) when there is no difference at the population level are .184 or 18.4%.

Because the probability of finding more extreme *t*-values depends on df, statisticians do not use fixed *t*-values. Instead, they use the *t*-values that limit the probability of more extreme values to 5% if the null hypothesis is true. This 5% criterion is called the **level of significance** or the **alpha level**. It is the probability of finding a larger *t*-value given that $\mu_1 = \mu_2$. When a 5% criterion is used we write $\alpha = .05$. Nearly all psychological research is based on this level, although sometimes researchers have reasons to set their level of significance at 1%, in which case we have $\alpha = .01$. This will be discussed in Chapter 7.

The critical values for $\alpha = .05$ are those values that mark out the regions of the distribution that include the lowest 2.5% of scores and the highest 2.5% of

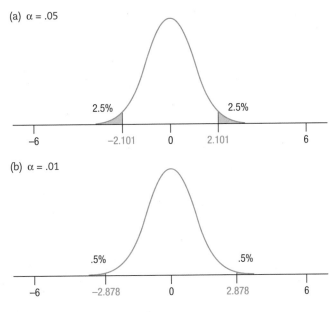

(a) $\alpha = .05$

2.5%   2.5%

−6   −2.101   0   2.101   6

(b) $\alpha = .01$

.5%   .5%

−6   −2.878   0   2.878   6

Figure 6.10 The t-distribution when $N_1 = N_2 = 10$ (df = 18), together with the critical values for $\alpha = .05$ and $\alpha = .01$

scores (Figure 6.10). Remember that the non-directional t-test does not specify whether $\mu_1 < \mu_2$ or $\mu_1 > \mu_2$. Therefore, the 5% extreme values are split into a lower half and an upper half.

To illustrate how the critical values are determined, let's have a look at Appendix A (p. 395), where the standard normal distribution is described in full. We see that p(lower) = .0250 for the z-score −1.96 and that p(higher) = .0250 for the z-score +1.96. Thus, the critical z-scores for $\alpha = .05$ ($z_{.05crit}$) are −1.96 and +1.96 (see also Figure 5.15).

Because the t-distribution approximates the standard normal distribution for large sample sizes, the critical t-values will be close to −1.96 and +2.96 for these samples. For instance, when $N_1 = N_2 = 100$, $t_{.05crit} = -1.98$ and +1.98. For smaller sample sizes we have to account for the flatter t-distribution (Figure 6.9) and thus the critical values will be more extreme. How extreme depends on the degrees of freedom, which as we have seen in the case of a t-test for independent samples are:

$df = N_1 - 1 + N_2 - 1$

So, for our example of error detection in young and old adults:

$df = 10 - 1 + 10 - 1 = 18.$

Table 6.4 lists the critical $\alpha = .05$ values for the most common sample sizes (see Appendix B for more values). Remember that $df = N_1 - 1 + N_2 - 1$. Also remember that in our discussions we always assumed that $N_1 = N_2$, so we will find that df = 2 when $N_1 = N_2 = 2$, df = 4 when $N_1 = N_2 = 3$ and so on. Finally, notice that these values are for two-tailed tests – the tests used in the vast majority of psychological research.

Table 6.4 Critical values for α = .05 (two-tailed) and df values for $N_1 = N_2$. The null hypothesis is rejected when the t-statistic is lower than the lower critical value or higher than the higher critical value. See Appendix B for the critical values of *t*-distributions with other df values and for a wider range of α-levels.

$N_1 = N_2$	df	lower $t_{.05crit}$	higher $t_{.05crit}$
2	2	–4.303	+4.303
3	4	–2.776	+2.776
4	6	–2.447	+2.447
5	8	–2.306	+2.306
6	10	–2.228	+2.228
7	12	–2.179	+2.179
8	14	–2.145	+2.145
9	16	–2.120	+2.120
10	18	–2.101	+2.101
11	20	–2.086	+2.086
12	22	–2.074	+2.074
13	24	–2.064	+2.064
14	26	–2.056	+2.056
15	28	–2.048	+2.048
16	30	–2.042	+2.042
20	38	–2.024	+2.024
30	58	–2.002	+2.002
40	78	–1.999	+1.999
50	98	–1.984	+1.984
∞	∞	–1.960	+1.960

For sample sizes N = 10 the critical t-values are –2.101 and +2.101 (df = 18). Remember that these are the sample sizes we used in our example of error detection by young and old adults. This means that we will reject the null hypothesis if we obtain a t-statistic lower than –2.101 or higher than +2.101. Given that our calculated t-statistic of +3.24 is higher than +2.101, we can say that the null hypothesis of no difference in error detection between young and old adults is likely to be wrong. The old adults are significantly worse than the young adults.

6.4.3 Rejection of the null hypothesis leads to a significant finding

Researchers are like prosecutors in a courtroom. In the same way as the court presumes that the defendant is free of guilt until the prosecuting counsel has convinced the jury of the opposite, so must researchers assume that the null hypothesis is true until they have demonstrated otherwise. They do this by obtaining a t-statistic that is more extreme than the critical value. Just as lawsuits are only initiated when there is enough suspicion against a person, so researchers only design experiments when they suspect that they will find a difference between two groups of people.

Therefore, when a researcher sets up an experiment in which the performances of two groups are compared, s/he expects (hopes) to find a difference. On the basis of previous research or a particular theory, the researcher has good reason to believe that the two groups should perform differently (just as a prosecuting attorney starts a court trial by presenting reasons to believe that the defendant is guilty). However, until the experiment is finished and a t-statistic that exceeds the critical value has been obtained, the researcher has to assume that the null hypothesis of no difference between the groups represents the reality. This is why so many researchers (and students!) are disappointed when their t-statistic turns out to be too small. They feel the same disappointment as prosecuting attorneys when a defendant is acquitted because they have not been able to prove their suspicion.

The first reason why researchers have to start from the assumption of no difference is that empirical evidence of a difference between two groups is much more convincing than evidence of no difference. The example that is usually given is the difficulty of proving the statement that 'all swans are white'. For centuries, Europeans were convinced that all swans were white and they even used the expression 'black swan' to refer to something which was impossible. Imagine their surprise when the Dutch explorer, Willem de Vlamingh, came across black swans on his voyage of discovery to Australia in 1697! So, even though you may have observed hundreds, even thousands, of swans that are all white, it is still possible that the next swan you observe is not white and, hence, invalidates your statement. On the other hand, to prove the statement that 'not all swans are white', you only need to find a single swan that is a different colour. As soon as you have found one such instance, you know your statement that 'not all swans are white' is correct. In a courtroom, too, evidence that the accused 'is guilty of something' is usually more persuasive than evidence that the accused 'is not guilty at all'.

There is a second reason why science requires researchers to show a difference between groups rather than requiring them to show that there is no difference. It is easy to find that there is no difference between groups by doing sloppy testing. The easiest way to 'prove' that all swans are white is to observe only a few swans and verify that they are all white. Similarly, the best way to 'prove' that someone is not guilty of a crime is not to look hard for evidence. So, the simplest way to fail to find a difference between two groups of people is to test small groups and/or to have a lot of noise (random variability) in your measurements. The smaller the groups, the larger the difference between the means has to be before the critical t-value is exceeded (and thus the higher the chances of not finding evidence against the null hypothesis). Similarly, the larger the standard deviations in the groups, the larger the difference in means has to be before the critical value is exceeded.

So, hypothesis testing in scientific research consists of stating a null hypothesis of no difference between conditions and trying to show that this null hypothesis is wrong. In this case, the null hypothesis has to be rejected and replaced by the alternative hypothesis. The null hypothesis can only be rejected when the *t*-statistic is larger than the critical value. At that point, researchers talk about 'a significant effect'. They usually add the significance level of their finding, which is typically 5% because they used $\alpha = .05$ as the cut-off value. An alternative way of communicating a significant finding at $\alpha = .05$ is to write $p < .05$. This means that, on the basis of the experimental results, the researcher estimates the probability of the null hypothesis being true to be smaller than .05. We will return to this issue in Section 6.5.

Alternatively, when the *t*-statistic is not larger than the critical value, the researcher fails to reject the null hypothesis. This does not mean that the researcher *proved* that there is no difference between the groups; it only means that there is not enough evidence to postulate a difference. This situation is very much the same as when an accused is acquitted by the jury. This does not prove that the accused is not guilty at all (unless there is indisputable evidence to the contrary); it just means that the evidence is too weak to convict him/her. When the null hypothesis cannot be rejected, researchers speak of an insignificant result.

Many students find it hard to grasp the underlying logic of hypothesis testing. The reason for this is quite simple: *Hypothesis testing is difficult to grasp because it goes against the way humans normally reason*. Think about it. What would be your first reaction if you were convinced that female students obtain higher grades than male students and somebody doubted this? Would you say: 'OK, you may have a point. Let's test this properly. We start by assuming that there is no difference. Then we look at a group of randomly selected males and a group of randomly selected females, and we check whether the difference in their grades is big enough to be reliable (significant), and whether in addition the observed difference is in favour of the female students.'? In all likelihood, you would defend your conviction by trying to find evidence in *favour* of your hypothesis. You would sum up all the evidence showing that females obtain better grades than males and try to find additional confirmation. You would not spontaneously go and search for evidence *against* your hypothesis. People's tendency to look for evidence that is in line with their convictions is well-known in psychology and is called the **confirmation bias**. It is the reason why people can maintain strong prejudices even if the real world provides overwhelming evidence to the contrary. They only pay attention to evidence that 'proves' their point.

Because researchers do not want to get stuck in prejudices, they constantly challenge each other's theories and ideas by trying to reject null hypotheses predicted by the theories. This has a very positive effect, because it means that science constantly evolves and – hopefully – reaches a more accurate understanding of reality (although not all philosophers agree with that statement). On the other hand, it also has a negative side: rejecting a null hypothesis is a destructive act. For this reason, at any moment in time and in any scientific area there are many more researchers who disagree with what others say (trying to reject their null hypotheses) than researchers who agree with one another. Anyone who has ever ventured into the real scientific literature has been astonished by the disagreement among researchers. Researchers quibble so much with each other because it is much easier to show that other people are wrong than to prove that they are right. Somewhat ironically, one could describe the scientific literature as a collection of a few theories and an avalanche of empirical studies claiming that all kinds of details of those theories are wrong because null hypotheses based on them have been rejected by empirical data. Because of this constant experimentation, only the strongest theories survive.

6.4.4 Reporting the results of a *t*-test in a manuscript

Generally, researchers do not report their statistical analyses in full. They summarise their findings in a few lines that allow other researchers to interpret and reconstruct them. To do so, they need to include the following information:

- the mean and the standard deviation of the first condition (M_1, SD_1),
- the mean and the standard deviation of the second condition (M_2, SD_2),
- the *t*-value,
- the degrees of freedom,
- whether or not the statistical test was significant.

The traditional way of reporting the significance level is to indicate whether the probability – the *p*-value – is smaller or larger than the .05 significance level. (See Chapter 7 for a more detailed discussion of why this is so.) So, researchers write $p < .05$ when they find a significant effect and $p > .05$ when they fail to obtain a significant effect. When the *p*-value is larger than .50, researchers may also write n.s., meaning *not significant*.

The findings of the error detection experiment would be reported more or less as follows: 'In our experiment, young adults detected significantly more errors ($M = 76.3\%$, $SD = 4.30$) than old adults ($M = 70.8\%$, $SD = 3.22$; $t(18) = 3.24$, $p < .05$).' Notice that the degrees of freedom are written in brackets after the letter t. Researchers do not write $t = 3.24$, df = 18, but $t(18) = 3.24$.

A second way of reporting the significance level is to make use of the exact *p*-value, which is given in all statistical software packages. So, rather than writing that $p < .05$ for the error detection experiment, researchers would write $p = .0046$. We will defer the discussion of this practice to the next chapter.

6.4.5 Step by step: hypothesis testing

 We have covered quite a lot of ground thus far. It is, therefore, a good time to recapitulate and organise this new information. We will do this by structuring the process of hypothesis testing in four steps. Each step will be illustrated with a fictional study in which a drug company wants to know whether a drug that successfully slows down the development of dementia also has a positive effect on memory performance in healthy individuals. One group of undergraduate students is given tablets consisting of carbohydrates and the drug for a week. This is the experimental group. A second group of undergraduates gets similar tablets, which only contain the carbohydrates but not the active substance. This group is called the placebo control group. Both groups take a memory test at the end of the week, in which they have to study 50 word pairs for 15 minutes (for example, book–pot, roof–line, …). After the study phase, they have to complete personality tests for one hour and then they are tested on the word pairs. On each trial, they are given the first word (for example, book–, roof–, …) and are asked to complete the pair (that is, –pot, –line, …). The number of correct responses is calculated for each individual (min = 0; max = 50).

The full hypothesis-testing procedure consists of four steps.

1 *The null hypothesis and the alternative hypothesis are outlined.*
The null hypothesis says that the experimental group will show the same distribution of performance as the placebo control group. Because the drug is assumed not to have an effect at the population level, both groups of participants come from the same distribution ($\mu_{experimental} = \mu_{control}$). The alternative hypothesis says that the drug has an effect and that the performance of the experimental group will differ from that of the placebo control group ($\mu_{experimental} \neq \mu_{control}$). At this moment, we are not considering whether the influence of the drug will be beneficial or detrimental. The researchers are simply starting from the assumption of no effect (null hypothesis) and examining whether the evidence is strong enough to reject that null hypothesis. Figure 6.11 illustrates the choice that will be made after the experiment.

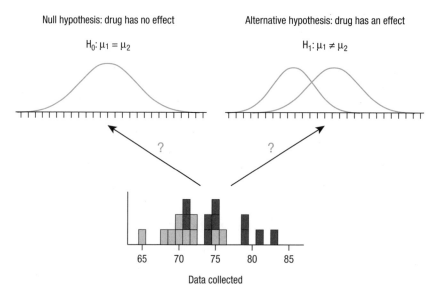

Figure 6.11 Figure illustrating the null hypothesis and the alternative hypothesis for the study on the effect of the drug. The null hypothesis says that the drug has no effect and, hence, that the data of the experimental and the control group should come from the same normal population distribution. The alternative hypothesis says that the drug has an effect (either beneficial or detrimental) and, therefore, that the population distribution of the experimental group has a different mean from the population distribution of the control group.

2 *Researchers determine the critical values for their t-statistic.*
These values will depend on three decisions:

☐ the sample sizes (we assume that $N_1 = N_2$);
☐ the α-level;
☐ whether the test is two-tailed or one-tailed.

The latter two decisions are easy because the default values in psychology are α = .05 and a two-tailed test. Only in exceptional circumstances (see Section 7.7) will other values be chosen. The sample sizes are a different matter because the sample size will determine the chances of finding a significant effect. We will discuss this more extensively in Section 7.5. For the time being, let's assume that the researchers have the funding and permission to test 24 participants (12 in each group). These participants will be distributed at random over the experimental and the placebo control condition so that, apart from the administration of the drug, both groups can be considered to be equivalent. Given that the researchers have $N_1 = N_2 = 12$, the degrees of freedom in their test will be df = $N_1 - 1 + N_2 - 1 = 12 - 1 + 12 - 1 = 22$.

According to Table 6.4, $t_{.05crit}$ for df = 22 is –2.074 or +2.074. So, if the researchers obtain a *t*-statistic (based on the difference between the experimental and the control condition) with a value between –2.074 and +2.074, they will be unable to reject their null hypothesis. They will have to conclude that the effect of the drug was not strong enough to be perceptible in the study. In other words, they will fail to reject the null hypothesis and will have to carry on assuming that the effect of the drug cannot be seen. They will not have proved that the drug is worthless for healthy students; they will only have shown that the effect was not strong enough to induce a reliable difference between the scores of the groups.

Alternatively, if the obtained *t*-statistic is smaller than –2.074 or larger than +2.074, then the null hypothesis can be rejected, and the researchers will conclude that the drug has had an effect. If the *t*-statistic based on the comparison of the experimental group with the control group is smaller than –2.074, then the scores of the experimental group are lower than those of the control group. This will indicate that the effect of the drug is *detrimental*, because it decreases the number of word pairs that are remembered. If the *t*-statistic is larger than +2.074, the researchers can conclude that the drug is *beneficial*, because the memory scores of the experimental group are reliably better than those of the control group.

Figure 6.12 illustrates the decisions made in Step 2. It illustrates the *t*-distribution for df = 22, shows the cut-off score for the lower 2.5% and the cut-off score for the upper 2.5% of the distribution, and indicates which decisions will be made for different values of the *t*-statistic.

6

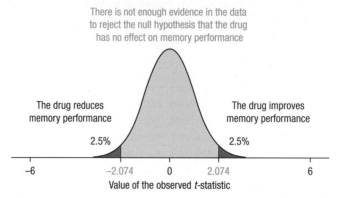

Figure 6.12 Illustration of the values of $t_{.05crit}$ and the decisions that will be made on the basis of the observed *t*-statistic. The critical t-values depend on the degrees of freedom (df), which are a function of N_1 and N_2. The critical t-values also depend on the significance level and whether the test is two-tailed or one-tailed. In this example, the default options in psychology have been used: $\alpha = .05$, two-tailed. The critical values then cut off the lower 2.5% of the distribution and the upper 2.5% of the distribution. For df = 22, $t_{.05crit}$ are −2.074 and +2.074. When the t-statistic falls between these two values, the researchers will conclude that there is not enough evidence to reject the null hypothesis. When the t-statistic is lower than −2.074, they will conclude that the drug has had a detrimental effect. When the t-value is larger than +2.074, they will conclude that the drug has had a beneficial effect.

3 *Researchers collect the data and calculate the various statistics.*

These statistics are the means, variances, standard deviations and standard errors of the two conditions, and the t-statistic that allows the researchers to assess the difference between the conditions. The hypothetical data are given in Table 6.5.

Table 6.5 Number of word pairs remembered (max = 50).

Experimental group	Placebo control group
27	14
5	19
34	3
19	17
13	16
41	13
19	36
21	8
22	14
8	29
24	1
19	22

To calculate the sample statistics of the experimental group, the auxiliary table in Table 6.6 is used.

$M_1 = 21$

$$SD_1{}^2 = \frac{\sum(X_1 - M_1)^2}{N_1 - 1}$$

$$= \frac{1116}{12 - 1} = 101.45$$

$$SD_1 = \sqrt{\frac{\sum(X_1 - M_1)^2}{N_1 - 1}}$$

$$= \sqrt{\frac{1116}{12 - 1}} = 10.07$$

$$SE_1 = \frac{SD_1}{\sqrt{N_1}}$$

$$= \frac{10.07}{\sqrt{12}} = 2.91$$

Table 6.6 Auxiliary table to calculate the sample statistics of the experimental group.

X_1	$X_1 - M_1$	$(X_1 - M_1)^2$
27	6	36
5	−16	256
34	13	169
19	−2	4
13	−8	64
41	20	400
19	−2	4
21	0	0
22	1	1
8	−13	169
24	3	9
19	−2	4
$\sum X_1 = 252$	$\sum(X_1 - M_1) = 0$	$\sum(X_1 - M_1)^2 = 1116$
$N_1 = 12$		
$M_1 = 252/12 = 21$		

The same calculations are done for the placebo control group (Table 6.7).

$M_2 = 16$

$$SD_2{}^2 = \frac{\sum(X_2 - M_2)^2}{N_2 - 1}$$

$$= \frac{1090}{12 - 1} = 99.09$$

$$SD_2 = \sqrt{\frac{\sum(X_2 - M_2)^2}{N_2 - 1}}$$

$$= \sqrt{\frac{1090}{12 - 1}} = 9.95$$

$$SE_2 = \frac{SD_2}{\sqrt{N_2}}$$

$$= \frac{9.95}{\sqrt{12}} = 2.87$$

Table 6.7 Auxiliary table to calculate the sample statistics of the placebo control group.

X_2	$X_2 - M_2$	$(X_2 - M_2)^2$
14	−2	4
19	3	9
3	−13	169
17	1	1
16	0	0
13	−3	9
36	20	400
8	−8	64
14	−2	4
29	13	169
1	−15	225
22	6	36
$\sum X_2 = 192$	$\sum(X_2 - M_2) = 0$	$\sum(X_2 - M_2)^2 = 1090$
$N_2 = 12$		
$M_2 = 192/12 = 16$		

On the basis of the sample statistics, the *t*-statistic can be calculated:

$$t = \frac{M_1 - M_2}{\sqrt{\dfrac{SD_1{}^2}{N_1} + \dfrac{SD_2{}^2}{N_2}}} = \frac{21 - 16}{\sqrt{\dfrac{101.45}{12} + \dfrac{99.09}{12}}} = 1.22$$

4 *The researchers compare the t-statistic they obtained in Step 3 with the* $t_{.05crit}$ *values they defined in Step 2 and decide whether the result is significant.* Remember that the critical values depend on the degrees of freedom (df = 22).

The *t*-statistic obtained in Step 3 (*t* = +1.22) falls in the range between –2.074 and +2.074. The researchers, therefore, fail to reject the null hypothesis (Figure 6.12). That is, the difference in numbers of word pairs remembered by the experimental group (M_1 = 21) and the placebo control group (M_2 = 16) is not large enough to conclude that it is unlikely to be due to sampling error. The reasons for this may be:

1 the large variability of the scores in each condition (SD_1 = 10.07, SD_2 = 9.95)
2 the small sample sizes,
3 the small difference in the mean scores of words remembered by the experimental and the control group ($M_1 - M_2$ = 5).

Because of these three characteristics of the experiment, the difference between the two groups is too small to be reliable. If the drug company thinks that a difference of 5 remembered words is important enough, it will have to repeat the study with larger sample sizes. The size of these new samples will be covered in the next chapter.

All in all, the conclusion of the drug experiment has to be that the researchers failed to find a significant difference between the experimental group and the control group. On the basis of the data, the drug company cannot decide that its drug which slows down the development of dementia, also has a beneficial effect on the memory performance of healthy undergraduate students. The variability in the samples is too large to exclude the possibility that the observed difference between the samples was due to sampling error. There is an unacceptably high chance that researchers would fail to replicate the difference if this study was repeated.

The results of the data analysis would be summarised as follows in a manuscript: 'There was no significant difference in the number of word pairs remembered by the experimental group (*M* = 21.0, *SD* = 10.07) and by the control group (*M* = 16.0, *SD* = 9.95; *t*(22) = 1.22, *p* > .05).'

Learning check 3

Do the *t*-test for the following data in which a group of four professors from Royal Holloway College compete against a group of four professors from the University of Oxford in an egg-and-spoon race. These are the times (in seconds) they took to run 200 m while holding a spoon with an egg in one hand. Before you start the analysis, have a look at the data. Do you expect to find a significant difference? Why? Or why not?

Then do the calculations. Make use of the four steps outlined in this section.

Time to run 200 m in an egg-and-spoon competition (secs):

Royal Holloway	Oxford
140	160
110	190
110	200
120	170

6.5 Calculating a *t*-test for independent samples with SPSS

On the basis of the preceding sections, you will have noticed that calculations by hand become quite tedious as soon as you have more than 10 participants per condition. Luckily, the computer on your desk can do most of these tasks for you. For instance, you can use a spreadsheet (such as Excel) to run the computations for you (see the website (www.palgrave.com/psychology/brysbaert) for an example of such a program). Here we discuss the use of SPSS. We will do so with the memory-test example of the percentages of errors noticed by young and old adults.

Further details about the use of the *t*-test for independent samples can be found in Chapter 5 of Brace, Kemp, and Snelgar, *SPSS for Psychologists*.

First, we enter the data. For an independent samples analysis, we always have to define the independent variable (the group to which the participant belongs) and the dependent variable (the score of the participant). Go to *Variable View* and give titles to the first two rows. The first row defines the age group (so we give it the name 'Group'); the second row contains the percentage of errors noticed. By default SPSS assumes that the variables are numeric with two decimal digits. Although we can keep these defaults, we will make the interpretation slightly easier by defining the age group as a string variable (so that we can enter names) and the percentage of errors noticed as numeric without decimal digits. This is how the screen looks if you entered everything correctly:

File   Edit   View   Data   Transform   Analyze   Graphs   Utilities   Add-ons   Window   Help

	Name	Type	Width	Decimals	Label	Values	Missing	Columns
1	Group	String	8	0		None	None	8
2	Percentage_noticed	Numeric	8	0		None	None	8
3								

Then enter the data. For this, you first have to click on *Data View*. Because we have 20 participants, we have to enter 20 rows: 10 for the young participants and 10 for the old participants.

File   Edit   View   Data   Transform   Analyze   Graphs

1 : Group   Young

	Group	Percentage_r oticed	var
1	Young	71	
2	Young	75	
3	Young	81	
4	Young	79	
5	Young	75	
6	Young	84	
7	Young	74	
8	Young	74	
9	Young	71	
10	Young	79	
11	Old	72	
12	Old	65	

Now click on Analyze, Compare Means, Independent-Samples T Test.

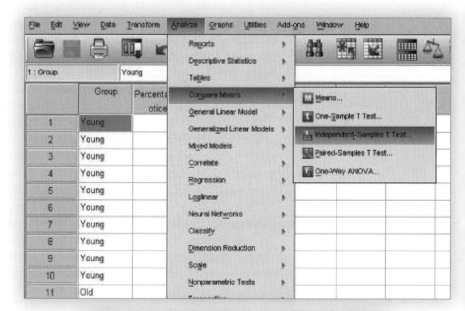

This opens the following dialogue box:

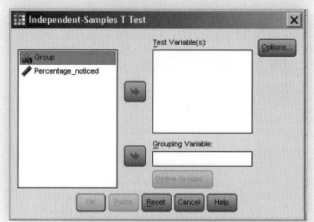

The Test Variable is the dependent variable; the Grouping Variable is the independent variable. Put your two columns in the correct place using the central arrows.

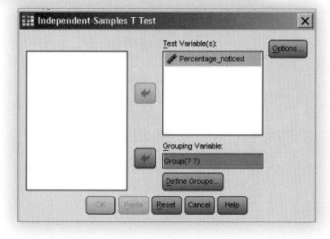

Now SPSS asks you to *Define Groups*. Click on the button () and give the correct names:

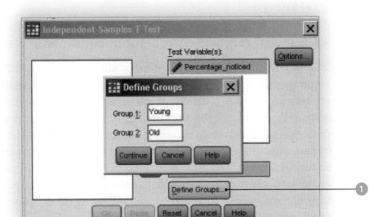

Then click on **Continue** and **OK**, to get the output.

Group Statistics

	Group	N	Mean	Std. Deviation	Std. Error Mean
Percentage_noticed	Young	10	76.30	4.296	1.359
	Old	10	70.80	3.225	1.020

Independent Samples Test

		Levene's Test for Equality of Variances		t-test for Equality of Means							
									95% Confidence Interval of the Difference	
		F	Sig.	t	df	Sig. (2-tailed)	Mean Difference	Std. Error Difference	Lower	Upper
Percentage_noticed	Equal variances assumed	1.607	.221	3.238	18	.005	5.500	1.699	1.931	9.069
	Equal variances not assumed			3.238	16.669	.005	5.500	1.699	1.911	9.089

In this output you will find the information you require: the *t*-test has 18 degrees of freedom, and a *t*-value of 3.238 that is significant at *p* = .005. Compare this to the values we calculated above.

Learning check 4
Do the analysis for the number of words remembered by the experimental group and the placebo control group in Table 6.5. Did you obtain the outcome you were looking for?

Also do the *t*-test for the example of the heights of males and females in Section 6.2.1. Is this difference significant?

⚕ 6.6　Going further: unequal sample sizes and unequal variances

6.6.1　A *t*-test that remains correct for unequal sample sizes

In this chapter we have considerably simplified the calculations by always requiring that $N_1 = N_2$. The results of a study are much more stable when they are based on equal numbers of observations in the different conditions. For instance, violations of the assumptions underlying a t-test (such as the requirement that the data in both conditions come from a normal distribution) have less impact when the *t*-test is based on equal numbers in both conditions. However, sometimes researchers have no control over the number of people in the different groups, and they are reluctant to reduce the number of participants in order to level the numbers. In addition, the underlying theory and calculations do not exclude the possibility of unequal numbers.

There are two things you must keep in mind when you go into the more advanced levels of statistics. The first is that degrees of freedom are much more important than sample sizes. The second is that, because of the square root transformation, the standard deviation is less interesting than the variance. Once you appreciate these two features, the t-statistic for unequal sample sizes looks quite straightforward:

$$t = \frac{M_1 - M_2}{\sqrt{\dfrac{\dfrac{df_1 SD_1{}^2 + df_2 SD_2{}^2}{df_1 + df_2}}{N_1} + \dfrac{\dfrac{df_1 SD_1{}^2 + df_2 SD_2{}^2}{df_1 + df_2}}{N_2}}}$$

$df_1 = N_1 - 1$, $df_2 = N_2 - 1$, $df = df_1 + df_2$

In this equation the individual variances of the samples have been replaced by an 'average' variance, the so-called pooled variance. As a matter of fact, this averaging of the variances of the samples is always required, but when $df_1 = df_2$, the denominator can be simplified. The equation then resembles the one we saw when we introduced the t-test:

$$t = \frac{M_1 - M_2}{\sqrt{\dfrac{SD_1{}^2}{N_1} + \dfrac{SD_2{}^2}{N_2}}}$$

6.6.2　A *t*-test that remains correct for unequal variances

Another assumption of the t-test is that it requires equal variances in the two samples: $SD_1{}^2 = SD_2{}^2$. (This is called the assumption of homogeneity of variance.) Although there is a statistical test to check whether both the variances are the same (called Levene's test), in practice the following rule of thumb works well:

The t-test presented thus far gives you a good estimate of *p*, as long as one variance is less than double the other. When one variance is more than twice the other, you have to use a correction. In particular, you will have to use a t-test with a df-value that is smaller than the one you would normally use.

Do not ask how statisticians have come to this conclusion. This requires really deep insights into the distribution of difference scores between two normal distributions (and at this level of detail, statisticians do not fully agree on which correction to use, even though these quibbles have negligible implications for the use of t-tests in practice).

The most commonly used correction is the Welch-Satterthwaite correction. Instead of using df $= N_1 - 1 + N_2 - 1$, we will use:

$$df' = \frac{\left(\dfrac{SD_1^2}{N_1} + \dfrac{SD_2^2}{N_2}\right)^2}{\dfrac{\left(\dfrac{SD_1^2}{N_1}\right)^2}{N_1 - 1} + \dfrac{\left(\dfrac{SD_2^2}{N_2}\right)^2}{N_2 - 1}}$$

Applied to the experiment of error detection in young and old adults, this would give:

$$df' = \frac{\left(\dfrac{18.4556}{10} + \dfrac{10.4}{10}\right)^2}{\dfrac{\left(\dfrac{18.4556}{10}\right)^2}{10 - 1} + \dfrac{\left(\dfrac{10.4}{10}\right)^2}{10 - 1}} = \frac{8.3265}{0.4986} = 16.70$$

So, rather than df $= N_1 - 1 + N_2 - 1 = 18$, we would use df $= 17$, the nearest integer to the df' we calculated. A look at Table 6.4 confirms that a t-statistic of 3.24 is still significant at $p < .05$ for df $= 17$ (as a matter of fact, the p-value has only changed from $p = .0046$ for df $= 18$ to $p = .0048$ for df $= 17$). This agrees with the recommendation that the Welch-Satterthwaite correction is not needed as long as one variance is not more than twice the other. It is also unlikely to make much of a difference for very high values of the t-statistic. However, it may make a difference when the t-statistic is close to the critical value.

Tip Be alert to unequal variances in SPSS.

In the SPSS output (Figure 6.13), you see two columns headed 'Levene's test for equality of variances'. When this test is significant (the value in the column Sig. is smaller than .05), you have to use the test for 'equal variances not assumed'. As you can see, the t-value is the same but the value for df is slightly lower, as indicated in Figure 6.13. Also notice that in SPSS the df-values don't have to be integers. We will return to this in the next chapter.

Independent Samples Test

		Levene's Test for Equality of Variances		t-test for Equality of Means					95% Confidence Interval of the Difference	
		F	Sig.	t	df	Sig. (2-tailed)	Mean Difference	Std. Error Difference	Lower	Upper
Percentage_noticed	Equal variances assumed	1.607	.221	3.238	18	.005	5.500	1.699	1.931	9.069
	Equal variances not assumed			3.238	16.669	.005	5.500	1.699	1.911	9.089

Figure 6.13

❓ 6.7 Answers to chapter questions

1 Why do psychologists need statistical tests to decide whether there is a difference between two groups?

Psychologists need statistical tests to decide whether there is a difference between two groups because most of the time the difference is not clear to the naked eye. The distributions of the X-values in the two conditions overlap. The difference between the conditions only comes to light when the means are compared. This, however, requires calculation of the standard errors of the means.

2 Why is the prediction that smokers die earlier than non-smokers not invalidated when you hear of a 100-year old who still smokes?

The distribution of the ages at which smokers die is a normal distribution that never really touches 0. So, if the life expectancy of smokers were 68 years (some 10 years shorter than that of non-smokers), you would still find the odd person who smokes and lives beyond 100, just as you find non-smokers who are older than 110.

3 What are inferential statistics?

Inferential statistics are statistics that help us decide whether a pattern observed in the limited empirical data of our sample (for example, a difference between two conditions) can be generalised to the population.

4 What is the standard error of the mean? Can we calculate this on the basis of a single sample?

The standard error of the mean is the standard deviation of the sample means we would observe if we took many samples and calculated their means. Usually, however, researchers do not take several samples, because they can estimate the standard error of the mean on the basis of the standard deviation of the X-values and the sample size N: $SE = SD/\sqrt{N}$. Therefore, it is better to describe the standard error of the mean as the *hypothetical* standard deviation of the sample mean calculated on the basis of the standard deviation of the scores and the sample size.

5 Why can we have more confidence in the mean of a large sample than in the mean of a small sample?

If M_1 is the mean of a sample we just calculated and M_2 is the mean of a new sample drawn from the same population, we can assume that most of the time the values of M_1 and M_2 will be closer together when they come from large samples than when they come from small samples. This directly follows from the finding that $SE = SD/\sqrt{N}$: the larger the sample sizes, the smaller the variability in their means (that is, the smaller SE).

6 Why can researchers be reasonably sure that the mean of a sample will be part of a normal distribution? What are the restrictions?

> The normal distribution is the distribution you expect when the X-values are the outcome of a large number of random choices. Because the sample mean is the outcome of N values drawn randomly from a population, we can expect the means to form a normal distribution, at least when (1) the data come from an interval/ratio scale, and (2) the means are based on a reasonably large sample size (certainly when the original X-scores are not randomly distributed).

7 What is sampling error and how does it relate to research?

> The sampling error is the discrepancy that exists between a sample statistic, such as the mean, and the corresponding population parameter. It is a direct consequence of the variability that is present in the data and the fact that a random sample of a population is not always a fully 'representative' sample of that population.

8 How do we calculate the t-statistic for independent groups?

$$t = \frac{M_1 - M_2}{\sqrt{\frac{SD_1^2}{N_1} + \frac{SD_2^2}{N_2}}}$$

> in which M_1 is the mean of the first sample, M_2 is the mean of the second sample, SD_1^2 is the variance (or the squared standard deviation) of the first sample, SD_2^2 is the variance (or the squared standard deviation) of the second sample, N_1 is the size of the first sample, and N_2 is the size of the second sample ($N_1 = N_2$).

9 Which three factors does the t-statistic for independent groups depend upon?

> (1) The difference between M_1 and M_2, (2) SD_1 and SD_2, and (3) N_1 and N_2.

10 How do we have to interpret a t-statistic?

> A t-statistic around 0 means that there is not much difference between the two observed conditions. A t-statistic below –2 or above +2 indicates a potentially significant difference between the conditions. This will be significant at the .05 level when $N_1 + N_2 \geq 60$. Otherwise, you have to consult Table 6.4 or Appendix B to verify whether your t-statistic is large enough to reach significance.

11 What is hypothesis testing and what has the t-statistic to do with this?

> Hypothesis testing uses a statistical method based on sample data to evaluate a hypothesis about population parameters. It typically involves four steps: (1) defining a null hypothesis and an alternative hypothesis, (2) determining the critical value of the statistic needed to reach a certain significance level, (3) collecting the data and calculating the statistics, and (4) verifying whether the obtained statistic exceeds the critical value needed for statistical significance. The t-statistic is the statistic often used to test whether the difference between the means of two conditions is significant (that is, large enough to be reliable).

12 **What are the null hypothesis and the alternative hypothesis? And what is their relationship to the courtroom?**

> The null hypothesis is the assumption of no difference between the conditions; the alternative hypothesis is the assumption that such a difference exists. (The direction of the difference is not usually specified and a two-tailed test is used.) The null hypothesis can be compared to the assumption of 'not guilty' in the courtroom, which remains true unless the prosecutor can convince the judge or the jury of the opposite.

13 **Why does a t-test depend on the degrees of freedom?**

> The t-statistic observed in a study can be thought of as one observation from the hypothetical distribution of t-statistics that would be obtained if the study were repeated many times. Under the null hypothesis, the distribution of t-statistics would be centred on 0 (because $M_1 = M_2$) and its exact shape would depend on the degrees of freedom (which are directly related to the sample sizes: $df = N_1 - 1 + N_2 - 1$). More specifically, there would be more variability in the observed t-statistics calculated on the basis of small samples than in the t-statistics calculated on the basis of large samples. This explains why the critical values for significance are higher for small dfs than for large dfs (Table 6.4.).

14 **What is the level of significance?**

> The level of significance refers to the risk that the researcher has wrongly decided that there is a significant difference between two conditions, when in reality (that is, at the population level) there is no such difference. In psychology, the level of significance is usually set at 5% ($\alpha = .05$). This means that researchers are willing to take a risk of 5% that an effect they believe to be significant in reality is not.

15 **When do researchers talk of a significant effect?**

> Researchers talk of a significant effect when the statistic they observe is so extreme that it is unlikely (probability of less than 5%) to be in line with the null hypothesis. Specifically, with respect to the t-test, researchers will talk of a significant effect when the t-statistic they observe is larger than the critical t-value needed to reach the significance level. Then, the assumption at the onset (the null hypothesis of no difference) can be rejected and replaced by the alternative hypothesis.

16 **What has the confirmation bias to do with hypothesis testing?**

> The confirmation bias refers to people's tendency to look for evidence that corroborates their convictions. Because this approach leads people to stick with their convictions (prejudices), such practice is not allowed in science. Instead scientists are urged to try to find evidence that would contradict their beliefs. If they can find such evidence, they know that their understanding is either incomplete or wrong.

☑ 6.8 Learning check solutions

Learning check 1

For 18-year olds $SD = 6.5$. The SE for a sample of $N = 10,000$ is $6.5/\sqrt{10,000} = 6.5/100 = .065$ cm. This implies that the mean heights of two samples of 10,000 particpants each would not be expected to differ by more than a few mm! For 12-year olds $SD = 7.6$. So, for a sample size of 400, $SE = 7.6/20 = .38$ cm.

Learning check 2

Figure 6.8 also illustrates why conclusions would have been easier to draw if the sample sizes had been larger (e.g., $N = 1,000$). If the difference between the population distributions of the young and the old adults is genuine, then increasing the sample sizes would decrease the SE of the means and the overlap of the theoretical distributions of the means. On the other hand, if the difference between the two distributions illustrated in Figure 6.8 is a fluke, due to sampling error, then additional data would decrease the difference between the distributions and make it clear that in reality there is no difference in performance between young and old adults. The t-test allows us to assess how sure we can be that the difference in the means observed in Table 6.1 is an indication of a genuine difference at the population level.

Learning check 3

We expect a difference because all the Oxford times are longer than the Royal Holloway times. On the other hand, the sample sizes are small. These are the statistics:

$M_1 = 120$ $M_2 = 180$
$SD_1 = 14.14$ $SD_2 = 18.26$

$t = -5.190$
$df = 6$
$p = .002$

Learning check 4

$M_1 = 163.3$ $M_2 = 177.1$
$SD_1 = 6.60$ $SD_2 = 7.30$

$t = -5.613$
$df = 30$
$p < .001$

Interpreting the results of a statistical test

7

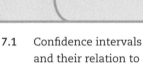

In the previous chapter we learned how to calculate a t-statistic and how to use it in a t-test for independent groups to decide between the null hypothesis and the alternative hypothesis. However, given that hypothesis testing is central to research in psychology (and many other sciences) and given that the subtleties of such testing require an approach that deviates from human intuitions, it is good to devote some more time to the interpretation of the outcome. What do we make of the p-value we obtain? Because we have so far only covered the t-test for independent groups, all of our examples will refer to this test. However, the principles apply to all instances of hypothesis testing and, therefore, we will return to them in later chapters.

The issues will be illustrated by the two experiments we introduced in Chapter 6. The first involved 10 young adults and 10 old adults pressing keys in response to light flashes and indicating whether or not they had made an error in the previous three trials. The dependent variable was the percentage of errors detected. The results are summarised in Table 7.1 (see also Tables 6.1–6.3).

Table 7.1 Summary of data from experiment on error detection in young and old adults (percentage of errors detected).

Young adults: $N_1 = 10$, $M_1 = 76.3$, $SD_1^2 = 18.4556$, $SD_1 = 4.2960$, $SE_1 = 1.3585$
Old adults: $N_2 = 10$, $M_2 = 70.8$, $SD_2^2 = 10.4000$, $SD_2 = 3.2249$, $SE_2 = 1.0198$
Hypothesis test $t = 3.2378$, df = 18 critical values ($\alpha = .05$) are –2.101 and +2.101 exact p-value : $p = .0046$

In the second experiment, an experimental group of 12 students was given a supposedly memory-enhancing drug and a control group of 12 other students took a placebo pill. The dependent variable was the number of word pairs the students could remember one hour after being shown the word pairs. The statistics are given in Table 7.2 (see also Tables 6.5–6.7).

Table 7.2 Summary of data from experiment on effectiveness of memory-enhancing drug (number of word pairs remembered).

Experimental group: $N_1 = 12$, $M_1 = 21.0$, $SD_1^2 = 101.4545$, $SD_1 = 10.0725$, $SE_1 = 2.9077$
Placebo control group: $N_2 = 12$, $M_2 = 16.0$, $SD_2^2 = 99.0909$, $SD_2 = 9.9544$, $SE_2 = 2.8736$
Hypothesis test $t = 1.2231$, df = 22 critical values ($\alpha = .05$) are –2.074 and +2.074 exact p-value : $p = .2342$

These two experiments provide us with one case in which the difference between the conditions is significant (the error detection experiment) and one in which the effect is not significant (the drug experiment). Notice that the absolute difference in means is more or less the same (5.5% error detection and

5 remembered word pairs). However, the variability of the scores is much higher in the drug experiment than in the error detection experiment (look at the values of SD^2, SD and SE). Because the t-test accounts for the variability of the scores within the conditions, as well as the difference in means, the evidence against the null hypothesis is much weaker in the drug experiment than in the error detection experiment. Below we will flesh out the implications of these findings.

7.1 Confidence intervals and their relation to statistical tests

One way to look at the data is to think of the condition means as estimates embedded in an area of uncertainty. If we repeated the experiment on error detection in young and old adults, we would not expect to find exactly the same means (because of the sampling error). Rather, we would expect to find values *close* to the ones we obtained (that is, around 76 for the young adults and around 71 for the old adults). Similarly, because of the sampling error, it is unlikely that the population values of the young and the old adults are exactly the same as the sample means. It is better to think of them as *quite close* to the sample means.

Statistics allow us to estimate how close the observed means are likely to be to the population values (i.e., the 'true' values). The range of uncertainty around a mean is called the **confidence interval**. If we find that M_2 is inside the confidence interval around M_1, we would not feel very certain about the difference between the conditions. If we were to replicate the experiment, M_2 could end up having exactly the same value as M_1. On the other hand, if M_2 is way outside the confidence interval around M_1, we can feel confident that we will again find a difference between the conditions if we repeat the experiment (see Figure 7.1).

Below, we will see how to calculate the confidence intervals around the means of conditions and how to use these intervals to interpret the result of a t-test.

7.1.1 The 95% confidence interval around the mean

To calculate the confidence interval of a mean, we start from SE, the standard error of the mean. Remember from Chapter 6 that this represents the variability we expect to find in the means if we run the experiment several times. In our examples, the SEs were slightly above 1 in the memory experiment ($SE_1 = 1.3585$, $SE_2 = 1.0198$; Table 7.1) and close to 3 in the drug experiment ($SE_1 = 2.9077$, $SE_2 = 2.8736$; Table 7.2).

To understand the relationship between the confidence interval and SE, it is helpful to recall what we discovered about the normal distribution in Chapters 4 and 5. There we saw that values below the mean minus two times the standard deviation ($M - 2SD$) are considered exceptional; the same is true for values above the mean plus two times the standard deviation ($M + 2SD$). They are considered exceptional because the chance of encountering them is less than 5%. This is

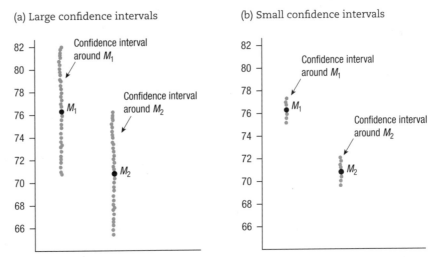

Figure 7.1 The confidence interval gives us information about how likely we are to find the same difference between M₁ and M₂ if we were to repeat the study. In (a) the confidence intervals around M₁ and M₂ are fairly large. We cannot, therefore, feel sure that the difference between M₁ and M₂ will be found again, because the population values estimated by M₁ and M₂ could easily be the same. In contrast, the difference between M₁ and M₂ in (b) is much more solid because of the small confidence intervals. If we were to repeat the study, we would again expect the value of M₁ to be higher than the value M₂.

why psychologists say that IQ scores below 70 and above 130 are exceptional, when the IQ test has a mean of 100 and a standard deviation of 15. Similarly, z-scores below –2.00 and above +2.00 are considered to be exceptional. (You may even remember that the exact z-values are –1.96 and +1.96.)

We can apply the same reasoning to the distribution of means. In Chapter 6 we saw that for a large sample size, the mean of the sample is a score from a normal distribution with $M = \mu$ (the population mean) and $SE = SD/\sqrt{N}$ (remember the central limit theorem). So, when N is large, we can define the **95% confidence interval** around the mean of the sample as the interval going from $M - 2SE$ to $M + 2SE$ (or more precisely from $M - 1.96SE$ to $M + 1.96SE$). This means that we expect the population mean μ to fall within this interval with a probability of .95.

The situation is slightly more complicated for smaller sample sizes (in particular, for sizes smaller than 40). Although we know that for these samples the mean is also likely to be part of a normal distribution with $M = \mu$ and $SE = SD/\sqrt{N}$, we have rather unreliable estimates of M and SD. The confidence interval based on the normal distribution is, therefore, likely to be an underestimate of the true confidence interval. However, we can solve this problem by using a t-distribution instead of the normal distribution. When both M and SD have to be estimated on the basis of sample data (which is nearly always the case in scientific research), the distribution of the sample mean is a t-distribution with $df = N - 1$. So, to calculate the 95% confidence interval of a sample mean based on sample size N, we have to use the .05 cut-off scores of the t-distribution with df $= N - 1$ (see Figure 6.12, Table 6.4 and Appendix B). For example, when the sample size is $N = 3$ (and df $= 2$), the 95% confidence interval around the mean is $M - 4.303*SE$ to $M + 4.303*SE$. When df $= 20$ ($N = 21$), the 95% confidence interval goes from $M - 2.086*SE$ to $M + 2.086*SE$.

> **Tip – the size of the confidence interval.** If the sample size is larger than 40, then the 95% confidence interval extends roughly from the mean minus twice the standard error ($M - 2SE$) to the mean plus twice the standard error ($M + 2SE$). For smaller sample sizes, the 95% confidence interval is larger (use a table of t-values to determine exactly how large). For instance, for sample size $N = 3$ (df $= 2$), the confidence interval will range from $M - 4.3SE$ to $M + 4.3SE$.

The confidence interval is a very important concept in opinion polls, for example, because it indicates the region of uncertainty around the values that have been obtained. Suppose an opinion poll indicates that 48% of the people from a particular European country are against membership of the European Union. As researchers we would immediately want to know the 95% confidence interval of the mean. Does it range from 43% to 53%, or is it limited to the range from 47% to 49%? As you can probably guess, the main factor that determines the confidence interval is the sample size on which the estimate is based. The larger the sample size, the smaller the interval. The second factor that determines the width of a confidence interval is the standard deviation of the scores within the sample.

Confidence intervals are also important in other areas of research. For each study, they indicate the reliability of our sample mean and tell us how much of a difference we can expect if we were to repeat the study with the same sample size. For example, for the drug experiment the 95% confidence interval of the experimental group's mean score is:

$N_1 = 12$

$df_1 = N_1 - 1 = 11$

Cut-off scores of t-distribution $= -2.201$ and $+2.201$ (Appendix B)

$M_1 = 21$

$SE_1 = 2.91$

Lower limit of the interval $= M_1 - 2.201*SE_1 = 21 - 2.201*2.91 = 14.6$

Upper limit of the interval $= M_1 + 2.201*SE_1 = 21 + 2.201*2.91 = 27.4$

Thus, the 95% confidence interval of the experimental group's mean in the drug experiment goes from a memory score of 14.6 to a memory score of 27.4. Notice that the performance of the placebo control ($M_2 = 16$) falls within this confidence interval. This is a sure sign that the t-test will not be significant (as we found in our t-test: $p = .2342$). When M_2 falls within the 95% confidence interval around M_1, then the t-statistic will never be significant. The t-test is significant only when M_2 falls in a region outside 1.5 times the confidence interval, as we will see in the next section.

For the sake of completeness, check whether the mean of the experimental group in the drug study falls within the 95% confidence interval of the placebo group. This interval is given opposite.

$N_2 = 12$

$df_2 = N_2 - 1 = 11$

Cut-off scores of t-distribution = –2.201 and +2.201 (Appendix B)

$M_2 = 16$

$SE_2 = 2.87$

Lower limit of the interval = $M_2 - 2.201*SE_1 = 16 - 2.201*2.87 = 9.68$

Upper limit of the interval = $M_2 + 2.201*SE_1 = 16 + 2.201*2.87 = 22.32$

Learning check 1
Calculate the 95% confidence intervals for the young and old adults in the experiment on error detection. Does the mean of each group fall outside the confidence interval around the other mean, as predicted by the significant t-test?

7.1.2 Adding confidence intervals to graphs

Because confidence intervals (CIs) include so much information, it is a good idea to add them to your graphs. Figure 7.2 shows how this is done in a bar chart (using the data of the error detection experiment). Figure 7.3 shows how this is done in a line graph (using the data of the drug experiment).

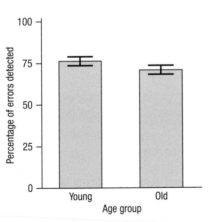

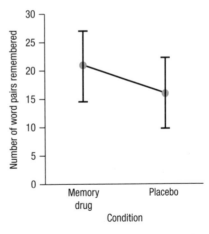

Figure 7.2 Bar chart of the error detection experiment with the 95% confidence intervals added. The confidence interval for the young adults goes from 73.2 to 79.4; that for the old adults from 68.5 to 73.1. These intervals are represented by the whiskers around the means. Because the whiskers of the two conditions do not overlap, we immediately know that the difference between the conditions is significant.

Figure 7.3 Line graph of the memory drug experiment with the 95% confidence intervals added. The confidence interval for the participants who were given the drug goes from 14.6 to 27.4; that for the participants in the placebo condition from 9.7 to 22.3. Because the mean of each condition falls within the confidence interval of the other, we immediately know that the difference between the conditions is not significant.

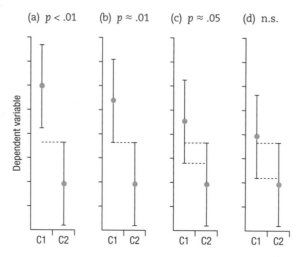

Figure 7.4 The interpretation of confidence intervals. The four graphs show possible differences between the means of two conditions. In (a) there is no overlap at all between the two confidence intervals. Then the difference between the means will always be significant ($p < .01$). When the two confidence intervals touch each other (b), there is significance at around $p \approx .01$. We have significance ($p < .05$) as long as the overlap of the two intervals is smaller than half a whisker (c). As soon as the overlap is larger than half a whisker (d), there is no longer any significance ($p > .05$ or n.s.). Adapted from Cumming and Finch (2005).

Cumming and Finch (2005) reported some rules of thumb for correctly interpreting 95% confidence intervals in graphs (Figure 7.4). They are:

☐ if the two confidence intervals do not overlap, then $p < .01$,
☐ if the two confidence intervals overlap by less than half a whisker, then $p < .05$,
☐ if the overlap between the confidence intervals is larger than half a whisker, then there is no significant difference between the conditions (n.s.).

7.1.3 Using *SE* bars instead of confidence intervals

Not all researchers use confidence intervals in their graphs. Some draw SE bars around the means. These graphs look deceptively similar to those in Figures 7.2 and 7.3, but the whiskers around the means have been halved (or more if the sample sizes are small). At first sight this looks more impressive (which is why authors are attracted to SE bars), but of course the use of SE bars does not change anything in the underlying data or statistical tests. All that happens is that readers are easily misled if they are not attentive. So, be attentive when you are looking at bars in figures. Do they represent confidence intervals or standard errors? To interpret figures with SE bars rather than confidence intervals, use Figure 7.5 (at least when the sample sizes are reasonably large).

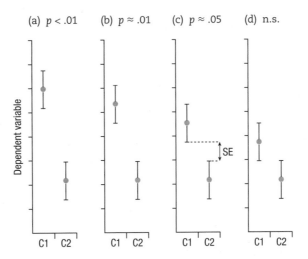

(a) $p < .01$ (b) $p \approx .01$ (c) $p \approx .05$ (d) n.s.

Figure 7.5 The interpretation of SE bars. The four graphs show possible differences between the means of two conditions. The data are the same as in Figure 7.4 but the bars around the means represent SEs rather than confidence intervals (i.e., they have been halved). The most important differences are in (c) and (d). When two SE bars touch each other, there is no significance. You only get significance ($p < .05$) when there is a gap between the two bars that is at least one standard error wide. Adapted from Cumming and Finch (2005).

7.1.4   Why is the interpretation of *CIs* and *SE* bars so difficult? The confidence interval of the difference score

You may wonder why statisticians have defined CIs and SEs in such a counterintuitive way. As Cumming and Finch (2005) discovered, even professional psychology researchers tend to misinterpret them!

The crux of the strange relationship between the *p*-value and the CIs or SEs of the means lies in the fact that the standard deviation of a difference between two scores is larger than the standard deviation of the individual scores. Think again about an IQ score. As we have seen a number of times IQ scores form a normal distribution with $M = 100$ and $SD = 15$. So, we expect 95% of the data to fall between IQ = 70 and IQ = 130. Now, if we took the difference in IQs between two random persons, we could expect to find most differences between −60 (IQ person 1 = 70, IQ person 2 = 130) and +60 (IQ person 1 = 130, IQ person 2 = 70). This is larger than our original range.

The exact relationship between the standard deviation of the difference scores and the standard deviations of the individual scores has a complex derivation that is beyond the scope of an introductory book such as this. Suffice it to say here that if you have two normal distributions, one with M_1 and SD_1 and another with M_2 and SD_2, and you take a random sample from the first distribution and a random sample from the second distribution, then the difference between the two sample means is part of a new normal distribution with $M = M_1 - M_2$ and $SE = \sqrt{SE_1^2 + SE_2^2}$

The standard error of the difference between the old and the young adults in Table 7.1 is therefore:

$$SE_{diff} = \sqrt{SE_1{}^2 + SE_2{}^2} = \sqrt{1.3585^2 + 1.0198^2} = 1.70$$

Similarly, the standard error between the experimental and the control condition in the drug study is:

$$SE_{diff} = \sqrt{SE_1{}^2 + SE_2{}^2} = \sqrt{2.9077^2 + 2.8736^2} = 4.09$$

You may remember from Chapter 6 that we can usually assume that $SE_1 \approx SE_2$. So, we can also write that:

$$SE_{diff} \approx \sqrt{2SE_1{}^2} \approx \sqrt{2SE_2{}^2} \approx \sqrt{2}SE_1 \approx \sqrt{2}SE_2$$

In other words, the standard error of the difference score will roughly be $\sqrt{2}$ or 1.414 larger than the mean SE of the means. This is the reason why there must be a gap of roughly 1 SE between the SE bars of the means to have $p = .05$ (Figure 7.5: $2SE_{diff} \approx 3SE_1 \approx 3SE_2$).

The relationship between the SE of the difference score and the SEs of the sample means further allows us to calculate the confidence interval of the difference. All we need to know is the degrees of freedom of the t-distribution. Given that the SE of the difference score is based on the sum of the SEs of the mean, the degrees of freedom will be $df = df_1 + df_2$. So, for the experiment of error detection in old and young adults, $df = 9 + 9 = 18$ (which was also the df of the t-test). For the drug study, $df = 11 + 11 = 22$.

This gives us a 95% confidence interval of the difference score equal to $CI_{diff} = M_1 - M_2 \pm t_{.05crit}(df) * SE$. Applied to the error detection experiment in old and young adults, this gives:

Lower limit $CI_{diff} = 5.5 - 2.101 * 1.70 = 1.93$,
Upper limit $CI_{diff} = 5.5 + 2.101 * 1.70 = 9.07$.

For the drug study, the values are:

Lower limit $CI_{diff} = 5 - 2.074 * 4.09 = -3.48$,
Upper limit $CI_{diff} = 5 + 2.074 * 4.09 = 13.48$.

From these CIs you can easily see that the first difference is significant at the .05 level, because the confidence interval around the mean does not include 0 (the point where $M_1 = M_2$). As this value is included in the second difference score, we quickly see that the difference between the two groups in the drug study is not significant.

7.2 More on the interpretation of significant effects

The goal of hypothesis testing is to evaluate hypotheses about population parameters on the basis of sample data. In particular, the goal of the t-test for independent groups is to decide whether the performance of two groups at

7

Tip You can calculate the exact *p*-values with a spreadsheet. For instance, if you have Microsoft Excel on your computer, this is how you do it.

Open Excel and write 't-value', 'df', and 'p' in the first row:

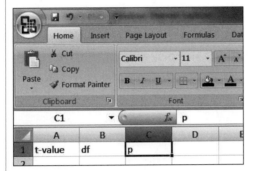

Then enter the *t*-value (e.g., 3.2378) and the df value (e.g., 18) in the first two cells of the second row. Put your cursor in the third cell of the second row and write =TDIST(ABS(A2);B2;2) in this cell, as shown below:

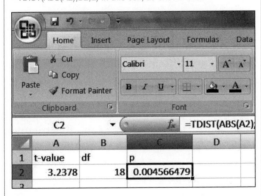

If you now press enter, you get the value 0.004566479 in the cell, which is the *p*-value associated with the *t*-value and the df. By changing the value of *t* or df, you can now calculate all *p*-values of *t*-tests!

the population level is the same or different. The starting position (null hypothesis) is that of no difference. Researchers must stay with this assumption unless the data of their study are so compelling that the difference between the two groups is unlikely to be due to sampling error alone. Then, researchers are allowed to abandon the null hypothesis and accept the alternative hypothesis as a better explanation of their findings.

To determine whether the obtained difference is large enough, researchers calculate the *t*-statistic and check whether the *t*-value is larger than predetermined critical scores. Usually, the critical values are set at a significance level of .05 (two-tailed; see below). This means that psychologists will reject the null hypothesis only when they obtain a *t*-statistic so large that there is a less than 5% chance that it could be due to sampling error. In practice, for sample sizes larger than 10, this will be the case for *t*-values below −2.1 and above +2.1 (see Table 6.4).

The basis of a hypothesis test is the assumption that a difference between two groups is significant when the *t*-statistic exceeds the .05 cut-off score; otherwise it is insignificant. However, the advent of computer programs has made more information available than a simple yes/no decision on the basis of whether or not the *t*-statistic exceeds the cut-off score (see the SPSS output in Chapter 6). Virtually all statistical software packages will tell you that the *p*-value for the error detection experiment is $p = .0046$, whereas the *p*-value in the drug experiment is $p = .2342$. What do these values mean?

7.2.1 The interpretation of *p*-values

To understand what $p = .2342$ means, we have to return to Figure 6.10 and how the .05 cut-off values of Table 6.4 were defined. Remember, these were the values that cut off 2.5% of the lower tail of the *t*-distribution and 2.5% of the upper tail. A more formal definition of this process is: the .05 cut-off values are defined in such a way that if the null hypothesis is true, the probability of finding a *t*-statistic that is as extreme as or more extreme than the cut-off values is equal to 5%.

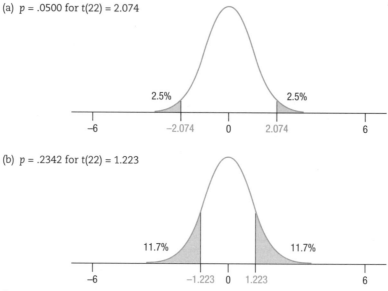

(a) $p = .0500$ for $t(22) = 2.074$

2.5%   2.5%

−6   −2.074   0   2.074   6

(b) $p = .2342$ for $t(22) = 1.223$

11.7%   11.7%

−6   −1.223 0 1.223   6

Figure 7.6 The interpretation of p-values: (a) $p = .0500$ for $t(22) = 2.074$ and (b) $p = .2342$ for a $t(22) = 1.223$

If the t-statistic of your test falls exactly on one of the cut-off values (e.g., $t(22) = -2.074$ or $t(22) = +2.074$), then the computer will tell you that $p = .0500$, because that is the proportion of the t-distribution that falls beyond your t-statistic (Figure 7.6a). Similarly, when the computer returns a p-value of $p = .2342$ for $t(22) = 1.223$, this means you have a probability of .2342 of obtaining a t-statistic of this size or larger given that the null hypothesis is true (Figure 7.6b). The percentage is equally distributed over the part of the t-distribution below the value −1.223 and the part of the distribution above +1.223.

As we have already seen, psychologists do not find a probability of .23 low enough to allow them to reject the null hypothesis. Therefore, the effect is insignificant. Only when the computer returns a p-value smaller than .05 ($p < .05$) is the effect significant.

Learning check 2
What does the computer output $t(18) = 3.2378$, $p = .0046$ for the error detection experiment mean?

7.2.2 Is there a difference between $p = .049$ and $p = .00000037$?

In the psychology literature (and also in the wider statistical literature) there is a huge debate going on about whether any meaning should be attached to the precise p-value that is obtained. Is a p-value of .00000037 'more significant' than a p-value of .049 (which after all just scrapes into the .05 significance region)? For a long time, psychologists were told not to attach any importance to the precise p-value of their studies, even if this seemed to go against their intuitions. They were told that statistics was all about setting a significance level in Step 2 of the hypothesis testing cycle, and checking in Step 4 whether the obtained t-statistic exceeded the cut-off scores. So, if the .05 significance level was chosen at Step 2, the conclusion for both $p = .049$ and $p = .00000037$ would simply be that $p < .05$.

The main reason why psychologists were urged not to pay attention to the exact p-level was that this represented a post-hoc measure. In other words, it was obtained after the experiment had been run and analysed, and was not predicted beforehand. Research is about the prediction of future events (before they happen) and not about the post-hoc explanation of past events. So, if researchers want to conclude that their effect is 'very significant', for instance at the .01 significance level, they must predict this at Step 2 and select the appropriate cut-off scores before running and analysing the experiment. (For $df = 18$, the .01 cut-off scores are -2.878 and $+2.878$; see Appendix B; for $df = 22$, the .01 cut-off scores are -2.819 and $+2.819$.) In this view, setting the significance level at .05 in Step 2 and concluding in Step 4 that the effect is significant at the $p < .01$ level is cheating. In a similar way, someone who has played the lottery four times and wins at the fourth attempt would conclude that the chances of winning the lottery are 1/4!

In recent years, however, psychologists are starting to accept that p-values yield information, even though they were not predicted beforehand. For example, as a boss of a pharmaceutical company, I would feel much more confident about the effect of a new drug when my researchers come to tell me that the drug has the desired beneficial effect at $p = .0000000000001$ than if they came to tell me that the new drug has the desired effect at $p = .009$, even though I had asked them to set the significance level at .01 in step 2 (more about my reactions later).

In a series of publications, Peter Dixon (for example, Dixon, 2003) argued that the p-value does make a difference. In particular, he proposed that we calculate the likelihood of the alternative hypothesis relative to the null hypothesis, in addition to the p-value.

To calculate the **likelihood ratio** of the alternative hypothesis relative to the null hypothesis for a t-test of two independent samples, the following equation is used:

$$\text{Likelihood ratio} = \sqrt{\left(1 + \frac{t^2}{N_1 + N_2 - 2}\right)^{N_1 + N_2}}$$

This equation can be simplified and rewritten as:

$$\text{Likelihood ratio} = \left(1 + \frac{t^2}{N_1 + N_2 - 2}\right)^{(N_1 + N_2)/2}$$

Applied to the error detection experiment, this gives:

$$\text{Likelihood ratio} = \left(1 + \frac{(3.2378)^2}{10 + 10 - 2}\right)^{(10+10)/2} = \left(1 + \frac{10.4833}{18}\right)^{10} = 98.44$$

This likelihood ratio tells us that on the basis of our data we can conclude that the alternative hypothesis of a difference between old and young participants is 98 times more likely than the null hypothesis of no difference between the groups.

If the t-value had been 2.111 (p = .049) instead of 3.2378 (p = .0046), we would have found that:

$$\text{Likelihood ratio} = \left(1 + \frac{(2.111)^2}{10 + 10 - 2}\right)^{(10+10)/2} = \left(1 + \frac{4.4563}{18}\right)^{10} = 9.13$$

The likelihood ratio tells us that when the t-value falls on the border of the $p < 05$ confidence interval, the alternative hypothesis is only 9 times more likely than the null hypothesis. The difference between 98 times more likely and 9 times more likely agrees with our intuition that we can feel more confident about an effect with a p-value of .0046 than about an effect with a p-value of .049.

Because Dixon's likelihood ratio provides valuable information in addition to the t-test, you may want to include it in your analysis. For its interpretation, use the following guidelines:

1 When there is no difference between the samples (i.e., t = 0), then the likelihood ratio is 1, meaning that the null hypothesis and the alternative hypothesis are equally likely on the basis of the data. (Notice that the likelihood ratio adequately informs us that an insignificant effect is not necessarily evidence for the null hypothesis!)

2 A t-statistic equal to the .05 cut-off score yields a likelihood ratio close to 10. So, a likelihood ratio of 10 can be interpreted as evidence in favour of the alternative hypothesis (cf. the ratio was 9.13 for our t-statistic at p = .049).

3 The higher the t-statistic, the higher the likelihood ratio. It is not uncommon in psychological research to find likelihood ratios above 100 or even 1000. The higher the likelihood ratio, the more confident we can be that the difference between the conditions would be found again if we replicated the experiment **in exactly the same way**. (The importance of exact replication will become clear in Section 7.2.3).

In conclusion, it looks like Dixon's reasoning adds interesting information to the usual distinction between significant and insignificant effects (which is the reason why it has been included here). However, for two reasons it is better practice to report the likelihood ratio information in *addition to* the conventional t-test rather than *instead of* the t-test. First, the likelihood is a post-hoc measure, one that is obtained after the data have been collected. As indicated at the beginning of this section, there is a difference between *predicting* a high likelihood ratio before you start the experiment and boasting about a large ratio *after* you obtained it. There are two possible reasons why you obtained your high likelihood ratio: either there is a large difference between the two conditions at the population level or the sampling error played in your favour. If your high likelihood ratio is partly due to sampling error, you will be unlikely to replicate it in a new study.

The second reason why exclusive reliance on the likelihood ratio may cause confusion is that a ratio of 10 seems to be rather high. So, before long, we might see people claiming they found evidence for a certain theory because their alternative hypothesis was *twice* as likely as the null hypothesis! The strength of a t-test is precisely that it warns us not to consider small differences between groups as significant because they are likely to be due to sampling error.

For the above two reasons, it is recommended always to do a proper t-test and then to calculate the likelihood ratio on the basis of the t-statistic. This approach gives you information on whether the difference between your groups is reliable and on the size of the difference in terms of the likelihood ratio between the alternative and the null hypothesis.

Learning check 3

Calculate the likelihood ratio for the drug experiment. Is the value smaller than 10, as suggested by the finding that we failed to find a significant difference between the experimental group and the placebo control group?

7.2.3 The relationship between *p* and *N*

Remember that the t-statistic depends on three properties of the data:

1 the difference between M_1 and M_2
2 the magnitudes of SD_1 and SD_2
3 the sample sizes N_1 and N_2 (although we assume that $N_1 = N_2$)

Up to now, our discussion of the sample size has been limited to the facts that the larger N, the better the estimates of M and SD, the smaller the confidence interval around M, and the lower the critical values for the t-test. All these are positive aspects of N. The larger the sample size, the more reliable are the statistics and the more likely you are to obtain a significant effect if there is a difference at the population level.

However, you should be careful about an interpretation danger related to N. To illustrate this danger, let's make use of a hypothetical example. Assume that we know the population parameters of an IQ test (M = 100, SD = 15) and that there is a gender difference of 1 IQ unit in favour of the girls. So, for boys the mean IQ score is 99.5, and for girls it is 100.5. This difference is very small. It means that 95% of the boys will have scores between 70.1 (99.5 – 1.96*15) and 128.9 (99.5 + 1.96*15) and 95% of the girls' scores will be between 71.1 and 129.9. To illustrate it differently, if we sampled one boy at random and one girl at random, we would have a 51.9% chance that the girl has a higher IQ score than the boy. (If there were no difference between the populations, the chance would be 50%.) Figure 7.7 illustrates the difference between the populations.

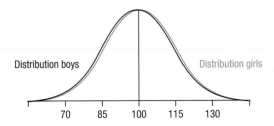

Figure 7.7 The distribution of IQ scores for boys and girls under the assumption that there is a difference of 1 in favour of the girls. Notice the large overlap of the distributions.

Hopefully, you will agree that this difference has very few practical implications. Now look at what happens when we calculate the t-test for various sample sizes, always assuming that the obtained sample statistics are exactly the same as the population parameters.

$N_1 = N_2 = 5$

$$t = \frac{M_1 - M_2}{\sqrt{\dfrac{SD_1{}^2}{N_1} + \dfrac{SD_2{}^2}{N_2}}} = \frac{100.5 - 99.5}{\sqrt{\dfrac{15^2}{5} + \dfrac{15^2}{5}}} = 0.1054$$

$df = 5 - 1 + 5 - 1 = 8$, $p = .9187$

$N_1 = N_2 = 50$

$$t = \frac{M_1 - M_2}{\sqrt{\dfrac{SD_1{}^2}{N_1} + \dfrac{SD_2{}^2}{N_2}}} = \frac{100.5 - 99.5}{\sqrt{\dfrac{15^2}{50} + \dfrac{15^2}{50}}} = 0.3333$$

$df = 50 - 1 + 50 - 1 = 98$, $p = .7396$

$N_1 = N_2 = 500$

$$t = \frac{M_1 - M_2}{\sqrt{\dfrac{SD_1{}^2}{N_1} + \dfrac{SD_2{}^2}{N_2}}} = \frac{100.5 - 99.5}{\sqrt{\dfrac{15^2}{500} + \dfrac{15^2}{500}}} = 1.0541$$

$df = 500 - 1 + 500 - 1 = 998$, $p = .2921$

$N_1 = N_2 = 5000$

$$t = \frac{M_1 - M_2}{\sqrt{\dfrac{SD_1{}^2}{N_1} + \dfrac{SD_2{}^2}{N_2}}} = \frac{100.5 - 99.5}{\sqrt{\dfrac{15^2}{5000} + \dfrac{15^2}{5000}}} = 3.3333$$

$df = 5000 - 1 + 5000 - 1 = 9998$, $p = .0009$

$N_1 = N_2 = 50000$

$$t = \frac{M_1 - M_2}{\sqrt{\dfrac{SD_1{}^2}{N_1} + \dfrac{SD_2{}^2}{N_2}}} = \frac{100.5 - 99.5}{\sqrt{\dfrac{15^2}{50000} + \dfrac{15^2}{50000}}} = 10.5409$$

$df = 50000 - 1 + 50000 - 1 = 99998$, $p < 1.0E{-}20$

Notice that our effect becomes the more 'significant' as N increases. When we test a total of 100,000 participants (50,000 boys and 50,000 girls), our p-value becomes so small that we can no longer calculate it properly because of rounding errors. Similarly, if we calculate Dixon's likelihood ratio, we find that:

$$\text{Likelihood ratio} = \left(1 + \frac{t^2}{N_1 + N_2 - 2}\right)^{(N_1 + N_2)/2}$$

$$= \left(1 + \frac{10.5409^2}{50000 + 50000 - 2}\right)^{(50000 + 50000)/2}$$

$$= 1.30E{+}24$$

This likelihood ratio tells us that the alternative hypothesis is more than a trillion trillion times more likely than the null hypothesis (1 trillion = 1.0E+12), even though we are still talking about a tiny difference of 1 IQ unit. What is happening here?

To understand this, we must return to the meaning of p (and the likelihood ratio). This tells us how likely a finding is on the basis of the null hypothesis. Now, the probability of finding a difference of 1 IQ unit between a sample of 50,000 boys and another sample of 50,000 girls given that there is no difference at the population level is very small indeed. The standard error of each mean is $SE = SD/\sqrt{N} = 15/\sqrt{50000} = .067$. So, the 95% confidence interval of the mean of the boys is $99.50 \pm 1.96 * .067$, and goes from 99.37 to 99.63. Similarly, the 95% confidence interval around the girls' mean goes from 100.37 to 100.63. There is no overlap whatsoever between these two confidence intervals even though the difference in means remains a single IQ unit.

This demonstration shows us an interpretation fault that is sometimes made with respect to p-values: the tendency to interpret small p-values as an indication of big effects ('very significant findings'). In fact, p-values only indicate how likely it is that you will find no difference between the two conditions if you were to repeat the same experiment. And the chances of not finding a difference between 50,000 boys and 50,000 girls in a replication of the study described above are very small indeed.

Learning check 4

Calculate the 95% confidence intervals around the mean IQ of boys and girls for $N_1 = N_2 = 5$ and 500 in the example above.

How do they compare to one another? Can you explain this?

7.3 The effect size

7.3.1 Measuring the effect size

Because the interpretation of p-values depends on the sample sizes, researchers have looked for measures that inform them about the size of an effect, independent of the sample size.

One way to decide whether a difference between two groups is large is to forget everything you have learned about statistical tests for a moment, and to look at the means of the two conditions. If you knew nothing about statistics and p-values and someone told you that girls are 1 IQ unit more intelligent than boys, your spontaneous reaction probably would be: So what? Does this have any visible consequences? This is the first approach you must take, regardless of the p-value you obtain. If you find a difference of 20 IQ units between two groups, you must tell yourself that this may be a big difference with serious implications in real life, regardless of the p-value. (Remember that the p-value only gives you an idea of the likelihood that this difference is due to sampling error, as when the two groups are very small.) Similarly, if there is only a tiny difference between the two conditions, you must keep this in mind, even if your p-value turns out to be extremely small (always think of the IQ example above!)

So, if you want to know whether there is a big difference between the groups you tested, first have a look at the means. Are they far apart or close together? Is there an IQ difference of 1 between your two groups or an IQ difference of 40?

(In the latter case you probably won't even need statistics to know that the intelligence of your groups differs!)

Look again at the two examples we have been discussing. In the error detection experiment, there was a difference between the errors detected by young (76%) and old (71%) adults. Is this difference important in practical and clinical terms, even though it is statistically significant? Does it make a difference in everyday life?

In the experiment on the effectiveness of the memory-enhancing drug, there was a difference between the number of word pairs remembered by those who got the drug (21) and those who received the placebo (16). This could have a huge effect in everyday life (a memory improvement of 31%, from 16 to 21), even though it cannot be interpreted because of the lack of statistical significance (so that we are not sure whether the difference would be replicated if we repeated the experiment). In such a situation a good pharmaceutical company would repeat the study with more participants to see whether the difference persists (see the discussion of the power of experiments below).

Raw difference scores between means have two limitations, however. First, they are expressed in different units. For the error detection experiment, the difference score is expressed in percentage error detection. For the drug experiment, it is the number of word pairs remembered. For the IQ study, it is the IQ score.

A second limitation of a raw difference score is that it does not take into account the variability of the data in the groups. There was more variability in the data from the drug experiment than in the data from the error detection experiment. Somehow, this difference in variability must be taken into account.

In summary, a good measure of the difference between two conditions has to be a **standardised measure** – a measure that has the same meaning for all dependent variables and one that takes into account the variability of the data.

Hopefully, at this moment you remember that we have come across such a standardised measure before, in Chapter 5 when we discussed z-scores. These scores were obtained by dividing the difference between an observation and a sample mean by the standard deviation: $z = (X - M)/SD$.

The difference between two conditions can be standardised in a similar way: we simply divide the $M_1 - M_2$ difference by an appropriate standard deviation. This measure is called the **d-statistic** or Cohen's d (after Jacob Cohen who introduced it). The d-statistic is a measure of the **effect size**, a standardised measure of the difference between two conditions. (See Chapter 13 for another measure of effect size.)

The equation to calculate d is:

$$d = \frac{M_1 - M_2}{\sqrt{\dfrac{SD_1{}^2 + SD_2{}^2}{2}}}$$

This equation is very similar that of the t-statistic. The only things that have changed are (a) we no longer work with the standard errors of the means but with the standard deviations of the scores within the samples, and (b) we take the average of the variances in sample 1 ($SD_1{}^2$) and sample 2 ($SD_2{}^2$). Because of the similarities in the calculation of d and t, we can calculate one if we know the other:

$$d = \frac{2t}{\sqrt{N_1 + N_2}}$$

In this equation we clearly see that the t-value is 'corrected' for the sample sizes.

We will illustrate the d-statistic by calculating its value for our examples:

Error detection:

$M_1 = 76.3$, $M_2 = 70.8$, $SD_1 = 4.2960$, $SD_2 = 3.2249$, $N_1 = N_2 = 10$

$$d = \frac{M_1 - M_2}{\sqrt{\dfrac{SD_1{}^2 + SD_2{}^2}{2}}} = \frac{76.3 - 70.8}{\sqrt{\dfrac{4.2960^2 + 3.2249^2}{2}}} = \frac{5.5}{3.798} = 1.45$$

$$d = \frac{2t}{\sqrt{N_1 + N_2}} = \frac{2 * 3.2378}{\sqrt{10 + 10}} = \frac{6.4756}{4.4721} = 1.45$$

Drug experiment:

$M_1 = 21$, $M_2 = 16$, $SD_1 = 10.0725$, $SD_2 = 9.9544$, $N_1 = N_2 = 12$

$$d = \frac{M_1 - M_2}{\sqrt{\dfrac{SD_1{}^2 + SD_2{}^2}{2}}} = \frac{21 - 16}{\sqrt{\dfrac{10.0725^2 + 9.9544^2}{2}}} = \frac{5}{10.0136} = 0.50$$

$$d = \frac{2t}{\sqrt{N_1 + N_2}} = \frac{2 * 1.2231}{\sqrt{12 + 12}} = \frac{2.4462}{4.8990} = 0.50$$

IQ difference between boys and girls ($N_1 = N_2 = 5$):

$M_1 = 100.5$, $M_2 = 99.5$, $SD_1 = SD_2 = 15$, $N_1 = N_2 = 5$

$$d = \frac{M_1 - M_2}{\sqrt{\dfrac{SD_1{}^2 + SD_2{}^2}{2}}} = \frac{100.5 - 99.5}{\sqrt{\dfrac{15^2 + 15^2}{2}}} = \frac{1}{15} = 0.07$$

$$d = \frac{2t}{\sqrt{N_1 + N_2}} = \frac{2 * 0.1054}{\sqrt{5 + 5}} = \frac{0.2108}{3.1623} = 0.07$$

IQ difference between boys and girls ($N_1 = N_2 = 5,000$):

$M_1 = 100.5$, $M_2 = 99.5$, $SD_1 = SD_2 = 15$, $N_1 = N_2 = 5000$

$$d = \frac{M_1 - M_2}{\sqrt{\dfrac{SD_1{}^2 + SD_2{}^2}{2}}} = \frac{100.5 - 99.5}{\sqrt{\dfrac{15^2 + 15^2}{2}}} = \frac{1}{15} = 0.07$$

$$d = \frac{2t}{\sqrt{N_1 + N_2}} = \frac{2 * 3.3333}{\sqrt{5000 + 5000}} = \frac{6.6666}{100} = 0.07$$

These calculations show that the effect size is bigger in the experiment on age differences in error detection, which shows smaller variability, than in the experiment on drug effectiveness. The calculations also show that differences in sample sizes have no impact on the effect size. The effect size is exactly the same for the IQ study with 10 participants as for the IQ study with 10,000 participants.

Learning check 5

Calculate the effect size for the following experiment.

Fifty male and fifty female participants had to indicate as quickly as possible whether faces shown on a computer screen were smiling or had a neutral expression. Their reaction times were measured and yielded the following results:

Female participants: $M = 810$ ms, $SD = 165$ ms
Male participants: $M = 840$ ms, $SD = 171$ ms

7.3.2 The interpretation of the effect size

The effect size indicates how much the distribution of one condition is shifted relative to that of the other when the measurements are coded as z-scores. Figure 7.8 illustrates this for d = +.2, +1.0, +2.0, and +3.0.

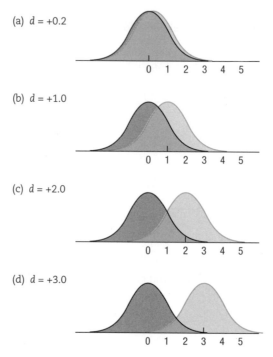

(a) d = +0.2

(b) d = +1.0

(c) d = +2.0

(d) d = +3.0

Figure 7.8 The meaning of the effect size. The d-statistic indicates how much the distribution of results in one condition is shifted relative to that of the other condition when the measurements are coded as z-values. When d = 0.0, there is no difference at all between the conditions. When d = .2, there is a shift of only 2/10 of a standard deviation and both distributions still largely overlap (a). In contrast, when d = 3.0, there is a difference of 3 standard deviations and the difference between the conditions is obvious: nearly all participants in one condition perform better than the participants in the other condition.

When d = 0.0, there is no difference between the two conditions of the study. The larger d becomes, the more one condition is shifted relative to the other and the easier it will be to see the difference between the two conditions. To help you with the interpretation, Table 7.3 lists the chances that a randomly chosen participant from condition B (the condition with the highest scores) has a higher score than a randomly chosen participant from condition A. For instance, the effect size in height between 20-year old men and 20-year old women is about d = 2.0 (in favour of men). This means that if you went to a busy shopping centre and you compared randomly chosen men with randomly chosen women, you would find that in 92% of the cases the man is taller than the woman. In contrast, the difference in conscientiousness between men and women is about d = 0.2 (this time in favour of women). This means that if you measured the

Table 7.3 The meaning of group differences as expressed by the d-statistic. If $d = +3.0$ then a randomly chosen person from condition B has a higher score than a randomly chosen person from condition A in 98% of the comparisons. If $d = +0.2$, then a randomly chosen person from condition B will have a higher score than a randomly chosen person from condition A in 56% of the cases only. Negative values of d are also possible and have the same meaning, except that they indicate that the participants of condition A performed better than those of condition B.

Effect size (d)	Interpretation: What are the chances that a randomly chosen person from condition B has a higher score than a randomly chosen person from condition A?
0.0	50%
+0.2	56%
+0.5	64%
+0.8	71%
+1.0	76%
+2.0	92%
+3.0	98%

conscientiousness of randomly chosen pairs of men and women, you would find that the woman has the higher score in 56% of the pairs (she would score higher on statements like 'I make plans and stick to them', 'I pay attention to details', and 'I get chores done right away').

In general, d-values will be defined in such a way that they are positive. So, if experimenters expect females to perform better on a task than males, they will define the B group as the females and the A group as the males and say that there is an effect size of 0.2 between females and males on conscientiousness. Alternatively, when the males perform better than the females, group B will be defined as the males and researchers will conclude that there is an effect size of 2.0 between males and females as far as height is concerned.

However, it is also possible to work with negative d-values. This will be done, for instance, when two groups of people are compared on a wide range of variables, some of which are better in one group and others in the other group. Table 7.4 (overleaf) shows an excerpt from a much longer table of gender differences for a number of different attributes (Hyde, 2005). To make this table, the females have been defined as group A and the males as group B. Therefore, an effect size of $d = -0.40$ for smiling implies that women in general smile slightly more than men. (More specifically, there is a shift of 0.4 standard deviations of the A distribution relative to the B distribution, meaning that the degree of smiling in a randomly chosen female will be higher than the degree of smiling in a randomly chosen male in 60% of cases; Table 7.3.)

7.3.3 What effect sizes can we expect in psychology?

One of the main errors made by psychology students is that they intuitively expect big effect sizes (in the order of 2.0 and more). That is, they expect that all the differences between the groups under investigation will be of the same

Table 7.4 Gender differences
A review of the literature of gender differences confirms a number of intuitively expected differences (for example, women smile more and men are more willing to have sex outside a love relationship) and also shows a number of unexpected findings (for example, men interrupt a conversation more often than women). The most important finding, however, was that most gender differences were very small. Of the 100 characteristics tested, 78 had values between $d = -0.35$ and $d = +0.35$. Notice that the characteristics in this table are ordered from more in women to more in men. Adapted from Hyde, 2005.

Smiling	−0.40
Mathematics anxiety	−0.15
Mathematics computation	−0.14
Reading comprehension	−0.08
Vocabulary	−0.02
Mathematics problem solving	+0.08
Attribution of success to ability	+0.13
Helping behaviour	+0.13
Self-esteem	+0.14
Interruptions in conversation	+0.15
Aggression	+0.50
Mental rotation of pictures	+0.56
Sexuality: attitudes about casual sex	+0.81

order as gender difference in height. However, if you come to think of it, you do not need statistics to know that men in general are taller than women do you? And how many other differences between males and females are as obvious as the difference in stature?

Most of the time psychologists are looking for group differences that are much subtler. As a matter of fact, the person who introduced the d-statistic, Jacob Cohen (for example, Cohen, 1988), noted that very few of the group differences found by psychologists are larger than 1.0. Most are even smaller than 0.5, as shown in Table 7.4 (gender differences) and Table 7.5 (other group differences that have been reported in the literature). On the basis of this observation, Cohen made a distinction between three types of effect sizes in psychological research:

1 small effect size: $d = 0.2$
2 medium effect size: $d = 0.5$
3 large effect size: $d = 0.8$

A look at Figure 7.8 and Table 7.3 indicates that in most psychological research there will be a large overlap in the distribution of the scores in condition A and the distribution of the scores in condition B. Even for the large effect sizes psychologists are probing ($d = .8$), there is only a 71% chance of that a randomly selected person from condition B will have a higher score than a randomly selected person from condition A. This has consequences for the number of participants you have to investigate in a good study – a topic we turn to later.

Table 7.5 Typical effect sizes of group differences (*d*-statistics)

Effect of systematic phonics instruction v. whole word instruction on reading comprehension (Torgerson et al., 2006)	0.28
Stress in children at centre day care v. children in home setting as measured by the cortisol level (Vermeer and van IJzendoorn, 2006)	0.37
Nonword reading in dyslexics v. normal readers (Herrmann et al., 2006)	0.65
Alcohol use in sensation seekers v. non-sensation seekers (Hittner and Swickert, 2006)	0.54
Effect of cognitive training on Alzheimer's disease (Sitzer et al., 2006)	0.47
Effectiveness of academic admission interviews (Goho and Blackman, 2006)	0.17
Effect of intervention in note-taking on learning from lectures (Kobayashi, 2006)	0.02
Impact of antipsychotic medications on long-term memory deficits in schizophrenia (Thornton et al., 2006)	0.17
Depression in mothers of children with and without developmental disabilities (Singer, 2006)	0.39
Impact of safer sexual communication on condom use (Noar et al., 2006)	0.45

7.4 How to interpret non-significant effects

The starting position of a statistical test is that the null hypothesis represents reality. Only when the statistical evidence is strong enough are we allowed to reject the null hypothesis and accept the alternative hypothesis as a better description of reality. However, quite often researchers have high hopes that they will be able to reject the null hypothesis (that is, they will find a significant effect). They run the study precisely because they predict a difference between the conditions. Therefore, failing to find the predicted significant effect is frequentlly a big disappointment for researchers. What to do then?

Suppose you have just finished a study of a new gender difference you think you have discovered and you are quite excited about. You administered a test to 30 men and 30 women and analysed your data. However, to your dismay, you found that there was no significant difference between the groups (M_{men} = 16.2 [maximum score = 20]; M_{women} = 17.1; $t(38)$ = 1.56, p = .1271). What do you do now? Is your prediction wrong? Did you misunderstand the differences between men and women? Or could it be that the difference you hypothesised is there in reality (at the population level) but did not show up in your study (sample level)?

For a start, it is good to know that, unless you did a very careful experiment with many participants, failing to find a significant effect in a study does **not** allow you to conclude that the two conditions are the same at the population level. In statistical terms, failing to reject the null hypothesis in an experiment does not mean that there is no difference between the conditions at the population level. There are tens of reasons why you may have failed to find an effect, the most mundane (and frequent!) being that you did not test carefully enough. Revealing small effects requires skilful hands, precise measurements, an eye for detail and dedication. If you measured imprecisely and exposed your participants to a lot of distractions (so that the variance in their performance was high), you should not be surprised if you fail to find a significant difference. As an extreme example, it would be like trying to determine whether men run faster than women by asking them to run 50 metres and measuring their times with a sundial!

TIP Why did I obtain a null effect, although I expected to find a significant difference?
The most frequent reason why students fail to obtain an expected effect is that they did not test enough participants. The second most frequent reason is that they did not test carefully enough. Therefore, unless you tested very carefully with lots of participants, you usually cannot conclude anything from a null effect.

Another common reason why researchers fail to obtain a significant effect is that they tested too few participants. All too often, students test their hypotheses by comparing 10 participants from one group with 10 participants from another group. As we will see below, they are unlikely to find anything with such small numbers unless they are looking at a very big effect size ($d \gg 1.0$). This raises the question of how many participants we should include in an experiment with two independent groups.

7.5 How many participants should I include in my experiment?

Failing to reject a null hypothesis is a nuisance because you cannot conclude anything. It is something that should be avoided. The first way to increase your chances of finding a predicted effect is by reducing, as much as possible, the variability due to extraneous variables – 'noise' that is unrelated to the effect you are testing. This can be achieved by standardising the test conditions and by trying to have several measurements per participant (the more the better, unless repeated testing makes the participants behave differently). The reason for multiple observations per participant is the same as the reason for having many participants in an experiment: the standard error of a mean is always smaller than the standard deviation of the individual observations. So, if you can take several measurements per participant and average them, the random differences between the participants become smaller because the measures are less influenced by noise.

The second way to increase your chances of finding a predicted effect is by increasing the sample size. Look at Figure 7.9. It shows the exam marks of two samples of 5 pupils who attend different schools with different approaches to education. Do you think there is any difference between the schools?

If you think there is no difference between the schools in Figure 7.9, your assessment is in line with the results of the t-test ($M_{\text{school A}} = 9.9$, $M_{\text{school B}} = 10.4$, $t(8) = -.12$, $p = .91$).

Now look at Figure 7.10. It shows the same 10 pupils, but now they are supplemented with the remaining 490 pupils from the schools ($N = 250$ per school). A t-test of the data in Figure 7.10 indicates that the difference between the schools is now significant ($M_{\text{school A}} = 9.7$, $M_{\text{school B}} = 11.2$, $t(498) = -3.52$, $p < .001$).

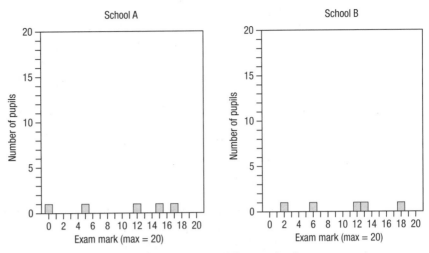

Figure 7.9 Exam results of 10 pupils from 2 different schools.
Do you think there is a difference between the schools?

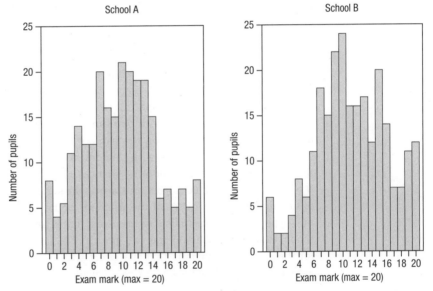

Figure 7.10 Exam results of 500 pupils from 2 different schools.
Do you think there is a difference between the schools?

What Figures 7.9 and 7.10 illustrate is a difference in **power** between two experiments. The power of an experiment refers to the chances of finding a significant effect, given that such a difference exists at the population level.

Suppose we knew the population distributions of school A and school B. Suppose the exam results of school A came from a normal distribution with $\mu = 10$ and $\sigma = 5$, and the exam results of school B from a normal distribution with $\mu = 11$ and $\sigma = 5$. How many chances would we then have of obtaining a significant difference when we test two groups of 5 pupils each? And how high would the probability be with two groups of 250 pupils each?

Statistics give us the answer, although the numbers are quite difficult to calculate (way outside the realm of this introductory book!). Luckily, statisticians have developed computer programs to help us. (You can even find some for free on the internet; see the accompanying website, www.palgrave.com/psychology/brysbaert.) When we do the calculations, we find something quite surprising: the probability of finding a significant difference between the two schools in our example ($p < .05$) with 5 pupils from each is only .06! That is, if we ran 100 such studies, we would expect to find a statistically significant effect in only 6 studies. Of these, 5 would be due to the alpha level we chose ($\alpha = .05$) and only 1 to the difference between the two schools. Remember that the alpha-level is the risk we take in rejecting a null hypothesis, given that there is no difference at the population level.

In other words, any statistician can tell you that running a study to compare the performance of two schools on the basis of two samples of 5 pupils is foolish, unless you expect to find a huge difference between the schools (e.g. $\mu_{school\ A} = 5$ and $\mu_{school\ B} = 15$, $\sigma_{school\ A} = \sigma_{school\ B} = 3$). If the expected difference is quite small, you have virtually no chance of finding a significant effect and you can conclude nothing on the basis of such a null effect. Even worse, if you find a significant effect, there is a good chance that it is a fluke, due to the alpha-level of .05. In other words, the power of your experiment is way too low to conclude anything sensible, except when the difference between your conditions is so large that you can see it with the naked eye. Have a good look at Figure 7.9 to understand why this is so. How on earth could statistics tell us whether there is a difference between the schools if the evidence is so sparse?

How does an experiment with two samples of 250 pupils fare? Actually, not as well as you would expect on the basis of Figure 7.10. We were quite 'lucky' there (which can be the case with random numbers). A power analysis shows that for this particular situation the chances of finding a significant effect with $N_1 = N_2 = 250$ are only .60. So, before starting the study we had only a 60% chance of finding the effect; in 40% of the trials we would expect to 'fail' to reject the null hypothesis. Further calculations reveal that if we want a power of .95 in the school example, we should test two groups of 650 individuals each! The reason for these large numbers is that the effect size in our example is quite small. Remember this is how the effect size is calculated:

$$d = \frac{M_1 - M_2}{\sqrt{\dfrac{SD_1{}^2 + SD_2{}^2}{2}}}$$

So, in the school example:

$$d = \frac{10 - 11}{\sqrt{\dfrac{5^2 + 5^2}{2}}} = .2$$

According to Cohen, this is the typical small effect size psychologists are trying to tackle (see above). Power analysis tells us that for this effect size it is futile to start an experiment if you can't include more than 250 participants per condition.

How does the situation look if the effect size is .5 rather than .2 (if the average difference between the schools is 2.5 marks rather than 1)? For two groups of 5 pupils, we now have a power of .11, which is still not very exciting because we will obtain a null effect in 89% of the studies we run. For two groups of 250 pupils, the power is much better (.99), meaning that, for an effect size of $d = .5$, we expect to find a significant difference between groups of 250 participants in nearly every study.

Life further improves if the effect size is $d = .8$ (which is equivalent to an average difference of 4 marks between the schools). Then the power of an experiment with two groups of 5 pupils rises to .20 and the power of an experiment with two groups of 250 pupils approaches 1.00.

On the basis of these findings, statisticians have formulated recommendations for psychologists to design good experiments. In a nutshell they are:

- ☐ If you don't know the effect size of the effect you are testing beforehand (as will be the case in most studies), assume that $d = .5$ (a medium effect size) and include two samples of 64 participants in your study. This will give you an 80% chance of finding a significant effect.
- ☐ If you have reasons to believe that your effect size is large (i.e., $d > .8$), 26 participants per group will suffice.
- ☐ If you have reasons to believe that your effect size is small (perhaps because no one has noticed it before), you must have two groups of at least 393 participants.

You may be tempted to think that a power of .80 is rather stingy and that it would be a better idea always to include some 1000 participants per group, as this would ensure that you observe virtually all differences with an effect size $d \geq .2$. This is true, but in most circumstances it would be needlessly expensive and often not feasible. Therefore, statisticians have sought a kind of optimal balance between the power and the cost of an experiment. There is little merit in running an experiment on 2000 participants rather than 1000 if this merely increases the power from .88 to .99. That is, after a certain point, the extra costs outweigh the increase in power you can expect. (This is what economists call 'the effect of diminishing returns'.)

Tip How many participants do I have to include in an experiment with two independent groups?
If you have no information beforehand, you are advised always to use a minimum of 64 participants per condition. If you have reasons to expect a big effect size ($d \geq .8$), you can go down to 26 per group. If you have reasons to assume that you are after a small effect size ($d \geq .2$), you need at least 393 participants per condition.

 Recap | **A code of practice for the interpretation of *p*-values**

On the basis of what we have seen in this chapter, the following code of practice for the interpretation of a *p*-value can be used. First, we have to decide whether a particular effect was predicted or not. This may seem odd at the moment because you may wonder why anyone would want to set up a study if no effect is expected. However, many studies in psychology involve more than one independent variable (that is, they are multifactorial), and researchers do not always have explicit expectations for all of the variables they include in their design (or for the interactions between these variables; see Chapter 13).

▷

▷

When the effect was **predicted** on the basis of a coherent theory, then:

☐ If $p < .05$ (a significant effect), you can safely assume that the effect is there, certainly the smaller p becomes. Calculate the effect size so that you have an idea of the extent to which the significance is due to a substantial difference between the populations or to the size of the participant samples.

☐ If $p > .05$ (a non-significant effect), then check whether there are reasons why the experiment may not have been sensitive enough to detect a difference. Calculate your effect size, determine the power of your design and find out whether there is room for improvement. Possible actions would be to:

(a) increase the sample sizes (this will be particularly interesting if the data go in the right direction and $d \geqslant .2$),

(b) try to find ways of decreasing the variability in the scores (for example, by more stringent testing)

(c) find out whether there are ways to make the manipulation of the independent variable stronger. (Some null effects are due to the fact that the groups did not differ enough on the independent variable – for example, the young adults were in their twenties and the old in their fifties – or because both groups performed so well or so poorly that no difference between them could be found.)

☐ If, after several serious attempts to prove the null hypothesis wrong, you still fail to obtain a significant effect, there is growing evidence for the possibility that the null hypothesis is an adequate representation of reality after all. This is the time to accept that even your most cherished research hypothesis may be wrong and that you will have to change your theory.

When the effect was **not predicted** and the study was exploratory, then:

☐ If $p < .05$, start by having a critical look at the data. How strong is the evidence, both in terms of p and d? Are the standard deviations of the samples in the expected range or did they suddenly drop (which can be an indication of random fluctuations)? Be cautious in your interpretation and, if you think you are really on to something, try to design a new experiment that reformulates your idea into an explicit null hypothesis (and alternative hypothesis) so that you can test your idea properly.

☐ If $p > .05$, just assume that for the time being there is no evidence against the null hypothesis. Do not start to interpret.

7.6   Adding confidence intervals to your graphs in SPSS

Because confidence intervals are so informative, it is good know how to add them to your graphs in SPSS. To illustrate this, we will make a bar chart and a line graph for the example of the number of words remembered in the memory-enhancing drug study (Table 6.5). First, we enter the data in SPSS (if you have not yet done so) and then we click on *Graphs*, *Chart Builder*.

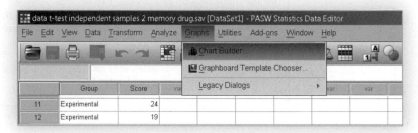

This gives you the dialogue box:

In the *Gallery* section ① go to *Bar* ②, put your cursor on the picture showing a bar graph ③, hold down the left mouse button and drag the picture into the upper box ④.

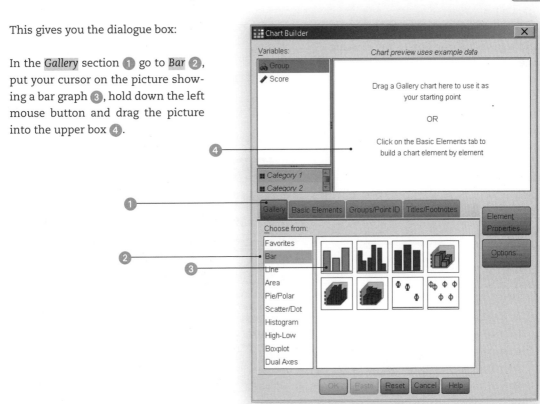

This is what you should get.

Drag the variable *Group* to the X-axis ① and *Score* to the Y-axis ②.

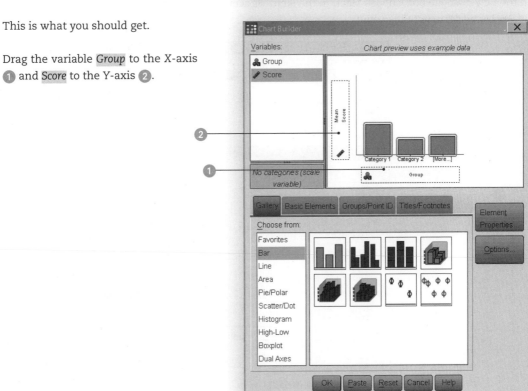

Click on *Element Properties* ①. This will add a new dialogue box to the existing one.

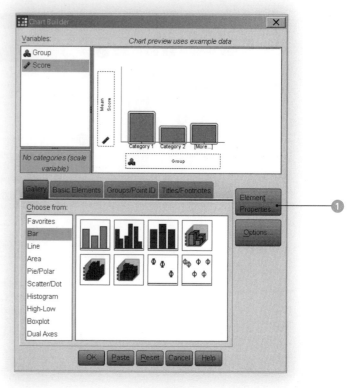

In the new dialogue box, choose Mean in the *Statistics* section ① and check *Display error bars* ②. Click on *Apply* and *OK* to get the output.

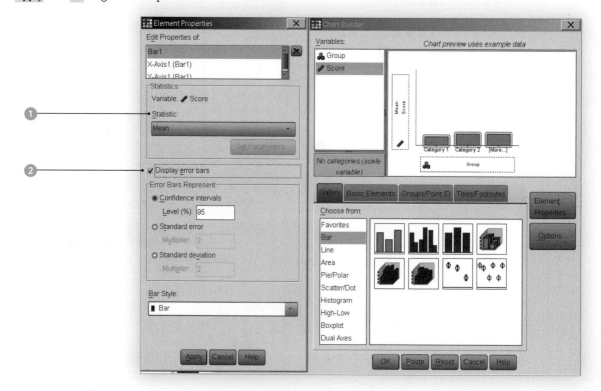

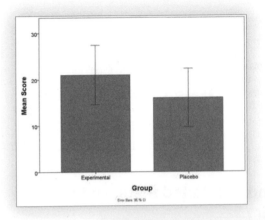

To make a line graph, select *Line* ① in the *Gallery section* ② and proceed as before.

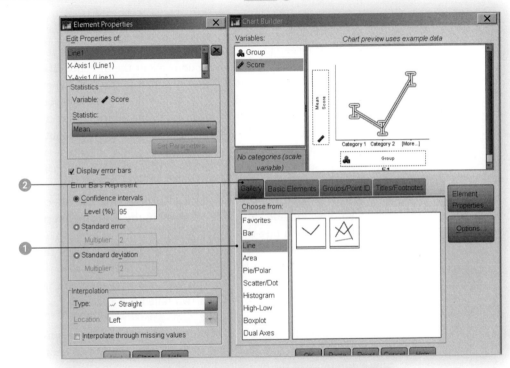

This gives you the output:

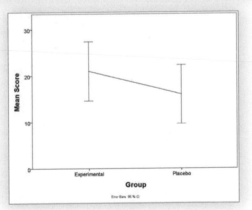

Learning check 6

Run all analyses we have covered so far on the following data. They come from an experiment in which 20 female undergraduates and 20 male undergraduates generated as many words starting with the letter T as they could in one minute. The usual finding with this task is that the females outperform the males. Is this also the case here?

Females: 29, 30, 41, 40, 39, 37, 31, 37, 24, 30, 31, 31, 38, 29, 20, 23, 29, 33, 32, 29

Males: 24, 26, 34, 33, 37, 21, 30, 13, 39, 16, 36, 24, 31, 27, 38, 18, 22, 16, 18, 25

Notice how simple statistics suddenly becomes if you can make use of a software package!

 ## 7.7   Going further: one- and two-tailed tests, and a mathematical summary

7.7.1   A two-tailed v. a one-tailed test

In psychology researchers normally use two-tailed statistical tests. These are tests that do not make prior assumptions about the direction of the difference in the alternative hypothesis. All that is stated is the null hypothesis $M_1 = M_2$ and the alternative hypothesis $M_1 \neq M_2$. This is the reason why you must always check whether the difference in means is in the expected direction when you find a significant effect! The *p*-value does not inform you about the direction of the $M_1 - M_2$ difference. So be careful! You wouldn't be the first student who erroneously used a significant difference in the *opposite* direction as evidence for their hypothesis.

If you have good reason *beforehand* to believe that the effect will be in a particular direction and cannot be observed in the opposite direction, then you are allowed to use a one-tailed test. In this test the α-level is not divided over the two tails of the *t*-distribution, but is fully located in one of the tails. Figure 7.11 shows the difference between a two-tailed test and a one-tailed test for the expected direction of $M_1 - M_2$. This effectively means that the *p*-values can be halved. For example, $p = .064$ in a two-tailed test becomes $p = .032$ in a one-tailed test

The crux of a one-tailed test, of course, is that you must be sure of the direction of $M_1 - M_2$ *before* you start your research. You must have theoretical reasons why a difference in the opposite direction is impossible. Otherwise, using a one-tailed test is the same type of *post hoc* cheating as we've seen before. (Remember the person who claims that the chances of winning the lottery are ¼ because he won after 4 attempts.) For this reason, fellow psychologists are unlikely to accept your one-tailed test if it is not well supported by prior reasoning. On the other hand, a one-tailed test increases the power of an experiment and so can be defended when the effect size is small and the data are difficult to obtain.

7.7.2   A mathematical summary

If you are mathematically-minded, the discussion in this chapter probably annoyed you. Because the text stays close to intuitive feelings and describes

(a) Two-tailed test

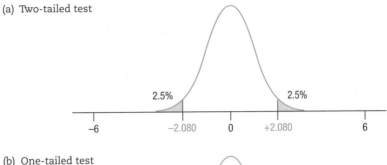

(b) One-tailed test

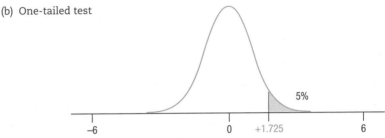

Figure 7.11 A two-tailed v. a one-tailed test. In a two-tailed t-test (a) the exceptional 5% t-values are divided equally over the lower and the upper tail of the t-distribution. Statisticians do this because they usually cannot guarantee that $M_1 - M_2$ will go in only one direction. If they can guarantee this (that is, if they have very strong theoretical evidence that only positive or negative $M_1 - M_2$ values can be observed), they are allowed to use a one-tailed test. Then the whole 5% of the exceptional t-values are situated in the predicted tail. This means that you will find significance earlier. For instance, the .05 cut-off value for t(20) is 1.725 instead of 2.086.

statistical tests in broad-brush terms from a practical point of view, very few solid facts have been presented (and you would doubtless prefer to use a book that gave a mathematical treatment of the issues). However, for you, everything that has been said in this chapter can be summarised in a few sentences.

As you already know, parametric tests (to which the t-test belongs) are based on the assumption that observations come from normal distributions. So:

1 $X_1 \sim N(\mu1,\sigma1)$ (in which N refers to a normal distribution)
2 $X_2 \sim N(\mu2,\sigma2)$.
3 μ and σ have to be estimated on the basis of the sample data, so we have to use t-distributions rather than normal distributions, with dfs equal to the number of values that are free to vary.
4 The two-tailed confidence interval around M is $CI_\alpha = M \pm t_{\alpha/2}(df) * SE$.
5 The sum of two normally distributed variables is a variable that is also normally distributed. More specifically, $X_1 - X_2 \sim N(\mu_1 - \mu^2, \sqrt{\sigma_1^2 + \sigma_2^2})$. Because it is assumed that $\sigma_1 = \sigma_2 = \sigma$ this can be rewritten as $X_1 - X_2 \sim N(\mu_1 - \mu_2, \sqrt{2}\sigma)$, which explains the discrepancy between the CIs of the means and the significance of the t-tests in Figures 7.4 and 7.5.

6 There are various tests to check whether the assumptions of a t-test (independent observations, normal distributions, equal variances) are met. If you are worried about this, you can supplement your t-test with the non-parametric tests discussed in the next chapter.

7 The difference between the t-statistic and the d-statistic should be clear to you and you should understand why each provides independent information.

❓ 7.8 Answers to chapter questions

1 What is a confidence interval?

A confidence interval is the region of uncertainty around a sample statistic. There is always some level of uncertainty around a statistic, which occurs because, as a result of sampling errors, sample statistics do not always coincide with the population parameters they try to estimate. The 95% confidence interval of a sample mean is the region in which we can expect to find the population parameter in 95% of the cases. Similarly the 95% confidence interval of the difference between two conditions defines the range of values we can expect to find for the difference between the population means.

2 What is the relationship between a confidence interval and the standard error (SE)?

The confidence interval is calculated on the basis of the standard error of the statistic. When the sample sizes are reasonably large ($N > 30$) and $\alpha = .05$ (two-tailed), the approximate confidence interval will range from the statistic minus 2SE to the statistic plus 2SE. (See Appendix B for the exact values.)

3 What is the difference between a 95% confidence interval and a 99% confidence interval?

A 95% confidence interval is the interval in which you expect the population parameter to fall in 95% of the cases. This is the default value in psychological research. The 99% confidence interval is the interval in which you expect to find the population parameter in 99% of the cases. This interval is larger than the 95% confidence interval. For sample sizes $N > 12$, it roughly coincides with the range from the statistic minus 3SE to the statistic plus 3SE. (See Appendix B for the exact values.)

4 Why is the confidence interval of a mean larger when the sample size is small than when the sample size is large, assuming that all samples come from the same population?

There are two reasons why the CI around the mean of a small sample is larger than the CI of a large sample. First, the standard error of the mean is larger for a small sample than for a large sample (remember the central limit theorem). Second, because the estimates of the mean and the standard error are less secure for a small sample than for a large sample, the critical t-values will be bigger. When N = 5 (df = 4) you have to multiply the SE by 2.776; when N = 20 (df = 19) you only have to multiply the SE by 2.093. So, even when you have the same SE value for N = 5 and N = 50, your CI will still be considerably larger for the smaller sample size than the larger.

5   What is the relative position of the confidence interval around M_1 and the confidence interval around M_2 when $p \approx .05$ in the t-test?

The CIs will partly overlap. The overlap will not be larger than roughly half a whisker (see Figure 7.4).

6   What is the relative position of the error bars around M_1 and the error bars around M_2 when $p \approx .05$ in the t-test?

The SE bars must not overlap. As a matter of fact, the gap between them should be roughly equal to 1SE (see Figure 7.5)

7   What can you say about the confidence interval of the difference between M_1 and M_2 when the effect is not significant in the t-test?

The confidence interval of the $M_1 - M_2$ difference will include the value of 0 because, when a t-test is not significant, the observation of $\mu1 = \mu2$ is among the possible scenarios.

8   What does the value $p = .40$ mean?

A p-value of .40 means that you have 40% chance of finding this difference or a larger difference on the assumption that the null hypothesis is true. This means that you fail to reject the null hypothesis. The chances are too high that this small difference cannot be replicated if you repeat the study.

9   Is there a difference between $p = .043$ and $p = .00001$? What has the likelihood ratio to do with this?

Both values are significant if you used the $p < .05$ significance level. In all likelihood, however, the difference between the conditions will be more obvious and you will feel surer about the existence of an effect at the population level for the smaller p-value. You can use the likelihood ratio to calculate how much more likely the alternative hypothesis is relative to the null hypothesis. As a rule of thumb, only when the alternative hypothesis is more than 10 times more likely than the null hypothesis is the effect safe to interpret. (Otherwise it could be due to sampling error.)

10   Why is an effect that is significant at $p < .001$ level in a t-test for independent groups sometimes not perceptible in practical terms?

The p-value not only depends on the difference between the two groups and the variability within each group, it also depends on the number of participants in each condition. When the numbers are very large, you can find 'very significant' p-values even though there is little difference between the X-values in both conditions.

11　**What does Cohen's d-statistic mean and why is this important information?**

Cohen's d-statistic is a standardised measure of the difference between two conditions. This is achieved by dividing the raw difference score by the average standard deviation.

12　**How do you calculate Cohen's d-statistic for a t-test for independent groups?**

$$d = \frac{M_1 - M_2}{\sqrt{\dfrac{SD_1{}^2 + SD_2{}^2}{2}}}$$

13　**How large are typical d-values in psychological research and how should these be interpreted?**

Although d-values can in principle be larger than 5.0, in the field of psychology, they are usually smaller than 1.0. Most of the time you can expect $d = .5$ (medium effect size). Occasionally, an effect is bigger (it is defined as a big effect size as soon as $d \geq .8$). Alternatively, researchers may be looking for a more subtle difference (for example, $d = .2$) in which case they will have to measure very precisely and include many participants in their groups.

14　**What can researchers conclude from non-significant effects?**

Usually very little, except that they must try anew and work harder if they believe the effect is there (that is, more participants, more precise measurements). Only after repeated careful and powerful experiments can researchers start to accept the idea that the null hypothesis might be a correct description of the reality (or, at least, that they are looking for a very small difference). Usually the story about the black swans is given here as a precaution not to conclude too hastily that the null hypothesis is correct.

15　**How many participants do you have to include in a design with two independent groups?**

As a rule of thumb, go for $2 \times 64 = 128$ participants. This allows you to find effects that are as small as $d = .5$. Only when you have reasons to expect d to be considerably larger than .5, can you decrease the number (for example, for $d \geq .8$, you can go down to 26 per group). Do not trust your intuitions to postulate a big effect size, though! Experience tells us that researchers always tend to be way too optimistic about the size of the effects they are testing. The assessment must be based on an analysis of previous studies on the topic.

☑ 7.9 Learning check solutions

Learning check 1

Young adults:

$N_1 = 10,$

$df = 9$

$t_{.05crit} = -2.262$ and $+2.262$

$M_1 = 76.3, \ SE_1 = 1.3585$

Lower limit of the interval $= M_1 - 2.262*SE_1 = 76.3 - 2.262*1.3585 = 73.23$

Upper limit of the interval $= M_1 + 2.262*SE_1 = 76.3 + 2.262*1.3585 = 79.37$

Old adults:

$N_1 = 10,$

$df = 9$

$t_{.05crit} = -2.262$ and $+2.262$

$M_1 = 70.8, \ SE_1 = 1.0198$

Lower limit of the interval $= M_1 - 2.262*SE_1 = 70.8 - 2.262*1.0198 = 68.49$

Upper limit of the interval $= M_1 + 2.262*SE_1 = 70.8 + 2.262*1.0198 = 73.11$

You can see that M_2 falls outside CI of M_1 and vice versa. This agrees with the finding of $p < .01$ (see Figure 7.4).

Learning check 2

This computer output means that the difference between the two conditions is significant: The p-value is less than .05 or $p < .05$, as scientists would write. The chances of finding a t-value that equals 3.2378 or is larger under the assumption that $\mu_1 = \mu_2$ are .0046. To calculate this value, you must know to which t-distribution the t-statistic belongs. This information is given by the degrees of freedom expressed as $t(18)$ for a t-distribution with $df = 18$.

Learning check 3

$$\text{Likelihood ratio} = \left(1 + \frac{t^2}{N_1 + N_2 - 2}\right)^{(N_1+N_2)/2}$$

$$= \left(1 + \frac{1.2231^2}{12 + 12 - 2}\right)^{(12+12)/2}$$

$$= 2.2$$

The low value of the likelihood ratio (< 10) agrees with the fact that the t-test was not significant.

Learning check 4

Boys:

$N_1 = 5,$

$df = 4$

$t_{.05crit} = -2.776$ and $+2.776$

$M_1 = 99.5, \ SE_1 = SD_1/\sqrt{N_1} = 15/\sqrt{5} = 6.7$

Lower limit of the interval $= M_1 - 2.776*SE_1 = 99.5 - 2.776*6.7 = 80.9$

Upper limit of the interval $= M_1 + 2.776*SE_1 = 99.5 + 2.776*6.7 = 118.1$

Girls:

M_2 = 100.5 (everything else is the same as for the boys)

Lower limit of the interval = M_2 – 2.776*SE_2 = 100.5 – 2.776*6.7 = 81.9

Upper limit of the interval = M_2 + 2.776*SE_2 = 100.5 + 2.776*6.7 = 119.1

Boys:

N_1 = 500,

df = 499

$t_{.05crit}$ = -1.97 and +1.97

M_1 = 99.5, SE_1 = $SD_1/\sqrt{N_1}$ = 15/$\sqrt{500}$ = .67

Lower limit of the interval = M_1 – 1.97*SE_1 = 99.5 – 1.97*.67 = 98.2

Upper limit of the interval = M_1 + 1.97*SE_1 = 99.5 + 1.97*6.7 = 100.8

Girls:

M_2 = 100.5 (everything else is the same as for the boys)

Lower limit of the interval = M_1 – 1.97*SE_1 = 100.5 – 1.97*.67 = 99.2

Upper limit of the interval = M_1 + 1.97*SE_1 = 100.5 + 1.97*6.7 = 101.8

Learning check 5

$$d = \frac{M_1 - M_2}{\sqrt{\dfrac{SD_1{}^2 + SD_2{}^2}{2}}} = \frac{819 - 840}{\sqrt{\dfrac{165^2 + 171^2}{2}}} = \frac{-30}{168.0} = -.18$$

Most of the time d will be written as a positive number, so d = .18. This is a small effect size.

Non-parametric tests of difference between independent groups

8

?

1 Why are the Mann-Whitney U-test and the chi-square test called non-parametric tests?
2 Why does the Mann-Whitney U-test have a wider range of applications than the t-test for independent groups?
3 What is the basic idea behind the Mann-Whitney U-test?
4 Why do people who are familiar with the t-test tend to draw the wrong conclusion on the basis of the Mann-Whitney U-test?
5 What are tied data and why do they present a difficulty for the Mann-Whitney test?
6 What is a boxplot and why is it interesting?
7 When can you use a one-way chi-square test?

In Chapter 6 we introduced the t-test for independent groups. This test is based on the assumption that the data of the two conditions come from normal distributions, the parameters of which have to be estimated on the basis of the sample data. Therefore, the t-test is called a **parametric test**. Another feature of the t-test is the need for arithmetic operations: adding, averaging, squaring numbers and taking square roots. As we saw in Chapter 1, all this is only possible when the numbers are part of an interval/ratio scale. So, what do we do when none of the above assumptions applies to the data we want to test? What do we do when our data come from an ordinal scale, when the difference between the numbers 1 and 2 can have a different meaning from the difference between the numbers 2 and 3? In Chapters 3 and 4, we saw that it not sensible in such a situation to calculate means and standard deviations. Instead, we have to work with medians and ranges. Does this mean, however, that there are no tests to assess whether the data of two groups of people differ significantly from one another? Don't underestimate statistics!

The t-test was developed in the early 1900s by William Gosset (who published under the pseudonym 'Student', in order not to identify his employer, Guinness Brewing Company). The details of its calculations were further explored and extended in the following decades by a close-knit group of eminent statisticians in the UK. In the 1940s, however, three Americans proposed a series of tests that started from a completely different set of assumptions. They were Frank Wilcoxon, a chemist, and Henry Mann and D. Ransom Whitney, an economist and his graduate student. Mann and Whitney worked independently of Wilcoxon, but developed a test that was equivalent to Wilcoxon's (who was first). As sometimes happens, the Mann-Whitney test became more popular than Wilcoxon's (even though it is slightly more complicated to calculate) and, therefore, it will be presented here. Luckily for Wilcoxon, his non-parametric test for related groups did not have a competitor and so we will encounter him again in Chapter 10.

Because the Mann-Whitney and the Wilcoxon test do not make assumptions about the underlying distributions of the scores, they are called **non-parametric tests**.

8.1   The Mann-Whitney *U*-test for ordinal data

8.1.1   The *U*-statistic

The Mann-Whitney U-test is used for data that form at least an ordinal scale (see Section 8.2 for a test that can be used when the data are nominal). The basic reasoning is deceptively simple (so simple that the authors could not believe that no one had thought of it before!). The assumption is that if the data form an ordinal scale, then you can replace them by their rank scores and see whether the ranks in condition 1 are lower or higher than the ranks in condition 2.

Let's illustrate the approach with an example. Suppose you ask 10 psychology students and 10 sociology students to indicate on a scale from 1 to 100 how

Table 8.1 The data to the question 'Indicate on a scale from 1 to 100 how confident you are that the world will still exist in 2000 years' time (1 = very sure it will no longer exist; 100 = very sure it will still exist)'.

Psychology students	Sociology students
80	91
96	28
65	64
75	57
58	55
88	70
85	72
92	35
74	76
36	30

confident they are that the world will still exist in 2000 years' time (1 = very sure it will no longer exist; 100 = very sure it will still exist). The data are shown in Table 8.1.

Is there any difference between psychology and sociology students in their view of mankind's future? Given the nature of the numbers you get from the participants, it is a big stretch to assume that they come from a normal distribution and that the difference between 50 and 60 has the same meaning as the difference between 1 and 10 or between 90 and 100. So, running a *t*-test would be a shaky business, even though every statistical package will happily provide you with a *t*-statistic and a *p*-value! So, what is the alternative?

If the data come from an ordinal scale, then their rank numbers are important. In addition, the difference between rank 1 and rank 2 is the same as the difference between rank 2 and rank 3. So, it would make sense to replace the data by their ranks, starting with the lowest and ending with the highest. In our example the lowest score of 28 was given by a sociology student. So, this student gets rank 1. The second and third lowest scores, 30 and 35, were also given by sociology students and get the ranks 2 and 3. The fourth lowest score 36 was given by a psychology student, who gets rank 4, and so on. Table 8.2 (overleaf) shows the ranks of all 20 students. It also shows you an easy calculation check of the outcome: the sum of the ranks should be equal to $N * (N + 1)/2$, where N is the number of participants in the study. The origin of this check will be explained in more detail below.

If there is no difference in the world views of psychology and sociology students, we expect the ranks of the psychology students to be fully intermixed with those of the sociology students because they come from the same distribution. On the other hand, if the sociology students think it is less likely that the world will still exist in 2000 years' time, their ranks should be lower than those of the psychology students. The Mann-Whitney *U*-test is just a measure of how

Table 8.2 Ranks for the questionnaire study 'How likely is it that the world will still exist in 2000 years' time?'

Psychology students		Sociology students	
Raw score	Rank	Raw score	Rank
80	15	91	18
96	20	28	1
65	9	64	8
75	13	57	6
58	7	55	5
88	17	70	10
85	16	72	11
92	19	35	3
74	12	76	14
36	4	30	2
Σ ranks = 210 = (20*21)/2			

much the two distributions of ranks differ from one another. This is how you calculate the statistic:

$U = \min(U_1, U_2)$ (that is, $U = U_1$ if $U_1 < U_2$, and $U = U_2$ if $U_2 < U_1$)

$$U_1 = N_1 N_2 + \frac{N_1(N_1 + 1)}{2} - R_1$$

$$U_2 = N_1 N_2 + \frac{N_2(N_2 + 1)}{2} - R_2$$

in which N_1 = the number of observations in condition 1, N_2 = the number of observations in condition 2, R_1 = the sum of the ranks in condition 1, and R_2 = the sum of the ranks in condition 2.

Applied to our example this gives:

$R_1 = 15 + 20 + 9 + 13 + 7 + 17 + 16 + 19 + 12 + 4$

$\quad = 132$

$R_2 = 18 + 1 + 8 + 6 + 5 + 10 + 11 + 3 + 14 + 2$

$\quad = 78$

$U_1 = 10 * 10 + \dfrac{10(10 + 1)}{2} - 132 = 100 + 55 - 132 = 23$

$U_2 = 10 * 10 + \dfrac{10(10 + 1)}{2} - 78 \quad = 100 + 55 - 78 \quad = 77$

$U = \min(23, 77) = 23$

In order to understand the calculations behind the U-statistic, you should know that:

$$1 + 2 + 3 + 4 + \ldots + N = \frac{N(N + 1)}{2}$$

For instance, $1 + 2 + 3 + 4 + 5 + 6 = (6 * 7)/2 = 21$. The reason for this equation is easy to understand. Start at the extremes and take the sum of both numbers (1+6). Then go one number towards the middle and again take the sum (2+5). Each time, the two numbers add up to N + 1. So, we can rewrite 1 + 2 + 3 + 4 + 5 + 6 as (1 + 6) + (2 + 5) + (3 + 4). There are 3 pairs that add up to 7. This can be expressed in general terms, when N is even, as N/2 pairs of numbers that add up to N + 1. When N is odd, there will be (N – 1)/2 pairs that add up to N + 1 and the middle number is always equal to (N + 1)/2. With a bit of reshuffling this produces the same expression, namely N(N + 1)/2, as you can see in the following example: 1 + 2 + 3 + 4 + 5 = (1 + 5) + (2 + 4) + 3 = (5 * 6)/2.

Now, the significance of the middle term in the equations to calculate U_1 and U_2 becomes clear. It is the sum of ranks you would expect if all the lowest ranks were in that condition. For instance, if the ranks of the psychology students in our example had been 1 to 10, we would have found that $R_1 = N_1 * (N_1+1)/2 = 55$.

Once you know this, it is easy to see that the U-statistic basically looks at the sum of ranks of the higher condition and subtracts this from the minimum sum expected. You can profit from this insight and immediately calculate the smaller of U_1 and U_2. When it is clear which condition has the higher ranks, calculate the U statistic for this condition alone. In our example it was clear that the ranks of the psychology students in general were higher than those of the sociology students. So, simply calculating U_1 suffices because $U_1 < U_2$. Of course you have to make sure that you are not making a mistake in judging which condition has the higher ranks. If in doubt, always calculate both U_1 and U_2!

The fact that R_1 and R_2 are calculated over the N_1+N_2 samples, means that you have a quick check to see whether you calculated R_1 and R_2 correctly. All you have to do is to add them and check whether:

$$R_1 + R_2 = \frac{(N_1 + N_2)(N_1 + N_2 + 1)}{2}$$

For our example: 132 + 78 = (20 * 21)/2 = 210.

The term $N_1 * N_2$ is added to the calculation of the U-statistic to ensure that it is always positive.

 Performance checks for the Mann-Whitney U-test

1	Do the ranks add up to $\frac{(N_1 + N_2)(N_1 + N_2 + 1)}{2}$?
2	Is $R_1 + R_2 = \frac{(N_1 + N_2)(N_1 + N_2 + 1)}{2}$?
3	Are U_1 and U_2 positive?
4	Did you take the smaller of U_1 and U_2 as the value of U?
5	Does the U-value correspond to the U-value of the condition with the highest ranks?

8.1.2 When is the U-statistic significant?

Knowing that U = 23 for our example with psychology and sociology students is interesting, but does not tell us very much. How are we to interpret this value?

For a start, because the U-statistic is calculated by subtracting R from the other two terms, we can predict that the larger the difference between two conditions, the smaller U will be. Let's illustrate this with our example. Suppose that all sociology students had given lower scores than all psychology students. Then, the ranks of the sociology students would have been 1–10 and the ranks of the psychology students 11–20. We would then find that

$$R_1 = 1 + 2 + 3 + 4 + 5 + 6 + 7 + 8 + 9 + 10 = 55$$

$$U_1 = 10 * 10 + \frac{10 * 11}{2} - 55 = 100$$

$$R_2 = 11 + 12 + 13 + 14 + 15 + 16 + 17 + 18 + 19 + 20 = 155$$

$$U_2 = 10 * 10 + \frac{10 * 11}{2} - 155 = 0$$

$$U = \min(U_1, U_2) = \min(100, 0) = 0$$

Thus, in the case of the largest possible difference between 2 conditions, U equals 0. Or to put it differently, the smaller U becomes, the larger the difference between the two conditions. Be careful here because the interpretation of the U-statistic is exactly opposite to that of the t-statistic! Whereas larger t-values mean that the difference between the two conditions is more significant, for U, smaller U-statistics reflect a more significant difference!

Now that we know that a small U is good in terms of significance, the next questions are: 'How small does U have to be in order to attain significance?' and 'How do we calculate the p-value?'

Unfortunately, there are no easy guidelines for the U-test. We can only say that the critical value is higher for larger sample sizes. For instance, when $N_1 = N_2 = 5$, $U_{.05crit} = 2$; for $N_1 = N_2 = 10$, $U_{.05crit} = 23$; and for $N_1 = N_2 = 20$, $U_{.05crit} = 127$. Appendix C shows the critical values for all possible combinations of N_1 and N_2 up to 20. From this table, we see that the U-statistic we obtained for the example with psychology and sociology students ($U = 23$) agrees with $U_{.05crit}$, which means that the difference we observed is just significant at the $p < .05$ level.

For sample sizes larger than 20, we can use the following equation, which yields a good approximation:

$$z = \frac{U - \dfrac{N_1 N_2}{2}}{\sqrt{\dfrac{N_1 N_2 (N_1 + N_2 + 1)}{12}}}$$

in which z is a z-value from the standard normal distribution.

As you may remember from Chapter 5, z-scores higher than 1.96 are significant at the .05 level. For instance, if we apply the approximation to the example $N_1 = N_2 = 20$, $U = 127$, we find that:

$$z = \frac{127 - \dfrac{20 * 20}{2}}{\sqrt{\dfrac{20 * 20 * (20 + 20 + 1)}{12}}} = -1.975$$

which is more extreme than the critical value -1.96, making the difference significant at $p < .05$. If you look at Appendix C, you will see that 127 is indeed $U_{.05crit}$ when $N_1 = N_2 = 20$.

> **Be careful!** For the *t*-statistic we have seen that *p* becomes smaller as *t* increases. In practice, *t*-values of more than 2.2 imply significance at the .05 level (unless *N* is very small, in which case you need higher *t*-values for significance).
>
> For the *U*-statistic, however, you must remember that the smaller *U*, the smaller *p*. A *U*-statistic of 0 means maximum significance (unless N_1 and N_2 are smaller than 4, in which case you can never get significance).

8.1.3   The problem of ties

Thus far, we have sidestepped a thorny issue in the assignment of ranks, namely the fact that the raw data rarely all differ from one another, as 'conveniently' happened in our example of psychology and sociology students. Most of the time, one or more observations overlap, so that we have so-called **tied data**. Table 8.3 repeats Table 8.1 but with different data – this time some values are the same.

Table 8.3 New data on the question 'Indicate on a scale from 0 to 100 how confident you feel that the world will still exist in 2000 years' time'. These data contain ties.

Psychology students	Sociology students
80	90
95	30
65	65
75	60
60	55
90	70
85	70
90	35
75	75
40	30

The ties in Table 8.3 become obvious when we order the data from small to large:

30, 30, 35, 40, 55, 60, 60, 65, 65, 70, 70, 75, 75, 75, 80, 85, 90, 90, 90, 95

To assign ranks to these raw data, you must know that the ranks of tied data equal the mean rank of the tied data. (Strictly speaking, the ranks must be the median rank, but you can easily show that the median rank and the mean rank are the same in this situation.)

The best way to avoid errors in the assignment of the correct ranks is to start with the usual ranking. So, we have:

Data: 30, 30, 35, 40, 55, 60, 60, 65, 65, 70, 70, 75, 75, 75, 80, 85, 90, 90, 90, 95
Rank: 1,   2,   3,   4,   5,   6,   7,   8,   9, 10, 11, 12, 13, 14, 15, 16, 17, 18, 19, 20

Next, we tackle the ties. This is shown below, with the ties underlined:

Data: 30, 30, 35, 40, 55, 60, 60, 65, 65, 70, 70, 75, 75, 75, 80, 85, 90, 90, 90, 95
Rank: 1,   2,   3,   4,   5,   6,   7,   8,   9, 10, 11, 12, 13, 14, 15, 16, 17, 18, 19, 20

Now we replace the ranks of tied data by their mean rank. So, values of 30 are both ranked at 1.5 rather than 1 and 2, the ranks of 60 are both 6.5 instead of 6 and 7, and so on. We leave the ranks of untied values exactly as they are. This gives us the following result:

Data: 30, 30, 35, 40, 55, 60, 60, 65, 65, 70, 70, 75, 75, 75, 80, 85, 90, 90, 90, 95
Rank: 1.5, 1.5, 3,   4,   5, 6.5, 6.5, 8.5, 8.5, 10.5, 10.5, 13, 13, 13, 15, 16, 18, 18, 18, 20

If you assign ranks in this way, you will not make the beginners' error of accidentally dropping a few ranks. A good check to see whether you have correctly assigned the ranks is to verify that the sum of the ranks still equals $N * (N + 1)/2$. Does the sum of the ranks above equal 210? (Check if you are not sure!)

Table 8.4 lists the ranks for the example with tied data (Table 8.3).

Table 8.4 Ranks for the questionnaire study with tied data.

Psychology students		Sociology students	
Raw score	Rank	Raw score	Rank
80	15	90	18
95	20	30	1.5
65	8.5	65	8.5
75	13	60	6.6
60	6.5	55	5
90	18	70	10.5
85	16	70	10.5
90	18	35	3
75	13	75	13
40	4	30	1.5
Σ ranks = 210 = (20*21)/2			

If we repeat the calculations, we get:

$R_1 = 15 + 20 + 8.5 + 13 + 6.5 + 18 + 16 + 18 + 13 + 4$
$\quad = 132$

$R_2 = 18 + 1.5 + 8.5 + 6.5 + 5 + 10.5 + 1.5 + 3 + 13 + 1.5$
$\quad = 78$

$U_1 = 10 * 10 + \dfrac{10(10 + 1)}{2} - 132 = 100 + 55 - 132 = 23$

$U_2 = 10 * 10 + \dfrac{10(10 + 1)}{2} - 78 \ = 100 + 55 - 78 \ = 77$

$U = \min(23, 77) = 23$

$U_{\text{crit}}(N_1 = 10, N_2 = 10) = 23$, so $p < .05$

Because the tied values did not change anything in the ordering of the data, the U-statistic stays the same.

8.1.4   Reporting the results of a Mann-Whitney test

In reporting your study you must indicate that a Mann-Whitney test was used, and you have to give enough information for the reader to have full knowledge of what happened. So, if we were to report the results of our study with psychology and sociology students, we would write something like:

> 'A sample of 10 psychology students and 10 sociology students were asked to indicate on a scale from 1 to 100 how confident they felt that the world will still exist in 2000 years' time (1 = very sure it will no longer exist; 100 = very sure it will still exist). The scores given by the sociology students (median = 60.5) were significantly lower than those of the psychology students (median = 77.5), as indicated by a Mann-Whitney test ($U = 23$, $N_1 = N_2 = 10$, $p < .05$).'

In the discussion section we would then say how this finding is to be interpreted and whether or not it agrees with the predictions made beforehand. Notice that, because we are dealing with ordinal data, we have to use the medians rather than the means (Chapter 3).

Because the Mann-Whitney test does not make assumptions about the underlying distribution, it is not really possible to calculate a measure of effect size or a confidence interval as we can for the t-test. However, this does not mean that we cannot give the reader more information than simply reporting the medians and the U-statistic.

A particularly informative graphical tool is a **boxplot** (sometimes called a box-and-whisker plot). This plot makes use of the following information:

1   The median of each condition, Mdn: As discussed in Chapter 3, this is the score that divides the frequency distribution in half.
2   The first quartile, Q1: This is the score that divides the frequency distribution in ¼ v. ¾. It is the median of the lower half of the data.
3   The third quartile, Q3: This is the score that divides the frequency distribution in ¾ v. ¼. It is the median of the upper half of the data.
4   The minimum value.
5   The maximum value.

If we calculate these for Table 8.1, we get:

$\text{Mdn}_{\text{psychology}} = 77.5$
$\text{Q1}_{\text{psychology}} = 65$
$\text{Q3}_{\text{psychology}} = 88$
$\text{Min}_{\text{psychology}} = 36$
$\text{Max}_{\text{psychology}} = 96$

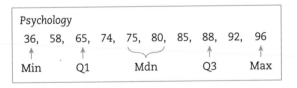

$\text{Mdn}_{\text{sociology}} = 60.5$
$\text{Q1}_{\text{sociology}} = 35$
$\text{Q3}_{\text{sociology}} = 72$
$\text{Min}_{\text{sociology}} = 28$
$\text{Max}_{\text{sociology}} = 91$

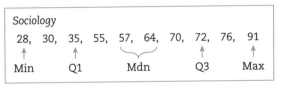

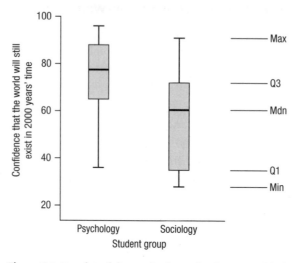

Figure 8.1 Boxplot of the study about the future world views of psychology and sociology students. The meaning of the different lines is indicated for the sociology students (Max = maximum value observed, Q3 = third quartile, Mdn = median, Q1 = first quartile, Min = minimum value observed). The whiskers indicate the range. The boxes contain 50% of the data observed.

Figure 8.1 shows how we can use these values to build a very informative graph of our findings. This boxplot not only informs us about the range of the observations in each condition (as indicated by the whiskers), but also about the median and the range within which 50% of the data fall (shown by the box). If we add such a graph to the usual statistics, readers have all the information they need to understand what has been found in the study. As for the interpretation, the further the two boxes are separated from each other, the surer we are that the difference will be found again in a replication of the study. (The interpretation is similar to that for confidence intervals in Chapter 7.)

8.1.5 The Mann-Whitney test as an alternative for the *t*-test for independent groups

The Mann-Whitney test and the t-test for independent groups start from different assumptions (overlapping ranks v. a shift in the normal distribution), but should in general return very similar results, certainly when the data come from an interval/ratio scale. So, each t-test can be replaced by a Mann-Whitney test. (The reverse is not true, as the Mann-Whitney test can be used for ordinal data and for data that do not come from a normal distribution.) A highly significant effect in one test should be accompanied by a highly significant effect in the other. Similarly, an effect that is far from significant in one test should not be significant in the other. Only on the $p = .05$ borderline can we expect some differences, with one test edging into the significance region while the other does not.

For some time it was thought that the Mann-Whitney had less power than the *t*-test for independent groups, so that it would be more difficult to reach significance with it. However, careful analysis of both tests has indicated that, although this difference in power exists, it is very small. In addition, the Mann-Whitney test is less influenced by **outliers** – values that are much lower or higher than the remainder. For instance, assume we ask 5 participants to name a word and time their responses. The results are (ordered from small to large): 587 ms, 621 ms, 648 ms, 663 ms and 1498 ms. For a *t*-test, the last value will be a problem, because it hugely increases the standard deviation. For the Mann-Whitney test, however, its impact will be much more limited, because the raw data are translated into ranks. As a matter of fact, extreme data were the reason why Wilcoxon and Mann-Whitney were searching for an alternative to the *t*-test.

A nice way to see how Mann-Whitney compares to the *t*-test is to repeat the analyses of the two studies we analysed in Chapters 6 and 7 on *t*-tests. Remember, one was an experiment on error detection in young and old adults. The other was a study on the effectiveness of a memory drug. In this section we will deal with the error detection experiment. The drug experiment will be discussed in the next section.

The data are given again in Table 8.5..

Table 8.5 Data from experiment on error detection in young and old adults (percentage of errors detected).

Young adults
$X = 71, 75, 81, 79, 75, 84, 74, 74, 71, 79$
$N_1 = 10$, $M_1 = 76.3$, $SD_1^2 = 18.4556$, $SD_1 = 4.2960$, $SE_1 = 1.3585$

Old adults
$X = 72, 65, 70, 76, 72, 75, 68, 69, 71, 70$
$N_2 = 10$, $M_2 = 70.8$, $SD_2^2 = 10.4000$, $SD_2 = 3.2249$, $SE_2 = 1.0198$

$t(18) = 3.2378$, $p = .0046$
$d = 1.45$
likelihood ratio = 98

Be careful! The correspondence between the Mann-Whitney test and the *t*-test for independent samples should remind us that power is as much an issue for the Mann-Whitney test as it is for the *t*-test (Chapter 7). Remember that in real life samples of $N = 10$ are unlikely to yield significant effects because the differences psychologists are examining are much more subtle than the ones used in statistics books (including this one)! The number of observations in an experiment with a Mann-Whitney test should be at least as high as the number for an experiment with a *t*-test (that is, more than 64 participants per condition if you are after a medium effect size).

When we run a Mann-Whitney test on the data (please do it as a learning check!), we get $U = 16$, $N_1 = N_2 = 10$, $p < .01$, as we could have expected if the Mann-Whitney was a valid alternative of the *t*-test. Figure 8.2 (overleaf) shows the results of the boxplot. Compare it with the graph of the confidence intervals on the basis of the *t*-test (Figure 7.2).

8

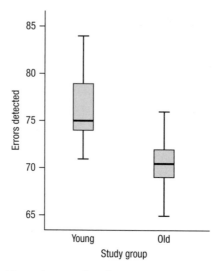

Figure 8.2 Boxplot of the error detection experiment (young v. old adults). Compare it to Figure 7.2 showing the confidence intervals on the basis of the t-test.

8.1.6 Step by step: hypothesis testing with the Mann-Whitney test

In this final section on the Mann-Whitney test we will revise the important parts of the test. We will use the same format and data as we used in Chapter 6 when we summarised the t-test for independent groups (see Section 6.4.5). In this way, it is easier for you to see the commonalities and differences between the tests.

The study to illustrate the different steps in hypothesis testing was a study on the effectiveness of a memory drug. For one week, one group of undergraduate students took tablets containing the drug and another group received placebo tablets. Both groups took a memory test at the end of the week, in which they had to study 50 word pairs for 15 minutes. In the test session they were given the first word of each pair and were asked to name the second word. For each individual the number of correct responses was calculated (min = 0; max = 50).

The hypothesis testing procedure consists of the following four steps:

1 *The null hypothesis and the alternative hypothesis are outlined.*
The null hypothesis says that the experimental group will show the same distribution of performance scores as the placebo control group because the drug has no effect. The alternative hypothesis says that the drug has an effect and that the performance of the experimental group will differ from that of the placebo control group. Initially, it is not specified whether the influence of the drug will be beneficial or detrimental. The null hypothesis states that the researchers start from the assumption of no effect and will examine whether the evidence is strong enough to reject it.

2 *The researchers determine their statistic and the corresponding cut-off value.*
They decide to use a Mann-Whitney test and an α-level of .05. They have money and permission to test 24 participants (12 in each group). Given that $N_1 = N_2 = 12$, $U_{.05crit} = 37$ (Appendix C).

3 *The researchers collect the data and calculate the various statistics.*
The data are given in Table 8.6.

Table 8.6 Number of word pairs remembered (max = 50).

Experimental group	Placebo control group
27	14
5	19
34	3
19	17
13	16
41	13
19	36
21	8
22	14
8	29
24	1
19	22

First, the ranks are determined. We list the scores from low to high and assign ranks.

1,   3,   5,   8,   8,   13, 13, 14, 14, 16, 17, 19, 19, 19, 19, 21, 22, 22, 24, 27, 29, 34, 36, 41

1,   2,   3,   4,   5,   6,   7,   8,   9,   10, 11, 12, 13, 14, 15, 16, 17, 18, 19, 20, 21, 22, 23, 24

We identify the ties and replace the tied ranks by the mean of the ranks:

1,   3,   5,   8,   8,   13, 13, 14, 14, 16, 17, 19, 19, 19, 19, 21, 22, 22, 24, 27, 29, 34, 36, 41

1,   2,   3,   4,   5,   6,   7,   8,   9,   10, 11, 12, 13, 14, 15, 16, 17, 18, 19, 20, 21, 22, 23, 24

1,   3,   5,   8,   8,   13, 13, 14, 14, 16, 17, 19, 19, 19, 19, 21, 22, 22, 24, 27, 29, 34, 36, 41

1,   2,   3,   4.5, 4.5, 6.5, 6.5, 8.5, 8.5, 10, 11, 13.5,13.5,13.5,13.5,16, 17.5,17.5, 19, 20, 21, 22, 23, 24

We check whether the sum of the ranks = $N(N + 1)/2 = (24 * 25)/2 = 300$.
We enter the ranks in the original table.

Table 8.7

Experimental group		Placebo control group	
Word pairs	Rank	Word pairs	Rank
27	20	14	8.5
5	3	19	13.5
34	22	3	2
19	13.5	17	11
13	6.5	16	10
41	24	13	6.5
19	13.5	36	23
21	16	8	4.5
22	17.5	14	8.5
8	4.5	29	21
24	19	1	1
19	13.5	2	17.5

We calculate:

$R_1 = 20 + 3 + 22 + 13.5 + 6.5 + 24 + 13.5 + 16 + 17.5 + 4.5 + 19 + 13.5 = 173$

$R_2 = 8.5 + 13.5 + 2 + 11 + 10 + 6.5 + 23 + 4.5 + 8.5 + 21 + 1 + 17.5 = 127$

Check whether $R_1 + R_2 = N * (N + 1)/2 = 300$

$$U_1 = N_1 N_2 + \frac{N_1(N_1 + 1)}{2} - R_1 = 12 * 12 + \frac{12 * 13}{2} - 173 = 49$$

$$U_2 = N_1 N_2 + \frac{N_2(N_2 + 1)}{2} - R_2 = 12 * 12 + \frac{12 * 13}{2} - 127 = 95$$

$$U = \min(U_1, U_2) = 49$$

4 *The researchers compare the U-statistic they obtained in step 3 (U = 49) with the cut-off values they defined in step 2 (U_{crit} = 37) and make a decision on the basis of the data.*

Because 49 > 37 the difference between the two conditions is not significant at the .05 level ($p > .05$; $p = .183$ to be exact). Remember that you have to be careful at this stage because smaller U-values are more significant (in contrast to t-values, where larger is more significant)!

In addition, we will add a boxplot to give a better idea of the data (Figure 8.3).

$Mdn_{drug} = 20$ $Mdn_{placebo} = 15$

$Q1_{drug} = 16$ $Q1_{placebo} = 10.5$

$Q3_{drug} = 25.5$ $Q3_{placebo} = 20.5$

$Min_{drug} = 5$ $Min_{placebo} = 1$

$Max_{drug} = 41$ $Max_{placebo} = 36$

The results of the data analysis are summarised as follows in a report: 'There was no significant difference in the number of word pairs remembered by the experimental group (Mdn = 20) and the control group (Mdn = 15, U = 49, $N_1 = N_2 = 12$, $p > .05$).'

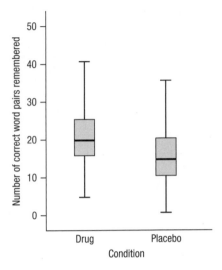

Figure 8.3 Boxplot of the data from the drug experiment. Notice the large overlap of the two conditions. This is in line with the lack of a significant difference.

Learning check 1

To investigate the effects of severe sleep deprivation on creativity, researchers persuaded 5 individuals not to sleep for 96 hours. They compared them to 10 control participants on a task in which the participants had to generate as many uses of a brick as they could in 2 minutes.

These are the results (number of different uses generated):

Sleep deprived : 11, 9, 15, 20, 7
Control : 20, 18, 26, 40, 37, 24, 37, 26, 12, 26

Calculate the Mann-Whitney U-test and interpret the findings.

8.1.7 The Mann-Whitney *U*-test for independent samples in SPSS

For further guidance on carrying out the Mann-Whitney U-test in SPSS, I recommend that you consult Chapter 5 of the Brace, Kemp and Snelgar, SPSS *for Psychologists*.

Interestingly, the Mann-Whitney test does not work in SPSS if you define the group condition as a string variable (Young v. Old). You have to redefine it as a numeric variable (go to *Variable View*) and give it the values 1 (Young) and 2 (Old).

Next click on *Analyze*, *Nonparametric Tests*, *Legacy Dialogs*, and *2 Independent Samples*.

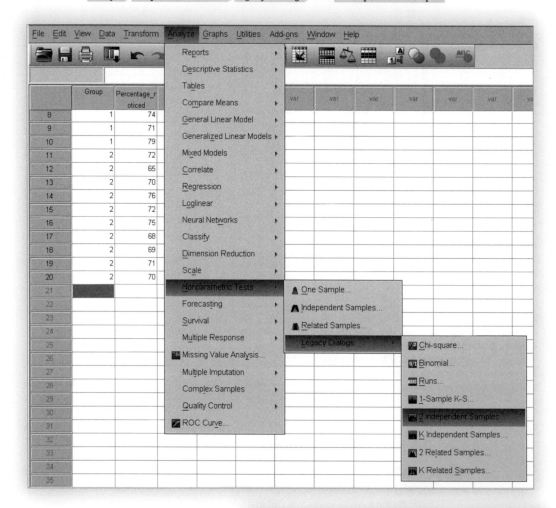

Put 'Percentage_noticed' in the Test Variable List and 'Group' in the Grouping Variable box.

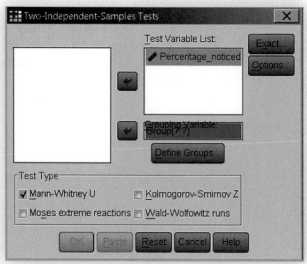

Then *Define Groups* (group1 = 1, group2 = 2) and click on *Continue* and *OK* to get the output.

Ranks				
	Group	N	Mean Rank	Sum of Ranks
Percentage_noticed	1	10	13.90	139.00
	2	10	7.10	71.00
	Total	20		

Test Statistics[b]	
	Percentage_ noticed
Mann-Whitney U	16.00
Wilcoxon W	71.00
Z	-2.582
Asymp. Sig. (2-tailed)	.010
Exact Sig. [2*(1-tailed Sig.)]	.009[a]

a. Not corrected for ties
b. Grouping Variable: Group

From these panels, you can see that $U = 16$, and that the exact *p*-value is $p = .009$, whereas the approximation through the normal distribution is $p = .010$.

Learning check 2
Do the analysis for all the datasets we have seen thus far.

8.1.8 Making a boxplot with SPSS

To make a boxplot, open *Graphs*, *Chart Builder*.

	Group	Percentage_r oticed	var					var	var	
8	1	74								
9	1	71								
10	1	79								
11	2	72								
12	2	65								
13	2	70								
14	2	76								
15	2	72								
16	2	75								
17	2	68								
18	2	69								
19	2	71								
20	2	70								

*Data Mann Whitney U-test.sav [DataSet2] - PASW Statistics Data Editor

File Edit View Data Transform Analyze Graphs Utilities Add-ons Window Help

Chart Builder...
Graphboard Template Chooser...
Legacy Dialogs

In the Gallery choose Boxplot and drag the boxplot and the variables to the work field, so that you have the following outcome.

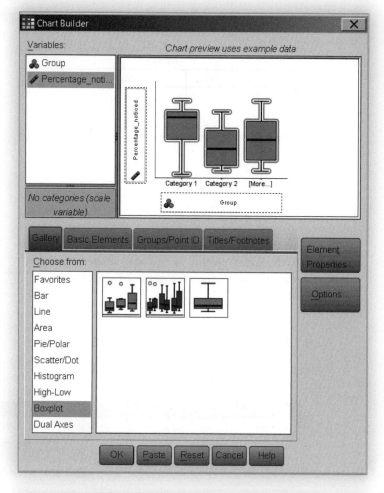

Click on OK to get the following output.

(Notice that I am still working with the data file in which the groups were defined as 1 and 2; this is not necessary, you can also work with Young v. Old.)

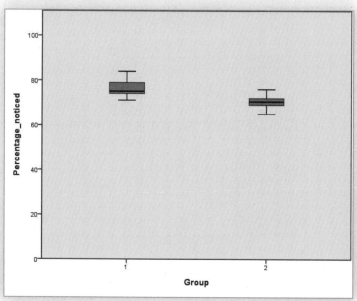

By clicking on the graph, you can make the changes you want. For instance, you can change the Y-axis, so that the values only vary between 60 and 90, and you can give other names to the age groups, so that you get something like this output.

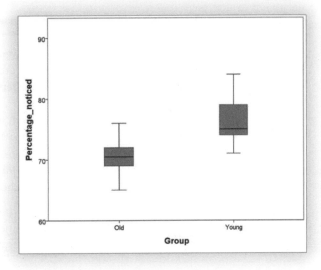

8.2 The one-way chi-square test for nominal data

Thus far we have seen tests for assessing a difference between two independent groups when the data come from an ordinal scale (Mann-Whitney) or an interval/ratio scale (t-test, Mann-Whitney). What do we do when all we have are the frequencies of people in two different groups who show a particular behaviour or who have a particular feature? For instance, how do we test whether men are more likely than women to help someone? And how do we test whether they are more or less willing to help another man than to help a woman?

The test mostly used for the above questions is the two-way chi-square test for an association between two variables (for example, between the gender of the participant and helping v. not helping), as we will see in Chapter 12. However, under some circumstances, we will calculate the one-way chi-square test, which is a simple test of differences in frequencies between two groups. This test can only be used when the sample is divided into complementary groups. In line with the rest of the book, we limit our discussion to the situation in which there are two (complementary) groups.

8.2.1 The one-way chi-square test

An example of a situation where the one-way chi-square test is applicable is the question: 'Are women more successful crime writers than men?' Because there are only two genders, the sample will always comprise two complementary groups.

To answer our question, we can look at a sample of successful crime writers and see whether there are significantly more women among them than men. For instance, we can look at the winners' list of the Gold Dagger award, granted yearly by the Crime Writers' Association for the best crime novel of the previous year (see www.thecwa.co.uk). This award was given for the first time in 1955 (to Winston Graham) and we will use the data up to 2009 (William Brodick), so we have a total of 55 names. Let's see how many of them are female and how many male.

Of the 55 awards, 37 were received by men against 18 by women. This looks like a significant difference but, in order to be sure, we have to check whether it passes a proper statistical test. Otherwise, the chances are too high that we are simply looking at sampling error.

To do a one-way chi-square test, we must first decide what frequencies are to be expected under the null hypothesis. In the example this is quite simple. Given that the null hypothesis states there is no difference between men and women in the number of award winners, both genders should have half of the 55 awards. So, under the null hypothesis we predict that:

expected number of female prize winners = 27.5,
expected number of male prize winners = 27.5.

Next we look at the observed frequencies:

observed number of female prize winners = 18,
observed number of male prize winners = 37.

To calculate the difference between the observed and the expected numbers, we use the following equation:

$$\chi^2 = \frac{(\text{Observed}_{female} - \text{Expected}_{female})^2}{\text{Expected}_{female}} + \frac{(\text{Observed}_{male} - \text{Expected}_{male})^2}{\text{Expected}_{male}}$$

in which χ^2 stands for chi-square and Observed and Expected represent the observed and expected frequencies. Applied to our example, this gives:

$$\chi^2 = \frac{(18 - 27.5)^2}{27.5} + \frac{(37 - 27.5)^2}{27.5}$$
$$= 6.56$$

Look carefully at the equation and its application to the data of the Gold Dagger award. The reasoning behind a chi-square test is pretty straightforward. It is based on the deviations between what is observed and what is expected. These deviations are squared, so that they do not cancel each other out (see our discussion of the standard deviation in Chapter 4). They are then divided by the expected frequencies because a difference of 5 between 10 and 15 is bigger than the same difference between 1010 and 1015. Finally, the deviation scores are summed to give a single statistic.

To know whether the chi-square statistic of 6.56 is significant, we must either compare it to a critical value or directly compute the p-value. Statisticians have shown that if the null hypothesis is true and the deviations observed between two groups are due to sampling error, then 95% of the values fall between $\chi^2 = 0$ and $\chi^2 = 3.84$. So, when two groups are compared, $\chi^2_{.05crit} = 3.84$. Notice that due to the squaring of the differences, χ^2 will never be negative. Also notice that the magnitude of χ^2 has the same interpretation as the t-statistic: the larger its value the more significant the difference in frequencies.

Given that the observed value in our example, $\chi^2 obs = 6.56$, is larger than the critical value $\chi^2_{.05crit}$ (df = 1) = 3.84, we can assume that the observed gender difference in awards bestowed on male and female writers is unlikely to be due to chance. It will either be due to a difference in quality between male and female writers or to the gender-biased criteria which may have been used to judge the winners.

We can also calculate the exact *p*-value associated with the observed chi-square statistic. This can easily be done in a spreadsheet, such as Excel (see Chapter 7 for how to calculate the exact *p*-value of a *t*-statistic with Excel). We just have to use the CHIDIST function, as shown below.

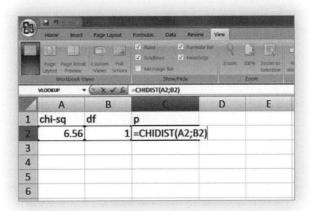

When you press enter, you get the value $p = 0.010429637$, meaning that the gender difference is significant at the .05 level, but would not have been significant if we had set the α-level at .01.

Learning check 3
A university wants to introduce new exam regulations. The university's good practice guidelines stipulate that the new set of rules must get student approval. A sample of 100 students is asked to vote, of which 56 vote against the regulation.

Surprisingly, the university claims it can still introduce the new legislation, because 56 out of 100 does not differ significantly from 50%. Evaluate the statistical evidence on the basis of which this claim is made.

8.3 Answers to chapter questions

1 Why are the Mann-Whitney U-test and the chi-square test called non-parametric tests?

Parametric tests like the *t*-test make assumptions about the frequency distribution of the scores in the conditions. Mostly in parametric tests these distribution are assumed to be normal (and, for instance, to have the same standard deviations) and to be based on a variable from an interval/ratio scale. Non-parametric tests do not make such assumptions. The Mann-Whitney U-test does this by replacing the raw scores by their ranks. The chi-square test simply counts the number of instances in the different conditions.

8

2 Why does the Mann-Whitney U-test have a wider range of applications than the t-test for independent groups?

> The Mann-Whitney U-test can also be applied to ordinal data and to data that are not normally distributed.

3 What is the basic idea behind the Mann-Whitney U-test?

> The basic idea behind the Mann-Whitney U-test is that, if there is no difference between two conditions, then there will be a large overlap in the scores of the conditions. The overlap is estimated by converting the raw X-scores into ranks and comparing the sum of the ranks in one condition with the sum of ranks in the other condition. If there is a big difference between the conditions, then the values (and their ranks) will be higher in one condition than in the other. In contrast, if there is no big difference, the sums of ranks will be nearly equal.

4 Why do people who are familiar with the t-test tend to draw the wrong conclusion on the basis of the Mann-Whitney U-test?

> The significance of a t-statistic (and many other statistics) depends on the magnitude of the statistic: the higher the statistic, the more evidence against the null hypothesis. In contrast, for the Mann-Whitney test (and the Wilcoxon test) small values mean big differences in ranks and are therefore associated with significance. So, whereas you have to check whether the observed t-statistic is larger than the critical value, for the Mann-Whitney test you must check whether the obtained U-value is smaller than the critical value.

5 What are tied data and why do they present a difficulty for the Mann-Whitney test?

> Tied data are X-scores with the same value. They present a difficulty because they must be given the same rank, which has to be the mean of the ranks involved. Many inattentive students (or students who are trying to work quickly) make errors in the assignment of tied ranks.

6 What is a boxplot and why is it interesting?

> A boxplot is a graphical technique to present readers with information about the central tendency and the variability in a condition. It has the same function as the mean and confidence intervals in parametric tests, but can be applied to a wider range of situations. The measure of central tendency is the median. There are two measures of variability: (1) the difference between Q1 and Q3 (the range of the central half of the observations; indicated by the box), and (2) the range between the minimum and the maximum value (indicated by the whiskers; see Figure 8.1). Boxplots are ideal for non-parametric tests and ordinal data.

7 When can you use a one-way chi-square test?

> You can use a one-way chi-square test when the dependent variable is the frequency of a certain observation (that is, nominal data) and when the groups are complementary (that is, a person who is not

part of one condition is automatically part of the other condition). If the groups are not complementaty, you must use a chi-square test of association (Chapter 12). One-way chi-square tests are rare, so be careful about whether you are allowed to use it. (Always check whether the data would not be more in line with the chi-square test of association.)

☑ 8.4 Learning check solutions

Learning check 1

Replace the X-scores by ranks:

7, 9, 11, 12, 15, 18, 20, 20, 24, 26, 26, 26, 37, 37, 40
1, 2, 3, 4, 5, 6, 7, 8, 9, 10, 11, 12, 13, 14, 15

Calculate the ties

7, 9, 11, 12, 15, 18, 20, 20, 24, 26, 26, 26, 37, 37, 40
1, 2, 3, 4, 5, 6, 7.5, 7.5, 9, 11, 11, 11, 13.5, 13.5, 15

Check whether everything is correct:

$1 + 2 + 3 + 4 + 5 + 6 + 7.5 + 7.5 + 9 + 11 + 11 + 11 + 13.5 + 13.5 + 15 = 120$
$(5 + 10) * (5 + 10 + 1)/2 = 15 * 16/2 = 120$

Assign the ranks to the conditions

Sleep deprived		Control	
11	3	20	7.5
9	2	18	6
15	5	26	11
20	7.5	40	15
7	1	37	13.5
		24	9
		37	13.5
		26	11
		12	4
		26	11

Calculate R_1 and R_2

$R_1 = 3 + 2 + 5 + 7.5 + 1 = 18.5$
$R_2 = 7.5 + 6 + 11 + 15 + 13.5 + 9 + 13.5 + 11 + 4 + 11 = 101.5$
Calculation check: $18.5 + 101.5 = 120$

Calculate U

$$U_1 = N_1 N_2 + \frac{N_1(N_1 + 1)}{2} - R_1 = 5 * 10 + \frac{5 * 6}{2} - 18.5 = 46.5$$

$$U_2 = N_1 N_2 + \frac{N_2(N_2 + 1)}{2} - R_2 = 5 * 10 + \frac{10 * 11}{2} - 101.5 = 3.5$$

$U = 3.5$

Compare to $U_{.05crit}$

$N_1 = 5, N_2 = 10: U_{.05crit} = 11$

Because $U_{obs} < U_{crit}$ effect is significant ($p < .05$)

Learning check 2

Observed: 56 no, 44 yes

Expected : 50 no, 50 yes

$$\chi^2 = \frac{(Observed_{no} - Expected_{no})^2}{Expected_{no}} + \frac{(Observed_{yes} - Expected_{yes})^2}{Expected_{yes}}$$

$$\chi^2 = \frac{(56 - 50)^2}{50} + \frac{(44 - 50)^2}{50} = 1.44$$

Given that 1.44 < 3.84 [$\chi^2_{.05crit}$(df=1)], you cannot say that 56 out of 100 is sufficiently different from 50 to be certain that it would be replicated in another study. The chi-square value has too high a chance ($p = .230$) of being observed under the assumption that the null hypothesis is true. This, of course, does not condone the university's policy. Democracy has never been defined in terms of a 'significant' majority. If the university believes there is no majority against the new exam regulation, it should test more students, not misuse stats!

Using the *t*-test to measure change in related samples

9

?

1. What is the difference between an independent groups design and a related samples design?
2. Why is the *t*-test for related samples based on difference scores?
3. How do you calculate the *t*-statistic for related samples?
4. How many degrees of freedom has a *t*-statistic for related samples?
5. How do you calculate the effect size (*d*-statistic) for a *t*-test for related samples?
6. How many participants do you have to include in a design with related samples? How does this compare to a *t*-test for independent groups?
7. How do you calculate the confidence intervals around the means on the basis of a *t*-statistic for related samples?

Thus far we have discussed how you can decide whether two groups of people differ significantly from each other. However, much psychological research does not look at differences between groups but at changes within individuals. Does a person's depression improve after psychotherapy? Do people recognise taboo words more easily than neutral words? Do I study better in a silent environment than when I am listening to my favourite music?

We cannot analyse this type of person-related change with a *t*-test for independent samples, a Mann-Whitney U-test or a chi-square test, because those tests assume that each observation is *independent* of the other. Individual observations (participants) can be added or dropped without influencing the other observations. Such an assumption cannot be made when we are measuring the same individuals repeatedly. A person who is slow at recognising words will be slow at recognising both neutral words and taboo words. A good student will perform better than a poor student, irrespective of the study conditions. So, if we want to replace the observation of a student in one condition, we have to replace the corresponding observation in the other condition as well. The observations from every participant are yoked; they form pairs. A design in which the observations are linked is called a **related samples design** or a **repeated measures design** (because the same participant is tested 'repeatedly').

TIP How do you decide whether a design involves independent groups or related samples?

To decide which design has been used, ask yourself the question: Did the participants take part in both conditions or were different people involved in condition 1 and condition 2? If the same participants take part in both conditions, then you are dealing with a related samples design. If condition 1 and condition 2 involve different participants, then you are dealing with an independent groups design. You can also ask yourself the question: Is it possible to change one value in condition 1 without having to change a corresponding value in condition 2? If this is possible, then you are dealing with independent groups. If not, because the observations come from the same participants and are yoked in pairs, then you are dealing with a related samples design. A related samples design is also called a repeated measures design, because the same participant is tested repeatedly.

In this and the next chapter we will see how to analyse data from related samples. First, we discuss the *t*-test, which can be used with data from an interval/ratio scale. In the next chapter, we discuss the non-parametric alternatives which can also be used with data from ordinal and nominal scales.

9.1　The *t*-statistic for repeated measures

Although this may be hard for you to believe, the *t*-statistic for repeated measures is easy to understand on the basis of what we have covered so far in this book. All you need to know is that we will work with difference scores rather than with the raw observations. Remember that the observations in a related samples design are not independent; they are yoked in pairs. However, the participants' difference scores between condition 1 and condition 2 are independent, and will be used.

Let's explain the reasoning with an example. Suppose I want to test the effectiveness of a new therapy for depression. In order to see whether my therapy has any effect, I need a dependent variable that measures the degree of depression. A widely used test is the Beck Depression Inventory (BDI). It consists of 21 depression symptoms (e.g., sadness, dislike of self) and asks to what extent each symptom applies to the individual under investigation (indicated with a score going from 1 to 3). The maximum score is 63 and the score is interpreted as follows:

≤ 4	Possible denial, faking that all is well; this is a score not usually given by healthy people
5–9	Ups and downs within the normal range
10–18	Mild to moderate depression
19–29	Moderate to severe depression
30–63	Severe depression

Suppose there are 12 people taking part in the study. Before the therapy starts, I ask a relative of each patient to complete the BDI for that patient. Then the patients take part in the therapy which lasts for 12 weeks. Six months after the therapy I ask the same relatives to complete the BDI once more, so that I can measure the long-term effect of the therapy. (Notice that in real life, I would also include a placebo control condition in my study, to make sure that any difference I am finding is due to the therapy and not to the fact that nine months have passed since the initial intake.)

Table 9.1 lists the data I obtained. Before we start running the statistical analysis, it is always good to have a close look at the data. Not unexpectedly, most patients fell in the range of severe depression before the onset of the therapy, although there were quite substantial individual differences. The most

Table 9.1 Beck Depression Inventory scores of 12 patients before the start of a therapy and 6 months after the end of the therapy. Maximum score = 63. Any score above 30 is considered a sign of severe depression. A score between 5 and 9 indicates absence of depression.

	Before	6 months after
patient 1	36	24
patient 2	27	18
patient 3	45	30
patient 4	25	8
patient 5	34	27
patient 6	28	14
patient 7	51	47
patient 8	30	31
patient 9	33	5
patient 10	47	27
patient 11	32	16
patient 12	26	23
	$M_1 = 34.5$	$M_2 = 22.5$

depressive person had a score of 51, the least depressive had a score of 25 (which indicates moderate to severe depression). A second interesting finding is that all but one patient (patient 8) improved, although again to varying extents. Finally, even though the vast majority of patients improved, they cannot be considered symptom-free at the end of the study. Three patients remained in the range of severe depression; only two were in the range of normal ups and downs.

Now that we have a feeling for the data, let's look at what the statistical analysis says.

Hopefully, it will be clear to you that the study in Table 9.1 is a related samples or repeated measures study. The same patients were assessed repeatedly (twice) and if one person's data in condition 2 were missing you could not simply replace it with a value from another person, without at the same time replacing the corresponding value in condition 1 (assuming you had 'spare' data). So, the observations are not independent.

Although the individual observations are not independent, the improvement scores per patient are. You can replace any patient by another patient without influencing the remaining observations. So, the first thing we will do for our repeated measures t-test is to replace the raw scores by difference scores: before – after, showing how much each has patient improved. This is shown in Table 9.2.

Table 9.2 Beck Depression Inventory scores of 12 patients before the onset of a therapy and 6 months after the end of the therapy, together with each patient's improvement score.

	Before	After	Improvement (D = Before – After)
patient 1	36	24	12
patient 2	27	18	9
patient 3	45	30	15
patient 4	25	8	17
patient 5	34	27	7
patient 6	28	14	14
patient 7	51	47	4
patient 8	30	31	−1
patient 9	33	5	28
patient 10	47	27	20
patient 11	32	16	16
patient 12	26	23	3
	$M_1 = 34.5$	$M_2 = 22.5$	$M_D = 12.0$

Because the improvement scores are independent, we can calculate their mean (M_D) and standard deviation (SD_D). For these, we use the auxiliary tables introduced in Chapter 4 (see Table 4.1). This is shown in Table 9.3.

Table 9.3 Calculating the mean and the standard deviation of the improvement scores.

	Improvement (D)	$D - M_D$	$(D - M_D)^2$
patient 1	12	0	0
patient 2	9	−3	9
patient 3	15	3	9
patient 4	17	5	25
patient 5	7	−5	25
patient 6	14	2	4
patient 7	4	−8	64
patient 8	−1	−13	169
patient 9	28	16	256
patient 10	20	8	64
patient 11	16	4	16
patient 12	3	−9	81
	$\Sigma D = 144$	$\Sigma(D - M_D) = 0$	$\Sigma(D - M_D)^2 = 722$

$N = 12$

$M_D = 144/12 = 12$

$$SD_D = \sqrt{\frac{\Sigma(D - M_D)^2}{N - 1}} = \sqrt{\frac{722}{11}} = 8.10$$

We now need the definition of the *t*-statistic for repeated measures:

$$t = \frac{M_{\text{difference score}}}{\frac{SD_{\text{difference score}}}{\sqrt{N}}} = \frac{M_D}{\frac{SD_D}{\sqrt{N}}} = \frac{M_D}{SE_{M_D}}$$

where M_D stands for the mean difference score, SD_D for the standard deviation of the difference scores, N for the number of difference scores (the number of participants) and SE_{MD} for the standard error of the mean difference score.

On the basis of everything you have learned thus far, you should be able to understand the reasoning behind this equation. We are simply dividing the mean difference score (in our example the improvement score) by the standard error of the mean difference score. The standard error of the mean equals the standard deviation divided by the square root of the sample size (Chapter 6).

For large samples, a *t*-value lower than −2 or higher than +2 will imply significance. For smaller sample sizes, we must know the degrees of freedom so that we can look up the exact cut-off scores in Appendix B. The degrees of freedom for a repeated measures *t*-test with N particpants is:

$df = N - 1$

And that's all we need to run a *t*-test for related samples! Applied to our example, this gives:

$$t = \frac{12}{\frac{8.1}{\sqrt{12}}} = \frac{12}{\frac{8.1}{3.46}} = \frac{12}{2.34} = 5.13$$

$df = N - 1 = 12 - 1 = 11$

The critical .05 value for $t(11)$ is 2.179 (see Appendix B), so $p < .05$ (as a matter of fact $p = .000328$). The fact that the improvement score is (highly) significant should not surprise us, given that all but one patient improved between the assessment before the therapy and the assessment six months after the therapy.

Notice how simple statistical tests have become now that we have mastered the basics of statistical reasoning. The same concepts come back again and again. In the next section we discuss how we calculate the effect size and the likelihood ratio of a *t*-test with repeated measures and how many participants we have to examine in order to have a test with sufficient power.

Learning check 1

Calculate the *t*-test for a study in which 5 right-handed participants (2 men and 3 women) squeeze a hand grip dynamometer. They do so with the right hand and the left hand. The results are measured in kilograms. These are the findings:

	Right hand	Left hand
participant 1	45	43
participant 2	62	61
participant 3	28	24
participant 4	21	22
participant 5	27	25

9.2 The effect size, likelihood ratio and power of a *t*-test with repeated measures

9.2.1 The effect size

As discussed in Chapter 7, the significance of a t-test is important, but should not be the only aspect of interest to researchers. Apart from knowing that our therapy has a statistically significant effect on the patients' depressive symptoms, we also want to know the magnitude of the effect in practical terms. Part of this information comes from directly looking at the data, as we did at the beginning of the analysis. As we noted there, although most patients improved, only two of the twelve became symptom-free; three even stayed within the range of severe depression. This is already a serious qualification of our statistically significant effect.

Further insight can be gained by looking at the standardised effect size. Are we talking about a large, a medium or a small effect size? To answer that question, we need to calculate Cohen's *d* statistic:

$$d_{\text{repeated measures}} = \frac{M_{\text{difference score}}}{SD_{\text{difference score}}}$$
$$= \frac{M_D}{SD_D}$$

As you can see, the effect size for repeated measures is just the z-value of the mean difference score (that is, the mean difference score divided by the standard deviation of the difference scores). Applied to our example of the effectiveness of therapy, this gives:

$$d = \frac{12}{8.1} = 1.48$$

Table 9.4 The meaning of individual changes as expressed by the *d*-statistic, explained as the percentage of patients that feel better after a therapy.

Effect size (d)	Interpretation
<0.0	More than half of the patients have a lower quality of life at the end of the therapy than at the beginning.
0.0	At the end of the therapy there is no overall difference in the quality of life; half of the patients feel (slightly) better, half (slightly) worse.
+0.5	At the end of the therapy 70% of the patients feel (slightly) better; 30% feel (slightly) worse; most changes are small; only a few patients feel a clear improvement.
+1.0	At the end of the therapy 84% of the patients feel (slightly) better; about half of the patients feel a real improvement.
+2.0	At the end of the therapy 98% of the patients feel better; most patients experience a clear improvement; a good number are symptom-free.
+3.0	At the end of the therapy 99.8% of the patients feel better; many are symptom-free.

This is a very large effect size in Cohen's terms and, as a matter of fact, comes pretty close to the average effect size obtained with therapies for depression. Still, the data show us that it does not mean everybody is cured after the therapy. For a complete cure we would need effect sizes of 3.0 and more, as shown in Table 9.4.

On the basis of your statistical knowledge, you will be able to understand where the numbers in Table 9.4 come from. The *d*-statistic represents a normal distribution that is shifted *d* standard deviations away from the point of no change. This is shown in Figure 9.1 (see also Appendix A).

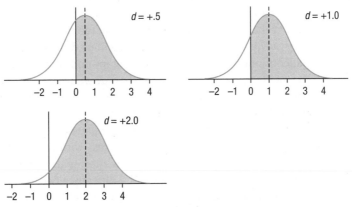

Figure 9.1 What do effect sizes of +.5, +1.0, and +2.0 mean in a repeated measures design? When *d* = +.5, 70% of the difference scores are positive, and 30% are negative. In contrast, when *d* = +2.0, 98% of the difference scores are positive. Remember that in psychological research *d*-values of .5 and smaller are much more common than *d*-values of +1.0. This means that the expected effect will not be observed in all participants!

9.2.2   The likelihood ratio for related samples

Another question we may ask concerns the likelihood of the alternative hypothesis relative to the null hypothesis (Chapter 7). This information is not particularly necessary in this example, where the effect is obvious. However, it is important when researchers are investigating a more subtle effect and are comparing two theories against one another (for example, when the null hypothesis is in line with one theory and the alternative hypothesis is predicted by a rival theory). In such cases, the likelihood ratio is extremely instructive. The equation for the likelihood ratio based on the repeated measures *t*-test again strongly resembles that of the independent groups *t*-test:

$$\text{Likelihood ratio}_{\text{repeated measures}} = \left(1 + \frac{t^2}{N-1}\right)^{N/2}$$

in which N is the number of participants taking part in the study (that is, the number of observations per condition). Applied to the example:

$$\text{Likelihood ratio}_{\text{repeated measures}} = \left(1 + \frac{5.13^2}{12-1}\right)^{12/2} = 1524$$

So, the alternative hypothesis of a helpful effect of the depression therapy is 1524 times more likely than the null hypothesis of no effect, which agrees with the low *p*-value we observed.

9.2.3   How many participants do we need to include in a repeated measures design?

Researchers are very interested in repeated measures designs, not only because they allow them to measure changes in individuals, but also because they are more powerful. Researchers require fewer participants to find a statistically significant effect in a repeated measures design than in an independent groups design, if the difference exists at the population level. To understand this, look at the data in Table 9.1 which shows the large variability between individuals, both at the onset of the therapy and six months after the end of the therapy. If the study had been an independent groups design with two different groups of patients (one without having had therapy and another after having taken part in the therapy), the *t*-statistic of the therapy would have been considerably smaller, because the standard deviations in the two groups would have been included in the *t*-statistic. This is shown in Table 9.5.

Because the differences between the patients are included in the *t*-test with independent groups but not in the *t*-test with related samples, its value will usually be lower than the value of the *t*-test with related samples. For the same data in Tables 9.1 and 9.5, we had a difference between $t(11) = 5.13$ and $t(22) = 2.90$. The degrees of freedom are larger in the *t*-test for independent groups, but this difference does not make up for the loss in *t*-value.

The larger the differences in overall performance between participants, the bigger the difference between the independent groups *t*-value and the related samples *t*-value. (See the Going further section if you want to know why.) Just try it out with a few SPSS analyses. Change the overall scores of the individual

Table 9.5 Independent groups *t*-test for the data of Table 9.1, on the assumption that two different groups of patients have been compared: one group without therapy and the other 6 months after therapy.

Group without therapy	Group with therapy
36	24
27	18
45	30
25	8
34	27
28	14
51	47
30	31
33	5
47	27
32	16
26	23
$M_1 = 34.5$ $SD_1 = 8.69$	$M_2 = 22.5$ $SD_2 = 11.37$

$$t = \frac{M_1 - M_2}{\sqrt{\dfrac{SD_1^2}{N_1} + \dfrac{SD_2^2}{N_2}}} = \frac{34.5 - 22.5}{\sqrt{\dfrac{8.69^2}{12} + \dfrac{11.37^2}{12}}} = 2.90$$

$df = N_1 + N_2 - 2 = 22, \quad p = .008$

patients while keeping their differences constant and see what happens to a related samples *t*-test and to an independent groups *t*-test. For instance, what happens if the first row of data is changed from 36–24 to 64–52 and the second from 27–18 to 11–2? Does it have an effect on the related samples *t*-test? What happens to the independent samples *t*-test? Why is this so?

The higher power of a related samples *t*-test also shows in the minimum number of participants we must test in order to have an 80% chance of finding a significant effect given that there is an effect at the population level. Remember from Chapter 7 that for independent groups we need 786 participants (2 × 393) if we are investigating a small effect size, 128 participants if we are looking at a medium effect size, and 52 participants if we have reasons to believe the effect size will be large. What are the numbers for a related *t*-test?

Table 9.6 lists the minimum numbers of participants you need for the different effect sizes. From this table you can conclude that a typical study with repeated measures can be done with slightly over 30 participants. This allows you to find medium effect sizes. Notice that 30 participants is one-quarter of the number of participants you need for an independent groups study! So, when you plan a study it is worth asking yourself whether it is possible to use a repeated measures design rather than an independent groups design. This will make your study much more feasible (and cheaper).

Table 9.6 Minimum number of participants needed in a related samples study with two conditions as a function of the effect size (α = .05, two-tailed; power of finding the effect = 80%).

Small effect size (*d* = .2)	N = 198
Medium effect size (*d* = .5)	N = 33
Large effect size (*d* = .8)	N = 14

Why are the numbers of participants required for repeated measures designs so much lower than for independent groups designs? For a start, because the same participants are tested twice in a repeated measures design, the number of participants can already be halved. The rest of the reduction is due to the fact that, in a repeated measures design, only the difference scores matter, taking away the variability due to the overall differences in performance between the participants.

Learning check 2
Calculate the effect size and the likelihood ratio of the handgrip study (see Learning check 1). Can you also say something about the power of this experiment?

9.3   The confidence interval for a design with repeated measures

In Chapter 7 we saw how much extra information confidence intervals (CIs) give us in addition to the usual *t*- and *p*-values. So, how do we calculate the confidence interval for a *t*-test with repeated measures?

At this point we are again confronted with a distinction that was introduced in Chapter 7. There are two types of confidence intervals: the confidence intervals of the means of the conditions and the confidence interval of the difference between the conditions. Whereas, for a *t*-test for independent groups, it was easier to calculate and understand the confidence intervals of the means than the confidence interval of the difference, for a repeated measures *t*-test the reverse is true. Because the *t*-test is based on the difference scores of the participants, it is easy to calculate the confidence interval of the mean difference between condition 1 and 2, whereas extra calculations are involved in the confidence intervals of the means. We start with the easiest part: the confidence interval of the difference score.

9.3.1   The confidence interval of M_D, the difference between M_1 and M_2

Because the significance of a repeated measures *t*-test depends on the difference scores, it is easy to calculate the confidence interval on the basis of the difference scores. All we need is the standard error of the difference $M_1 - M_2$.

Remember that $SE = SD/\sqrt{N}$. Therefore, $SE_{MD} = SD_D/\sqrt{N}$. So, the confidence interval around M_D is:

lower limit $CI_{MD} = M_D - t_{.05crit}(df) * SE_{MD}$
upper limit $CI_{MD} = M_D + t_{.05crit}(df) * SE_{MD}$

in which df = N − 1 (where N is the number of participants or data pairs in the study).

Applied to the example of the therapy effectiveness for depression, the confidence interval is:

$M_1 = 34.5; \quad M_2 = 22.5$
$M_D = 12$
$df = N - 1 = 12 - 1 = 11$
$t_{.05crit}(11) = -2.201 \text{ and } +2.201 \text{ (Appendix B)}$
$SE_{MD} = \dfrac{SD_D}{\sqrt{N}} = \dfrac{8.1}{\sqrt{12}} = 2.34$

So, the confidence interval of M_D will be:

lower limit $CI_{MD} = M_D - t_{.05crit}(df) * SE_{MD} = 12 - 2.201 * 2.34 = 6.85$
upper limit $CI_{MD} = M_D + t_{.05crit}(df) * SE_{MD} = 12 + 2.201 * 2.34 = 17.15$

The fact that the confidence interval does not include 0 agrees with the significant effect we found in the t-test.

Learning check 3
Calculate CI_{MD} for the handgrip study (see Learning check 1). Does it include 0?

9.3.2   The confidence intervals around M_1 and M_2

Remember that confidence intervals are particularly useful in graphs if we can add them to the values of M_1 and M_2 (see Figures 7.2 and 7.3). So, how do we get from CI_{MD} to confidence intervals around M_1 and M_2?

One option is to use CI_{MD} in our graphs. To some extent this would make the interpretation of the confidence interval easier than the approach we discussed in Chapter 7 (pp. 167–170). However, to keep the interpretation of confidence intervals of related t-tests in line with all other tests, we have to 'correct' CI_{MD}. The easiest way is to divide CI_{MD} or SE_{MD} by $\sqrt{2}$. Remember from Section 7.1.4 that the standard error of the difference equals the sum of the standard errors of the means: $SE_{diff} = \sqrt{SE_1{}^2 + SE_2{}^2} \approx \sqrt{2}SE_1 \approx \sqrt{2}SE_2$. So, rather than use the values of CI_{MD} and SE_{MD}, we use:

confidence interval of $M_1 = M_1 \pm t_{.05crit}(df) * \dfrac{SE_{MD}}{\sqrt{2}}$

confidence interval of $M_2 = M_2 \pm t_{.05crit}(df) * \dfrac{SE_{MD}}{\sqrt{2}}$

So,

lower limit confidence interval $M_1 = 34.5 - 2.201 * 1.41 = 30.86$
upper limit confidence interval $M_1 = 34.5 + 2.201 * 1.41 = 38.14$

lower limit confidence interval $M_2 = 22.5 - 2.201 * 1.41 = 18.86$
upper limit confidence interval $M_2 = 22.5 + 2.201 * 1.41 = 26.14$

This may seem like a needless detour to you – you have to 'correct' the CIs so that they are more difficult to understand – and to some extent it is. However, this value of CI is the value you get when you calculate the confidence interval on the basis of an analysis of variance (Masson and Loftus, 2003), as we will see in Chapter 13. Because analyses of variance are used much more frequently than t-tests and because the 'corrected' confidence intervals have the same meaning as those of between-groups, most software packages calculate them rather than CI_{MD}.

Figure 9.2 shows the graphs with the 'corrected' values For this particular example it does not make much difference, as the effect was very significant ($p = .000328$). However, for effects that hover around the $p = .05$ border, the difference is more conspicuous.

Finally, notice that even when SE and CI are properly calculated, there is still an important difference between the interpretation of SEs and CIs for related groups designs and independent groups designs. Whereas in the latter, the confidence intervals around the means indicate where the population values are likely to be situated, for a related groups design the confidence intervals

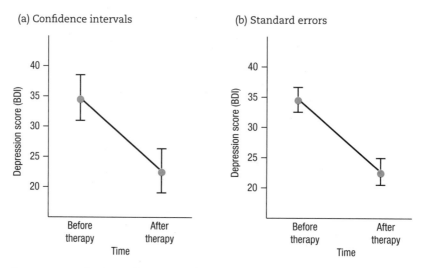

Figure 9.2 Graph of the efficacy of depression therapy with .05 confidence intervals (a) or standard errors (b) that have the same interpretation as for designs with independent groups (Figures 7.2 and 7.3). These are the values you will obtain if you base your calculations on the results of an analysis of variance (Chapter 13). However, when you use a t-test for related groups you must divide SE_{MD} or CI_{MD} by $\sqrt{2}$ to get the correct value of SE and CI.

only give an indication of the size of the population difference between M_1 and M_2. So, if we repeated the therapy effectiveness study of Table 9.1, we would not expect the depression scores to be between 30.85 and 38.15 before the therapy starts and between 18.185 and 16.15 six months after the therapy (these values depend on the specific group of patients we test). However, we would expect to find improvement scores between 6.85 and 17.15, and this is what the confidence intervals in the graph convey.

Learning check 4
Calculate the correct confidence intervals around the means for the handgrip study so that we can include them in a graph (see Learning check 1).

9.4 Step by step: a *t*-test for repeated measures

 We've covered quite a lot of ground in this chapter so this would be a good opportunity to summarise it all with another example. In that way you can easily check whether you have understood everything.

The new example features a psychologist who wants to test whether it is true that students' intelligence is lower after the summer holidays than before. Such a claim has been made on the basis that students do not exercise their brains much over the summer and therefore show a decline in their brain power. To find out whether the claim is correct, the psychologist tests a sample of 20 first-year students at the end of term 3 (after the exams) and at the beginning of term 1 of the following academic year. In each session, the students complete the Raven's progressive matrices test. This is an IQ test that primarily measures fluid intelligence (the use of working memory to solve unknown reasoning problems). The raw test scores are converted to IQ scores with a mean of 100 and a standard deviation of 15.

There are four steps in the hypothesis test.

1 *Define the null hypothesis and the alternative hypothesis.*
In this example the null hypothesis is that of no difference in IQ scores before and after the holidays, so the mean difference score will not differ from 0. The alternative hypothesis is that a significant difference in IQ scores will be observed between the two assessments. This difference will be large enough that it is unlikely to be due to sampling error.

2 *Define the critical values for the t-statistic.*
The psychologist uses an α-level of .05 and a two-tailed test. (These are the default options in psychological research; Chapter 7). Given that 20 students will be tested, df = N − 1 = 19 and $t_{05crit}(19) = -2.093$ or +2.093.

3 *Collect the data and calculate the statistics.*
These steps are shown in the Tables 9.7 and 9.8.

Table 9.7 IQ scores of first year psychology students immediately before and after the summer holidays.

	Before	After	Difference
student 1	106	98	8
student 2	135	131	4
student 3	124	123	1
student 4	111	119	–8
student 5	128	112	16
student 6	119	125	–6
student 7	107	113	–6
student 8	114	114	0
student 9	156	140	16
student 10	110	116	–6
student 11	124	121	3
student 12	109	113	–4
student 13	118	117	1
student 14	122	119	3
student 15	123	124	–1
student 16	115	118	–3
student 17	133	129	4
student 18	123	124	–1
student 19	117	111	6
student 20	128	125	3
	$M_1 = 121.1$	$M_2 = 119.6$	$M_D = 1.5$

Table 9.8 Auxiliary table to calculate the *t*-statistic.

	D	D – M$_D$	(D – M$_D$)^2
student 1	8	6.5	42.25
student 2	4	2.5	6.25
student 3	1	–0.5	.25
student 4	–8	–9.5	90.25
student 5	16	14.5	210.25
student 6	–6	–7.5	56.25
student 7	–6	–7.5	56.25
student 8	0	–1.5	2.25
student 9	16	14.5	210.25
student 10	–6	–7.5	56.25
student 11	3	1.5	2.25
student 12	–4	–5.5	30.25
student 13	1	–0.5	.25
student 14	3	1.5	2.25
student 15	–1	–2.5	6.25
student 16	–3	–4.5	20.25
student 17	4	2.5	6.25
student 18	–1	–2.5	6.25
student 19	6	4.5	20.25
student 20	3	1.5	2.25
	$\Sigma D = 30$	$\Sigma(D - M_D) = 0$	$\Sigma (D - M_D)^2 = 827$

$$N = 20, \quad M_D = 1.5, \quad SD_D = \sqrt{\frac{\Sigma(D - M_D)^2}{N - 1}} = \sqrt{\frac{827}{19}} = 6.597, \quad t = \frac{M_D}{\dfrac{SD_D}{\sqrt{N}}} = \frac{1.5}{\dfrac{6.597}{\sqrt{20}}} = 1.017$$

4 *Compare the obtained t-value with the critical value.*

Because $t_{obt}(19) = 1.017$ does not exceed $t_{.05crit}(19) = 2.179$, the difference is not significant at the .05 level (the exact *p*-value = .322). On the basis of the available evidence, the psychologist is not able to reject the null hypothesis that students' IQ scores remain the same over the summer holidays.

As well as the hypothesis test, we will calculate measures that help us to better understand the finding. These measures are the effect size, the likelihood ratio and the confidence intervals to be included in a graph. In addition, always look at the raw data themselves. Given that we found a difference in IQ scores between 121.1 and 119.6 (a difference of 1.5), this is unlikely to have a big impact in practical terms! Keep this in mind when you do your analyses and when you discuss your findings.

First we calculate the effect size:

$$d = \frac{M_D}{SD_D} = \frac{1.5}{6.597} = .23$$

This is a small effect size, meaning that a study with only 20 participants may lack the power to find the effect even if it is present at the population level. We would want to see at least 198 participants. The calculation of the effect size is a good reminder of the fact that failing to reject a null hypothesis does not imply that the alternative hypothesis is wrong. We just fail to find enough evidence for it. The situation would be different if we had tested 1000 participants. If we then still fail to observe a significant effect, we can be sure that any effect at the population level must be very small. This study only suggests that if holidays have an effect on the intelligence of students, the effect is likely to be small.

The status of the alternative hypothesis vis-à-vis the null hypothesis is better understood if we calculate the likelihood ratio:

$$\text{Likelihood ratio}_{\text{repeated measures}} = \left(1 + \frac{t^2}{N-1}\right)^{N/2} = \left(1 + \frac{1.017^2}{20-1}\right)^{20/2} = 1.7$$

This means that the alternative hypothesis is 1.7 times more likely than the null hypothesis, which is too small a margin to attach any weight. (Remember that the ratio must be around 10 in order to be safe enough to interpret.)

Finally, we calculate the confidence intervals we need for our graph. First, we calculate SE_{MD}:

$$SE_{MD} = \frac{SD_D}{\sqrt{N}} = \frac{6.597}{\sqrt{20}} = 1.475$$

Next we divide SE_{MD} by $\sqrt{2}$ to get the values of error bars around the means:

$$SE = \frac{SE_{MD}}{\sqrt{2}} = \frac{1.475}{1.414} = 1.04$$

Finally, we calculate the confidence intervals around the means:

lower limit $CI_1 = M_1 - t_{.05\text{crit}}(19) * SE = 121.1 - 2.093 * 1.04 = 118.9$
upper limit $CI_1 = M_1 + t_{.05\text{crit}}(19) * SE = 121.1 + 2.093 * 1.04 = 123.3$

lower limit $CI_2 = M_2 - t_{.05\text{crit}}(19) * SE = 119.6 - 2.093 * 1.04 = 117.4$
upper limit $CI_2 = M_2 + t_{.05\text{crit}}(19) * SE = 119.6 + 2.093 * 1.04 = 121.8$

When we add these confidence intervals to the graph of our data (Figure 9.3), we can easily see why the difference in IQ is not significant, and how large the difference would have to be in order to reach significance.

Figure 9.3 Results of the study in which students' IQs were tested before and after the summer holidays with the CIs added. The bars represent the .05 confidence intervals.

9.5   Running a *t*-test with repeated measures in SPSS

The *t*-test with repeated measures is called the paired *t*-test in Brace, Kemp, and Snelgar, *SPSS for Psychologists*. It is discussed in section 3 of Chapter 4.

For a repeated measures analysis in SPSS all observations of a person must be written on the same line. So, for the therapy example we have two columns: one with the depression scores before the therapy and one with the depression scores six months after the therapy. Enter the data in SPSS, by first defining the variables in Variable View and then entering the data in Data View.

After entering and saving the data, click on *Analyze*, *Compare Means* and *Paired-Samples T Test*.

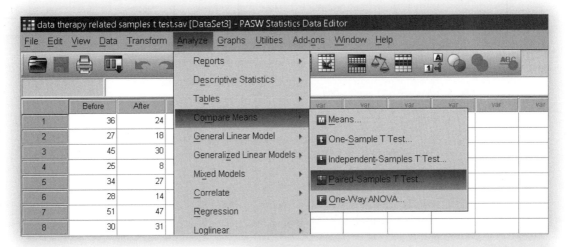

This will open the dialogue box:

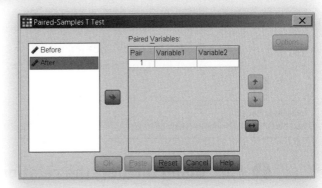

Assign 'Before' to Variable1 and 'After' to Variable2 by clicking on the variable name and the central arrow.

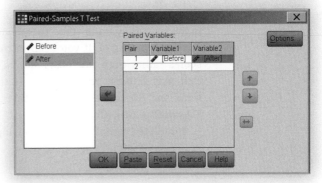

Click on **OK** to get the output.

Paired Samples Statistics

		Mean	N	Std. Deviation	Std. Error Mean
Pair 1	Before	34.50	12	8.692	2.509
	After	22.50	12	11.374	3.283

Paired Samples Test

		Paired Differences							
					95% Confidence Interval of the Difference				
		Mean	Std. Deviation	Std. Error Mean	Lower	Upper	t	df	Sig. (2-tailed)
Pair 1	Before – After	12.000	8.102	2.339	8.852	17.148	5.131	11	.000

These tables contain all the information you need for your analyses. To reiterate:

$$t(11) = 5.131, \quad p < .001$$

$$d = \frac{M_D}{SD_D} = \frac{12}{8.102} = 1.48$$

$$\text{Likelihood ratio} = \left(1 + \frac{t^2}{N-1}\right)^{N/2} = \left(1 + \frac{5.13^2}{12-1}\right)^{12/2} = 1524$$

$$SE = \frac{SE_{MD}}{\sqrt{2}} = \frac{2.339}{1.414} = 1.65$$

confidence interval of $M_1 = M_1 \pm t_{.05crit}(11) * SE$
confidence interval of $M_2 = M_2 \pm t_{.05crit}(11) * SE$

So,

lower limit confidence interval $M_1 = 34.5 - 2.201 * 1.65 = 30.86$
upper limit confidence interval $M_1 = 34.5 + 2.201 * 1.65 = 38.14$

lower limit confidence interval $M_2 = 22.5 - 2.201 * 1.65 = 18.86$
upper limit confidence interval $M_2 = 22.5 + 2.201 * 1.65 = 26.14$

Learning check 5
Run the SPSS analysis for the study on IQ loss as a result of holidays (Table 9.7). Do you obtain the correct values?

9.6 Going further: the relationship between SD_D, SD_1 and SD_2

If you have fully understood the previous chapters, nothing in this chapter will have surprised you. If you keep in mind that we are working with difference scores rather than raw observations, all the rest follows logically. One thing that may interest you, however, is the relationship between SD_D on the one hand and SD_1 and SD_2 on the other. Remember that for independent groups $SD_D{}^2 = SD_1{}^2 + SD_2{}^2$ (Chapter 7).

For related samples, the relationship is:

$$SD_D{}^2 = SD_1{}^2 + SD_2{}^2 - 2r * SD_1 * SD_2$$

The only new term is *r*, which stands for the Pearson product-moment correlation between the scores in condition 1 and 2. This correlation will be discussed in Chapter 11, so you may want to defer reading the remainder of this section until you have studied Chapter 11. Everything will be much clearer then.

The relationship between SD_D and SD_1 and SD_2 shows that the variability of the difference scores depends on the correlation between the scores in condition 1 and condition 2. The more positive this correlation, the lower SD_D will be, with a limit of 0 when $r = +1.00$. (This will be the case when the difference score is exactly the same for each participant; then $r = +1.00$, $SD_D = 0$, and $t = \infty$.)

The relationship between SD_D and SD_1 and SD_2 also informs you that SD_D will not always be lower than SD_1 and SD_2. When there is a negative correlation between the scores, SD_D will be larger. However, one would have to search hard to find such a situation in reality!

❓ 9.7 Answers to chapter questions

1 **What is the difference between an independent groups design and a related samples design?**

A design with independent groups involves different people in each condition (that is, two groups of different people when two conditions are compared with one another). Because of this, each observation is independent of all the others and can be replaced without problem. In contrast, a design with related samples involves the same group of participants taking part in all conditions (that is, in both conditions when two conditions are compared). In such a design, it is not possible to replace an observation in one condition without at the same time having to replace the corresponding observation in the other condition(s), because the observations are yoked for each participant.

2 **Why is the *t*-test for related samples based on difference scores?**

Because the values in the two conditions come from the same participants, they are not independent. However, the difference score between the conditions for each participant is independent (and can be replaced without problem). Therefore, the *t*-test for related samples is based on the difference scores of the participants.

3 **How do you calculate the *t*-statistic for related samples?**

$$t = \frac{M_{\text{difference score}}}{\frac{SD_{\text{difference scores}}}{\sqrt{N}}} = \frac{M_D}{\frac{SD_D}{\sqrt{N}}} = \frac{M_D}{SE_{M_D}} \quad \text{(where N = number of participants)}$$

4 **How many degrees of freedom has a *t*-statistic for related samples?**

df = N − 1 (where N = number of participants)

5 **How do you calculate the effect size (*d*-statistic) for a *t*-test for related samples?**

$$d_{\text{repeated measures}} = \frac{M_{\text{difference score}}}{SD_{\text{difference score}}} = \frac{M_D}{SD_D}$$

6 How many participants do you have to include in a design with related samples? How does this compare to a t-test for independent groups?

The number depends on the effect size you are measuring. If you expect to find a medium effect size ($d = .5$), you need 33 participants; for a small effect size ($d = .2$) you need 198 participants; and for a large effect size ($d = .8$) you can get away with 14 participants. These numbers are roughly one-quarter of those needed in a design with independent groups. The reasons for this are: (1) the participants take part in both conditions, and (2) the differences in overall performance between the participants are not included in the variability of the difference scores.

7 How do you calculate the confidence intervals around the means on the basis of a t-statistic for related samples?

This is a bit tricky because it is much easier to calculate the confidence interval of the mean difference than the confidence intervals around the means. The simplest option (unless you know how to calculate an analysis of variance) is first to calculate the standard error of the difference and then to divide this by $\sqrt{2}$.

$$SE_{M_D} = \frac{SD_D}{\sqrt{N}}$$

$$SE \text{ for the means} = \frac{SE_{M_D}}{\sqrt{2}}$$

CI around the means =
    $$\text{Mean} \pm t_{.05crit}(df = N - 1) * SE \text{ for the means}$$

☑ 9.8 Learning check solutions

Learning check 1

$M_1 = 36.6$, $M_2 = 35$, $D = 1.6$, $SD_D = 1.82$, $t(4) = 1.97$, $t_{.05crit}(4) = 2.776$; so, no significant effect ($p = .12$)

Learning check 2

$d = .88$, likelihood ratio = 5.4. The estimated effect size is big, meaning that with 14 participants we have an 80% chance of obtaining significance (provided that this estimate on the basis of a small sample is not too far off the effect size at the population level). If the researcher wants to be sure about the difference in grip strength between the left and the right hand, she/he is advised to test another 10 participants to see whether the effect turns out to be significant.

Learning check 3

The 95% confidence interval of the difference between the right and the left hand or $CI_{\bar{D}}$ goes from $-.66$ to $+3.86$. It includes 0, as we could expect from the fact that the t-statistic was not significant.

Learning check 4

The confidence interval around the mean of the right hand goes from 35.01 to 38.19; that around the mean of the left hand goes from 33.41 to 36.59. The overlap between the CIs is in line with the finding of a non-significant difference.

Non-parametric tests to measure changes in related samples

10

?

1 What is the difference between the Mann-Whitney U-test and the Wilcoxon signed-rank test?
2 Why does the Wilcoxon signed-rank test have a wider range of applications than the t-test for related samples?
3 What is the basic idea behind the Wilcoxon signed-rank test?
4 Why do people who are familiar with the t-test tend to misinterpret the W-statistic in the Wilcoxon signed-rank test?
5 Why do you have to be careful with the N used in the Wilcoxon signed-rank test?
6 What is a boxplot of the differences and why is it interesting?

The t-test for related samples makes a number of (reasonable) assumptions about the data. Two of these are that the difference scores come from a normal distribution and are part of an interval/ratio scale. Otherwise, there is no point in calculating standard deviations of difference scores and using t-distributions. If you have reasons to doubt these assumptions, or if you just wish to see whether your data pass a non-parametric test as well as a parametric test, the Wilcoxon signed-rank test is your alternative.

10.1 The Wilcoxon signed-rank statistic

Just like the Mann-Whitney U-test, the Wilcoxon signed-rank test avoids the problem of unequal intervals between numbers by replacing the raw data by their ranks. So rather than using the raw difference scores, the Wilcoxon signed-rank test works with the ranks of the difference scores. We will again explain the process by using an example.

Suppose I want to test the efficacy of a self-esteem booster session. Such a session involves employees of an international company learning to focus on the positive things they have done in the past day, rather than on the negative things that have happened. As an easy assessment measure, I simply ask the participants to indicate on a scale from 0 to 100 how satisfied they are with their performance (0 = not satisfied at all, 100 = fully satisfied). Participants give a rating before the session and one month after the session. Twenty-four employees take part. Table 10.1 gives the data.

As always, before we start the statistical analysis it is good practice to have a look at the data themselves. We see that, before the booster session, most employees are reasonably satisfied with their performance. Most participants have a score above 50, although two had rather low scores (19 and 22). There seems to be improvement for some (with a highlight of 46 for participant 9), but a slight deterioration for others (with a maximum difference of 10 for participant 19, who had a high score in condition 1). If we look at the medians (which we have to do if we think the scale may not be interval/ratio; Chapter 2), we see little difference between the first and the second measurement. Will this imply that there is no statistically significant difference?

To find out, we have to run a statistical test. Because of the nature of the dependent variable (rating scale) we may not be confident that the data form an interval scale. The difference between 40 and 60 may not be the same as the difference between 80 and 100. Therefore, we prefer to use a non-parametric test. Because the data are not independent from each other but are yoked in pairs (Chapter 9), we have to use a non-parametric test for related samples. The one used most often is the **Wilcoxon signed-rank test**.

For the Wilcoxon signed-rank test we first calculate the difference scores. In this particular example, it is more interesting to define the difference score as 'after minus before'. Then positive scores indicate an improvement, whereas negative scores indicate a decrease in satisfaction (Table 10.2). The results of the Wilcoxon signed-rank test, just like those of the related-samples t-test, do not

Table 10.1 Efficacy of a self-esteem booster session for employees of a company. Dependent variable is participants' satisfaction rating of their performance (0 = not satisfied at all, 100 = fully satisfied). Measures were obtained before the booster session and 1 month after the session.

	Before	After
participant 1	70	75
participant 2	81	78
participant 3	76	83
participant 4	94	89
participant 5	45	54
participant 6	53	60
participant 7	22	18
participant 8	67	70
participant 9	19	65
participant 10	52	56
participant 11	82	83
participant 12	75	79
participant 13	95	99
participant 14	84	85
participant 15	74	69
participant 16	66	72
participant 17	55	62
participant 18	52	52
participant 19	89	79
participant 20	57	56
participant 21	81	85
participant 22	48	41
participant 23	73	77
participant 24	65	66
Mdn =	68.5	71.0

depend on the direction of the differences, So, we are free to choose. Be careful, however, to make sure you know the direction of the differences, so that you can see whether the findings are in line with your expectations or go against them! (Remember that a [two-tailed] statistical test does not tell you whether the difference is in the right direction; it only tells you whether the difference is large enough to be reliable.)

Next, we rank the difference scores from minimum to maximum on the basis of their ABSOLUTE values. These are the scores independent of the sign. So, we rank the participants from those who showed no difference after the booster session to those who showed the largest difference. This is shown in Table 10.3, columns 3 and 4.

Table 10.2 Difference scores for the self-esteem booster session example.

	Before	After	Difference: After – Before
participant 1	70	75	5
participant 2	81	78	–3
participant 3	76	83	7
participant 4	94	89	–5
participant 5	45	54	9
participant 6	53	60	7
participant 7	22	18	–4
participant 8	67	70	3
participant 9	19	65	46
participant 10	52	56	4
participant 11	82	83	1
participant 12	75	79	4
participant 13	95	99	4
participant 14	84	85	1
participant 15	74	69	–5
participant 16	66	72	6
participant 17	55	62	7
participant 18	52	52	0
participant 19	89	79	–10
participant 20	57	56	–1
participant 21	81	85	4
participant 22	48	41	–7
participant 23	73	77	4
participant 24	65	66	1

When we assign ranks, we first have to discard the participants with zero difference, because this score cannot be assigned a positive or a negative value.[1] So, we will discard participant 18 from our ranking. Next, we give each person an increasing rank number according to their absolute difference score (column 6 of Table 10.3). Finally, we correct for ties (Chapter 8; see column 7 of Table 10.3). We do this by taking the average rank of the tied scores. Be careful with the tie correction, because many students make errors here! Control your outcome by ensuring that the sum of the ranks equals $N*(N+1)/2$ both for the original ranks and the ranks with ties, as also shown in Table 10.3. (Remember N is the number of participants with non-zero difference scores.)

1 Some authors include the ranks of 0 differences and divide them equally over W+ and W–. This makes sense, but has not been done in the statistical packages I have been checking.

Table 10.3 Ranks of the absolute difference scores for the self-esteem booster session example.

	Before	After	$D_{After - Before}$	Abs(D)	Rank	Rank$_{with ties}$
participant 18	52	52	0	(0)		
participant 11	82	83	1	1	1	2.5
participant 14	84	85	1	1	2	2.5
participant 20	57	56	−1	1	3	2.5
participant 24	65	66	1	1	4	2.5
participant 2	81	78	−3	3	5	5.5
participant 8	67	70	3	3	6	5.5
participant 7	22	18	−4	4	7	9.5
participant 10	52	56	4	4	8	9.5
participant 12	75	79	4	4	9	9.5
participant 13	95	99	4	4	10	9.5
participant 21	81	85	4	4	11	9.5
participant 23	73	77	4	4	12	9.5
participant 1	70	75	5	5	13	14
participant 4	94	89	−5	5	14	14
participant 15	74	69	−5	5	15	14
participant 16	66	72	6	6	16	16
participant 3	76	83	7	7	17	18.5
participant 6	53	57	7	7	18	18.5
participant 17	55	62	7	7	19	18.5
participant 22	48	41	−7	7	20	18.5
participant 5	45	54	9	9	21	21
participant 19	89	79	−10	10	22	22
participant 9	19	65	46	46	23	23
					ΣR = 276	ΣR = 276

$$\frac{N(N+1)}{2} = \frac{23 * 24}{2} = 276$$

Be careful: N has been calculated on the basis of the participants with non-zero difference scores!

If the booster session has had no effect, then we would expect roughly equal numbers of positive and negative difference scores. In addition, we would expect the absolute magnitudes of the difference scores to be roughly the same for the positive and negative scores. In contrast, if the booster session has had a positive effect, we would expect to find more positive difference scores than negative ones and their magnitudes will probably be larger. Finally, if the booster session has had a harmful effect, we would expect to find more negative difference scores than positive and they will be larger.

So, by comparing the sum of ranks of the positive difference scores with the sum of ranks of the negative difference scores, we can estimate the impact of the intervention. At one extreme, if the effect is positive for each and every participant, we will find a sum of zero for negative differences and a sum equal to $N*(N+1)/2$ for positive differences (N is the number of participants with non-zero difference scores). At the other extreme, if the effect is negative for all participants, we will find a sum of zero for positive differences and a sum equal to $N*(N+1)/2$ for negative differences. In reality, we will mostly find sums of ranks between these two extremes.

In our example, the sum of the positive ranks is:

$\Sigma R_+ = 3*2.5 + 5.5 + 5*9.5 + 14 + 16 + 3*18.5 + 21 + 23 = 190$

The sum of the negative ranks is:

$\Sigma R_- = 2.5 + 5.5 + 9.5 + 2*14 + 16 + 18.5 + 22 = 86$

> **Tip** Two errors often made in the calculation of the Wilcoxon signed-rank statistic are:
>
> 1 The ranks and N are not corrected for participants with zero difference scores.
> 2 The W-statistic is not based on the smallest sum of ranks.
>
> Make sure you are not making these errors! Check your solution.

As a control, we can check whether $\Sigma R_+ + \Sigma R_- = N*(N+1)/2$, in which N = the number of participants with a non-zero difference score. In our example N = 23, so $N*(N+1)/2 = 23*24/2 = 276 = 190 + 86$.

The Wilcoxon signed-rank statistic W is the minimum of ΣR_+ and ΣR_-. So, in our example W = $min(\Sigma R_+, \Sigma R_-) = min(190, 86) = 86$.

10.2   The Wilcoxon signed-rank test

Knowing the value of the Wilcoxon signed-rank statistic is necessary to do a Wilcoxon signed-rank test, but not enough. We also need to assign a p-value to the statistic to find out whether the effect is statistically significant.

Either we can do this with SPSS (see below) or a freely available website that does the calculation for us (see the website that accompanies this book, www. palgrave.com/pschology/brysbaert), or we can make use of a table with critical values, as in Appendix D.

Before we look at the critical values, let's first think for a minute about the meaning of the Wilcoxon signed-rank statistic. As we said in the previous section, when there are no positive or negative difference scores, then either the sum of positive ranks will be zero ($\Sigma R_+ = 0$) or the sum of negative ranks will be zero ($\Sigma R_- = 0$). In both cases W = 0 because it is the minimum of ΣR_+ and ΣR_-. So, just like the Mann–Whitney test, but unlike the t-test and the chi-square test, **the smaller the Wilcoxon signed-rank statistic W, the greater the likelihood that the effect is significant**. Keep this in mind!

How small the Wilcoxon signed-rank statistic has to be before it becomes significant depends on N, the number of participants with non-zero difference scores in the study.

> **Be careful!** As for the Mann-Whitney U-statistic, you must remember that the smaller the Wilcoxon signed-rank statistic, the smaller is p. A statistic of W = 0 means significance (unless N is smaller than 6). This differs from the interpretation of the t-statistic and the χ^2 statistic!

For N smaller than 6, there is no point in running the Wilcoxon signed-rank test, because it can never be significant. (The chances of finding 5 or fewer negative or positive differences in a row are simply too high.).

For N = 6, we have significance when the observed W statistic, W_{obs}, equals 0 (because $W_{.05crit}$ = 0). That is, all difference scores above 0 must be in the same direction.

For larger Ns, we have significance whenever the observed W-value is **smaller than or equal to** the critical W-value listed in Appendix D. For instance, for N = 10, $W_{.05crit}$ = 8. This means that we will have significance when $W_{obs} \leq 8$. For N = 20, $W_{.05crit}$ = 52, and for N = 50, $W_{.05crit}$ = 434. Appendix D lists critical values for all values of N up to 50.

Because in our example $W_{.05crit}$ = 73 (N = 23) and W_{obs} = 86, we fail to reject the null hypothesis at the .05 level (as a matter of fact, p = .117).

For N > 15, a good approximation is given by the equation:

$$z = \frac{W - \dfrac{N*(N+1)}{4}}{\sqrt{\dfrac{N*(N+1)*(2N+1)}{24}}}$$

in which z is a standard normal score (Chapter 5). For our example:

$$z = \frac{86 - \dfrac{23*24}{4}}{\sqrt{\dfrac{23*24*47}{24}}} = -1.58$$

As you can see in Appendix A, this z-score has an associated p-value of .114 (that is, twice the p-value of the smallest tail; see Section 7.7 for more information about how to calculate the p-value of a two-tailed test).

10.3   How to report a Wilcoxon signed-rank test

When we report the results of a Wilcoxon signed-rank test in a manuscript, we have to inform the reader about the number of participants, the number of participants with a zero difference score, the W-value and the p-value. For the self-esteem example we would write something like:

'We studied the usefulness of a booster session on the self-esteem of employees in a multinational company. Participants indicated on a rating scale from 0 to 100 how satisfied they were with their performance (0 = not satisfied at all, 100 = fully satisfied). They completed the rating scale before the session and one month after the session. The results were analysed with the Wilcoxon signed-rank test for related samples. From the analysis it emerged that there was no significant difference between the self-esteem ratings before the session (Mdn = 68.5) and one month after the session (Mdn = 71; W = 86, N = 23 (excluding 1 person with a zero difference score), p = .12).'

10.4   Adding a confidence interval to your graph

As for the other tests we discussed, you may wonder how best to convey the information to the reader. How do we include information about the confidence interval around the medians, so that the reader can see at a glance the magnitude of the effect that was found?

Here things are getting difficult, because there is no generally recommended procedure for this in the literature. What we can do, however, is to make a boxplot of the difference scores.

10.4.1 A boxplot of the difference scores

Remember from Chapter 8 that a boxplot contains information about the median, Q1 and Q3 (together giving the range in which half of the data fall), the minimum value and the maximum value (giving the range of all the data). A boxplot of difference scores is calculated on the basis of the differences between condition 1 and condition 2 for all participants (that is, the improvement scores in our example). The position of the boxplot relative to 0 indicates the strength

Table 10.4 Ranked difference scores (minimum to maximum) for the self-esteem booster session example. These ranks are needed to draw a boxplot of the differences.

	Before	After	$D_{After-Before}$	
participant 19	89	79	−10	minimum value = −10
participant 22	48	41	−7	
participant 4	94	89	−5	
participant 15	74	69	−5	
participant 7	22	18	−4	
participant 2	81	78	−3	Q1 = (−3 − 1)/2 = −2
participant 20	57	56	−1	
participant 18	52	52	0	
participant 11	82	83	1	
participant 14	84	85	1	
participant 24	65	66	1	
participant 8	67	70	3	median = (3 + 4)/2 = 3.5
participant 10	52	56	4	
participant 12	75	79	4	
participant 13	95	99	4	
participant 21	81	85	4	
participant 23	73	77	4	
participant 1	70	75	5	Q3 = (5 + 6)/2 = 5.5
participant 16	66	72	6	
participant 3	76	83	7	
participant 6	53	57	7	
participant 17	55	62	7	
participant 5	45	54	9	
participant 9	19	65	46	maximum value = 46

of the evidence for a significant effect. If 0 lies within the box between Q1 and Q3, then there certainly is no significant effect; if 0 falls outside the full range, then there certainly is a significant effect.

This is the information we need for the boxplot:

1. The median of the difference scores, Mdn. As discussed in Chapter 3, this is the score that divides the frequency distribution in half.
2. The first quartile of the difference scores, Q1. This is the score that divides the frequency distribution in ¼ v. ¾. It is the median of the lower half of the data.
3. The third quartile of the difference scores, Q3. This is the score that divides the frequency distribution in ¾ v. ¼. It is the median of the upper half of the data.
4. The minimum value.
5. The maximum value.

To calculate the above values, we rank the difference scores from the smallest to the largest, as is shown in Table 10.4. Be careful here! This time we do not rank according to the absolute values as in Table 10.3, but according to the raw values, going from the most negative difference score to the most positive. The values needed for the boxplot can then easily be read or calculated from the table.

Notice that the value of the median of the difference scores we obtain ($\text{Mdn}_{\text{difference scores}}$ = 3.5) is slightly different from the value $\text{Mdn}_2 - \text{Mdn}_1$ we had in Table 10.1 ($\text{Mdn}_2 - \text{Mdn}_1 = 71 - 68.5 = 2.5$). This is due to the way in which the measures are calculated. It is not a problem, although it is not arithmetically pleasing (which is one of the reasons why researchers prefer to use means whenever they can).

Figure 10.1 shows the box plot of the difference scores for the example of the self-esteem booster session. You can easily see that the effect is not significant, as 0 falls within the box.

Incidentally, as we will see below, when you make a boxplot with a commercially available statistical software package (such as SPSS), the upper whisker of the example will not go all the way up to +46, because this value will be seen as an outlier (indicated by an unconnected symbol, such as a star).

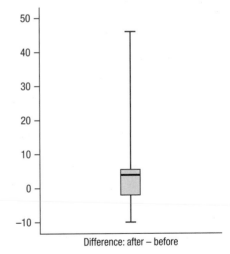

Difference: after – before

Figure 10.1 A boxplot of the difference scores for the self-esteem study. Because the zero difference score is part of the box, we immediately see that the booster session has had no significant effect.

10.4.2   Integrating the boxplot of the differences in a bar graph

We can further integrate the information provided by the boxplot of the differences within a bar graph representing the medians of the conditions. This is done by placing the boxplot between the two bars of the medians in such a way that the zero difference coincides with the median of the condition that is subtracted (that is, condition 1 if the difference scores are defined as condition 2 minus condition 1). You must make sure that you use the same scale for the boxplot and the bar graph!

Figure 10.2 shows how such a graph looks when we integrate the boxplot of Figure 10.1 into a bar graph representing the medians of the conditions. It is immediately obvious that the difference between the conditions is not significant because the box of the difference scores is wider than the difference between the conditions. In this figure, however, you get information both about the median values and the range of difference scores.

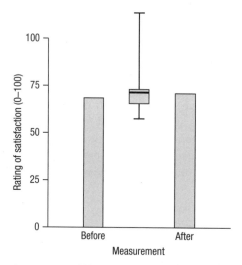

Figure 10.2 Adding a boxplot of the difference scores to the bar graph of the medians. In this way, we provide readers with information about the uncertainty range around the difference between the two medians, so that they can easily see the reliability of the difference. Notice that the box is placed in such a way that a zero difference coincides with the median of the condition that is subtracted.

10.5   The Wilcoxon signed–rank test as an alternative to the *t*-test for related samples

Because the Wilcoxon signed-rank test makes fewer assumptions than the related samples t-test, it can be used as an alternative test. Most of the time it will be slightly less powerful (that is, the p-values will be slightly higher), but the test is less sensitive to outliers and, therefore, provides interesting additional information. To see how well the Wilcoxon signed-rank test does relative to the related samples t-test, we can apply it to the two examples we used in Chapter 9.

These were the summary data of the two examples:

Efficacy depression therapy:
Before M_1 = 34.5
After M_2 = 22.5
N = 12
$t(11) = 5.13, p = .00033$

IQ scores of students:
Before summer holidays M_1 = 121.1
After summer holidays M_2 = 119.6
N = 20
$t(19) = 1.02, p = .322.$

These are the results of the Wilcoxon signed-rank test (please verify them as a learning check):

Efficacy depression therapy: $W = 1, N = 12, p = .00098$

IQ scores of students: $W = 78.5, N = 19$ (excluding 1 person with a zero difference score), $p = .505$

So, the Wilcoxon signed-rank test can indeed be used as an alternative to the related samples t-test. In the vast majority of situations it will yield exactly the same conclusion. Only when the p-value is close to the .05 boundary, is it possible that one test is just over the significance 'threshold' whereas the other is not. This is in line with the insight that the .05 cut-off score should not be seen as a strict border but as an area of uncertainty around which an effect starts to gain enough statistical credit to be taken seriously. Given the ease with which the related samples t-test and the Wilcoxon signed-rank test can be computed nowadays, it is always a good idea to run both tests, just to be sure that the effect you are observing is significant/non-significant in both.

To show you how a graph with a boxplot of the difference scores looks when the effect is significant, Figure 10.3 illustrates the findings of the efficacy study

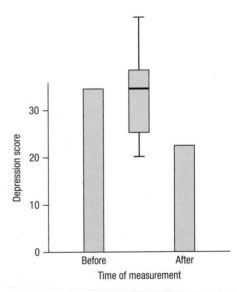

Figure 10.3 A boxplot showing the differences in the therapy efficacy study. Because the lower condition falls outside the box, you know that the effect has a high chance of being significant (verify the W-statistic to be sure). The graph also indicates that not all participants showed the effect, because the median of the measurement after the therapy does not fall outside the lower whisker.

for depression. As you can see, the median of the lowest condition falls outside the box of the differences, suggesting significance. The figure also shows that there was one participant who did not show an improvement (the median of the measurements after the therapy does not fall outside the lower whisker).

10.6 Step by step: the Wilcoxon signed-rank test

An environmental psychologist investigates whether refurbishing a home for the elderly increases their well-being. A Likert-scale with 20 questions is administered two weeks before the refurbishment and two weeks after. Each question has to be answered on a 7-point scale, going from 1 – totally disagree to 7 – totally agree. The total score is the sum of the ratings (max = 140). These are the four steps that should be made in the research:

1   *Define the null hypothesis and the alternative hypothesis.*
In this example the null hypothesis is that of no difference in well-being before and after the refurbishment. In this case, the mean difference score will not differ from zero. The alternative hypothesis is that of a significant difference in well-being between the two assessments. This difference will be large enough that it is unlikely to be due to sampling error.

2   *Define the cut-off value for the Wilcoxon signed-rank test.*
The cut-off value can be found in Appendix D. The psychologist intends to test all 10 residents of the home. She uses an α-level of .05 and a two-tailed test. (These are the default options in psychological research; Chapter 7). Be careful at this stage: the number of participants is not necessarily the same as the N under which you will have to search in Appendix D. Remember that N is the number of non-zero differences! So, it is better not to choose $W_{.05crit}$ yet, but to wait until you know how large N is after step 3.

3   *Collect the data and calculate the statistics.*

	Before	After	$D_{After - Before}$
Resident 1	86	95	9
Resident 2	54	53	−1
Resident 3	79	77	−2
Resident 4	66	73	7
Resident 5	20	20	0
Resident 6	35	52	17
Resident 7	67	64	−3
Resident 8	56	49	−7
Resident 9	47	68	21
Resident 10	63	90	27
	Mdn = (56 + 63)/2 = 59.5	Mdn = (64 + 68)/2 = 66	

Ranking and statistics

	$D_{\text{After − Before}}$	Abs(D)	Raw Rank	Tied Rank
Resident 5	0	0	—	
Resident 2	−1	1	1	1
Resident 3	−2	2	2	2
Resident 7	−3	3	3	3
Resident 4	7	7	4	4.5
Resident 8	−7	7	5	4.5
Resident 1	9	9	6	6
Resident 6	17	17	7	7
Resident 9	21	21	8	8
Resident 10	27	27	9	9
			$\Sigma R = 45$	$\Sigma R = 45$

$$\frac{N(N+1)}{2} = \frac{9 * 10}{2} = 45$$

$\Sigma R_- = 1 + 2 + 3 + 4.5 = 10.5$

$\Sigma R_+ = 4.5 + 6 + 7 + 8 + 9 = 34.5$

$\Sigma R_- + \Sigma R_+ = 10.5 + 34.5 = 45$

$W_{\text{obs}} = \min(\Sigma R_-, \Sigma R_+) = \min(10.5, 34.5) = 10.5$

N = number of non-zero difference scores = 9

4   *Compare the observed statistic with the critical value and determine whether the effect is statistically significant.*

First, $W_{.05\text{crit}}$ is established on the basis of the number of non-zero difference scores. In the example this is 9 (and not 10, because one participant had a difference of zero). $W_{.05\text{crit}} = 5$ for N = 9. Next, the position of W_{obs} relative to W_{crit} is determined. Be careful! For the Wilcoxon signed-rank test, like for the Mann-Whitney U-test, the observed value must be *smaller than or equal to* the critical value to be significant. Given that $W_{\text{obs}} = 10.5$ is larger than $W_{.05\text{crit}} = 5$, the psychologist fails to reject the null hypothesis. In her report, the psychologist would write that 'Although there was a trend towards higher well-being after the refurbishment (Mdn = 66) than before (Mdn = 59.5), the difference was not significant in a Wilcoxon signed-rank test (W = 10.5, N = 9 (one participant showed no difference), p > .05).'

If the psychologist had taken a proper course on statistics, she would have known that the chances of finding a significant effect with only 10 participants at the outset of the study were pretty low unless there was an effect size of *d* > 1.0 at the population level (Table 9.5). Otherwise, the test lacks the necessary power (Chapter 7). Figure 10.4 summarises the findings.

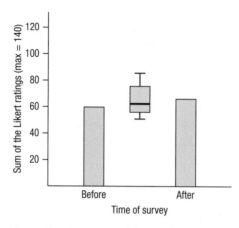

Figure 10.4 Summary of the findings from a study of well-being in residents of a home for elderly before and after a refurbishment.

10.7   The Wilcoxon signed-rank test in SPSS

The Wilcoxon signed-rank test is discussed in section 6 of Chapter 3 in Brace, Kemp, and Snelgar, *SPSS for Psychologists*.

To run the Wilcoxon signed-rank test in SPSS for the self-esteem booster study, we first enter the data and then select *Analyze*, *Nonparametric Tests*, *Legacy Dialogs*, *2 Related Samples*.

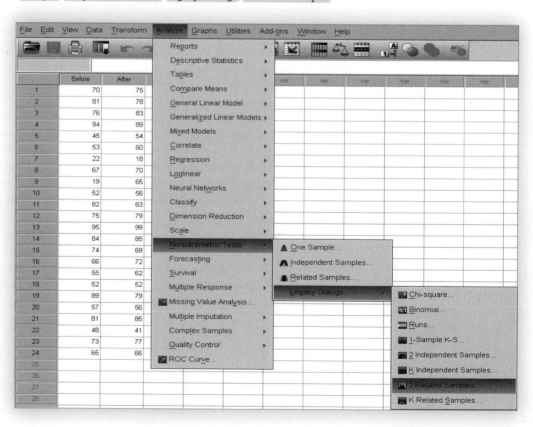

This opens the dialogue box:

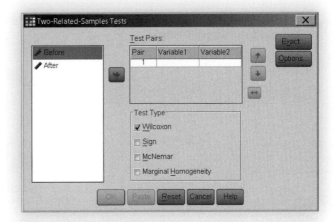

Put Before in Variable1 and After in Variable2 by using the central arrow, so that you get following.

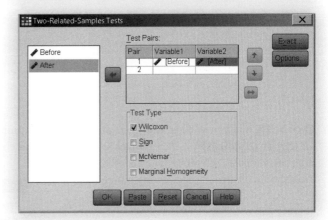

Click on **OK** to get the output.

Ranks

		N	Mean Rank	Sum of Ranks
After – Before	Negative Ranks	7[a]	12.29	86.00
	Positive Ranks	16[b]	11.88	190.00
	Ties	1[c]		
	Total	24		

a. After < Before
b. After > Before
c. After = Before

Test Statistics[b]

	After – Before
Z	−1.587[a]
Asymp. Sig. (2-tailed)	.112

a. Based on negative ranks.
b. Wilcoxon Signed Ranks Test

If you also want the exact rather than the approximate probability, click on *Exact* in the upper panel of the Two-Related-Samples test.

To make a boxplot of the difference scores, start by defining a new variable called Difference. Click on *Transform* and *Compute Variable*.

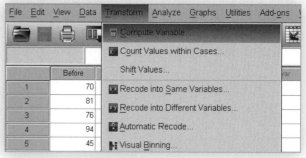

Define a new variable 'Difference' as After – Before.

Click on *OK* and you will see that your data window contains a new column named Difference. Click on *Graphs*, *Chart Builder*. Select *Boxplot* and drag it to the chart preview box in the upper right. Then drag the variable Difference to the Y-axis.

This should give you the following panel.

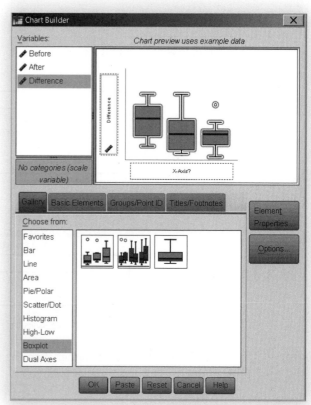

Click on OK to get the output, which looks as follows.

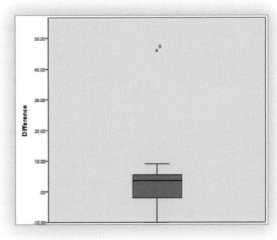

By double clicking on the graph, you can edit it to your liking. Also notice that in this graph the value +46 is considered to be an outlier (which it truly is).

10.8 Answers to chapter questions

1 What is the difference between the Mann-Whitney U-test and the Wilcoxon signed-rank test?

Both are non-parametric tests, but the Mann-Whitney U-test is used with independent groups, whereas the Wilcoxon signed-rank test is used with related samples (that is, paired data that come from participants who take part in both conditions).

2 Why does the Wilcoxon signed-rank test have a wider range of applications than the t-test for related samples?

The Wilcoxon signed-rank test is a non-parametric test. This means that it can be used in all situations in which the related-samples t-test can be used. However, it can also be used in situations where the data are not normally distributed or come from an ordinal scale.

3 What is the basic idea behind the Wilcoxon signed-rank test?

The basic idea is that if the null hypothesis is true, some participants will show a positive difference between the conditions and others a negative difference. To check whether this is the case, we look at the distribution of the ranks of the positive and the negative differences by calculating the sum of the positive ranks and the sum of the negative ranks. If the sums are more or less the same, we know that there is no (big) difference between the conditions. If one sum is considerably larger than the other, then we know that one condition yielded substantially larger or smaller values than the other.

4 Why do people who are familiar with the t-test tend to misinterpret the W-statistic in the Wilcoxon signed-rank test?

In a t-test large values of t point to a bigger difference between the conditions and, hence, increased chances of a significant effect. In contrast, for the signed-rank test the smaller the W-statistic (with a minimum of zero), the more significant the difference becomes.

5 Why do you have to be careful with the N used in the Wilcoxon signed-rank test?

In the Wilcoxon signed-rank test, differences of zero are not included in the test. Therefore N does not refer to the number of participants that took part in the study, but to the number of participants with a non-zero difference between the two conditions.

6 What is a boxplot of the differences and why is it interesting?

A boxplot of the differences is a graphic representation of the difference scores obtained in the sample of participants. It indicates the median difference score, the difference between Q3 and Q1 (the central half of the differences scores), and the range between the minimum and the maximum difference score. The boxplot can be integrated within the bar graph representing the median values of the conditions and allows the reader to immediately grasp the significance of the difference between the conditions. If the box of the boxplot is larger than the difference between the median of condition 1 and the median of condition 2, you immediately know that the effect is not significant. If the box is considerably smaller than the difference, you know that the effect is significant (see Figure 10.3).

Improving predictions through the Pearson correlation coefficient

11

In Chapter 1 we saw how correlations help us to improve our predictions. If we are asked to guess the height of a mystery person and we are allowed three questions, we will ask questions that improve our estimate because they *are correlated with* a person's height. One question could be about the age of the person because we know that children are generally smaller than adults. (Up to the age of 16 (girls) or 18 (boys) there is a positive correlation between age and height.) The second question might be about the gender of the person because we know that men are taller than women, at least from the age of 13 years. Finally, we could ask about the height of the person's mother or father, because there is a positive correlation between the height of parents and the height of the offspring: Tall parents in general have tall children. On the basis of the answers to these three questions, we would expect our guess to be closer to the real height of the mystery person. This does not mean that our guess will always be correct, but it increases our chances of being closer to the target.

In the same way, psychologists will search for correlations to enable them to understand and predict phenomena. Which variables make a person more vulnerable to depression? Which variables predict whether a person may become a good athlete? Which variables tell us whether a child needs special provisions for education? To answer these questions, psychologists will look at correlations. Two questions are important: (1) how strong is the correlation, and (2) is the correlation significant? We deal with these questions successively.

11.1 The Pearson product-moment correlation coefficient

11.1.1 The discovery of the correlation coefficient

The development of the **correlation coefficient** started with Sir Francis Galton, a relative of Charles Darwin and a great scientist in his own right. Galton was particularly interested in the heredity of characteristics of living organisms. If Darwin's evolution theory was right, he reasoned, parents had to be able to pass on their qualities to their offspring. Galton is famous (and, some say, notorious) for his research on the heredity of human intelligence and how this could be measured. However, his need for a correlation coefficient started with a much simpler question: How could he study the heredity of seed sizes in sweet peas? Galton was interested in sweet peas because they show considerable variety and because they can self-fertilise. It was, therefore, possible to look at the similarity between mothers and daughters without having to take into account the murky interference of fathers (see Salsburg (2001) and Stanton (2001)).

In 1875 Galton gave packets of sweet pea seeds to seven friends. Each friend was given a packet with seeds of a particular size, and different packets contained different seed sizes. After the summer, the friends returned the newly harvested seeds to Galton, who measured the first 100 of them (that is, for each mother size, $N = 100$) and made a table of the observations (Table 11.1).

Table 11.1. Raw data on the diameters of parent and daughter seeds, based on the table published by Galton in 1894. Each cell contains the number of mother-daughter pairs. For instance, the value in the upper left cell (0) means that there were no pairs in which the mother had a diameter of 15 and the daughter a diameter of 22. The second cell of the first column (2) indicates that there were two pairs of mothers with diameter 15 and daughters with diameter 20.5; and so on. The rows are ordered from largest daughter size (top) to smallest daughter size (bottom), to increase the correspondence with Figure 11.1. The second last row of the table contains the number of observations per mother diameter (this was always 100). The last row gives the mean diameter of the daughters per column (for example, the mean diameter of the daughters from mothers with diameter 15 was 15.80).

		Diameter of parent seed (0.01 inch)						
		15	16	17	18	19	20	21
Diameter of daughter seed (0.01 inch)	22.0	0	0	0	0	1	2	2
	20.5	2	1	1	2	2	3	6
	19.5	4	3	4	6	10	13	13
	18.5	14	13	13	16	11	20	21
	17.5	11	16	16	17	13	17	18
	16.5	9	18	13	13	12	12	10
	15.5	14	15	16	12	16	10	8
	14.0	46	34	37	34	35	23	22
	N	100	100	100	100	100	100	100
Mean daughter diameter, M		15.80	16.05	15.99	16.28	16.25	17.01	17.21

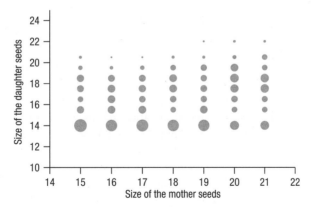

Figure 11.1. Graphical representation of Galton's data based on Table 11.1. The number of pairs in each cell is indicated by the magnitude of the circle. For instance, the lower left circle represents the 46 mother-daughter pairs with sizes 15–14 (see the lower left cell of Table 11.1). Similarly, the upper dot of the leftmost column represents the 2 mother-daughter pairs with sizes 15–20.5 (second cell of column 1 in Table 11.1).

Galton's problem was how to interpret his data, which are shown graphically in Figure 11.1. From the graph we see that there is some 'correlation' (a word introduced by Galton) between the size of the mother seeds and the size of the daughter seeds: on average, daughters from big mothers are larger than daughters from small mothers. This becomes clear when we plot mean daughter diameter against mother diameter (see Figure 11.2).

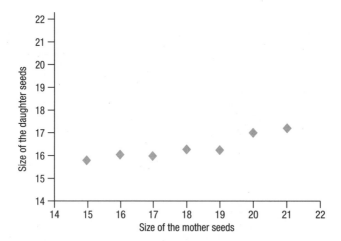

Figure 11.2. Graphical representation of Galton's data based on mean daughter diameters rather than the raw data. The increase in average daughter diameter with increasing mother size indicates that there is a correlation between the sizes of the mother and daughter seeds.

At the same time, Galton could not deny that there was considerable variability in the data. The largest daughters of the small mothers were larger than the smallest daughters of the large mothers. (Compare the highest left dot with the lowest right dot in Figure 11.1.) Galton did not know how to communicate this aspect of the data except by showing a table like Table 11.1. (He made some rudimentary attempts to come up with a more appropriate correlation coefficient, but he lacked the mathematical sophistication to do so properly.)

Finally, Galton noticed that the daughters of small mother peas on average were larger than their mothers, whereas the daughters of large mother peas on average were smaller than their mothers. If you look at Table 11.1, you see that mothers of size 15 have daughters of 15.8, whereas mothers of 21 have daughters of 17.21.

One of Galton's collaborators, Karl Pearson, developed in 1895 a measure that would describe the relationship between the two variables, which he called the **product-moment correlation**. He was helped in this endeavour by a paper that had been published in 1846 by the French scientist Auguste Bravais.

11.1.2   Pearson's product-moment correlation coefficient

So, how does Pearson's measure look? Actually, it is a very straightforward extension of what we already know. Basically, we are trying to understand the variability in the scores. Remember from Chapter 4 that the variability is captured as the variance or the standard deviation of the scores. These are the equations we defined:

$$\text{variance}_{\text{sample}} = \frac{\Sigma(X - M)^2}{N - 1}$$

$$SD_{\text{sample}} = \sqrt{\text{variance}_{\text{sample}}}$$

$$= \sqrt{\frac{\Sigma(X - M)^2}{N - 1}}$$

In Galton's data we have two distributions of variables: the sizes of the mother peas and the sizes of the daughter peas. So, we have two variances (or standard deviations).

In addition to the variances of the variables, we also need to know the extent to which the two variables co-vary. For instance, if the mother pea is small, is the daughter pea small as well? Or is it large? Or is it sometimes small, sometimes of a medium size and sometimes large? One way to capture the co-variation of the two variables is to look at the values of the variables relative to their means. Rather than looking at the raw data, we look at the deviation between each observation and the mean of that variable. (Notice that this is also what we do when we calculate the variance and the standard deviation.) In particular, we will look at the values of $(X_1 - M_1)(X_2 - M_2)$.

To illustrate this, we will work with a simplified example. Suppose Galton only had data from three pairs of mother and daughter peas, as in Table 11.2.

Table 11.2 Simplified example of the relationship between the size of mother peas and the size of daughter peas

	Size of mother	Size of daughter
Pair 1	15	16
Pair 2	18	17
Pair 3	21	18

To calculate $(X_1 - M_1)(X_2 - M_2)$, we first must know M_1 and M_2. In this example they are pretty easy to calculate: $M_1 = (15 + 18 + 21)/3 = 18$, $M_2 = (16 + 17 + 18)/3 = 17$. This gives us the auxiliary table (Table 11.3).

Table 11.3 Auxiliary table to calculate the values of $(X_1 - M_1)(X_2 - M_2)$ for the data in Table 11.2. Also included is the sum of these values.

	X_1	X_2	$X_1 - M_1$	$X_2 - M_2$	$(X_1 - M_1)(X_2 - M_2)$
Pair 1	15	16	−3	−1	−3 * −1 = 3
Pair 2	18	17	0	0	0 * 0 = 0
Pair 3	21	18	3	1	3 * 1 = 3
	$M = 18$	$M = 17$			$\Sigma(X_1 - M_1)(X_2 - M_2) = 6$

Because the value of X_2 is smaller than M_2 when X_1 is smaller than M_1 and because it is larger than M_2 when X_1 is larger M_1, the product $(X_1 - M_1)(X_2 - M_2)$ is always positive (see Table 11.3). So the sum of $(X_1 - M_1)(X_2 - M_2)$ becomes a reasonably high positive number. In other words, a positive value of $\Sigma(X_1 - M_1)(X_2 - M_2)$ indicates that X_1 and X_2 co-vary in the same direction:

☐ if one is high, the other is also high;
☐ if one is low, the other is also low; and
☐ if one is medium, the other is medium too.

Now, how does the situation look when X_1 and X_2 vary in opposite directions? In that case, each time X_1 is smaller than the mean M_1, X_2 will be larger than the mean M_2, and vice versa. Table 11.4 shows the implications of this situation.

Table 11.4 Auxiliary table to calculate $\Sigma(X_1 - M_1)(X_2 - M_2)$ when X_1 and X_2 vary in opposite directions.

	X_1	X_2	$X_1 - M_1$	$X_2 - M_2$	$(X_1 - M_1)(X_2 - M_2)$
Pair 1	15	18	−3	+1	−3 * 1 = −3
Pair 2	18	17	0	0	0 * 0 = 0
Pair 3	21	16	3	−1	3 * −1 = −3
	$M = 18$	$M = 17$			$\Sigma(X_1 - M_1)(X_2 - M_2) = -6$

As you can see, $\Sigma(X_1 - M_1)(X_2 - M_2)$ now becomes a negative number, because each time $(X_1 - M_1)$ is positive $(X_2 - M_2)$ is negative and vice versa, so that the end result is a high negative value.

A third situation arises when there is no unidirectional relationship between X_1 and X_2, as shown in Table 11.5.

Table 11.5 Auxiliary table to calculate $\Sigma(X_1 - M_1)(X_2 - M_2)$ when there is no unidirectional relationship between X_1 and X_2.

	X_1	X_2	$X_1 - M_1$	$X_2 - M_2$	$(X_1 - M_1)(X_2 - M_2)$
Pair 1	15	16	−3	−1	−3 * −1 = 3
Pair 2	18	19	0	2	2 * 0 = 0
Pair 3	21	16	3	−1	3 * −1 = −3
	$M = 18$	$M = 17$			$\Sigma(X_1 - M_1)(X_2 - M_2) = 0$

In such a situation $\Sigma(X_1-M_1)(X_2-M_2)$ has a value close to zero because sometimes (X_2-M_2) is negative when (X_1-M_1) is negative, but at other times it is negative when (X_1-M_1) is positive. In the end, the negative and the positive values of $(X_1-M_1)(X_2-M_2)$ cancel each other out.

In summary, the sum of $(X_1-M_1)(X_2-M_2)$ will be positive when both variables vary in the same direction. It will be negative when the variables vary in opposite directions. And it will be close to zero when there is no unidirectional relationship between the first and the second variable.

The sum of $(X_1-M_1)(X_2-M_2)$ is a good measure of the co-variation of X_1 and X_2 but it has two major disadvantages. First, its value depends on the number of data pairs. If we add a new data pair to our examples, the chances are high that $\Sigma(X_1-M_1)(X_2-M_2)$ will become larger (unless the new data pair contradicts the co-variation that is present in the other data pairs). You can try this out: add the data pair 12–15 or 14–17 to Table 11.3 and see what happens to $\Sigma(X_1-M_1)(X_2-M_2)$.

The second problem is that the value of $\Sigma(X_1-M_1)(X_2-M_2)$ depends on the magnitude of the X_1-M_1 and X_2-M_2 values. For instance, when the standard deviation of X_1 increases, the X_1-M_1 values will be larger and result in a higher value of $\Sigma(X_1-M_1)(X_2-M_2)$, as shown in Table 11.6. All that has changed in this table relative to Table 11.3 is that the values of X_1 are further apart. For the rest, the relationship between X_1 and X_2 stays exactly the same.

Table 11.6 Table indicating what happens to $\Sigma(X_1-M_1)(X_2-M_2)$ when the standard deviation in X_1 is increased by changing two values: X_1 changes from 15, 18, 21 to 14, 18, 22.

	X_1	X_2	X_1-M_1	X_2-M_2	$(X_1-M_1)(X_2-M_2)$
Pair 1	14	16	–4	–1	$-4*-1=4$
Pair 2	18	17	0	0	$0*0=0$
Pair 3	22	18	4	1	$4*1=4$
	M = 18	M = 17			$\Sigma(X_1-M_1)(X_2-M_2)=8$

At this point, the standard deviations (or variances) of X_1 and X_2 come into play because you can prove that $\Sigma(X_1-M_1)(X_2-M_2)$ will never be larger than $\sqrt{\Sigma(X_1-M_1)^2}*\sqrt{\Sigma(X_2-M_2)^2}$. As you may notice, the terms in the latter expression are closely related to the standard deviations of X_1 and X_2. All you have to do is take the denominator $\sqrt{N-1}$ from the definition of the standard deviation.

If we divide $\Sigma(X_1-M_1)(X_2-M_2)$ by $\sqrt{\Sigma(X_1-M_1)^2}*\sqrt{\Sigma(X_2-M_2)^2}$, we get an expression that will never be more negative than –1 or more positive than +1. In other words, we have a measure that standardises the co-variation. The value of this measure is independent of the number of data pairs that are entered and it is also independent of the standard deviations of X_1 or X_2, as shown in Table 11.7.

Table 11.7 Demonstration that $\Sigma(X_1 - M_1)(X_2 - M_2)\Big/\sqrt{\Sigma(X_1 - M_1)^2} * \sqrt{\Sigma(X_2 - M_2)^2}$ does not differ when the standard deviation of X_1 changes.

	X_1	X_2	X_1-M_1	X_2-M_2	$(X_1-M_1)(X_2-M_2)$
Pair 1	15	16	−3	−1	−3 * −1 = 3
Pair 2	18	17	0	0	0 * 0 = 0
Pair 3	21	18	3	+1	3 * 1 = 3

$\Sigma(X_1 - M_1)(X_2 - M_2) = 3 + 0 + 3 = 6$

$\Sigma(X_1 - M_1)^2 = (-3)^2 + (0)^2 + (3)^2 = 18 \qquad \Sigma(X_2 - M_2)^2 = (-1)^2 + (0)^2 = (1)^2 = 2$

$SD_1 = \sqrt{\dfrac{\Sigma(X_1 - M_1)^2}{N - 1}} = \sqrt{\dfrac{18}{3 - 1}} = \sqrt{9} = 3 \qquad SD_2 = \sqrt{\dfrac{\Sigma(X_2 - M_2)^2}{N - 1}} = \sqrt{\dfrac{2}{3 - 1}} = \sqrt{1} = 1$

$r = \dfrac{\Sigma(X_1 - M_1)(X_2 - M_2)}{\sqrt{\Sigma(X_1 - M_1)^2}\sqrt{\Sigma(X_2 - M_2)^2}} = \dfrac{6}{\sqrt{18} * \sqrt{2}} = \dfrac{6}{\sqrt{18 * 2}} = \dfrac{6}{\sqrt{36}} = 1.00$

	X_1	X_2	X_1-M_1	X_2-M_2	$(X_1-M_1)(X_2-M_2)$
Pair 1	14	16	−4	−1	−4 * −1 = 4
Pair 2	18	17	0	0	0 * 0 = 0
Pair 3	22	18	4	+1	4 * 1 = 4

$\Sigma(X_1 - M_1)(X_2 - M_2) = 4 + 0 + 4 = 8$

$\Sigma(X_1 - M_1)^2 = (-4)^2 + (0)^2 + (4)^2 = 32 \qquad \Sigma(X_2 - M_2)^2 = (-1)^2 + (0)^2 = (1)^2 = 2$

$SD_1 = \sqrt{\dfrac{\Sigma(X_1 - M_1)^2}{N - 1}} = \sqrt{\dfrac{32}{3 - 1}} = \sqrt{16} = 4 \qquad SD_2 = \sqrt{\dfrac{\Sigma(X_2 - M_2)^2}{N - 1}} = \sqrt{\dfrac{2}{3 - 1}} = \sqrt{1} = 1$

$r = \dfrac{\Sigma(X_1 - M_1)(X_2 - M_2)}{\sqrt{\Sigma(X_1 - M_1)^2}\sqrt{\Sigma(X_2 - M_2)^2}} = \dfrac{8}{\sqrt{32} * \sqrt{2}} = \dfrac{8}{\sqrt{32 * 2}} = \dfrac{8}{\sqrt{64}} = 1.00$

The equation shown in Table 11.7 is the **Pearson product-moment correlation**. It is given the symbol r (introduced by Galton) and defined as:[1]

$$r = \frac{\Sigma(X_1 - M_1)(X_2 - M_2)}{\sqrt{\Sigma(X_1 - M_1)^2 \Sigma(X_2 - M_2)^2}}$$

As indicated above, the meaning of the correlation is simply:

$$r = \frac{\text{degree to which } X_1 \text{ and } X_2 \text{ vary together}}{\text{degree to which } X_1 \text{ and } X_2 \text{ vary separately}}$$

1 If you're mathematically minded, you may have guessed that the actual equation is slightly more complicated. On the other hand, it is more transparent:

$$r = \frac{\dfrac{\Sigma(X_1 - M_1)(X_2 - M_2)}{N - 1}}{\sqrt{\dfrac{\Sigma(X_1 - M_1)^2}{N - 1}\dfrac{\Sigma(X_2 - M_2)^2}{N - 1}}}$$

Needless to say, the $(N - 1)$ terms in the numerator and the denominator cancel each other out. $(N - 1)$ in the numerator corrects for the number of data pairs by taking the (corrected) mean of the $(X_1 - M_1)(X_2 - M_2)$ values, as for the calculation of the variances.

Let's apply the equation to the two other possible situations. For the data in Table 11.4, the auxiliary table to calculate $\Sigma(X_1 - M_1)(X_2 - M_2)$ when X_1 and X_2 vary in opposite directions, we find:

$$r = \frac{\Sigma(X_1 - M_1)(X_2 - M_2)}{\sqrt{\Sigma(X_1 - M_1)^2 \Sigma(X_2 - M_2)^2}}$$

$$= \frac{-6}{\sqrt{18 * 2}} = \frac{-6}{\sqrt{36}} = -1.00$$

For Table 11.5, the auxiliary table to calculate $\Sigma(X_1 - M_1)(X_2 - M_2)$ when there is no unidirectional relationship between X_1 and X_2, we have:

$$r = \frac{\Sigma(X_1 - M_1)(X_2 - M_2)}{\sqrt{\Sigma(X_1 - M_1)^2 \Sigma(X_2 - M_2)^2}}$$

$$= \frac{0}{\sqrt{18 * 2}} = \frac{0}{\sqrt{36}} = 0.00$$

Finally, we can also calculate the Pearson product-moment correlation for Galton's peas in Table 11.1.[2] This gives:

$N = 700$

$M_1 = 18.0$

$M_2 = 16.37$

$\Sigma(X_1 - M_1)(X_2 - M_2) = 641.5$

$\Sigma(X_1 - M_1)^2 = 2800$

$\Sigma(X_2 - M_2)^2 = 2963.43$

$$r = \frac{\Sigma(X_1 - M_1)(X_2 - M_2)}{\sqrt{\Sigma(X_1 - M_1)^2 \Sigma(X_2 - M_2)^2}}$$

$$= \frac{641.5}{\sqrt{2800 * 2963.43}} = .223$$

So, Galton found a Pearson correlation of +.223 between the sizes of the mother peas and the sizes of the daughter peas. The next question, of course, is: What does this Pearson correlation coefficient mean?

⟳ **Recap**

The calculation of the Pearson product-moment correlation (r)

The Pearson correlation is calculated with the equation:

$$r = \frac{\Sigma(X_1 - M_1)(X_2 - M_2)}{\sqrt{\Sigma(X_1 - M_1)^2 \Sigma(X_2 - M_2)^2}}$$

This equation takes into account how much the variables X_1 and X_2 co-vary (the numerator) and how much variability there is in X_1 and X_2 (the denominator). The denominator is needed to standardise the correlation, so that the values stay within the interval between −1.00 and +1.00.

---

2 There are some peculiar aspects to Galton's data. For each size of mother pea, the frequencies of the smallest daughter peas are higher than the frequencies of the other sizes. This is because Galton added all seeds with a diameter of less than 15. Because of this practice, it may be argued that the Spearman rank correlation is more appropriate for the analysis of Galton's data than the Pearson correlation (see the next chapter).

11.1.3 The interpretation of Pearson's correlation coefficient

To understand the meaning of a correlation, it is best to plot a graph like the one we made for Galton's data (Figure 11.1). This graph will show the **scatterplot** of the data pairs.[3] We start by defining the abscissa (the horizontal line) and the ordinate (the vertical line). When there is a clear predictor and a predicted variable, the predictor is placed on the abscissa and the predicted variable on the ordinate. So, in Galton's example the size of the mother peas (the predictor) is put on the abscissa and the size of the daughter peas (the predicted variable) on the ordinate, as shown in Figure 11.3.

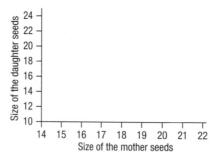

Figure 11.3 Making a scatterplot of two correlated variables.
Step 1: assign the abscissa and the ordinate. The predictor is placed on the abscissa and the predicted variable on the ordinate.

We will illustrate the placement of the dots by using the data from Table 11.2. The first data pair is a mother size of 15 and a daughter size of 16. To place the dot at the correct place, we draw a vertical line through 15 on the abscissa and a horizontal line through 16 on the ordinate, as shown in Figure 11.4.

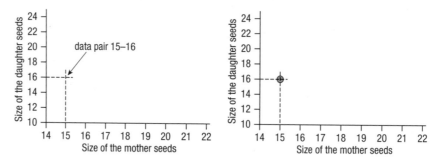

Figure 11.4 Making a scatterplot of two correlated variables.
Step 2: calculate the placement of the dot representing the data pair 'size of mother = 15 and size of daughter = 16'.

Next, we plot the other two data pairs from Table 11.2: 18–17 and 21–18 (Figure 11.5).

3 Notice that in scatterplots we usually do not change the size of the dots as a function of the number of observations covered by the dot, as we did in Figure 11.1. This is because in scatterplots each dot usually represents a single observation.

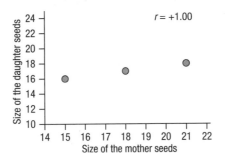

Figure 11.5 Making a scatterplot of two correlated variables.
Step 3: plot the remaining dots for the data pairs of Table 11.2.

In the same way we can make the scatterplots for the data in Table 11.4 ($r = -1.00$) and in Table 11.5 ($r = .00$). These are shown in Figure 11.6.

(a) Data in Table 11.4   (b) Data in Table 11.5

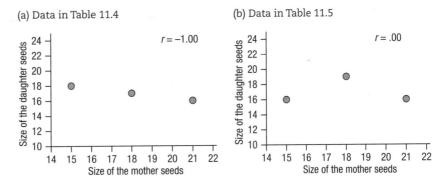

Figure 11.6 Scatterplots of the data in Table 11.4 (a) and 11.5 (b). For the sake of clarity, the help-lines to determine the positions of the dots have been deleted.

Figures 11.5 and 11.6 illustrate a first important aspect of the correlation coefficient. Remember that $r = +1.00$ for Figure 11.5, $r = -1.00$ for Figure 11.6a and $r = .00$ for Figure 11.6b. So, when all the data pairs fall on a straight line going from left low to right high, we have a correlation of $r = +1.00$. This makes sense because the value of X_2 becomes larger as the value of X_1 increases. In Figure 11.6a, the value of X_2 decreases as X_1 increases. So, we have a correlation coefficient $r = -1.00$ and a line going from left high to right low. Finally, the only straight line we can draw through the dots of Figure 11.6b is horizontal (as defined by $r = .00$), indicating that X_2 does not change in a unidirectional way as X_1 increases. This is shown in Figure 11.7. (In Section 11.1.4 we will discuss how to calculate the best fitting line.) Notice that the Pearson correlation assumes that the relationship between X_1 and X_2 is best represented by a straight line. Therefore the Pearson correlation is called a **linear correlation**.[4]

4 If you are not happy with the assumption of a linear relationship, you are foreseeing one of the shortcomings of Pearson's correlation coefficient. Notice, however, that you can easily correct this shortcoming by assuming that X_2 is predicted not only by X_1 but also by X_1^2. This allows you to draw a parabola connecting X_1 and X_2. However, then you are in the realm of multiple regression (Chapter 14).

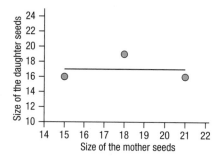

Figure 11.7 A correlation of $r = .00$ implies that the line connecting X_1 and X_2 is horizontal.

Figure 11.8 illustrates one last point about Pearson's correlation coefficient. Although the dots are differently positioned in the two graphs, the lines are nearly identical. In (a) the dots are closer to the straight line so we can better predict the value of X_2 if we know the value of X_1. In other words, there is less 'noise' in Figure 11.8a than 11.8b.

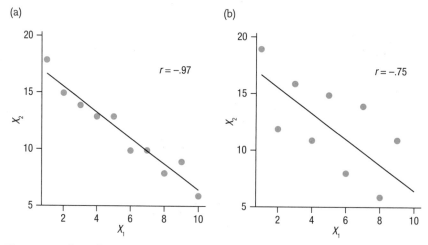

Figure 11.8 Figure illustrating the random noise in data. In both graphs the regression line is nearly the same. However, in (a) the dots are closer to the line than in (b). This is captured in the value of r. The closer r is to -1.00 or $+1.00$, the closer the dots are to the regression line and the better we can predict X_2 on the basis of X_1. The more error there is in the data, the more the value of r approximates zero.

You can imagine that Galton did not like the variability in the sizes of the daughters that came from mothers of the same size. He would have been much happier if the sizes of the daughters had been exactly the same as the sizes of their mothers. Then he would have found rock-solid evidence that the sizes of pea seeds are inherited. As his findings showed, the mean size of the daughters was not only smaller than that of the mothers, they also showed a lot of variability. A mother with size 15 could produce daughters with a size ranging from 14 to 20.5! This variability is captured in Pearson's product-moment correlation coefficient as well. The more noise there is in the data, the more r will shift away from –1.00 or +1.00 and the closer it will get to $r = 0$. Because of the large variability in the daughters' sizes, Galton obtained a correlation of only +.223. Apparently, Galton's friends (or more likely their gardeners) were not good pea growers. Apart from the small sizes of the daughter peas, they also showed a large variability, as if the different plants had not been looked after equally well. (Fairness obliges us to acknowledge that we know little about the weather that year. Maybe it was just one of those bad pea years.)

You are probably wondering how to draw the lines in Figures 11.7 and 11.8 and what exactly they mean. This will be covered in the next section.

⊘ Recap

> **The interpretation of r**
>
> For the interpretation of r, two aspects are important:
>
> 1 The sign of r: a positive sign indicates that X_2 changes in the same way as X_1; a negative sign indicates that X_2 changes in the opposite direction of X_1; zero correlation indicates that X_2 does not change linearly as a function of the value of X_1.
> 2 The magnitude of r: the closer r is to –1.00 or +1.00, the more accurately X_2 can be predicted on the basis of X_1. The closer r is to zero, the less informative X_1 is to predict X_2.

11.1.4 Drawing and interpreting the linear regression line

Previously in this chapter we have stated that correlations help to predict outcomes and in Chapter 1 we warned that students must be careful not to interpret a correlation as a cause-consequence relationship until they have further information. However, don't you wonder how researchers are able to predict X_2 on the basis of X_1? If Galton had been asked to predict the size of the daughter peas on the basis of the size of the mother peas, which formula should he have used? Clearly, he could not simply state that the daughters were likely to be the same size as their mothers, because this is not what he observed in his data. He found that the daughters of the smallest mothers were slightly larger than their mothers, whereas the daughters of the largest mothers were substantially smaller than their mothers. So, what would his best prediction have been?

Fortunately, the information included in the correlation allows us to answer that question. To illustrate this, we will use the data in Figure 11.8. Tables 11.8 and 11.9 include all the information you need to calculate the two correlations (Please do the calculations yourself to check whether you've understood everything up to now!)

Tables 11.8 and 11.9 contain all the information we need to calculate the predicted scores. The linear regression line – the straight line we want to find – is given by:

$$X_{2pred} = \text{intercept} + \text{regression weight} * X_1$$

where X_{2pred} is the predicted value of X_2 for each value of X_1. The intercept is the value which X_{2pred} will have when $X_1 = 0$ (because then $X_{2pred} = \text{intercept} + \text{regression weight} * 0$). The regression weight is the amount by which X_{2pred} will increase or decrease when X_1 increases by one unit.

Table 11.8 Data from Figure 11.8a, plus the auxiliary table to calculate SD_1, SD_2, and r.

	X_1	X_2	X_1-M_1	X_2-M_2	$(X_1-M_1)(X_2-M_2)$	$(X_1-M_1)^2$	$(X_2-M_2)^2$
Pair 1	1	18	−4.5	6.4	−28.8	20.25	40.96
Pair 2	2	15	−3.5	3.4	−11.9	12.25	11.56
Pair 3	3	14	−2.5	2.4	−6.0	6.25	5.76
Pair 4	4	13	−1.5	1.4	−2.1	2.25	1.96
Pair 5	5	13	−0.5	1.4	−0.7	0.25	1.96
Pair 6	6	10	0.5	−1.6	−0.8	0.25	2.56
Pair 7	7	10	1.5	−1.6	−2.4	2.25	2.56
Pair 8	8	8	2.5	−3.6	−9.0	6.25	12.96
Pair 9	9	9	3.5	−2.6	−9.1	12.25	6.76
Pair 10	10	6	4.5	−5.6	−25.2	20.25	31.36
	M = 5.5	11.6	Σ = 0.0	0.0	−96.0	82.50	118.4

$$\Sigma(X_1 - M_1)(X_2 - M_2) = -96$$
$$\Sigma(X_1 - M_1)^2 = 82.5 \qquad\qquad \Sigma(X_2 - M_2)^2 = 118.4$$

$$SD_1 = \sqrt{\frac{\Sigma(X_1 - M_1)^2}{N-1}} = \sqrt{\frac{82.5}{10-1}} = 3.03 \qquad SD_2 = \sqrt{\frac{\Sigma(X_2 - M_2)^2}{N-1}} = \sqrt{\frac{118.4}{10-1}} = 3.63$$

$$r = \frac{\Sigma(X_1 - M_1)(X_2 - M_2)}{\sqrt{\Sigma(X_1 - M_1)^2}\sqrt{\Sigma(X_2 - M_2)^2}} = \frac{-96}{\sqrt{82.5}\sqrt{118.4}} = \frac{-96}{\sqrt{82.5 * 118.4}} = -.97$$

Table 11.9 Data from Figure 11.8b, plus the auxiliary table to calculate SD_1, SD_2, and r.

	X_1	X_2	X_1-M_1	X_2-M_2	$(X_1-M_1)(X_2-M_2)$	$(X_1-M_1)^2$	$(X_2-M_2)^2$
Pair 1	1	19	−4.5	7.4	−33.3	20.25	54.76
Pair 2	2	12	−3.5	0.4	−1.4	12.25	0.16
Pair 3	3	16	−2.5	4.4	−11.0	6.25	19.36
Pair 4	4	11	−1.5	−0.6	0.9	2.25	0.36
Pair 5	5	15	−0.5	3.4	−1.7	0.25	11.56
Pair 6	6	8	0.5	−3.6	−1.8	0.25	12.96
Pair 7	7	14	1.5	2.4	3.6	2.25	5.76
Pair 8	8	6	2.5	−5.6	−14.0	6.25	31.36
Pair 9	9	11	3.5	−0.6	−2.1	12.25	0.36
Pair 10	10	4	4.5	−7.6	−34.2	20.25	57.76
	M = 5.5	11.6	Σ = 0.0	0.0	−95.0	82.50	194.4

$$\Sigma(X_1 - M_1)(X_2 - M_2) = -95$$
$$\Sigma(X_1 - M_1)^2 = 82.5 \qquad\qquad \Sigma(X_2 - M_2)^2 = 194.4$$

$$SD_1 = \sqrt{\frac{\Sigma(X_1 - M_1)^2}{N-1}} = \sqrt{\frac{82.5}{10-1}} = 3.03 \qquad SD_2 = \sqrt{\frac{\Sigma(X_2 - M_2)^2}{N-1}} = \sqrt{\frac{194.4}{10-1}} = 4.65$$

$$r = \frac{\Sigma(X_1 - M_1)(X_2 - M_2)}{\sqrt{\Sigma(X_1 - M_1)^2}\sqrt{\Sigma(X_2 - M_2)^2}} = \frac{-95}{\sqrt{82.5}\sqrt{194.4}} = \frac{-95}{\sqrt{82.5 * 194.4}} = -.75$$

To explain this equation, suppose that the predicted sizes of the daughter peas are exactly the same as the sizes of the mother peas. Then the regression line would be:

$$X_{2pred} = 0 + 1 * X_1$$

You can easily check the validity of this equation: when $X_1 = 0$, X_{2pred} will be 0 too; when $X_1 = 1$, X_{2pred} will be 1, and so on. For all values of X_1, $X_{2pred} = X_1$.

In order to calculate the intercept and the regression weight we need for the regression lines in Figure 11.8, we use the following equations:

$$\text{regression weight} = \frac{\Sigma(X_1 - M_1)(X_2 - M_2)}{\sqrt{\Sigma(X_1 - M_1)^2}}$$

$$\text{intercept} = M_2 - \text{regression weight} * M_1$$

Let's apply these equations to the data of Table 11.8:

$$\text{regression weight} = \frac{-96}{82.5} = -1.16$$

$$\text{intercept} = 11.6 - (-1.16 * 5.5) = 11.6 + 6.4 = 17.9$$

$$\text{So, } X_{2pred} = 17.9 - 1.16\, X_1$$

Thus, if we want to predict X_2 for $X_1 = 1$, we calculate that $X_{2pred} = 17.9 - 1.16 * 1$ = 16.7. Similarly, for $X_1 = 2$ we would predict $X_{2pred} = 17.9 - 1.16 * 2 = 15.6$, and so on. Table 11.10 shows the X_{2pred} values for all values of X_1, together with the observed values.

Table 11.10 Predicted X_{2pred} data for all the values of X_1 in Figure 11.8a (see also Table 11.8).

X_1	X_{2pred}	X_{2obs}
1	17.9 – 1.16 * 1 = 16.7	18
2	17.9 – 1.16 * 2 = 15.6	15
3	17.9 – 1.16 * 3 = 14.4	14
4	17.9 – 1.16 * 4 = 13.3	13
5	17.9 – 1.16 * 5 = 12.1	13
6	17.9 – 1.16 * 6 = 10.9	10
7	17.9 – 1.16 * 7 = 9.8	10
8	17.9 – 1.16 * 8 = 8.6	8
9	17.9 – 1.16 * 9 = 7.4	9
10	17.9 – 1.16 * 10 = 6.3	6
M = 5.5	M = 11.6	M = 11.6

If you look carefully at the regression line in Figure 11.8a, you will see that this line contains all the predicted values of X_2. In other words, the regression line is the set of X_{2pred} you obtain for all possible values of X_1 between the minimum and the maximum value of X_1. For instance X_{2pred} for $X_1 = 7.67$ is $17.9 - 1.16 * 7.67$ = 9.0.

Now calculate the regression line for the data of Table 11.9, to see whether you have understood everything. Do you get more or less the same values of X_{2pred} as the ones we calculated in Table 11.10? (You should if the graphs in Figure 11.8 are correct!)

Finally, what would the regression line of Galton's peas be? Let's find out. Here are the descriptives of his sample data again:

$N = 700$

$M_1 = 18.0$

$M_2 = 16.37$

$\Sigma(X_1 - M_1)(X_2 - M_2) = 641.5$

$\Sigma(X_1 - M_1)^2 = 2800$

$\Sigma(X_2 - M_2)^2 = 2963.43$

$$\text{regression weight} = \frac{\Sigma(X_1 - M_1)(X_2 - M_2)}{\Sigma(X_1 - M_1)^2}$$

$$= \frac{641.5}{2800}$$

$$= +.229$$

$$\text{intercept} = M_2 - \text{regression weight} * M_1$$

$$= 16.37 - (+.229) * 18$$

$$= 12.25$$

So, for a mother size of 15, the predicted daughter size = 12.25 + .229 * 15 = 15.68. For a mother pea of 21, the predicted daughter size = 12.25 + .229 * 21 = 17.06. We can compare these with the observed mean values, which were 15.8 and 17.21 respectively (Table 11.1).

Actually, we do not have to calculate X_{2pred} for all possible X_1 values. Once we know X_{2pred} for the lowest and the highest X_1 value, we simply draw a straight line through these two dots in the plot. This line includes all the values of X_{2pred}!

To end this section on the regression line, you may notice something else of interest in Galton's data. Although the regression line describes the predicted X_2 values, researchers must be careful about how they use this information. For example, if Galton had extended the regression line to its intercept, he would have had to explain how a mother pea with a size of 0 can produce a daughter with a size of 12.25! Regression lines are nice summaries of sample data, but it is extremely dangerous to extrapolate them for X_1 values beyond the range observed in the sample.

 Recap

Drawing the regression line

The regression line indicates the values of X_2 that are predicted on the basis of the correlation with X_1. To draw this line, you must know the predicted X_2 values for the smallest and the largest X_1 values, so that you can draw a line between them. To calculate these, you need the values of the intercept and the regression weight. They are given by the formulas:

$$\text{regression weight} = \frac{\Sigma(X_1 - M_1)(X_2 - M_2)}{\Sigma(X_1 - M_1)^2}$$

$$\text{intercept} = M_2 - \text{regression weight} * M_1$$

11.1.5   The percentage of variance explained

When you are reading a scientific text you may encounter a claim like '60% of the variance in intelligence is due to genetics'. What does that mean? And how can we relate it to Galton's findings in Figure 11.1?

Remember that correlations are about better predictions. Knowledge of the predictor variable (intelligence of the parent) helps us to better anticipate the value of the predicted variable (intelligence of the offspring). Knowledge of the size of a mother pea helped Galton to better predict the size of a daughter pea. But how much better was his prediction?

To answer this question, we have to go back to the standard deviation (or more accurately the variance) of the predicted variable. Suppose Galton did not have information about the mother peas. What would then be his best estimate of the size of a particular daughter pea in his sample? As we have seen in Chapter 2, the best estimate in such a case is the mean of the sample. So, if Galton were asked about the size of a particular daughter pea, his best bet without any extra information about the mother's size would have been 16.37 hundredths of an inch (that is, M_2). On the basis of the standard deviation of the daughter sizes ($\sqrt{2963.43/(700 - 1)} = 2.06$), we know that on average the deviation between his estimate and the real size of the pea would be 2 hundredths of an inch.

In the previous section we saw how Galton could use knowledge of the size of the mother pea to improve his prediction regarding the daughter. Rather than using M_2, he could use the linear regression to find his best estimate. If he knew that the mother's size was 21, his estimate of the daughter would be 12.25 + .229 * 21 = 17.06, rather than 16.37. Similarly, if he knew that the mother was 15 hundredths of an inch, his estimate of the daughter would be 12.25 + .229 * 15 = 15.68, rather than 16.37. Only when the mother was 18, would his prediction coincide with the sample mean.

How big now would the difference be between Galton's predictions and the observed values? To explain this, we make use of the data in Table 11.9 (see also Figure 11.8b). These data are repeated in Table 11.11 (overleaf) for your convenience, and extended with some other information we will need. Remember that for these data $r = -.75$.

If we predict X_2 solely on the basis of M_2 for the data of Table 11.11, the standard deviation between our predictions and the observed values is:

$$\sqrt{\frac{\Sigma(X_{2obs} - M_2)^2}{N - 1}} = \sqrt{\frac{194.4}{10 - 1}} = 4.65$$

In contrast, if we predict X_2 on the basis of the regression line $17.9 - 1.15X_1$, the standard deviation between our predictions and the observed values is:

$$\sqrt{\frac{\Sigma(X_{2obs} - X_{2pred})^2}{N - 1}} = \sqrt{\frac{85}{10 - 1}} = 3.07$$

The smaller standard deviation between the predicted and the observed variables on the basis of the regression line rather than on the basis of M_2 indicates that these predictions are more accurate. This smaller standard deviation is consistent with the substantial correlation that was observed between X_1 and

Table 11.11 Data of Figure 11.8b, supplemented with the predicted X_2 values and the squared deviations between the observed and the predicted X_2 values.

	X_1	X_{2obs}	X_{2pred}	$(X_{2obs} - M_2)^2$	$(X_{2obs} - X_{2pred})^2$
Pair 1	1	19	16.75	54.76	5.06
Pair 2	2	12	15.60	.16	12.96
Pair 3	3	16	14.45	19.36	2.40
Pair 4	4	11	13.30	.36	5.29
Pair 5	5	15	12.15	11.56	8.12
Pair 6	6	8	11.00	12.96	9.00
Pair 7	7	14	9.85	5.76	17.22
Pair 8	8	6	8.70	31.36	7.29
Pair 9	9	11	7.55	.36	11.90
Pair 10	10	4	6.40	57.76	5.76
	$M = 5.5$	$M = 11.6$	$M = 11.6$	$\Sigma = 194.40$	$\Sigma = 85.00$

$\Sigma(X_{2obs} - M_2) = 194.4$

$$\text{regression weight} = \frac{\Sigma(X_1 - M_1)(X_2 - M_2)}{\Sigma(X_1 - M_1)^2} = \frac{-95}{82.5} = -1.15$$

$\text{intercept} = M_{2obs} - (-1.15) * M_1 = 11.6 - 1.15 * 5.5 = 17.9$

$X_{2pred} = 17.9 - 1.15 * X_1$

$\Sigma(X_{2obs} - X_{2pred})^2 = 85.0$

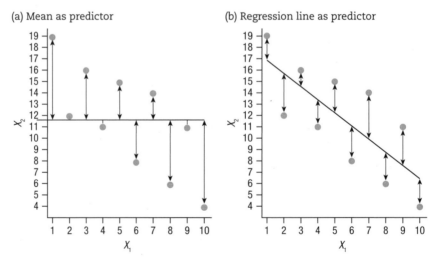

(a) Mean as predictor   (b) Regression line as predictor

Figure 11.9 Graph illustrating the fact that a significant correlation allows the researcher to reduce the unexplained variability in the data, measured as the squared deviations between the predicted and the observed values. When there is no predictor (a), then the mean is the point of comparison for each observed X_2 value. With a significant predictor, however, the regression line becomes the anchor point for the observed X_2 values (b). By calculating the reduction in variance, we can measure how much effect the predictor variable X_1 has had on the variance of X_2.

X_2 ($r = -.75$). Figure 11.9 illustrates the difference between the standard deviation on the basis of M_2 and the standard deviation on the basis of the regression line. As you can conclude yourself, when $r = +1.0$ or -1.0, the predicted values fully coincide with the observed values, and the standard deviation between the predicted and the observed values is zero.

Although the reduction in the standard deviation between the predicted and the observed values as a function of r is an interesting measure, for reasons that do not concern us here, statisticians prefer to work with the variances of the variables (that is, the values before the square root is taken). In particular, they look at the improvement in the prediction as a ratio:

$$\frac{\text{variance without linear regression} - \text{variance after linear regression}}{\text{variance without linear regression}}$$

$$= \frac{\dfrac{\Sigma(X_{2obs} - M_2)^2}{N-1} - \dfrac{\Sigma(X_{2obs} - X_{2pred})^2}{N-1}}{\dfrac{\Sigma(X_{2obs} - M_2)^2}{N-1}}$$

$$= \frac{\Sigma(X_{2obs} - M_2)^2 - \Sigma(X_{2obs} - X_{2pred})^2}{\Sigma(X_{2obs} - M_2)^2}$$

$$= \frac{194.4 - 85.0}{194.4} = .56$$

This ratio tells us how much of the original variance is explained by the introduction of the regression line. Without the regression line, the variance was 194.4. With the regression line, it is reduced to 85.0. This is a reduction of 56%. So, in our example X_1 predicts or explains 56% of the variance in X_{2obs}.

Interestingly, we do not have to do the full calculations of the variances in order to know the percentage of variance explained. You can show mathematically that

percentage variance explained $= (r)^2$.

So, in our example, the percentage variance explained $= (-.75)^2 = .56$ or 56%.

The fact that we can measure the percentage of variance explained by squaring the correlation coefficient means that we can easily see how much variance was explained in Galton's data. All we have to do is to square the correlation coefficient: $r^2 = (.223)^2 = .05$ or 5%. So, in Galton's data set, heredity accounted for 5% of the differences in the size of the second generation peas. Looking at Figure 11.1 this feels about right: the mother's size accounts for 5% of the variability in sizes. Needless to say, this was not the type of hard evidence Galton had hoped to find (and that would have swayed a sceptical public about the validity of evolutionary theory).

Because the explained variance equals the square of the correlation coefficient, researchers represent the proportion of explained variance as R^2 (called R square). Notice that you need a correlation of .70 before half of the variance is explained! The percentage of variance explained by the linear regression in Figure 11.8a is $(-.97)^2 = .94$ or 94%.

So far, we have discovered a lot that Galton would have loved to know before he collected his pea seeds, because it would have made it so much easier for him to understand the true impact of his findings. (Remember that he had

11

little more than a table to go on!) However, we still have not answered the most important question about Galton's findings: Is it likely that the correlation he observed between the sizes of the mother and the daughter peas was due to a coincidence, to sampling error? How likely was Galton to observe a correlation of +.223 between 700 pairs of peas if in reality heredity played no role at all in controlling the size of peas? Could it be that all the differences Galton observed were simply due to the growing conditions of the different plants and were not at all influenced by the size of the peas that were planted? These questions bring us back to hypothesis testing. Because of the importance of this topic, we devote a complete chapter section to it.

🔄 **Recap**

> ### The percentage of variance explained
>
> The percentage of variance explained refers to the reduction in unaccounted variance of the predicted variable X_2 when you take into account a correlated variable X_1 (see Figure 11.9). It is another measure of how well X_2 is predicted by X_1. In this section, we have gone through the various calculations needed to understand and calculate the value. However, for practical purposes we don't have to do this, as the percentage of variance is also given by simply squaring the correlation coefficient. So, the percentage of variance explained (also called R^2), is given by:
>
> $$R^2 = (r)^2$$

11.2 Significance of the Pearson product-moment correlation coefficient

At the end of many stats courses, students have a distorted perception of the magnitude of correlations found in real life. Because stats textbooks use clear examples, students expect to find these correlations in the real world as well. Although such situations exist, they are relatively rare. Much more often the correlations psychologists are looking for range from −.30 to +.30. (Remember that we encountered a similar misconception when we talked about the difference between two conditions.) In this respect, Galton's data are a much better representation of the situations that confront psychologists than the neat artificial data of Figure 11.8. This brings us to the question of how to determine the statistical significance of a Pearson product-moment correlation coefficient.

11.2.1 Hypothesis testing with the Pearson correlation

In order to be significant, how strong must a correlation be? Before we present the specific numbers, it may be worth giving this question some thought. What do you think is the primary variable determining the minimum degree of correlation that must be present in sample data before we can be confident that the correlation also exists at the population level? Think of Galton's data in Table 11.1. Are you confident that these data point to the existence of a heredity component in the size of sweet peas? If yes, why? If not, why not?

If you thought Galton's data were indicative of an inheritance component, you probably pointed to the fact that Galton's finding was based on quite a lot of pea pairs. If Galton had found his correlation of $r = +.223$ with only 10 pea pairs, you would have felt much less sure.

If you thought Galton's data were not strong enough to conclude that genetics play a role in determining the size of peas, you probably pointed to the rather low correlation. After all, 5% of the variance explained is not much to build a theory on.

In summary, two features of a correlation will decide whether we feel confident about its existence and usefulness in reality: the degree of the correlation (how close r is to -1.00 or $+1.00$) and the number of data pairs upon which the evidence is based. To take the most extreme example, a correlation of $r = +1.00$ is meaningless when it is based on two data pairs because you can always draw a straight line through two data points. Just do it. Write down your age and that of your friend (X_1, in months); then write down your shoe sizes (X_2). Now calculate the correlation between age and shoe size for the two of you. Unless both values of X_1 or X_2 are exactly the same, you will obtain a correlation of $+1.00$ or -1.00 (otherwise your correlation will be .00). Thus, a correlation of $+1.00$ or -1.00 means nothing if the evidence is based on two data pairs only. In contrast, a correlation of $+.10$ may be quite important when it is based on thousands of observations. For instance, the correlation between the use of antihistamine and the reduction in sneezing is .11 (Meyer et al., 2001). Despite this low correlation, thousands of allergic people feel better when they take their medicine than when they do not.

Hypothesis testing with Pearson correlations boils down to the following question: 'How strong must the correlation *minimally* be for a given number of data pairs N in order to be reliable (significant)?'

To decide the critical values, statisticians must know the distributions of the correlation coefficients for different values of N. Then they can establish from which value the chances of observing a more extreme correlation become less than the significance level (for example, $p < .05$ two-tailed).

Luckily for us we do not have to know the details of all these calculations. We can make use of published numbers, summarised in Table 11.12. This table gives, for different numbers of data pairs (N), the degree of correlation that minimally must be present in order for the correlation to be reliable at the .05 and .01 significance levels (two-tailed). Appendix E contains the same information. Notice that, although all correlation coefficients are given as positive numbers, the critical values also apply to negative correlation coefficients. So, for N = 20, the correlation must be lower than $r = -.444$ or higher than $r = +.444$ to be significant at the .05 α-level.

As we will see in the SPSS section, you can also calculate the exact p-value associated with a particular r and N, so that you know what p-value is associated with $r = -.444$ for N = 20. This value is $p = .04986$ (which is indeed smaller than .05). If you are interested in writing an Excel program to calculate this value yourself, you will find the necessary information in the **Going further** section.

Table 11.12 Minimal values of r needed to reach significance (two-tailed) for different numbers of data pairs. Notice that, although only the positive correlations are given, the critical values also apply to negative correlations.

Number of data pairs	$r_{.05crit}$ ($\alpha = .05$)	$r_{.01crit}$ ($\alpha = .01$)	Number of data pairs	$r_{.05crit}$ ($\alpha = .05$)	$r_{.01crit}$ ($\alpha = .01$)
1	—	—	30	.361	.463
2	—	—	35	.334	.430
3	.997	.9999	40	.312	.403
4	.950	.990	45	.294	.380
5	.878	.959	50	.279	.361
6	.811	.917	60	.254	.330
7	.754	.874	70	.235	.306
8	.707	.834	80	.220	.286
9	.666	.798	90	.207	.270
10	.632	.765	100	.197	.256
12	.576	.708	200	.139	.182
14	.532	.661	300	.113	.149
16	.497	.623	400	.098	.129
18	.468	.590	500	.088	.115
20	.444	.561	1000	.062	.081
25	.396	.505			

From Table 11.12 we can conclude that Galton's data are indeed unlikely to be due to sampling error (as a matter of fact, $p < .00000001$). So, Galton was quite right to claim that his finding was in line with the hypothesis that the size of a daughter pea is partly determined by the size of the mother pea. As long as the obtained correlation was equal to or higher than $r = .075$, he could defend the hypothesis that genetics were at play in shaping the seed size of sweet peas. This was because of his high number of data pairs. Notice in Table 11.12 that, if a study only involves 10 data pairs, we need a correlation of at least $-.632$ or $+.632$ before we are entitled to assume that there is a true relationship at the population level! We will return to this when we address the question of how many participants one must include in a study. First, however, we will review the hypothesis testing part with a cookbook example.

11.2.2   Step by step: hypothesis testing with the Pearson correlation

A psychologist wants to know whether there is a correlation between students' marks for exams in statistics and social psychology. On the one hand, you could expect such a correlation, given that both exams rely on the students' intelligence. On the other hand, the type of knowledge tested in the two courses is very different.

The psychologist has access to the exam marks of her 10 students and decides to correlate them. These are the four steps of the hypothesis testing.

1   *Formulate the null hypothesis and the alternative hypothesis.*

The null hypothesis states that there is no correlation between the marks of students in their stats and social psychology exams. The alternative hypothesis states that there is a correlation. It does not specify whether the correlation will be positive or negative. Therefore, it is a two-tailed test.

2   *Define the critical value of r (α = .05, two-tailed).*

Given that there are 10 data pairs (students), Table 11.12 informs us that $r_{.05crit}$ = –.632 or +.632. So, only correlations $\leq$ –.632 or $\geq$ +.632 will be significant.

3   *Collect and analyse the data.*

Because the exams have already been marked, the psychologist can simply copy the marks from her files. Each course has been marked out of 20. Table 11.13 shows the data.

Table 11.13 Marks obtained by 10 first-year psychology students in their statistics and social psychology exams (max = 20).

	Stats	Social psychology
student 1	13	15
student 2	15	16
student 3	10	17
student 4	10	12
student 5	17	16
student 6	14	14
student 7	12	14
student 8	9	11
student 9	11	15
student 10	13	12

To calculate the Pearson product-moment correlation coefficient, we need an auxiliary table with $\Sigma(X_1 - M_1)^2$, $\Sigma(X_2 - M_2)^2$, and $\Sigma(X_1 - M_1)(X_2 - M_2)$.

X_1	X_2	$(X_1-M_1)^2$	$(X_2-M_2)^2$	$(X_1-M_1)(X_2-M_2)$
13	15	.36	.64	.48
15	16	6.76	3.24	4.68
10	17	5.76	7.84	–6.72
10	12	5.76	4.84	5.28
17	16	21.16	3.24	8.28
14	14	2.56	.04	–.32
12	14	.16	.04	.08
9	11	11.56	10.24	10.88
11	15	1.96	.64	–1.12
13	12	.36	4.84	–1.32
M = 12.4	M = 14.2	Σ = 56.4	Σ = 35.6	Σ = 20.2

$$\Sigma(X_1 - M_1)(X_2 - M_2) = 20.2$$

$$\Sigma(X_1 - M_1)^2 = 56.4$$

$$\Sigma(X_2 - M_2)^2 = 35.6$$

$$SD_1 = \sqrt{\frac{\Sigma(X_1 - M_1)^2}{N - 1}} = \sqrt{\frac{56.4}{10 - 1}} = 2.50$$

$$SD_2 = \sqrt{\frac{\Sigma(X_2 - M_2)^2}{N - 1}} = \sqrt{\frac{35.6}{10 - 1}} = 2.00$$

$$r = \frac{\Sigma(X_1 - M_1)(X_2 - M_2)}{\sqrt{\Sigma(X_1 - M_1)^2}\sqrt{\Sigma(X_2 - M_2)^2}} = \frac{20.2}{\sqrt{56.4}\sqrt{35.6}} = \frac{20.2}{\sqrt{56.4 * 35.6}} = +.451$$

$$R^2 = (.451)^2 = .203$$

(that is, 20% of the variance of X_2 can be predicted on the basis of X_1)

4 *Compare the obtained r-value to the critical r-value.*

Because r_{obs} (.451) < r_{crit} (.632), the psychologist has to decide that the correlation is not significant (the exact p-value is $p = .191$). In other words, she cannot reject the null hypothesis that at the population level there is no correlation between the exam marks in stats and social psychology. At the same time, we can conclude that this study was not very well designed. The psychologist could have known beforehand that she only had a reasonable chance of finding a significant correlation, when the correlation at the population level was very high (that is, more than +.63 or less than –.63). Otherwise her study lacked the power to show the connection. We will see below how many data pairs you have to include to have an 80% chance of finding a significant correlation in a sample given that a correlation of a certain degree exists at the population level.

Because the correlation is not significant, the best predictions of the marks on the social psychology exam are the mean mark 14.2). For illustration purposes only, the calculations you need for the regression line, in case the correlation you find is significant, are:

$$\text{regression weight} = \frac{\Sigma(X_1 - M_1)(X_2 - M_2)}{\Sigma(X_1 - M_1)^2}$$

$$= \frac{20.2}{56.4}$$

$$= +.358$$

$$\text{intercept} = M_2 - \text{regression weight} * M_1$$

$$= 14.2 - .358 * 12.4$$

$$= 9.76$$

$$X_{2pred} = 9.76 + .358 * X_1$$

(that is, for $X_1 = 10$, $X_{2pred} = 9.76 + .358 * 10 = 13.3$)

Figure 11.10 shows the scatterplot of the data, together with the regression line of the predicted marks of the social psychology exam (X_2) based on the marks of the stats exam (X_1) and the assumption that there is a significant correlation.

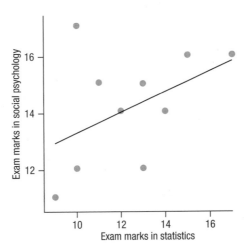

Figure 11.10 Illustration of the scatterplot and the regression line between the marks on the stats exam and the marks on the social psychology exam. Each dot represents the observed values for each student. The line represents the predicted social psychology marks on the basis of the stats marks. Remember that this line is only given for illustration purposes because the correlation was not significant. With a non-significant correlation, we should actually predict a flat line equal to $M_2 = 14.2$ (see Figure 11.9a)

11.2.3 Reporting a Pearson correlation

When we report a Pearson correlation, we have to inform the reader about:

1 the value of r,
2 the number of data pairs on which r is based, and
3 whether or not the correlation was significant.

For the study in the step by step example we would write something like:

> 'The correlation between the exam marks in statistics and social psychology failed to reach significance ($r = .451$, $N = 10$, $p = .191$). Therefore, we cannot reject the null hypothesis of no correlation.'

11.2.4 How many participants do we need to include in a study?

The examples of Galton's peas and the students' exam results illustrate that correlational studies are particularly interesting when they are based on large numbers of data pairs. Then, the study is able to pick up small correlations that exist at the population level (that is, in the real world).

As has been true with all the statistical tests we have covered thus far, the basic rule of thumb is 'the more observations the better'. However, after a certain point, extra data do not really provide additional information and simply increase the costs of a study (Chapter 7).

To calculate the desired minimum number of participants for a study, we must decide beforehand how strong the correlation is likely to be at the population level. When we have no further information, a good guess is that we are looking for a medium correlation coefficient. That is a correlation of $r = -.30$ or

$r = +.30$ (that is, $(.30)^2 = 9\%$ of the variance explained). When we have reasons to believe that the correlation is lower, we would be best to assume that the correlation will be $r = -.10$ or $r = +.10$ (that is, 1% of the variance explained). Finally, when we have reasons to assume that the correlation will be big, we can assume it will be at least $r = -.50$ or $r = +.50$ (that is, 25% of the variance explained). Table 11.14 lists the number of data pairs (participants) you need in each of these situations.

Table 11.14 What is the minimum number of data pairs (participants) that we have to include in order to have an 80% chance of finding a significant correlation in the sample ($\alpha = .05$, two-tailed)?

Correlation expected at the population level	Minimum N required
$r = .10$ (small effect size)	782
$r = .30$ (medium effect size)	84
$r = .50$ (big effect size)	29
Source: Retrieved 6 January 2011 from http://www.psycho.uni-duesseldorf.de/ abteilungen/aap/gpower3/	

A few interesting observations follow from Table 11.14. First, it is pointless to start a correlational study with fewer than 29 data pairs. Correlations of more than .50 are rare in psychological research. So, with less than 29 data pairs you are unlikely to find anything significant unless you are helped by the sampling error. Most of the time 84 data pairs is an absolute minimum. This will allow you to find correlations as low as .30. If, however, you also want to pick up smaller correlations, your number of data pairs must go as high as nearly 800. Interestingly, even though Galton did not know any of this, his intuitions about how many pea pairs he needed were surprisingly close to the mark!

Table 11.14 will not only help you to set up good correlational studies. It will also allow you to judge other people's research. If it is based on less than 30 data pairs, simply put it aside, unless you have good reasons to believe that the correlation they are looking for is higher than .50. As long as the numbers are lower than 100, keep a critical mind and remember that this only allows researchers to say anything about correlations from .30 upwards. Only with larger sample sizes are you starting to look with a reasonably fine-toothed comb!

11.3 Calculating the Pearson product–moment correlation in SPSS

Given that we need many observations and that the calculation of Pearson correlations requires a lot of repetitive and error-prone calculations, there are good reasons to automate the process. This is why software packages such as SPSS are so popular. The use of SPSS will be illustrated with the data from Table 11.13 on exam marks. Once you know the different steps, practise them by running all the other examples we discussed!

You can also find further details in Chapter 6 of Brace, Kemp, and Snelgar, SPSS for Psychologists.

We start by entering the data.

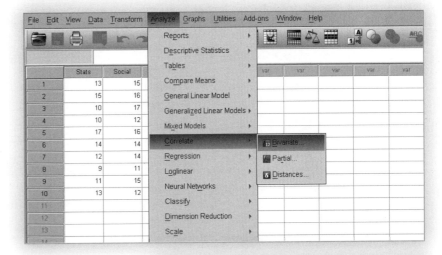

Then click on
Analyze, *Correlate*,
Bivariate.

In the panel that pops up, enter your
two variables in the Variables box and
click on **OK**.

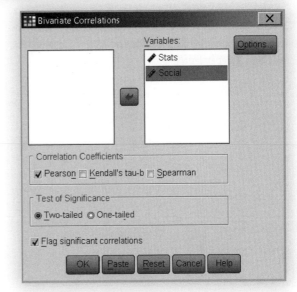

This is the output you get.

Correlations

		Stats	Social
Stats	Pearson Correlation	1	.451
	Sig. (2-tailed)		.191
	N	10	10
Social	Pearson Correlation	.451	1
	Sig. (2-tailed)	.191	
	N	10	10

From this output, you can easily conclude that $r = .451$, $N = 10$, $p = .191$.

To get information on the regression line, a better option is to use *Analyze*, *Regression*, *Linear*.

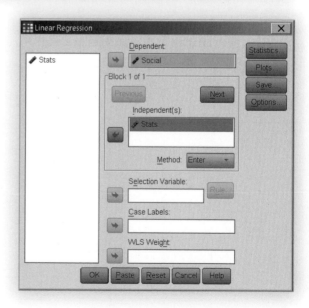

In the resulting panel you enter 'Social' (that is, the exam marks of the Social Psychology exam) in the box with the title *Dependent*, and 'Stats' in the box entitled *Independent(s)*.

Then click on *OK*.

The resulting outcome is quite complicated because now you are in the realm of (multiple) regression analysis (Chapter 14). However, the various panels allow you to find all the information you need.

In the first panel you find the value of the correlation ($r = .451$) and the variance explained ($R^2 = .451^2 = .203$).

Model Summary					
Model		R	R Square	Adjusted R Square	Std Error of the Estimate
1		.451[a]	.203	.104	1.883
a. Predictors: (Constant), Stats					

In the next panel, you find the significance value ($p = .191$)

ANOVA[b]						
Model		Sum of Squares	df	Mean Square	F	Sig.
1	Regression	7.235	1	7.235	2.040	.191[a]
	Residual	28.365	8	3.546		
	Total	35.600	9			
a. Predictors: (Constant), Stats						
b. Dependent Variable: Social						

Finally, there is a third panel with the intercept and the regression weight.

Coefficients[a]						
Model		Unstandardized Coefficients		Standardized Coefficients		
		B	Std. Error	Beta	t	Sig.
1	(Constant)	9.759	3.166		3.083	.015
	Stats	.358	.251	.451	1.428	.191[a]
a. Dependent Variable: Social						

To get to the scatterplot, click on *Graphs*, *Chart Builder*.

Compose a scatterplot with the stats exam marks on the X-axis and the social psychology exam marks on the Y-axis.

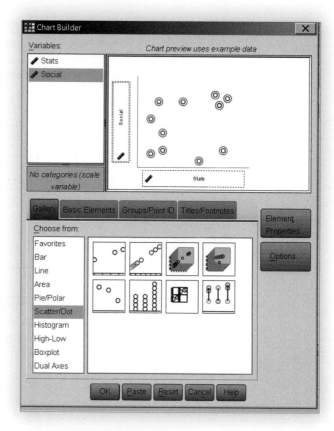

Click on OK to get the following output.

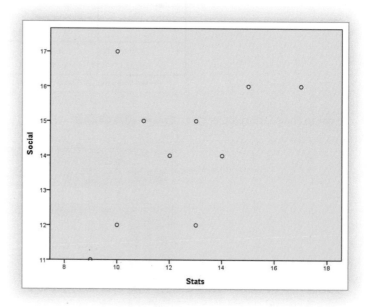

To add the regression line to the figure, double-click to activate it and then click on the right mouse button to get the following screen.

Choose the alternative *Add Fit Line at Total*.

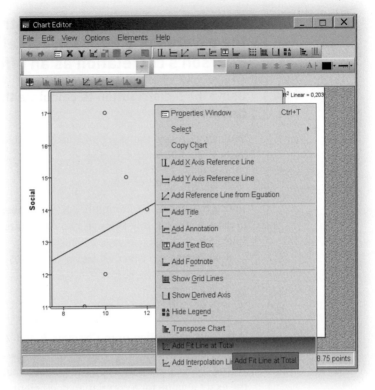

Select *Linear* and click on *Close* to get the linear regression analysis.

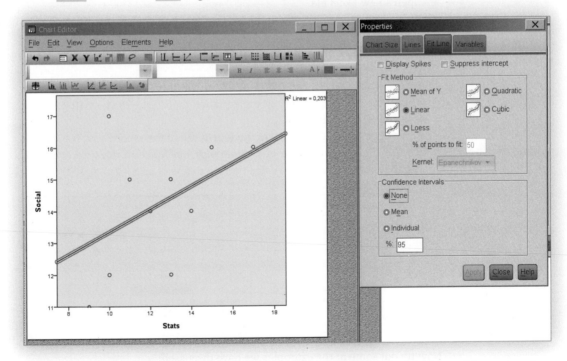

Now you can easily check all the calculations you have done thus far in this chapter! Or start analysing some other data you have found.

11.4 Going further: using the *t*-distribution to calculate the *p*-value of a Pearson correlation and using Pearson's correlation as an effect size

11.4.1 Using the *t*-distribution to calculate the *p*-value of a Pearson correlation

You can calculate the exact *p*-value associated with a particular *r* and N on the basis of the following equation:

$$t = \frac{r * \sqrt{N-2}}{\sqrt{1-r^2}}, \text{ with df} = N - 2$$

Notice that the *t*-distribution has N − 2 degrees of freedom. It is always possible to draw a straight line through two data pairs so the last two data pairs do not count for the *t*-test.

If we apply the *t*-test equation to the .05 critical value for N = 20 (that is, *r* = −.444 or +.444), we get

$$t = \frac{-.444 * \sqrt{20-2}}{\sqrt{1-(-.444)^2}} = -2.1023$$

Using our knowledge from Chapters 6 and 7 about the *t*-distribution, we can calculate the associated *p*-value, which is df = 18, *p* = .04986.

The equivalence between *r* and *t* means that we can use the *t*-test to calculate the exact *p*-value for a correlation coefficient and sample N with Excel.

☐ Open a new Excel file.

☐ Write in the top row *r*, N, *t* and *p*, so that you know what the different cells stand for.

☐ Enter the values of *r* and N in the first two cells of the second row (for example, *r* = −.444, N = 20).

☐ Enter =(A2*SQRT(B2-2))/SQRT(1-A2^2) in the third cell of the second row. This is the Excel equivalent of the equation $t = (r * \sqrt{N-2})/\sqrt{1-r^2}$ (the *r*-value is in cell A2 and N in cell B2).

☐ Enter =TDIST(ABS(C2);B2-2;2) in the fourth cell of the second row. Notice that we use the absolute value of *t*. Otherwise the function does not work for negative correlations. Also notice that we define df as N − 2

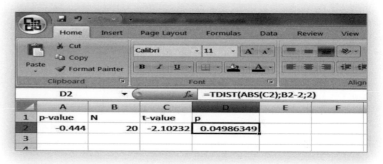

Now try out some of the examples we have discussed!

11.4.2   Using Pearson's correlation as an effect size

Because the Pearson correlation coefficient is so informative, an increasing number of statisticians prefer to use this measure as an index of effect size for experiments instead of Cohen's d-statistic. The Pearson correlation coefficient is the more interesting index because it is related to the percentage of variance explained and can easily be generalised to other situations, rather than just comparing two conditions (see Chapter 13 on analysis of variance). Cohen's d-statistic works fine as long as there are only two conditions to be compared (which was the case throughout this book), but runs into difficulties when three or more conditions are involved. An index based on the percentage of variance explained can easily be expanded to any number of conditions. So, you can use R^2 or derived measures such as η^2 (pronounced eta-squared) or ω^2 (omega-squared), which are alternatives to R^2 when more complicated statistical analyses are involved.

The interpretation of r as an effect size is very easy to understand for a design with two independent groups. Just imagine that condition 1 is represented by digit 1 and condition 2 by digit 2 and then calculate the correlation between the condition and the dependent variable.

Table 11.15 repeats the data from Table 6.1 (percentage of errors noticed by old and young adults) and shows the correspondence between the t-test and the Pearson correlation (all measures can be calculated by hand or with SPSS).

Table 11.15 The equivalence of a t-test and a Pearson correlation test for two independent groups.

t-test for independent groups		Correlation test for independent groups	
Young adults	**Old adults**		
71	72	1–71	2–72
75	65	1–75	2–65
81	70	1–81	2–70
79	76	1–79	2–76
75	72	1–75	2–72
84	75	1–84	2–75
74	68	1–74	2–68
74	69	1–74	2–69
71	71	1–71	2–71
79	70	1–79	2–70

$$t = \frac{M_1 - M_2}{\sqrt{\dfrac{SD_1{}^2}{N_1} + \dfrac{SD_2{}^2}{N_2}}}$$

$$= \frac{76.3 - 70.8}{\sqrt{\dfrac{(4.30)^2}{10} + \dfrac{(3.22)^2}{10}}} = 3.24$$

$$df = 10 + 10 - 2 = 18$$
$$p = .0046$$

$$r = \frac{\Sigma(X_1 - M_1)(X_2 - M_2)}{\sqrt{\Sigma(X_1 - M_1)^2}\sqrt{\Sigma(X_2 - M_2)^2}}$$

$$= \frac{-27.50}{\sqrt{410.95 * 5}} = -.607$$

$$df = N - 2 = 18$$
$$p = .0046$$

The situation is slightly more complicated for a related-samples t-test (because there you have to partial out the variance due to the differences between the participants), but this can be circumvented by using a shortcut. As we saw above, the t-statistic and the r-statistic can be converted into each other. The equation to convert a t-value into an r-value (both for independent groups and related samples) is:

$$r = \sqrt{\frac{t^2}{t^2 + df}}$$

Applied to the example in Table 11.15, we get:

$$r = \sqrt{\frac{(3.24)^2}{(3.24)^2 + 18}}$$
$$= .607$$

In this equation, the sign of the correlation (or the t-test) gets lost. So, you have to be careful about this. However, you obtain exactly the same value of r as when you calculate the statistic directly, and the same applies to the associated p-value.

In summary, by using the above equation, we can easily compute the correlation on the basis of the t-statistic we obtain. For instance, in Chapter 9 we discussed a related-samples t-test on the IQ scores of 20 students before and after the summer holidays (Table 9.6). We obtained a t-statistic of $t(19) = 1.017$, $p = .32$. Applying the equation to convert a t-statistic to an r-statistic, we get:

$$r = \sqrt{\frac{(1.017)^2}{(1.017)^2 + 19}}$$
$$= .227$$

Similarly, we can calculate the correlation coefficients for all the examples we have been discussing in the previous chapters. (Please do so as a learning check!)

A nice illustration of the r-statistic as an effect size was published by Anderson et al. (2003). They reviewed all experimental and correlational studies on the relationship between watching violence on television or in video games and the degree of aggression shown by the participants afterwards. Because the experimental studies were expressed as r-statistics, they could easily be compared to the correlational studies. Figure 11.11 shows the results. From this analysis, we can not only conclude that watching violence increases aggressive behaviour but we also know the degree of the relationship (i.e. $r \approx +.20$). This allows us to have a deeper understanding of the relationship than a simple yes/no answer.

(a) Correlation studies

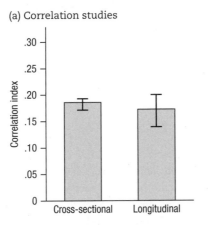

(b) Experimental studies

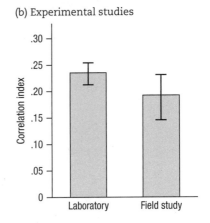

Figure 11.11 Correlations between exposure to media violence and aggression based on four types of study.
(a) Correlational studies between the amount of exposure to media violence and the degree of aggressive behaviour either measured immediately after the exposure or with a delay of several years.
(b) Experimental studies in which participants first saw a violent film or a non-violent film and were then put in a competitive situation in which they could 'punish' their opponent.
All four types of study yielded consistent correlations of around +.20.

11.5 Answers to chapter questions

1 What is a correlation?

> A correlation indicates the degree to which two variables are dependent. When two variables are correlated, they vary in a predictable way as a function of each other. This means that information on one variable can be used to improve the prediction of the other.

2 What is a correlation coefficient?

> A correlation coefficient is a standardised measure that represents the degree of correlation between two variables and the direction of the correlation. It varies from –1.00 (perfect negative correlation) to +1.00 (perfect positive correlation).

3 What is the Pearson product-moment correlation?

> The Pearson product-moment correlation is a parametric correlation coefficient. It assumes that the variables are normally distributed and and come from a ratio/interval scale.

11

4 **Which elements does the Pearson product-moment correlation contain and how do you calculate the coefficient?**

The Pearson product-moment correlation comprises three components: (1) the sum of the products of the deviation scores, (2) the variance of X_1, and (3) the variance of X_2, according to the equation:

$$r = \frac{\Sigma(X_1 - M_1)(X_2 - M_2)}{\sqrt{\Sigma(X_1 - M_1)^2 \Sigma(X_2 - M_2)^2}}$$

5 **What is the difference between a positive and a negative correlation?**

In both cases the variables are correlated (that is, they are not independent of each other). However, when the correlation is positive X_1 varies in the same direction as X_2 (if one increases the other increases as well). When the correlation is negative, the variables vary in opposite directions (X_2 decreases when X_1 increases and vice versa).

6 **What is a zero correlation?**

A zero correlation refers to a correlation coefficient equal to 0 or so close to 0 that the value is likely to be due to sampling error. You find a zero correlation when two variables are independent (that is, one does not vary systematically as a function of the other). In a scatterplot this is represented by a flat line (or a nearly flat line) surrounded by a cloud of dots representing the data pairs.

7 **What is a scatterplot?**

A scatterplot is a graph containing the data pairs of two variables between which a correlation is calculated. Each data pair is represented by a dot at the intersection of the value of X_1 (on the abscissa) and X_2 (on the ordinate); see Figures 11.3–11.8. A scatterplot can also include the regression line.

8 **What is the regression line and how do you calculate it?**

The regression line is a line representing the theoretical correlation between two variables. It indicates the predicted values of one variable as a function of the observed values of the other variable. For a Pearson product-moment correlation this is a straight line, because the correlation is linear. The regression line is calculated on the basis of the intercept and the regression weight using the equations:

$$\text{regression weight} = \frac{\Sigma(X_1 - M_1)(X_2 - M_2)}{\sqrt{\Sigma(X_1 - M_1)^2}}$$

$$\text{intercept} = M_2 - \text{regression weight} * M_1$$

9 **What does 'percentage of variance explained' mean?**

'Percentage of variance explained' refers to the reduction in unaccounted variance of the predicted variable by taking into account the correlated variable. It is calculated either by comparing the variance of the differences between the observed values and the predicted values relative to the total variance of the predicted variable, or by squaring the correlation coefficient. Both give the same value. When $r = +1.00$ or -1.00, all variance is accounted for (that is, the observed values coincide with the regression line; Figure 11.9). When $r = .00$, no variance is explained (that is, the regression line coincides with M_2 over the complete range of X_1 values).

10 Is a correlation always statistically significant?

No. A zero correlation is never significant in a statistical sense (that is, it always agrees with the null hypothesis of no correlation between the variables). The significance of higher correlation coefficients depends on the number of data pairs on which they are based. For a Pearson correlation, coefficients between $-.631$ and $+.631$ are not significant at the .05 level (two-tailed) if the evidence is based on only 10 data pairs. In contrast, when the number of data pairs equals 100, correlations are significant as soon as $r \leq -.197$ or $r \geq +.197$ (Table 11.12).

11 How many participants do you have to include in a study with a Pearson correlation coefficient?

This depends on the magnitude of the correlation coefficient at the population level. As a rule of thumb a minimum of 84 participants is required in a correlational study. This allows researchers to reliably detect correlations from -1.00 to $-.30$ and from $+.30$ to 1.00. If researchers have evidence that the correlation they are after is stronger, they can risk a lower number of participants (for example, 30 for an expected correlation of .50). When there is evidence for a lower correlation, the required number of participants may become as high as 800.

11

Improving predictions through non-parametric tests

12

?

1. When can you use the Spearman rank correlation and when the Pearson product-moment correlation ?
2. What does the Spearman rank correlation comprise?
3. Why is it always interesting to compare the results of a Pearson correlation with those of a Spearman correlation?
4. When can you use a chi-square test for independence? Why is this test useful for comparisons between two groups?
5. What is a contingency table?
6. With what are the observed frequencies compared in a chi-square test? Why is this interesting?
7. How many degrees of freedom does a chi-square test for independence have when the data form a 2×2 contingency table?

In the previous chapter we saw how it is possible to use the Pearson product-moment correlation to improve our prediction of a variable X_2 when we have knowledge of a correlated variable X_1. In particular, we discussed at great length how Galton could use the size of mother peas (X_1) to predict the size of daughter peas (X_2), because the variables were correlated.

The Pearson correlation is a parametric statistic. It assumes that the distributions of X_1 and X_2 are normal and tries to estimate the parameters of these distributions (means and standard deviations). It also assumes that the variables come from an interval/ratio scale. If these assumptions are untrue, the test should not be used (although it tends to be robust to small deviations).

Statisticians were not overly happy with the above restrictions and looked for alternatives that would have a wider applicability. This, as we have seen before, involves non-parametric tests. There are two types of non-parametric correlation test, depending on whether the data are ordinal or nominal. For ordinal data (and also applicable to interval/ratio scales), the tests are based on ranks. For nominal data, the tests are based on frequencies of occurrence. In this chapter, we discuss one test of each type. First, we deal with the Spearman rank correlation, which is used for ordinal data, then the chi-square test of independence, used for nominal data.

12.1 The Spearman rank correlation for ordinal data and interval/ratio data

When you have reasons to believe that your data do not form an interval/ratio scale, it is always good to run the Spearman rank correlation instead of (or in addition to) the Pearson correlation. For instance, this will be the case when you are using rating scales and you cannot be sure that the intervals between the ratings have the same meaning (for example, participants may feel that the difference between 4 and 5 on a 7-point scale is smaller than the difference between 1 and 2 or 6 and 7). Certainly, given the ease with which statistics can be calculated nowadays, you are strongly advised always to check whether there is a big difference between the Pearson correlation and its non-parametric equivalent and, if there is, to find the origin of the difference (see also Section 12.1.3).

12.1.1 The Spearman rank correlation coefficient

You will be happy to discover that the calculation of the Spearman rank correlation coefficient is a piece of cake if you understand how raw data are converted into ranks and how the Pearson correlation coefficient is calculated. In fact, the **Spearman rank correlation** is just the Pearson correlation of the ranks. This correlation is called rho and given the symbol ρ to distinguish it from the Pearson correlation r. If we use the symbols R_1 and R_2 for the ranks in condition 1 and 2, then we can define ρ as:

$$\rho = \frac{\Sigma(R_1 - M_{R_1})(R_2 - M_{R_2})}{\sqrt{\Sigma(R_1 - M_{R_1})^2 \Sigma(R_2 - M_{R_2})^2}}$$

12

in which R_1 represents the ranks of condition 1, R_2 represents the ranks of condition 2, M_{R_1} is the mean rank of condition 1, and M_{R_2} is the mean rank of condition 2. Notice that for ranks the mean equals the median because ranks make a symmetric distribution (Chapter 2).

Let's apply the Spearman rank correlation to an example. Suppose a psychologist wants to know whether or not teenage girls who have a close relationship with their mothers have a similar relationship with their fathers. On the one hand, you could imagine that girls who have good relationships with their mothers also have good relationships with their fathers, which would translate into a positive correlation. On the other hand, it could be that teenage girls who are close to their mothers are more distant from their fathers, and vice versa, which would hint at a negative correlation. Finally, it is possible that there is no relationship at all between the quality of the relationships with the mother and the father. To find out, the psychologist decides to ask 12 female students to rate the closeness of their relationships with their mother and father on a 10-point Likert scale. On the basis of what we have seen in Chapter 11, you should know that this is a very meagre sample size, which only allows the psychologist to pick up strong correlations at the population level. (Because non-parametric tests in general are slightly less powerful than their parametric alternatives, you need at least as many participants in your study as indicated for the parametric tests.) This number has been chosen for the sake of illustration and not to give you the illusion that you can do worthwhile correlational research on the basis of small samples! Table 12.1 lists the data.

Table 12.1 Closeness of the relationship between teenage girls and their parents, based on a 10-point rating scale: 'How close are you to your mother/father?' (1 = not close at all, 10 = very close).

	Mother	Father
student 1	8	7
student 2	5	6
student 3	9	8
student 4	5	4
student 5	10	8
student 6	7	7
student 7	8	2
student 8	9	6
student 9	5	4
student 10	6	3
student 11	4	5
student 12	8	3

As we indicated in previous chapters, it is always good to have a look at the data before running statistical analyses. In this example, we see that the relationships between daughters and their parents span virtually the entire range of possible values, going from 2 to 10. On average, however, it looks as if the relationships are quite close, particularly with the mothers. We can check this by calculating the median values ($Mdn_1 = 7.5$, $Mdn_2 = 5.5$). The difference in closeness with mothers and fathers can be verified by running a Wilcoxon signed-rank test ($W = 10.5$, $N = 11$ [excluding one person with a 0 difference score], $p = .042$). This test informs us that the difference in closeness is indeed significant at the .05 level.

To calculate the Spearman rank correlation, we have to replace the raw scores by their ranks. The ranks are calculated separately for each condition. So, we first establish the ranks for the relationships with the mothers and then the ranks for the relationships with the fathers. In our example both go from 1 to 12 (the number of students). To assign the ranks for the mothers, we use an auxiliary table in which we order the students in ascending order going from a low rating to a high rating (Table 12.2). As we saw in Chapter 8, such an auxiliary table helps to ensure that no mistakes are made with tied ranks.

Table 12.2

	Mother	Rank (raw)	Rank (tied)
student 11	4	1	1
student 2	5	2	3
student 4	5	3	3
student 9	5	4	3
student 10	6	5	5
student 6	7	6	6
student 1	8	7	8
student 7	8	8	8
student 12	8	9	8
student 3	9	10	10.5
student 8	9	11	10.5
student 5	10	12	12
		$\Sigma R = 78$	$\Sigma R = 78$
		$\dfrac{N(N+1)}{2} = \dfrac{12 * 13}{2} = 78$	

To prevent calculation errors, we check whether the sum of the ranks equals $N * (N + 1)/2$. Next, we establish the ranks of the girls' relationships with the fathers (Table 12.3).

Table 12.3

	Father	Rank (raw)	Rank (tied)
student 7	2	1	1
student 10	3	2	2.5
student 12	3	3	2.5
student 4	4	4	4.5
student 9	4	5	4.5
student 11	5	6	6
student 2	6	7	7.5
student 8	6	8	7.5
student 1	7	9	9.5
student 6	7	10	9.5
student 3	8	11	11.5
student 5	8	12	11.5
		$\Sigma R = 78$	$\Sigma R = 78$
		$\dfrac{N(N+1)}{2} = \dfrac{12 * 13}{2} = 78$	

Subsequently, we bring the ranks of the two conditions into the same table. Take care that you assign the correct ranks to the participants! Student 1 has rank 8 for the relationship with her mother and rank 9.5 for the relationship with her father. Student 2 has ranks 3 and 7.5, and so on. This results in Table 12.4.

Table 12.4

	R_1	R_2
student 1	8	9.5
student 2	3	7.5
student 3	10.5	11.5
student 4	3	4.5
student 5	12	11.5
student 6	6	9.5
student 7	8	1
student 8	10.5	7.5
student 9	3	4.5
student 10	5	2.5
student 11	1	6
student 12	8	2.5
	$\Sigma R = 78$	$\Sigma R = 78$
	$M_R = \dfrac{N+1}{2} = \dfrac{13}{2} = 6.5$	

Our next step is to make an auxiliary table for the calculation of the correlation coefficient (Table 12.5). For instance, the value of student 1 in the column $(R_1 - M_{R_1})^2$ is $(8 - 6.5)^2 = 2.25$.

Table 12.5

	R_1	R_2	$(R_1 - M_{R_1})^2$	$(R_2 - M_{R_2})^2$	$(R_1 - M_{R_1})(R_2 - M_{R_2})$
student 1	8	9.5	2.25	9.00	4.50
student 2	3	7.5	12.25	1.00	−3.50
student 3	10.5	11.5	16.00	25.00	20.00
student 4	3	4.5	12.25	4.00	7.00
student 5	12	11.5	30.25	25.00	27.50
student 6	6	9.5	.25	9.00	−1.50
student 7	8	1	2.25	30.25	−8.25
student 8	10.5	7.5	16.00	1.00	4.00
student 9	3	4.5	12.25	4.00	7.00
student 10	5	2.5	2.25	16.00	6.00
student 11	1	6	30.25	.25	2.75
student 12	8	2.5	2.25	16.00	−6.00
	$M = 6.5$	$M = 6.5$	$\Sigma = 138.50$	$\Sigma = 140.50$	$\Sigma = 59.50$

$$\rho = \frac{\Sigma(R_1 - M_{R_1})(R_2 - M_{R_2})}{\sqrt{\Sigma(R_1 - M_{R_1})^2 \Sigma(R_2 - M_{R_2})^2}} = \frac{59.5}{\sqrt{138.5 * 140.5}} = .43$$

12.1.2 Determining statistical significance of the Spearman rank correlation

Tip To calculate the Spearman rank correlation, simply replace the raw scores by ranks and calculate the Pearson product-moment correlation coefficient on the ranks. The p-value of the Pearson correlation provides you with the p-value of the Spearman rank correlation.

To see whether ρ is significant, we use the same table as we did for the Pearson correlation. (Remember that the Spearman rank correlation is just a Pearson correlation on the ranks.) Using Appendix E again, given that $N = 12$, $\rho_{.05crit} = .576$. Because $\rho_{obs} < \rho_{crit}$, we (or rather the psychologist who ran the study) fail to reject the null hypothesis. If we calculate the exact p-value, we find that $p = .167$.

12.1.3 The Spearman rank correlation as an alternative to the Pearson correlation

The Spearman rank correlation is not limited to ordinal data but can be used for interval/ratio data as well. This is particularly interesting because a comparison of the Spearman and the Pearson correlations tells us something about the data.

As a demonstration of the correspondence between the Pearson and Spearman correlations, let's calculate the Spearman rank correlation for the examples we used in Chapter 11. The first example was that of Galton's peas. Remember that for these data we found that $r = .346$ ($N = 700$, $p < .0001$). When we calculate the Spearman rank correlation for these data, we find that $\rho = .362$ ($N = 700$, $p < .0001$). These values are quite close (as we would expect), although ρ is slightly higher than r, probably because of the skewed distributions of the daughter sizes. (Remember that for each mother size there were more small daughters than medium-sized ones).

The next two examples we discussed in Chapter 11 were artificial data to illustrate the calculation of the Pearson correlation. The Pearson correlation for the data in Table 11.8 was $r = -.971$ ($N = 10$, $p < .0001$). If we calculate the Spearman rank correlation (please do so as a learning check!), we find that $\rho = -.982$ ($N = 10$, $p < .0001$). For the data in Table 11.9, r was $-.750$ ($N = 10$, $p < .0001$) and $\rho = -.754$ ($N = 10$, $p < .0001$). Finally, the Spearman rank correlation between the exam marks for statistics and social psychology (Table 11.13) is $\rho = +.423$ ($N = 10$, $p = .223$), while r was $+.451$ ($N = 10$, $p = .191$). For all these examples, we see the close proximity of the Pearson and the Spearman correlation coefficients.

In fact, some statisticians argue that the Spearman correlation is to be preferred to the Pearson for data from interval/ratio scales also. They prefer the Spearman correlation because it is better in two situations: when the sample includes outliers and when the relationship between X_1 and X_2 is curvilinear.

Outliers are data pairs that do not seem to be in line with the rest of the findings. Figure 12.1 shows a typical example. It includes the data on exam marks that we used in Table 11.13, supplemented with one extra student who had a mark of 20 on statistics and a mark of 0 on social psychology.

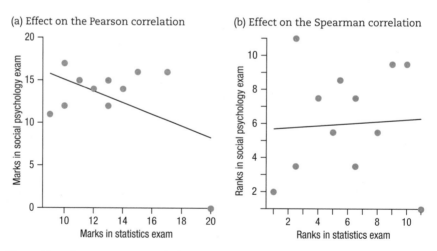

Figure 12.1 The Spearman correlation is less susceptible to outliers (data pairs with values widely diverging from the rest of the sample). (a) the effect on the Pearson correlation of an outlier that goes against the general trend in the data. (b) the effect of the same outlier on the Spearman correlation. Notice the different scales: (a) goes from 0 to 20 (the minimum and the maximum scores), whereas (b) goes from 1 to 11 (the minimum and the maximum ranks).

As you can see in Figure 12.1a, this outlier has a huge effect on the Pearson correlation. This has changed from $r = +.451$ ($N = 10$, $p = .191$) to $r = -.505$ ($N = 11$, $p = .113$), 'suggesting' a trend towards a negative correlation. In contrast, the effect on the Spearman correlation is much less severe because the values of the test are limited to the minimum and the maximum rank. The introduction of the outlier only shifts the Spearman correlation from $\rho = +.423$ ($N = 10$, $p = .223$) to $\rho = +.062$ ($N = 11$, $p = .856$; Figure 12.1b).

When the outlier does not go against the overall trend in the data but reinforces the trend, the effect on the Pearson correlation is again much more pronounced than for the Spearman correlation. Figure 12.2 shows what happens when a student with the exam marks 20,20 is added to the sample of students in Figure 11.13. Now, the Pearson correlation shifts from $r = +.451$ ($N = 10$, $p = .191$) to $r = +.710$ ($N = 11$, $p = .014$), 'suggesting' a substantial positive correlation. In contrast, the Spearman correlation only shifts from $\rho = +.423$ ($N = 10$, $p = .223$) to $\rho = +.569$ ($N = 11$, $p = .068$).

> **Tip** A big difference between the Pearson and the Spearman correlation is an indication that one or more outliers may be present in the data. Make a scatterplot of the data to check this possibility. In any case, you are strongly advised always to have a look at the scatterplot of the data in addition to the statistical analysis!

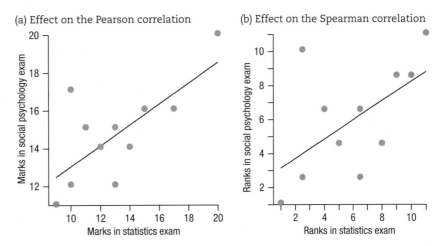

Figure 12.2 The effect of an outlier that reinforces the general trend in the data is again much stronger on the Pearson correlation than on the Spearman correlation.

The effect of the outlier on the Pearson correlation depends on the distance between the outlier and the rest of the data. For instance, if the maximum exam mark had been more than 20 and the outlying student had marks of 30,30, then the Pearson correlation would have been $r = +.916$ ($N = 11$, $p < .0001$). The Spearman correlation would still have been $\rho = +.569$ ($N = 11$, $p = .068$).

The second situation in which the Spearman correlation is superior to the Pearson correlation occurs when the relationship between X_1 and X_2 is curvilinear. That is, when the best fitting regression line between X_1 and X_2 is not a straight line but a curve. Such situations occur quite often in psychology. Figure 12.3 gives an illustration of what is meant using hypothetical data of a study on the relationship between the saltiness of water (X_1) and the palatability of the water (X_2). There is a negative correlation because the value of X_2 decreases

12

(a) Pearson correlation

(b) Spearman correlation

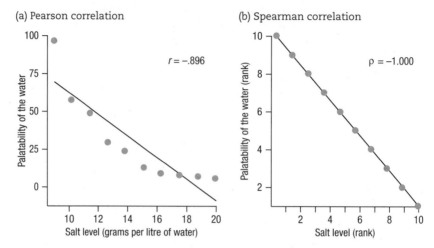

Palatability of the water

$r = -.896$

Salt level (grams per litre of water)

Palatability of the water (rank)

$\rho = -1.000$

Salt level (rank)

Figure 12.3 A Spearman rank correlation yields a higher coefficient than the Pearson correlation when the relationship between two variables is not linear but curvilinear. (a) the situation as assumed by a Pearson correlation; (b) the situation as assumed by a Spearman rank correlation.

as the value of X_1 increases. However, the drop is not the same for each increase in X_1 (that is, it is not linear). At low salt levels, the pleasantness drops sharply but at higher levels the drop becomes smaller (possibly because the participants do not taste much difference between a solution of 15 g salt per litre of water and 16 g salt per litre of water). The important fact for our present discussion is that in such a case the Spearman rank correlation results in a higher coefficient. Again, make use of a scatterplot to pick up this type of deviation from the linear relationship!

12.1.4 Calculating the Spearman rank statistic in SPSS

Chapter 6 of Brace, Kemp and Snelgar, *SPSS for Psychologists*, provides a useful guide to the Spearman rank correlation.

The Spearman rank correlation is available as an option in the Correlate analysis. We will illustrate it with the example of the closeness of daughters to their mothers and fathers, introduced in Table 12.1. Enter these data in SPSS and click on *Analyze*, *Correlate*, *Bivariate*.

Enter Mother and Father as the *Variables* of interest and click on *Spearman* ①.

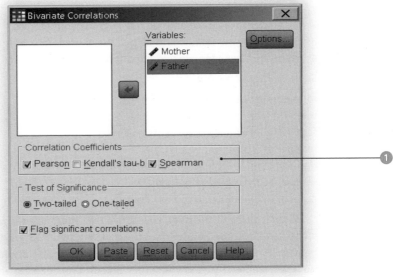

Click on **OK** and in the output you find a panel with the Spearman correlation.

Correlations			Mother	Father
Spearman's rho	Mother	Correlation Coefficient	1.000	.427
		Sig. (2-tailed)		.167
		N	12	12
	Father	Correlation Coefficient	.427	1.000
		Sig. (2-tailed)	.167	
		N	12	12

Have a look at the panel with the Pearson correlation as well and compare them.

12.2 The chi-square test of independence for nominal data

To illustrate the use of a chi-square test of independence for nominal data, suppose you want to know whether men are more (or less) likely than women to assist a person in need. To find out, a confederate of yours 'accidentally' drops a stack of papers in a university building when a student passes by. You are positioned out of sight and notice whether or not the student helps your confederate to pick up the papers. In addition you jot down the gender of the student.

12

After a few hours of observation, you summarise your data. You are likely to discover that you have four types of observations:

1 the student was male and helped the confederate,
2 the student was male and did not help the confederate,
3 the student was female and helped the confederate, and
4 the student was female and did not help the confederate.

Suppose these are your data:

total number of observations: 100
total number of male students observed: 43
total number of female students observed: 57
number of males that helped: 17
number of males that did not help: 26
number of females that helped: 29
number of females that did not help: 28

When looking at the data, you notice that there is a tendency for the female students to be more helpful than the male students: 51% of the female students helped (29 out of 57) against only 40% of the male students (17 out of 43). However, we need to know whether this difference is big enough to be reliable or whether it could simply be due to sampling error. This is what we will find out in the next sections.

12.2.1 The chi-square statistic of independence

The first step in the analysis of frequency data is the construction of a **contingency table**. This is a table with the observed frequencies of the different outcomes. In our example we have four types of observation, which form a 2×2 frequency table, as detailed in Figure 12.4.[1]

		Helping behaviour		
		Did help	Did not help	Total
Gender	Male	17	26	43
	Female	29	28	57
	Total	46	54	100

Figure 12.4 Contingency table for helping behaviour as a function of the participant's gender: observed frequencies.

Figure 12.4 shows the observed frequencies. In order to know whether they imply that women are more likely to help than men, we need to know the expected frequencies under the assumption of no difference between men and women. To find the expected frequency with which men help people under the assumption of no gender difference, we use the equation:

---

1 Notice that for this contingency table you can also use one-way chi-square tests (Chapter 8) to see whether more women were included in the sample than men, or to see whether significantly more or less than half of the sample helped.

$$\text{frequency}_{\text{men expected to help}} = \frac{\text{frequency}_{\text{men}} * \text{frequency}_{\text{people who help}}}{\text{all observations}}$$

In other words, the expected frequency of a cell equals the sum of the observations in the row times the sum of the observations in the column divided by the total number of observations, N. Applied to Figure 12.2, this gives:

$$f_{\text{men expected to help}} = \frac{f_{\text{men}} * f_{\text{helps}}}{f_{\text{all observations}}} = \frac{43 * 46}{100} = 19.78$$

Similarly, we can calculate the expected frequency of women who help under the assumption of independence. This is:

$$f_{\text{women expected to help}} = \frac{f_{\text{women}} * f_{\text{helps}}}{f_{\text{all observations}}} = \frac{57 * 46}{100} = 26.22$$

Next we calculate the expected frequencies of men and women who did not help:

$$f_{\text{men expected not to help}} = \frac{f_{\text{men}} * f_{\text{does not help}}}{f_{\text{all observations}}} = \frac{43 * 54}{100} = 23.22$$

$$f_{\text{women expected not to help}} = \frac{f_{\text{women}} * f_{\text{does not help}}}{f_{\text{all observations}}} = \frac{57 * 54}{100} = 30.78$$

Figure 12.5 shows the contingency table of the expected frequencies.

		Helping behaviour		
		Did help	Did not help	Total
	Male	19.78	23.22	43
Gender				
	Female	26.22	30.78	57
	Total	46	54	100

Figure 12.5 Expected frequencies under the assumption of independence.

The expected frequencies become more understandable when you express them as percentages of the total number of men and women observed in the study. 19.78 out of 43 men were expected to help. This is 46% of the men that took part in the study. Similarly, 26.22 out of 57 women were expected to help. This is also 46%. So, under the assumption of independence the percentages of helping do not differ between men and women and are equal to the overall percentage of people who helped.

Next, we make an auxiliary table to compare the observed and the expected frequencies for the four types of observation, as shown in Table 12.6:

Table 12.6 Auxiliary table comparing the observed and expected frequencies.

	f_{observed}	f_{expected}
men who helped	17	19.78
men who did not help	26	23.22
women who helped	29	26.22
women who did not help	28	30.78

12

In the next step we have to find out whether the observed and the expected frequencies differ significantly from each other. This is where the chi-square statistic comes in. The chi-square statistic is the sum of the squared differences between the observed and the expected frequencies divided by the expected frequencies. More formally:

$$\chi^2 = \sum \frac{(f_{obs} - f_{exp})^2}{f_{exp}}$$

To calculate χ^2, we use an auxiliary table (Table 12.7).

Table 12.7

	f_{obs}	f_{exp}	$(f_{obs} - f_{exp})^2$	$\dfrac{(f_{obs} - f_{exp})^2}{f_{exp}}$
men who helped	17	19.78	7.7284	.39
men who did not help	26	23.22	7.7284	.33
women who helped	29	26.22	7.7284	.29
women who did not help	28	30.78	7.7284	.25
				$\Sigma = 1.26$

The value of $(f_{obs} - f_{exp})^2$ is the same in each row, because the difference between the observed and the expected values is always +2.78 or –2.78, which both square to the value 7.7284.

The values of $(f_{obs} - f_{exp})^2/f_{exp}$ differ slightly because of the differences in the denominator (the expected frequencies). For instance, it is .39 in row 1 because 7.7284 is divided by 19.78.

The end result is the sum of the four numbers in the last column, which is the observed chi-square value. So, $\chi^2_{obs} = 1.26$. To know whether it is significant, we have to compare the observed value with the critical value. This is done in the next section.

12.2.2 The chi-square test of independence

To know whether the observed χ^2-value of 1.26 is large enough to be statistically significant, we must know the critical χ^2-value. For a 2×2 contingency table, the critical value at the .05 significance level is $\chi^2_{.05crit} = 3.841$. For the .01 significance level, it is $\chi^2_{.01crit} = 6.635$. If you look back to Chapter 8, you will notice that the .05 critical value is the same as the one for the one-way chi-square test for two samples. This is because, in a 2×2 contingency table, only one frequency is free to vary. As soon as one of the frequencies is fixed, the other frequencies become known as well. For instance, in this example, as soon as we know that the number of men who helped is 17, we know that the number of men who did not help is $43 - 17 = 26$, that the number of females who helped is $46 - 17 = 29$, and so on. Therefore, the chi-square test only has one degree of freedom (see also the **Going further** section).

Given that our observed chi-square value ($\chi^2_{obs} = 1.26$) is smaller than the .05 critical value ($\chi^2_{.05crit} = 3.841$, df = 1), we fail to reject the null hypothesis. That is, on the basis of the available data, the evidence is not strong enough to conclude that women are more likely to help than men. If we calculate the exact p-value, we find that $p = .262$ (see the SPSS section).

12.2.3 Reporting the results of a chi-square test

When we report the results of a chi-square test, we must give information about the number of people involved in the study, the χ^2-value that was observed, the degrees of freedom (df = 1 when we use a 2×2 contingency table), and either the significance level we used or the exact p-value. So, for the helping example we would write something like:

'A total of 100 students were observed when they passed by a confederate of the experimenter who dropped a pile of papers; 57 of the students were female. Forty-six of the students helped (29 females and 17 males). A chi-square test of independence indicated that the percentage of females who helped was not significantly different from the percentage of males who helped ($\chi^2(1) = 1.26$, $p = .260$).'

12.2.4 Another example of the chi-square test of independence

At the beginning of the 21st century, there was concern in the UK that the MMR vaccination might increase the chance of a child developing an autistic disorder. (The MMR vaccination is a combined injection against measles, mumps and rubella.) The scare was increased when the media published stories of children who had been injected with MMR and, shortly afterwards, had been diagnosed with autism. An increasing number of parents refused to have their children inoculated.

Smeeth et al. (2004) argued that the media had taken the wrong approach, which was based on a confirmation bias. If you want to show that there is an association between vaccination and autism, you cannot just demonstrate that some children who have been vaccinated will develop autism. Unfortunately, a certain proportion of children are bound to develop the disorder, whether they are inoculated or not. Instead, you must show that children who have been vaccinated are *more likely* to develop the disorder than children who have not been vaccinated.

Smeeth et al. analysed the National Health Service databases to locate all children with autistic disorders and to find a suitable control group of children living under the same socio-economic circumstances who had not developed an autistic disorder. They found 1294 children with autistic disorders and 4469 control children. In each group, the researchers calculated the number of children who had been vaccinated. The data are shown in Table 12.8 (overleaf).

Before we run the statistical test, we first look at the data. In these data something interesting and unexpected is observed: a higher percentage of children in the control condition had been vaccinated (82.1%) than children with autism (78.1%). That is, the data went *against* the hypothesis that MMR vaccination increases the chances of severe developmental disorders. To see whether the

Table 12.8 Data on autism in children.

	Children with autism	Children without autism	Total
given the vaccine	1010 (78.1%)	3671 (82.1%)	4681
not given the vaccine	284 (21.9%)	798 (17.8%)	1082
total	1294 (100%)	4469 (100%)	5763

Adapted from Smeeth et al. (2004.

evidence against the hypothesis could be due to sampling error, we have to run a chi-square test of independence.

For the calculation of the chi-square statistic we need to know the expected frequencies for each of the four types of observation under the assumption of independence. For the children who were given the vaccine and developed autism, this is:

$$f_{\text{vaccinated and autism expected}} = \frac{f_{\text{vaccinated}} * f_{\text{developed autism}}}{f_{\text{all observations}}}$$
$$= \frac{4681 * 1294}{5763} = 1051.05$$

We calculate the other expected frequencies in the same way:

expected frequency of vaccine + no autism = 3629.95
expected frequency of no vaccine + autism = 242.95
expected frequency of no vaccine + no autism = 839.05

Next, we calculate the chi-square statistic on the basis of deviations between the observed and the expected statistics. For this, we use an auxiliary table (Table 12.9).

Table 12.9

	f_{obs}	f_{exp}	$\dfrac{(f_{\text{obs}} - f_{\text{exp}})^2}{f_{\text{exp}}}$
vaccine + autism	1010	1051.05	1.60
vaccine + no autism	3671	3629.95	.46
no vaccine + autism	284	242.95	6.94
no vaccine + no autism	798	839.05	2.01
			$\Sigma = 11.01$

Finally, we check whether the observed χ^2-value is larger than the critical χ^2-value. Given that 11.01 > 3.841 ($\chi^2_{.05\text{crit}}$, df = 1), we find that the observed frequencies are significantly different from those that we would expect on the basis of no effect due to MMR vaccination. So, at least in this study, children who were given the MMR vaccine were significantly *less likely* to develop autistic disorder than the children who were not given the vaccine. Given that the observed χ^2-value is larger than the .01 cut-off value ($\chi^2_{.01\text{crit}} = 6.635$), the difference is even significant at the .01 level (when we calculate the exact p-value, we find that $p = .0009$).

12.2.5 Running the chi-square test of independence in SPSS

Chapter 7 of Brace, Kemp and Snelgar, *SPSS for Psychologists*, also contains a detailed guide to running the chi-square test in SPSS.

To run the chi square test, we must define three columns: (1) Vaccine (0 or 1 [no or yes]), (2) Autism (0 or 1 [no or yes]), and (3) the frequencies of the different combinations:

| File | Edit | View | Data | Transform | Analyze | Gr |

	Vaccine	Austism	Frequency	
1	0	0	798	
2	0	1	284	
3	1	0	3671	
4	1	1	1010	
5				

Next we have to indicate that the Frequencies show the number of observations in each cell of Vaccine * Autism. We do this by clicking on *Data*, *Weight Cases* ①.

| File | Edit | View | Data | Transform | Analyze | Graphs | Util |

Define Variable Properties...
Copy Data Properties...
New Custom Attribute...
Define Dates...
Define Multiple Response Sets...
Validation ▶
Identify Duplicate Cases...
Identify Unusual Cases...
Sort Cases...
Sort Variables...
Transpose...
Restructure...
Merge Files ▶
Aggregate...
Orthogonal Design ▶
Copy Dataset
Split File...
Select Cases...
Weight Cases... ①

This opens a dialogue box which you have to complete to make sure that the cells of the design are weighted by frequency:

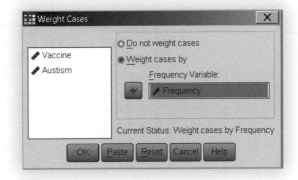

After clicking on OK, click on *Analyze*, *Descriptive Statistics* and *Crosstabs*.

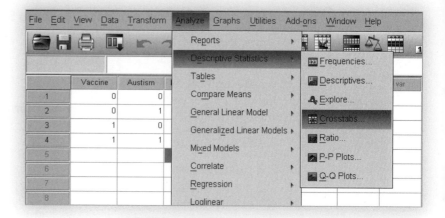

In the new panel, enter the correct variables in *Row(s)* and *Column(s)*, click on *Statistics* and *Exact* to get the exact *p*-value of the chi-square test.

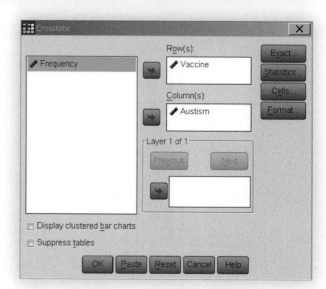

This will give the output:

Chi-Square Tests

	Value	df	Asymp. Sig. (2-sided)	Exact Sig. (2-sided)	Exact Sig. (1-sided)	Point Probability
Pearson Chi-Square	11.013ᵃ	1	.001	.001	.001	
Continuity Correctionᵇ	10.746	1	.001			
Likelihood Ratio	10.705	1	.001	.001	.001	
Fisher's Exact Test				.001	.001	
Linear-by-Linear Association	11.011ᶜ	1	.001	.001	.001	.000
N of Valid Cases	5763					

a. 0 cells (.0%) have expected count less than 5. The minimum expected count is 242.95.

b. Computed only for a 2×2 table.

c. The standardized statistic is -3.318.

The first row contains all the information you need for the chi-square test ($\chi^2 = 11.013$, df = 1, $p = .001$).

Learning check
Practise the calculation of the chi square test with the data on helping behaviour (Figure 12.2).

12.2.6 Going further: the chi-square test for independence when the contingency table is larger than 2 × 2

Although a 2×2 contingency table is the type of table we will encounter most often in research, the chi-square test for independence is not limited to this size. As a matter of fact, it can be applied to a contingency table of any possible size! All you need to know are the critical values for significance in larger tables.

For an $N_1 * N_2$ contingency table the chi-square statistic is part of a chi-square distribution with $(N_1 - 1) * (N_2 - 1)$ degrees of freedom. The chi-square distribution is a theoretical distribution of the same class as the normal distribution and the t-distribution. Its precise shape does not concern us here (although it is an interesting distribution!). We only need to know what chi-square values can be expected under the null hypothesis of independence. For a chi-square distribution with one degree of freedom, we have seen that 95% of the values fall between 0 and 3.841 and 99% fall between 0 and 6.635. (Notice that a chi-square statistic, unlike the z-statistic or the t-statistic, does not have negative values.) So, these are the critical values for a 2×2 contingency table.

The critical values for chi-square tests with other degrees of freedom are listed in Appendix F. Also notice that simple spreadsheets like Excel can give you the precise p-value associated with a particular χ^2-statistic. (Use the function CHIDIST(χ^2-value, df).)

To illustrate the use of the test for a larger contingency table, suppose a researcher wants to know whether husbands and wives resemble each other in birth order (first-borns prefer to marry other first-borns and later-borns prefer to marry other later-borns) or whether they complement each other (first-borns prefer to marry later-borns and vice versa). She asks several groups of students in lectures to indicate the birth orders of their parents.

Rather than making a dichotomous distinction between first-borns and later-borns, the researcher decides to keep a distinction between first-born, second-born, third-born, and later-born, both for the husbands and the wives. This gives a 4×4 contingency table like Table 12.10 (overleaf).

To calculate the χ^2-statistic, we need the expected frequencies. They are given by the product of the row and the column total divided by the overall total. So, the expected frequency of (birth order mother = 1st and birth order father = 1st) equals $(1206 * 1230)/3184 = 466$.

Table 12.11 contains the other expected values (rounded to the nearest integer).

Table 12.10 Observed frequencies of parents' birth order.

		Birth order of mother				
		1st	2nd	3rd	4th+	Total
Birth order of father	1st	575	364	137	154	1230
	2nd	384	301	106	140	931
	3rd	138	142	153	98	531
	4th+	109	94	124	165	492
	Total	1206	901	520	557	3184

Table 12.11 Expected frequencies of parents' birth order.

		Birth order of mother				
		1st	2nd	3rd	4th+	Total
Birth order of father	1st	466	348	201	215	1230
	2nd	353	263	152	163	931
	3rd	201	150	87	93	531
	4th+	186	139	80	86	492
	Total	1206	901	520	557	3184

Next we calculate the standardised squared deviation scores (Table 12.12).

Table 12.12 Values of $(f_{obs} - f_{exp})^2/f_{exp}$.

		Birth order of mother			
		1st	2nd	3rd	4th+
Birth order of father	1st	25.6	0.7	20.3	17.4
	2nd	2.8	5.4	13.9	3.2
	3rd	19.8	0.5	50.7	0.3
	4th+	32.1	14.7	23.7	72.4

These values sum to $\chi^2_{obs} = 303.4$. To find the critical χ^2-value, we must determine the degrees of freedom. These are given by $(N_{columns} - 1) * (N_{rows} - 1)$ $= (4 - 1) * (4 - 1) = 9$. Looking at Appendix F, we see that $\chi^2_{.05crit}(9) = 16.92$ and $\chi^2_{.01crit}(9) = 21.67$. This means that our observed χ^2-value is significant at the .01 level. (Actually it is way more significant than that: $p < 1.0E-10$.) In addition, a look at the data indicates that the differences between the observed and the expected frequencies are in line with the hypothesis that there are more same-rank marriages than would be expected by chance. So, the researcher is allowed to conclude that people tend to marry someone who resembles them in birth order ($\chi^2(9) = 303.4$, $p < .0001$).

12.3   Answers to chapter questions

1 When can you use the Spearman rank correlation and when the Pearson product-moment correlation?

>You can use a Spearman rank correlation in all situations where you can use a Pearson product-moment correlation (variables normally distributed from an interval/ratio scale). In addition, you can use the Spearman rank correlation when the two variables are not normally distributed or when they only form an ordinal scale. Only for nominal data is the Spearman rank correlation of no use. (In this case, you have to use a chi-square test.)

2 What does the Spearman rank correlation comprise?

>The Spearman rank correlation is a Pearson product-moment correlation of the ranks of the X-values. To calculate the Spearman rank correlation, you first have to convert the X-values of each variable to their respective ranks. (This is done separately for each variable.)

3 Why is it always interesting to compare the results of a Pearson correlation with those of a Spearman correlation?

>Usually, the Spearman correlation coefficient will be close to the Pearson correlation coefficient. If this is not the case, it is interesting to find out what causes the discrepancy. A rank correlation that is higher than the product-moment correlation is likely to be due to a few outliers or to the fact that the relationship between the two variables is curvilinear rather than linear. Use a scatterplot to find out which. A much higher Pearson correlation than Spearman rank correlation can also be due to a few outliers.

4 When can you use a chi-square test for independence? Why is this test useful for comparisons between two groups?

>You can use a chi-square test for independence to compare frequencies of occurrence in two (or more) groups. This is particularly interesting for nominal data. Because the frequencies in each group fall into a few categories (for example, a person who helps v. a person who does not help), the chi-square test for independence is used to investigate whether the distribution of the frequencies differs between the groups.

5 What is a contingency table?

>A contingency table is a table that represents the relationship between two (or more) categorical variables. In a two-dimensional contingency table, the rows represent the levels of one variable and the columns represent the levels of the other variable. Each cell includes the frequency of observations in that particular combination of 'variable 1 level' and 'variable 2 level' (see Figure 12.2).

12

6 With what are the observed frequencies compared in a chi-square test? Why is this interesting?

> The observed frequencies are compared with the frequencies that would be expected under the assumption of independence of the variables. In this way, the researcher can examine whether the distribution of data deviates from the distribution one would expect if the two variables were not correlated. If the deviations are big enough (that is, have a statistically significant χ^2-value), the researcher can conclude that the two variables are correlated.

7 How many degrees of freedom does a chi-square test for independence have when the data form a 2×2 contingency table?

> $df = 1$ [that is, $(\text{rows} - 1) * (\text{columns} - 1)$]

Using analysis of variance for multiple independent variables

13

?

1 When is analysis of variance (ANOVA) more interesting than t-tests?
2 What is the core mechanism underlying analysis of variance and why is this difficult to understand?
3 Which statistical test is used in analysis of variance and how does this relate to the t-test?
4 What is a split-plot design?
5 When do you have interaction terms in an analysis of variance?

So far we have covered the most important statistical tests to compare two conditions. These tests were developed at the beginning of the 20th century, and helped to establish psychology as a true science. However, they have one important limitation: they cannot be scaled up to more complex research designs. If researchers want to compare three levels of a variable rather than two (for example, pre-school children, primary school children and secondary school children), they have to run three t-tests or Mann-Whitney U-tests to compare the various groups. Similarly, these tests cannot be used to analyse the effects of two or more independent variables (for example, the effect of psychotherapy in older and younger individuals).

Another type of analysis, developed by the British mathematician Ronald Fisher, is capable of such generalisations. It is called **analysis of variance**, usually abbreviated as **ANOVA**. In this chapter, we first discuss how analysis of variance is equivalent to the t-tests covered in Chapters 6 and 9, and then we describe how it can be extended to a situation with one between-groups variable and one repeated measure. In Chapter 14 we will discuss how ANOVA can be applied to designs with variables of three and more levels.

In this chapter we also introduce the concepts you need to understand the outcome of an ANOVA. This will help you to read the output of computer programs, both for simple and complicated analyses. In this respect, this chapter goes way beyond Chapters 6 and 9, even though you will see the same examples. This has been done to make it easier for you to compare analysis of variance with the simpler t-tests.

13.1 Using analysis of variance to compare groups of people

In this section we illustrate how ANOVA can be used to compare two groups of people. We will do so by repeating the analysis of the percentages of errors noticed by young and old adults, introduced in Chapter 6.

13.1.1 Variance in means instead of differences between means

To understand analysis of variance, you must be aware of Fisher's counterintuitive insight that differences in means can be thought of as variance in means. When we compare conditions (for example, young people v. old people), we tend to look at the differences between the means. However, Fisher argued, we can also look at the variance of the means. When two (or more) means are the same, there is no variance between them. When the means are different, they exhibit variance. So, Fisher argued, a statistical analysis can be reformulated as a question of whether the variance between the conditions (the means) is sufficiently larger than the variance within the conditions.

To understand this, we repeat the example of the percentages of errors noticed by young and old adults, introduced in Table 6.1 and repeated here in Table 13.1. Remember that the example involved a study in which 10 young and 10 old adults were compared on the likelihood of remembering a mistake they

Table 13.1 Percentage of errors noticed by young and old adults.

Young adults	Old adults
71	72
75	65
81	70
79	76
75	72
84	75
74	68
74	69
71	71
79	70

$M_1 = 76.3$, $SD_1 = 4.30$
$M_2 = 70.8$, $SD_2 = 3.22$

$$t = \frac{M_1 - M_2}{\sqrt{\dfrac{SD_1^2}{N_1} + \dfrac{SD_2^2}{N_2}}} = \frac{76.3 - 70.8}{\sqrt{\dfrac{(4.30)^2}{10} + \dfrac{(3.22)^2}{10}}} = 3.24$$

$df = N_1 - 1 + N_2 - 1 = 18$
$p = .0046$

had made. The participants sat in front of a computer screen that displayed four boxes. Underneath the screen were four response keys. On each trial a light appeared in one of the boxes and the participants had to press the corresponding key as fast as possible. The trials succeeded each other rapidly. Occasionally, the computer program stopped and asked the participants whether they had made an error in the previous three trials (for example, the participants had pressed key 3 although the light was shown in box 2). The experiment was programmed in such a way that the program often stopped two trials after the participants made an error. These were the critical trials on which the results were based. There was a group of 10 young participants ($M = 20.1$ years) and a group of 10 old participants ($M = 71.2$ years). The t-test of independent groups we ran in Chapter 6 showed that the means of the two groups differed significantly: the young participants were more likely to notice the errors they had made than the old participants ($M_{young} = 76.3$, $M_{old} = 70.8$; $t(18) = 3.24$, $p = .0046$).

As we saw in Chapter 6, the t-test for independent groups takes into account the difference between the means (the numerator), the variances in the two groups and the sizes of the groups (the denominator).

The new insight Fisher introduced was that the difference in means can be replaced by the variance in means. Although this does not make much difference when only two groups are compared, it can be easily generalised to situations with more conditions. It is no more difficult to calculate the variance of three or four means than the variance of two means, as we will see in Chapter 14.

13

More specifically, in ANOVA a distinction is made between:

1 the total variance – the variance that is present in the full data set,
2 the treatment variance – the variance between the conditions,
3 the error variance – the variance within the conditions.

Let's apply this to the example of Table 13.1.

To calculate the **total variance**, we must know the grand mean. That is the mean of all 20 results (that is, the data of the 10 young adults and the data of the 10 old adults). As is shown in auxiliary Table 13.2, the grand mean equals $(71+75+...+71+70)/20 = 1471/20 = 73.55$. Another way to calculate the grand mean is by taking the average of M_1 and M_2: $(76.3+70.8)/2 = 73.55$.

Table 13.2 Auxiliary table to calculate the total variance of the study involving the percentages of errors noticed by young and old adults.

Condition	X	$(X - M_{grand})^2$
Young	71	$(71-73.55)^2 = 6.5025$
Young	75	$(75-73.55)^2 = 2.1025$
Young	81	$(81-73.55)^2 = 55.5025$
Young	79	$(79-73.55)^2 = 29.7025$
Young	75	$(75-73.55)^2 = 2.1025$
Young	84	$(84-73.55)^2 = 109.2025$
Young	74	$(74-73.55)^2 = .2025$
Young	74	$(74-73.55)^2 = .2025$
Young	71	$(71-73.55)^2 = 6.5025$
Young	79	$(79-73.55)^2 = 29.7025$
Old	72	$(72-73.55)^2 = 2.4025$
Old	65	$(65-73.55)^2 = 73.1025$
Old	70	$(70-73.55)^2 = 12.6025$
Old	76	$(76-73.55)^2 = 6.0025$
Old	72	$(72-73.55)^2 = 2.4025$
Old	75	$(75-73.55)^2 = 2.1025$
Old	68	$(68-73.55)^2 = 30.8025$
Old	69	$(69-73.55)^2 = 20.7025$
Old	71	$(71-73.55)^2 = 6.5025$
Old	70	$(70-73.55)^2 = 12.6025$
	$\Sigma X = 1471$	$\Sigma(X - M_{grand})^2 = 410.9500$

$N = 20$

$M_{grand} = 1471/20 = 73.55$

$\Sigma(X - M_{grand})^2 = 410.95$

$$\text{Variance} = \frac{\Sigma(X - M_{grand})^2}{N - 1} = \frac{410.95}{20 - 1} = 21.63$$

Table 13.3 Auxiliary table to calculate the treatment variance of the study involving the percentages of errors noticed by the young and the old adults.

Condition	M	$(M - M_{grand})^2$
Young	76.3	$(76.3 - 73.55)^2 = 7.5625$
Old	70.8	$(70.8 - 73.55)^2 = 7.5625$
	$\Sigma M = 147.1$	$\Sigma(X - M_{grand})^2 = 15.1250$

$N_{means} = 2$

$M_{grand} = 147.1/2 = 73.55$

$\Sigma(M - M_{grand})^2 = 15.125$

$\text{Variance} = \dfrac{\Sigma(M - M_{grand})^2}{N_{means} - 1} = \dfrac{15.125}{2 - 1} = 15.125$

The **treatment variance** is simply defined as the variance of the condition means. This is shown in auxiliary Table 13.3.

Finally, the **error variance** is the sum of the variances within the conditions. We will not re-iterate these calculations (see Tables 6.2 and 6.3) but simply copy them into auxiliary Table 13.4.

Table 13.4 Auxiliary table to calculate the error variance of the study involving the percentages of errors noticed by the young and the old adults.

Variance in the condition of the young adults (see Table 6.2)
$\Sigma X_1 = 763$
$N_1 = 10$
$M_1 = 76.3$
$\Sigma(X_1 - M_1)^2 = 166.10$
$\text{Variance}_1 = \dfrac{\Sigma(X_1 - M_1)^2}{N_1 - 1} = \dfrac{166.1}{10 - 1} = 18.46 \quad (SD = 4.30)$

Variance in the condition of the old adults (see Table 6.3)
$\Sigma X_2 = 708$
$N_2 = 10$
$M_2 = 70.8$
$\Sigma(X_2 - M_2)^2 = 93.60$
$\text{Variance}_2 = \dfrac{\Sigma(X_2 - M_2)^2}{N_2 - 1} = \dfrac{93.6}{10 - 1} = 10.40 \quad (SD = 3.22)$

13.1.2 Relationships discovered by Fisher

Fisher discovered that there is a systematic relationship between the total variance on the one hand and the treatment and error variances on the other hand. More specifically, he showed that:

$$\Sigma(X - M_{grand})^2 = N_{in\ cond} * \Sigma(M - M_{grand})^2 + \Sigma(X_1 - M_1)^2 + \Sigma(X_2 - M_2)^2$$

in which $N_{in\ cond}$ = the number of participants in each condition (that is, $N_{in\ cond} = N_1 = N_2$).

13

Applied to Tables 13.1–13.4, we can verify that:

$\Sigma(X - M_{grand})^2 = 410.95$ (Table 13.2)
$\Sigma(M - M_{grand})^2 = 15.125$ (Table 13.3)
$\Sigma(X_1 - M_1)^2 = 166.10$ (Table 13.4)
$\Sigma(X_2 - M_2)^2 = 93.60$ (Table 13.4)

and that:

$410.95 = 10 * 15.125 + 166.10 + 93.60$

Fisher further discovered that the ratio of the treatment variance to the error variance provided information analogous to the t-statistic. Before we can discuss this, however, we must introduce a few new concepts.

13.1.3   The ANOVA table

Although in the previous section we talked about total variance, treatment variance, and error variance, you may have noticed that the relationship discovered by Fisher actually involved the sums of squared deviations rather than variances. Remember that we said that $\Sigma(X - M_{grand})^2 = N_{in\,cond} * \Sigma(M - M_{grand})^2 + \Sigma(X_1 - M_1)^2 + \Sigma(X_2 - M_2)^2$. To capture this aspect, Fisher introduced the notion of the **sum of squares** (abbreviated to SS). In particular, we have:

$SS_{total} = \Sigma(X - M_{grand})^2$
$SS_{treatment} = N_{in\,cond} * \Sigma(M - M_{grand})^2$
$SS_{error} = \Sigma(X_1 - M_1)^2 + \Sigma(X_2 - M_2)^2$

The values for our example are:

$SS_{total} = 410.95$ (Table 13.2)
$SS_{treatment} = 10 * 15.125 = 151.25$ (Table 13.3)
$SS_{error} = 166.10 + 93.60 = 259.70$ (Table 13.4)

Every sum of squares has its own **degrees of freedom**. As you may remember from Chapters 4 and 6, these are the number of values that are free to vary (that is, variables that are not determined by the other values and the statistic calculated). For the different sums of squares the degrees of freedom are:

df for $SS_{total} = N - 1$
df for $SS_{treatment} = N_{levels} - 1$
df for $SS_{error} = N_1 - 1 + N_2 - 1$

where N_{levels} is the number of levels of the independent variable.

Given that we are comparing two conditions in our example (young v. old), N_{levels} is 2. So:

df for $SS_{total} = 20 - 1 = 19$
df for $SS_{treatment} = 2 - 1 = 1$
df for $SS_{error} = 10 - 1 + 10 - 1 = 18$

Next, Fisher introduced the notion of **mean square** values (abbreviated to **MS**). These are the sums of squares divided by their degrees of freedom. The MS values are only calculated for treatment and error, because MS_{total} does not provide any useful information. For our example, this gives:

$$MS_{treatment} = SS_{treatment}/(N_{levels} - 1)$$
$$= 151.25/(2 - 1)$$
$$= 151.25$$
$$MS_{error} = SS_{error}/(N_1 - 1 + N_2 - 1)$$
$$= 259.7/(10 - 1 + 10 - 1)$$
$$= 14.428$$

Finally, Fisher showed that the ratio of $MS_{treatment}$ to MS_{error} followed a distribution that was related to the normal distribution, the t-distribution and the chi-square distribution. This meant that p-values could be calculated in very much the same way as the p-values of the other statistics. In honour of Fisher this new distribution has been called the **F-distribution**. (Fisher called it the Z-distribution, but this caused confusion with the z-scores.) So, analysis of variance involves the calculation of an F-value and the associated p-value. The F-value is calculated as follows:

$$F = \frac{MS_{treatment}}{MS_{error}}$$

Applied to our example, this gives:

$$F = \frac{151.25}{14.428} = 10.483$$

To find out whether the observed F-value is significant, we must see whether it is larger than the critical F-value. The critical F-value depends on the degrees of freedom in the numerator (related to the number of treatments) and the degrees of freedom in the denominator (related to the error variance). These are called respectively df_1 and df_2. The critical F-values for various df_1s and df_2s are shown in Table 13.5 (overleaf).

Applied to our example, df_1 equals 1 (the df for $SS_{treatment}$); df_2 equals 18 (the df for SS_{error}). As can be seen in Table 13.5, the .05 critical value for the F(1,18) distribution is 4.41. Because the observed F-value exceeds the critical .05 F-value, the difference between the young and the old adults is significant at the .05 level (as we already knew from the t-test). Given that the .01 critical value of F(1,18) is 8.29, the difference is also significant at the .01 level.

As a matter of fact, the p-value associated with F(1,18) =10.483 is .0046, which it should be if the F-test is equivalent to the t-test. Even better, it can be shown that an F-value with one degree of freedom in the numerator is mathematically equivalent to the square of the corresponding t-value. So, for our example:

$$F(1,18) = [t(18)]^2$$
$$= 3.24^2 = 10.5$$

13

Table 13.5 Critical F-values at the .05 level. The columns indicate the degrees of freedom in the numerator (df1, related to the treatment variable); the rows indicate the degrees of freedom in the denominator (df2, related to the error variance). The critical values are equivalent to those of a two-tailed t-statistic (that is, they do not assume a particular direction in the differences between means).

	1	2	3	4	5	6
1	161.45	199.50	215.71	224.58	230.16	233.99
2	18.51	19.00	19.16	19.25	19.30	19.33
3	10.13	9.55	9.28	9.12	9.01	8.94
4	7.71	6.94	6.59	6.39	6.26	6.16
5	6.61	5.79	5.41	5.19	5.05	4.95
6	5.99	5.14	4.76	4.53	4.39	4.28
7	5.59	4.74	4.35	4.12	3.97	3.87
8	5.32	4.46	4.07	3.84	3.69	3.58
9	5.12	4.26	3.86	3.63	3.48	3.37
10	4.96	4.10	3.71	3.48	3.33	3.22
11	4.84	3.98	3.59	3.36	3.20	3.09
12	4.75	3.89	3.49	3.26	3.11	3.00
13	4.67	3.81	3.41	3.18	3.03	2.92
14	4.60	3.74	3.34	3.11	2.96	2.85
15	4.54	3.68	3.29	3.06	2.90	2.79
16	4.49	3.63	3.24	3.01	2.85	2.74
17	4.45	3.59	3.20	2.96	2.81	2.70
18	4.41	3.55	3.16	2.93	2.77	2.66
19	4.38	3.52	3.13	2.90	2.74	2.63
20	4.35	3.49	3.10	2.87	2.71	2.60
30	4.17	3.32	2.92	2.69	2.53	2.42
40	4.08	3.23	2.84	2.61	2.45	2.34
50	4.03	3.18	2.79	2.56	2.40	2.29
60	4.00	3.15	2.76	2.53	2.37	2.25
70	3.98	3.13	2.74	2.50	2.35	2.23
80	3.96	3.11	2.72	2.49	2.33	2.21
90	3.95	3.10	2.71	2.47	2.32	2.20
100	3.94	3.09	2.70	2.46	2.31	2.19
200	3.89	3.04	2.65	2.42	2.26	2.14
500	3.86	3.01	2.62	2.39	2.23	2.12
1000	3.85	3.00	2.61	2.38	2.22	2.11

Usually, the outcome of an F-test is summarised in an **ANOVA table**. This table contains all the information we have discussed. It contains three rows: the first row refers to the treatment variance, the second to the error variance and the third to the total variance. There are separate columns for SS, df, MS, F and p. So, for our example, the ANOVA table is:

	SS	df	MS	F	p
Treatment	151.25	1	151.25	10.483	.0046
Error	259.70	18	14.43		
Total	410.95	19			

Tip You can get the exact p-value associated with an F-value quite easily by making use of an applet on the internet or the spreadsheet of your computer. For instance, in Microsoft Excel, you need the function =FDIST(F-value;df1;df2), as shown in the screenshot.

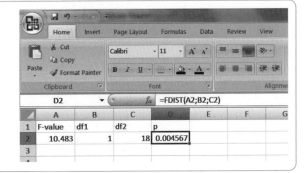

13.1.4 Reporting an *F*-test

When you report the outcome of an F-test, you must give enough information to enable a reader to reconstruct the ANOVA table. More specifically, you must give information about the F-value, the degrees of freedom, and the MS_{error}. Usually, the significance level is also reported. So, if we were to summarise the findings of our example of young and old adults, we would write something like: 'The old adults were less likely to notice the errors they made ($M = 70.8$) than the young adults ($M = 76.3$). This difference was significant ($F(1,18) = 10.48$, $MSe = 14.43$, $p < .01$).'

Notice that the abbreviation MSe is used for mean square of error. On the basis of MSe and F, you can calculate $MS_{treatment}$, and all the SS-values, making it possible for you to reconstruct the full ANOVA table.

13.1.5 Calculating confidence intervals, the effect size and the likelihood ratio on the basis of an ANOVA table

Because ANOVA is closely related to the t-test, it is very easy to calculate the confidence intervals, the effect size and the likelihood ratio of the alternative hypothesis v. the null hypothesis on the basis of an ANOVA table.

As for the **confidence intervals** around the means, remember from Section 7.1.1 that we calculated them on the basis of the critical t-values and the standard errors of the means. Table 13.6 repeats these calculations for the

Table 13.6 Confidence intervals around the means for the experiment on error detection in young and old adults (percentage of errors detected), when the calculations are based on the standard deviations of the samples.

Young adults:
$N_1 = 10$　$M_1 = 76.3$　$SD_1^2 = 18.4556$　$SD_1 = 4.2960$　$SE_1 = 1.3585$

Old adults:
$N_2 = 10$　$M_2 = 70.8$　$SD_2^2 = 10.4000$　$SD_2 = 3.2249$　$SE_2 = 1.0198$

critical t-value(df = 9, α = .05) is 2.262

lower bound confidence interval around M_1:
M_1 – critical t-value * SE_1 = 76.3 – 2.262 * 1.3585 = 73.23
upper bound confidence interval around M_1:
M_1 + critical t-value * SE_1 = 76.3 + 2.262 * 1.3585 = 79.37

lower bound confidence interval around M_2:
M_2 – critical t-value * SE_2 = 70.8 – 2.262 * 1.0198 = 68.49
upper bound confidence interval around M_2:
M_2 + critical t-value * SE_2 = 70.8 + 2.262 * 1.0198 = 73.11

---

confidence intervals around the mean percentages of errors made by the young and the old adults.

An ANOVA does not work with the standard deviations of the samples, but with the combined error variance. So, we do not calculate separate standard errors for M_1 and M_2 but a pooled SE based on MSe. More specifically:

$$SE_{mean} = \sqrt{\frac{MSe}{N_{in\ cond}}}$$

in which $N_{in\ cond}$ = the number of participants in each condition (that is, $N_{in\ cond} = N_1 = N_2$). For our example this gives:

$$SE_{mean} = \sqrt{\frac{14.43}{10}} = 1.201$$

To calculate the confidence intervals around M_1 and M_2, we must multiply the standard error by the critical t-values, as we did in Table 13.6. However, because SE_{mean} is based on the pooled variance, we have a more stable estimate and, therefore, we are allowed to use the degrees of freedom associated with MSe rather than the degrees of freedom associated with the condition means, which gives df = 18 instead of df = 9. The outcome of the various calculations is shown in Table 13.7.

Notice that the SE_{mean} based on the ANOVA table roughly agrees with the average of SE_1 and SE_2, which makes sense given that it is based on the pooled error term. This means that confidence intervals based on SE_{mean} only convey correct information when $SE_1 \approx SE_2$. The fact that the standard errors (and hence the standard deviations) of the different conditions must be roughly the same for an ANOVA to work properly is called *the assumption of the homogeneity of variance* (see Section 6.6.2 for a similar assumption with respect to the t-test). If there are clear differences in the standard deviations of the conditions, it is good to run another test or to correct the F-test, as is possible in SPSS.

The ANOVA table further allows you to easily calculate the **effect size**. Remember that in Section 7.3, we introduced Cohen's d-statistic as a standardised

Table 13.7 Confidence intervals around the means for the experiment on error detection in young and old adults (percentage of errors detected), when the calculations are based on the ANOVA table.

Young adults:
$N_1 = 10$ $M_1 = 76.3$

Old adults:
$N_2 = 10$ $M_2 = 70.8$

$MSe = 14.43$
$N_{in\ cond} = 10$

$$SE_{mean} = \sqrt{\frac{MSe}{N_{in\ cond}}} = \sqrt{\frac{14.43}{10}} = 1.201$$

critical t-value(df = 18, α = .05) is 2.101

lower bound confidence interval around M_1:
M_1 − critical t-value $* SE_{mean} = 76.3 - 2.101 * 1.201 = 73.78$
upper bound confidence interval around M_1:
M_1 + critical t-value $* SE_{mean} = 76.3 + 2.101 * 1.201 = 78.82$

lower bound confidence interval around M_2:
M_2 − critical t-value $* SE_{mean} = 70.8 - 2.101 * 1.201 = 68.28$
upper bound confidence interval around M_2:
M_2 + critical t-value $* SE_{mean} = 70.8 + 2.101 * 1.201 = 73.32$

---

estimate of the difference between two conditions. In Section 7.3.1 we showed that the effect size for the study with young and old adults was:

$$d = \frac{M_1 - M_2}{\sqrt{\frac{SD_1^2 + SD_2^2}{2}}} = \frac{76.3 - 70.8}{\sqrt{\frac{4.2960^2 + 3.2249^2}{2}}} = \frac{5.5}{3.798} = 1.45$$

$$d = \frac{2t}{\sqrt{N_1 + N_2}} = \frac{2 * 3.2378}{\sqrt{10 + 10}} = \frac{6.4756}{4.4721} = 1.45$$

Remember that in an ANOVA we use MSe as a combined estimate of the variance within the conditions. So, we can rewrite d as:

$$d = \frac{M_1 - M_2}{\sqrt{MSe}} = \frac{76.3 - 70.8}{\sqrt{14.43}} = \frac{5.5}{3.798} = 1.45$$

or

$$d = \frac{2\sqrt{F}}{\sqrt{N}} = \frac{2\sqrt{10.483}}{\sqrt{20}} = 1.45$$

In general, unless the samples are very small it does not make much difference whether one works with N or with the degrees of error associated with MSe. Some statisticians claim that the latter is better. Therefore, in an ANOVA you often find the effect size defined as:

$$d = \frac{2\sqrt{F}}{\sqrt{df_{MSe}}} = \frac{2\sqrt{10.483}}{\sqrt{18}} = 1.53$$

This calculation is more straightforward because the degrees of freedom of the error term are always given in the ANOVA table and the approach can easily be generalised to all F-statistics in more complicated designs (for which it is sometimes difficult to calculate the number of observations on which a particular F-statistic is based).

13

In Section 11.4.2 (**Going further**), we discussed how you can use the Pearson correlation as another measure of the effect size. Table 11.15 showed that the correlation between the percentages of error and the condition was $r = -.607$ ($df = 18$, $p = .0046$). This correlation can also be calculated from the ANOVA table on the basis of the equation:

$$r = \sqrt{\frac{F}{F + df_{MSe}}} = \sqrt{\frac{10.483}{10.483 + 18}} = .607$$

This means that $(.607)^2$ or .368 (36.8%) of the variance is due to the difference in the means between the conditions. Because the explained variance can be generalised to more situations than the Pearson correlation (see below) and is easier to calculate, the proportion of explained variance is a more interesting variable to calculate than the Pearson correlation. Explained variance (in ANOVA usually called eta squared and written as η^2) is given by the equation:

$$\eta^2 = \frac{F}{F + df_{MSe}} = \frac{10.483}{10.483 + 18} = .368$$

The proportion of explained variance is obtained by dividing $SS_{treatment}$ by SS_{total}:

$$\eta^2 = \frac{SS_{treatment}}{SS_{total}} = \frac{151.25}{410.95} = .368$$

This shows that the square of the Pearson correlation coefficient is indeed an estimate of the proportion of variance explained by the independent variable. It also illustrates how all parametric statistics are related to each other.

Finally, the **likelihood ratio** of the alternative hypothesis v. the null hypothesis is also easy to calculate on the basis of the ANOVA table. All you need is the equation:

$$\text{Likelihood ratio} = \left(1 + \frac{F}{df_{MSe}}\right)^{N/2}$$

in which N = the number of observations or the total number of participants in the experiment.

Applied to our example, this gives:

$$\text{Likelihood ratio} = \left(1 + \frac{10.483}{18}\right)^{20/2} = 98.4$$

The outcome indicates that the alternative hypothesis of a genuine difference between young and old adults is 98 times more likely than the null hypothesis of no difference, as we saw in Chapter 7 on the basis of the t-test. Indeed, a comparison with the equations used in Section 7.2.2 to calculate the likelihood ratio for the t-test shows how closely the t-test and the F-test are related to each other, at least as long as the F-test is limited to a comparison of two conditions (that is, $df_1 = 1$).

Before we look at the ANOVA of a repeated measure, you may be relieved to hear that all the above analyses are very easy to do with statistical software packages such as SPSS. So, in case you found the preceding paragraphs demanding, here is how you can get everything from your SPSS tables with a few mouse clicks!

13.1.6 Using SPSS for an ANOVA of independent groups

Analysis of variance using SPSS is treated extensively in Chapter 8 of Brace, Kemp and Snelgar's book, *SPSS for Psychologists*. Here we discuss the essentials you need to run the analyses discussed above.

Make an SPSS data file with the data of the memory error experiment with the young and old adults in Table 13.2 (or you may still have it saved on your computer).

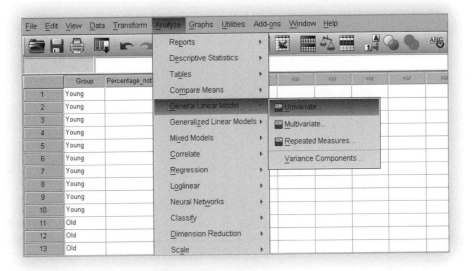

Click on **Analyze**, *General Linear Model* and *Univariate*. This opens the following dialogue box.

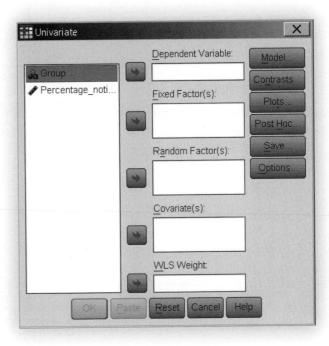

Put Percentage_noticed in the *Dependent Variable* box and Group in the *Fixed Factor(s)* box.[1]

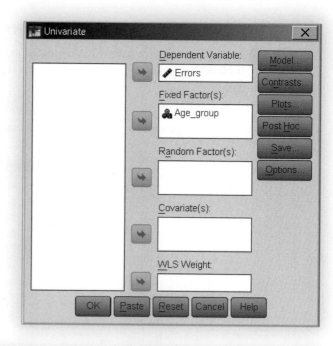

Click on **OK** to get the output.

Tests of Between-Subjects Effects

Dependent Variable: Percentage_noticed

Source	Type III Sum of Squares	df	Mean Square	F	Sig.
Corrected Model	151.250ᵃ	1	151.250	10.483	.005
Intercept	108192.050	1	108192.050	7498.871	.000
Group	151.250	1	151.250	10.483	.005
Error	259.700	18	14.428		
Total	108603.000	20			
Corrected Total	410.950	19			

a. R Squared = .368 (Adjusted R Squared = .333)

In this output, you can see the ANOVA table (amid some more information). In particular, the lines starting with Group and Error are important, as you can see by comparing them to the ANOVA table we calculated above (p. 327).

1 The term fixed factor is used for the independent variable(s) in an ANOVA because these factors have a limited (fixed) set of levels (for example, 2 for the age group). Factors that do not have this property (such as the participants in the experiment) are called 'random factors'. SPSS allows you to enter several random factors in a design, but you are unlikely to need this facility at this stage of your education (or indeed ever).

By clicking on *Options*, you can get further information about the means and the effect size. First use the arrow between the upper two boxes to get the variable Group into the box entitled *Display Means for* ❶. Then also check the option *Estimates of effect size* ❷.

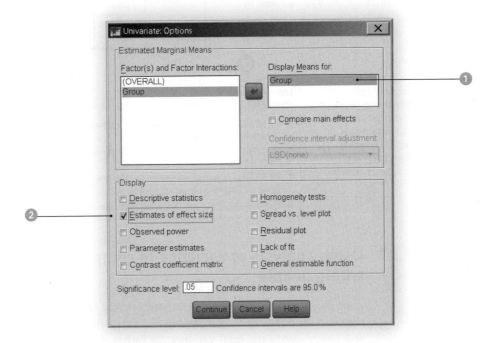

This gives you the following output.

Tests of Between-Subjects Effects

Dependent Variable: Percentage_noticed

Source	Type III Sum of Squares	df	Mean Square	F	Sig.	Partial Eta Squared
Corrected Model	151.250[a]	1	151.250	10.483	.005	.368
Intercept	108192.050	1	108192.050	7498.871	.000	.998
Group	151.250	1	151.250	10.483	.005	.368
Error	259.700	18	14.428			
Total	108603.000	20				
Corrected Total	410.950	19				

a. R Squared = .368 (Adjusted R Squared = .333)

In this panel you see that a new column has been added, called *Partial Eta Squared*. This is a measure that indicates how much of the variance is explained by the variable. When there are only two conditions, this measure is the same as R^2. Indeed, we have already calculated that the age group accounted for .368 of the variance in the data (see also the footnote to the table, which gives you the same information).

13

The next output panel is interesting because it contains the standard errors and the confidence intervals of the means based on the pooled variance, as you can see by comparing the panel to the calculations we did before.

Group				
Dependent Variable: Errors				
Group			95% Confidence Interval	
	Mean	Std Error	Lower Bound	Upper Bound
Old	70.800	1.201	68.276	73.324
Young	76.300	1.201	73.775	78.824

Tip By using the commands *Analyze, Compare Means, Means,* you can get the standard errors of the individual conditions (rather than those based on the pooled variance). Click on *Options* and add the *standard error of mean* to the output.

Learning check

Analyse the other data of between-group comparisons discussed in this book using SPSS. These are:

• the heights of male and female students (Section 6.2.1; see the solution to Learning check 4 of Chapter 6 for the answer),
• the number of word pairs remembered by participants after receiving a drug or a placebo (Table 6.5), and
• the outcome of an egg-and-spoon race between professors from Royal Holloway and Oxford University (Learning check 3 of Chapter 6).

Are you able to find the answers in the SPSS output?

13.2 Using analysis of variance to compare conditions within people

Another advantage of analysis of variance is that the same principles apply to repeated measures as to comparisons of independent groups. The researcher still has to divide the total variance (or rather the total sum of squares) into different components and to decide which of these components correspond to the treatment variance and the error variance. The only complication is that in a repeated measures design the overall differences between participants do not matter. As you may remember from Chapter 9, in the related-samples t-test this was achieved by using the difference scores of the participants rather than the raw scores. In an ANOVA this will be achieved by subdividing the error variance into (i) variance due to differences in the treatment effect between the participants, and (ii) variance due to the overall differences between the participants.

13.2.1 The variance components in a repeated measures design

Let us illustrate the various variance components with the example we introduced in Chapter 9. In this study 12 patients completed the Beck Depression Inventory before they started psychotherapy and six months after the therapy. Table 9.1 listed the results, which are repeated in Table 13.8.

To run an ANOVA on the data of Table 13.8, we first calculate the total sum of squares. For this we need the grand mean, which is $(34.5 + 22.5)/2 = 28.5$. Then we calculate $\Sigma(X - M_{grand})^2$ for all 24 data entries. This gives us:

$$SS_{total} = \Sigma(X - M_{grand})^2$$
$$= (36 - 28.5)^2 + (24 - 28.5)^2 + (27 - 28.5)^2 + (18 - 28.5)^2 + \ldots$$
$$\ldots + (26 - 28.5)^2 + (23 - 28.5)^2 = 3118.0$$

So, the total sum of squares for Table 13.8 is 3118.

Table 13.8 Beck Depression Inventory scores of 12 patients before the onset of a therapy and six months after the end of the therapy. Maximum score = 63. Any score above 30 is considered a sign of severe depression. A score between 5 and 9 indicates absence of depression.

	Before	6 months after	Difference
patient 1	36	24	12
patient 2	27	18	9
patient 3	45	30	15
patient 4	25	8	17
patient 5	34	27	7
patient 6	28	14	14
patient 7	51	47	4
patient 8	30	31	-1
patient 9	33	5	28
patient 10	47	27	20
patient 11	32	16	16
patient 12	26	23	3
	$M_1 = 34.5$	$M_2 = 22.5$	$M_{diff} = 12$

$M_{diff} = 12 \qquad SD_{diff} = 8.10$

$$t = \frac{M_{diff}}{\frac{SD_{diff}}{\sqrt{N}}} = \frac{12}{\frac{8.1}{\sqrt{12}}} = 5.13$$

$N = 12$, df $= N - 1 = 11$, $p = .000328$

Next, we calculate the sum of squares due to the treatment. This is the sum of the squared deviations between the condition means and the grand mean, multiplied by the number of observations per condition. Applied to the example, this gives (there are 12 data in each condition):

$$SS_{treatment} = N_{in\ cond} * \Sigma(M - M_{grand})^2$$
$$= 12 * \left[(34.5 - 28.5)^2 + (22.5 - 28.5)^2\right] = 12 * 72 = 864$$

The remainder between SS_{total} and $SS_{treatment}$ (i.e. 3118 – 864) is due to the variance in depression scores that is unrelated to the treatment. This variance can be divided into two parts:

1 the overall differences in depression scores between the patients, and
2 the differences in therapy efficacy across patients.

Only the latter component is important in a repeated measures analysis. (Remember that in Chapter 9 we worked with the difference scores for the t-test.)

To calculate the variance due to overall differences between patients, we have to follow the same logic as in the calculation of the variance due to treatment. That is, first we have to calculate the mean score per patient and then calculate the squared difference with the grand mean. Table 13.9 shows the auxiliary table we need for this.

Table 13.9 Auxiliary table to calculate the variance due to the overall differences between the participants.

	Mean score of the patient	Squared difference with the grand mean
patient 1	30.0	$(30.0-28.5)^2 = 2.25$
patient 2	22.5	$(22.5-28.5)^2 = 36$
patient 3	37.5	$(37.5-28.5)^2 = 81$
patient 4	16.5	$(16.5-28.5)^2 = 144$
patient 5	30.5	$(30.5-28.5)^2 = 4$
patient 6	21.0	$(21.0-28.5)^2 = 56.25$
patient 7	49.0	$(49.0-28.5)^2 = 420.25$
patient 8	30.5	$(30.5-28.5)^2 = 4$
patient 9	19.0	$(19.0-28.5)^2 = 90.25$
patient 10	37.0	$(37.0-28.5)^2 = 72.25$
patient 11	24.0	$(24.0-28.5)^2 = 20.25$
patient 12	24.5	$(24.5-28.5)^2 = 16$
		$\Sigma(M_{patient} - M_{grand})^2 = 946.5$

To calculate the sum of squares due to overall differences between participants, we again have to multiply the $\Sigma(M_{patient}-M_{grand})^2$ value with the number of observations per condition. In this case, this is 2 (that is, two values per person), so that we get:

$$SS_{participants} = N_{obs\ per\ patient} * \Sigma(M_{patient} - M_{grand})^2$$
$$= 2 * 946.5$$
$$= 1893$$

As it happens, we now already have all the information we need to make the ANOVA table because the remainder is the SS for the denominator of the F-test. So, we have:

$$SS_{total} = 3118$$
$$SS_{treatment} = 864$$
$$SS_{participants} = 1893$$
$$Remainder = 3118 - 864 - 1893 = 361$$

To understand what the remainder value represents, we have to appreciate where it comes from. This component stands for the divergences that remain between the observed values and the values predicted on the basis of the mean of the participant, the mean of the condition, and the grand mean. For instance, the predicted value for patient 1 before therapy is:

$$Predicted\ value_{patient1\ before} = M_{patient1} + M_{before} - M_{grand}$$
$$= 30 + 34.5 - 28.5$$
$$= 36$$

For this cell, the predicted value is the same as the observed value, so the squared deviation, (observed–predicted)^2, is 0. For patient 2, the predicted value before therapy is $M_{patient2} + M_{before} - M_{grand} = 22.5 + 34.5 - 28.5 = 28.5$, which is 1.5 more than the observed value of 27, giving a squared deviation of $(27 - 28.5)^2 = 2.25$. When the squared deviations of all 24 cells are calculated in this way and summed, you get a total of 361, which is the remainder. (Verify this if you don't believe it!)

If the above calculations frightened you, do not despair. The nice aspect about having good computer programs is that the programmers have done all the work for you. If you provide the software with the right input, it automatically calculates the different components and chooses the right numerator and denominator of the F-statistic, as we will see below when we discuss the SPSS analysis. Still, it is good to have an idea of the basic logic behind the calculations, which is essentially that the variability due to the treatment effect is compared to the error variability present in your data. For the independent-groups analysis, this was the variability within the groups. For a repeated measures analysis, this is the variability that is left after the overall differences between the participants have been taken out.

13.2.2   Calculating the ANOVA table and the *F*-statistic

We now have all the information to make the ANOVA table for the repeated measures analysis. Remember that the total sum of squares contains three components:

1   the variability due to the treatment effect,
2   the variability due to the overall differences between the participants, and
3   the variability due to differences in the treatment effect between the participants.

We want to know whether the treatment effect is big enough given the variability in treatment effects across participants.

In addition, we must know the degrees of freedom associated with each sum of squares. For the total sum of squares, this remains $N - 1$ (as is the case for all possible ANOVAs). For the treatment sum of squares this also remains $N_{levels} - 1$. However, because the error sum of squares has been divided into a sum of squares due to the overall differences between the participants and a sum of squares due to the variability in the treatment effects across participants, we have to share the degrees of freedom between these two components. For the overall differences between participants, the degrees of freedom equal the number of participants minus one ($N_{participants} - 1$). For the differences in treatment effects, the degrees of freedom equal $(N_{levels} - 1) * (N_{participants} - 1)$. If there are only two conditions, as in this example, this will also be $N_{participants} - 1$.

We now know enough to make our ANOVA table:

	SS	df	MS	F	p
Treatment	864.0	1	864.0	26.325	.000328
Error	361.0	11	32.82		
Differences between parts	1893.0	11			
Total	3118.0	23			

Notice that the F-value is obtained by taking $MS_{treatment}/MS_{variability\ in\ treatment}$ or 864/32.82. So, $MS_{variability\ in\ treatment}$ is the error term used in the denominator of F. For convenience, in the rest of this chapter we will also call this MSe. Be careful, however, that you understand the difference between this and the between-groups analysis (where the variance due to overall differences between the participants was not partialled out).

Given that the obtained F-value is higher than the critical .05 value for $F(1,11)$, as can be verified in Table 13.5, the overall treatment effect is significant at the .05 level, as we already knew on the basis of the t-test (Table 13.8). As a matter of fact, because the df of the numerator is 1, the F-value again is the square of the t-value, or $26.325 = 5.13^2$, not including the rounding-off errors. This means that the real p-value is $p = .000328$.

13.2.3   Confidence intervals, effect size and likelihood ratio

To calculate the **confidence intervals** around the means, we again start from the error MS used as the denominator of the F-statistic that is, $MS_{variability\ in\ treatment}$ (abbreviated in the remainder of this section to MSe). In our example, $MSe = 32.82$. From this value, we calculate the standard error of the means, SE_{mean} using the equation:

$$SE_{mean} = \sqrt{\frac{MSe}{N_{in\ cond}}}$$

in which $N_{in\ cond}$ is the number of observations in each condition or the number of participants who took part in the study. So, for our example we have

$$SE_{mean} = \sqrt{\frac{32.82}{12}} = 1.654$$

To get from SE to the .05 confidence interval, we need the critical t-value. For this we must know the degrees of freedom. As these comprise the df associated with MSe (or df_e), in this example $df = 11$, and the critical t-value is 2.201. This allows us to calculate the confidence intervals around M_1 and M_2. (See also Section 9.3.2 for a comparison with the related-samples t-test.)

lower limit confidence interval $M_1 = 34.5 - 2.201 * 1.654 = 30.86$
upper limit confidence interval $M_1 = 34.5 + 2.201 * 1.654 = 38.14$

lower limit confidence interval $M_2 = 22.5 - 2.201 * 1.654 = 18.86$
upper limit confidence interval $M_2 = 22.5 + 2.201 * 1.654 = 26.14$

To calculate the **effect size**, we can use one of the equations:

$$d = \frac{M_1 - M_2}{\sqrt{2MSe}} = \frac{34.5 - 22.5}{\sqrt{2 * 32.82}} = 1.48$$

or

$$d = \sqrt{\frac{F}{N_{in\ cond}}} = \sqrt{\frac{26.325}{12}} = 1.48$$

or approximately

$$d \approx \sqrt{\frac{F}{df_{MSe}}} = \sqrt{\frac{26.325}{11}} = 1.55$$

The proportion of variance explained can be calculated as follows:

$$\eta^2 = \frac{F}{F + df_{MSe}} = \frac{26.325}{26.325 + 11} = .705$$

$$\eta^2 = \frac{SS_{treatment}}{SS_{treatment} + SS_{variability\ in\ treatment}} = \frac{864}{864 + 361} = .705$$

Notice that the last equation clearly shows that in a repeated measures ANOVA the variance due to overall differences between participants is left out of consideration.

The **likelihood ratio** can also be calculated in two ways. The first method uses:

$$Likelihood\ ratio = \left(1 + \frac{F}{df_{MSe}}\right)^{N_{in\ cond}/2}$$

in which $N_{in\ cond}$ = the number of observations per condition or the number of participants who took part in the experiment. For the example, this gives:

$$Likelihood\ ratio = \left(1 + \frac{26.325}{11}\right)^{12/2} = 1526$$

The likelihood ratio can also be derived from the SS-values. Then we get

$$Likelihood\ ratio = \left(\frac{SS_{treatment} + SS_{variability\ in\ treatment}}{SS_{variability\ in\ treatment}}\right)^{N_{in\ cond}/2}$$

$$= \left(\frac{864 + 361}{361}\right)^{12/2} = 1526$$

As we will see in Chapter 14, the second equation can be generalised to variables with more than two levels. Now, however, it is time to see how we can do all the above analyses with SPSS.

13.2.4 Using SPSS for an ANOVA of repeated measures

Enter the data of the therapy example (Table 13.8) or open your previously saved file. Remember that for a repeated measures analysis all observations of a participant must be entered on the same line. So, we will have two columns in our data file: Before and After. Next click on *Analyze, General Linear Model, Repeated Measures.*

This opens a dialogue box that asks for the repeated measure(s). Fill in Effect_therapy and 2 as shown:

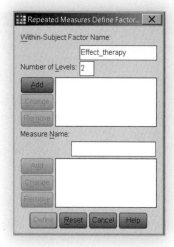

This names your repeated measure (or within-subject factor) as Effect_therapy and informs the program that it has two levels (before the therapy v. after the therapy). Click on **Add** to add the repeated measure to your design.

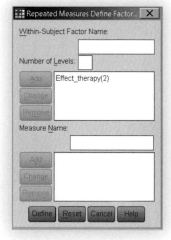

Now click on **Define** to go to the next panel.

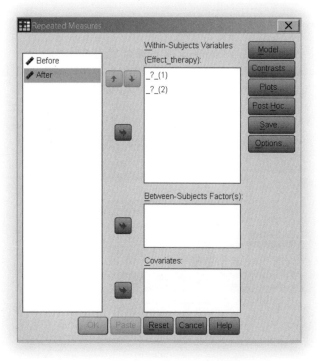

This box asks you for the two levels of the repeated measure Effect_therapy. Use the central arrow to enter Before and After.

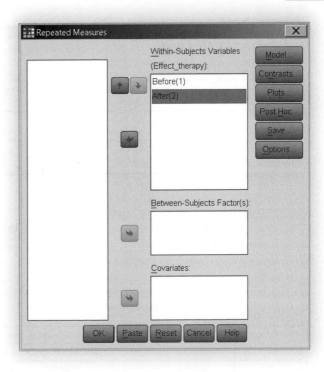

Click on **Options** to get extra information. You want information about the means of the conditions and their confidence intervals ❶. In addition, you want information about the effect size ❷.

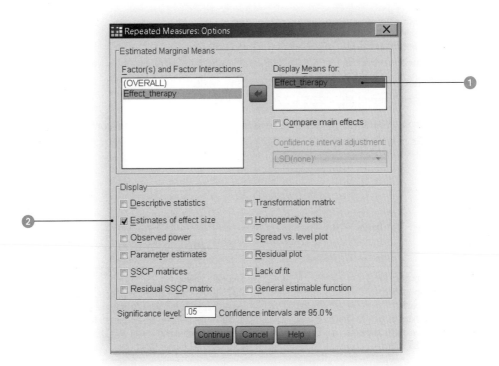

This returns you quite a bit of output, in which you can easily spot the essential panel on the basis of the calculations we did above.

Tests of Within-Subjects Contrasts

Measure: MEASURE_1

Source	Effect_therapy	Type III Sum of Squares	df	Mean Square	F	Sig.	Partial Eta Squared
Effect_therapy	Linear	864.000	1	864.000	26.327	.000	.705
Error (Effect_therapy)	Linear	361.000	11	32.818			

Verify it contains all the information you need!

Unfortunately, for repeated measures SPSS returns the wrong output with respect to the confidence intervals around the means! It gives you the confidence intervals from an independent samples analysis, as you can see from the table it generates.

Effect_therapy

Measure: MEASURE_1

Effect_therapy	Mean	Std. Error	95% Confidence Interval	
			Lower Bound	Upper Bound.
1	34.500	2.509	28.978	40.022
2	22.500	3.283	15.273	29.727

Compare this to the confidence intervals we calculated:

lower limit confidence interval M_1 = 34.5 − 2.201 ∗ 1.654 = 30.86
upper limit confidence interval M_1 = 34.5 + 2.201 ∗ 1.654 = 38.14

lower limit confidence interval M_2 = 22.5 − 2.201 ∗ 1.654 = 18.86
upper limit confidence interval M_2 = 22.5 + 2.201 ∗ 1.654 = 26.14

This means that with SPSS at present there is no alternative but to do some calculation work yourself on the basis of the equations:

$$SE_{mean} = \sqrt{\frac{MSe}{N_{in\ cond}}}$$

and

confidence interval $= M \pm t_{.05crit}(df_2) * SE_{mean}$

Be careful! At present SPSS gives the wrong confidence intervals for repeated measures. You have to calculate them yourself on the basis of the SPSS output.

Learning check
Run the SPSS analysis of the other repeated measures study we discussed in this book. This is the study of IQ scores before and after the summer break (Table 9.6). Are you able to find the same *p*-value and is your *F*-value the square of the *t*-value calculated in Chapter 9?

13.3 Analysis of variance with one between-groups variable and one repeated measure

Thus far, the ANOVAs have simply replicated the *t*-tests we discussed before. However, one of the appealing aspects of ANOVA is that it can be applied to studies in which more than one variable has been examined. (Another appealing aspect is that it can be used for studies with more than two levels per variable, as we will see in Chapter 14.) Suppose we ran a study on the efficacy of psychotherapy for depression in young and old adults. Let's say that the data in the example we discussed previously came from 12 patients in the age range 20–30 years and that we now add another group of 12 patients in the age range 60–70. Such a design with a between-groups variable and a repeated measure is often called a **split-plot design**.

Table 13.10 (overleaf) shows the data of a psychotherapy efficacy study in which the effect is compared for 12 younger patients (the data used thus far) and 12 older patients (new data). We will use these data to illustrate the ANOVA with one between-groups variable (age) and one repeated measure (therapy effect measured by comparing the depression scores before therapy and after therapy).

There are three questions we can ask about these data:

1 Is there a significant difference in depression scores between young and old patients?
2 Is there a significant therapy effect (that is, lower scores after the therapy than before)?
3 Is the therapy effect the same in young as in old patients?

The first question addresses the so-called **main effect** of the between-groups variable. Is there an overall difference in depression scores between the two groups of participants tested? The average depression score of the younger patients is (34.5 + 22.5)/2 = 28.5; that of the older patients is (26.0 + 18.0)/2 = 22. Is this difference significant?

The second question addresses the main effect of the repeated measure. Is there an overall difference in depression scores before and after the therapy? The average depression score before the therapy is (34.5 + 26.0)/2 = 30.25; after the therapy it is (22.5 + 18.0)/2 = 20.25. Is the difference between these two scores significant?

Finally, the third question asks whether there is an **interaction** between the between-groups variable and the repeated measures variable. Is the effect of the repeated measure the same for both groups or is it different? The therapy effect for the young participants is (34.5 − 22.5) = 12; that of the old participants is (26.0 − 18.0) = 8. Is the difference between these two effects significant?

In the next section we discuss how to build an ANOVA table for the data.

13

Table 13.10 Beck Depression Inventory scores of 12 younger and 12 older patients before the onset of a therapy and six months after the end of the therapy. Maximum score = 63. Any score above 30 is considered a sign of severe depression. A score between 5 and 9 indicates absence of depression. In this table the subscripts of the means first denote the group and then the level of the repeated measure. Thus, M_{11} refers to the young group (group 1) and the measurement before the therapy (measurement 1); M_{21} refers to the old group (group 2) and the measurement before the therapy (measurement 1). $M_{.1}$ refers to the mean score of the measurement before the therapy (measurement 1).

		Before	6 months after
Young group (20–30 years)			
patient 1		36	24
patient 2		27	18
patient 3		45	30
patient 4		25	8
patient 5		34	27
patient 6		28	14
patient 7		51	47
patient 8		30	31
patient 9		33	5
patient 10		47	27
patient 11		32	16
patient 12		26	23
$M_{11} = 34.5$	$M_{12} = 22.5$	$M_{1.} = (34.5 + 22.5)/2 = 28.5$	
Old group (60–70 years)			
patient 13		22	5
patient 14		20	28
patient 15		15	11
patient 16		35	25
patient 17		26	13
patient 18		41	9
patient 19		25	36
patient 20		16	17
patient 21		42	36
patient 22		23	5
patient 23		22	12
patient 24		25	19
$M_{21} = 26.0$	$M_{22} = 18.0$	$M_{2.} = (26.0 + 18.0)/2 = 22.0$	
$M_{.1} = (34.5 + 26.0)/2 = 30.25$		$M_{.2} = (22.5 + 18.0)/2 = 20.25$	

13.3.1 Calculating the ANOVA table and the *F*-statistics for an analysis with one between-groups variable and one repeated measure

Given that we have three questions to answer, we have three F-statistics to calculate:

☐ one for the difference between the two groups of patients,
☐ one for the difference between the scores before and after the therapy, and
☐ one for the interaction.

Each F-statistic involves a numerator (representing the variance due to the effect tested) and a denominator (representing the error variance).

We start by calculating the **total variance**. For this we need the grand mean. This can easily be calculated on the basis of the condition means:

$$M_{grand} = (M_{11} + M_{12} + M_{21} + M_{22})/4 = (34.5 + 22.5 + 26 + 18)/4 = 25.25$$

We use the grand mean to calculate SS_{total} by subtracting the grand mean from each observation:

$$SS_{total} = (36 - 25.25)^2 + (24 - 25.25)^2 + \ldots + (25 - 25.25)^2 + (19 - 25.25)^2$$
$$= 6199$$

The degrees of freedom associated with SS_{total} are: $N - 1 = 48 - 1 = 47$.

Next, we want the **sum of squares associated with the difference between the two age groups**. This is calculated by comparing the group means to the grand mean, and multiplying the summed squared deviations by the number of observations per condition ($N_{in\ cond}$) and the number of repeated measure conditions ($N_{levels\ repeated\ measure}$):

$$SS_{age} = \left[(M_{1.} - M_{grand})^2 + (M_{2.} - M_{grand})^2\right] * N_{in\ cond} * N_{levels\ repeated\ measure}$$
$$= \left[(28.5 - 25.25)^2 + (22 - 25.25)^2\right] * 12 * 2$$
$$= 21.125 * 24 = 507$$

Similarly, we calculate the **sum of squares associated with the therapy effect** (the repeated measure) by comparing the before and after means to the grand mean, and multiplying the summed squared deviations by the number of observations per condition ($N_{in\ cond}$) and the number of groups (N_{groups}):

$$SS_{therapy} = \left[(M_{.1} - M_{grand})^2 + (M_{.2} - M_{grand})^2\right] * N_{in\ cond} * N_{groups}$$
$$= \left[(30.25 - 25.25)^2 + (20.25 - 25.25)^2\right] * 12 * 2$$
$$= 50 * 24 = 1200$$

Finally, we calculate the **sum of squares associated with the interaction between group and therapy**. This is slightly more complicated because there is an overlap with the previous sums of squares we calculated. First, we compare the four condition means to the grand mean and multiply the summed squared deviations by the number of observations per condition ($N_{in\ cond}$):

$$SS_{cond}$$
$$= \left[(M_{11} - M_{grand})^2 + (M_{12} - M_{grand})^2 + (M_{21} - M_{grand})^2 + (M_{22} - M_{grand})^2\right] * N_{in\ cond}$$
$$= \left[(34.5 - 25.25)^2 + (22.5 - 25.25)^2 + (26 - 25.25)^2 + (18 - 25.25)^2\right] * 12$$
$$= 146.25 * 12 = 1755$$

13

Next, we must subtract from this value the SSs due to the main effects of age and therapy in order to get the SS uniquely associated with the interaction:

$$SS_{age \bullet therapy} = SS_{cond} - SS_{age} - SS_{therapy}$$
$$= 1755 - 507 - 1200$$
$$= 48$$

The numbers calculated thus far give us all the information we need for the numerators of the F-statistics. As you may have noticed, the underlying principles are quite straightforward: use the specific means of interest, compare them to the grand mean and multiply by the numbers of observations on which the means are based.

We still have to find the error terms needed for the denominators of the F-statistics. The calculations are again similar to those we did in the analyses with a single variable. For the between-groups variable, the error variance will be the variance within the groups. For the repeated measure, the error variance will be the variance in the effect across participants. The error term for the repeated measure is also used for the interaction F-statistic, because the interaction effect concerns the question of whether the therapy effect is different for the group of young participants than for the group of old participants. It makes sense to compare this variance to the individual variation in therapy effects as well.

The variability within the groups, needed for the **error term of the between-groups F-test**, is measured by summing the squared deviations between the observed values of each participant and their group mean. The calculation is similar to that for the between-groups analysis in Section 13.1. So, for each of the young participants, their average score is compared to the mean of the young group. The deviations are squared and summed. The same happens for the old group. Because each patient mean is calculated over the conditions of the repeated measure, we have to multiply by $N_{levels\ repeated\ measure}$. This gives us:

$$SSerror_{young\ group} = \Big[(M_{patient1} - M_{1.})^2 + (M_{patient2} - M_{1.})^2 + \ldots$$
$$+ (M_{patient12} - M_{1.})^2\Big] * M_{levels\ repeated\ measure}$$
$$= \Big[(30 - 28.5)^2 + (22.5 - 28.5)^2 + \ldots + (24.5 - 28.5)^2\Big] * 2$$
$$= 946.5 * 2$$
$$= 1893$$

$$SSerror_{old\ group} = \Big[(M_{patient13} - M_{2.})^2 + (M_{patient14} - M_{2.})^2 + \ldots$$
$$+ (M_{patient24} - M_{2.})^2\Big] * M_{levels\ repeated\ measure}$$
$$= \Big[(13.5 - 22.0)^2 + (24 - 22.0)^2 + \ldots + (22 - 22.0)^2\Big] * 2$$
$$= 717 * 2$$
$$= 1434$$

The error SS for the age effect is the sum of the SSerrors of the young and the old group:

$$SSerror_{age} = SSerror_{young\ group} + SSerror_{old\ group}$$
$$= 1893 + 1434 = 3327$$

The variability in therapy effects across participants, needed for the **error term of the repeated measure F-test and the interaction F-test**, is calculated by comparing the observed values to the values predicted on the basis of the participant's mean, the mean of the condition in the participant's group and the grand mean of the participant's group. Remember that we did something similar in Section 13.2 to calculate the error term for the repeated measurement test. There we had only one group. Here we must make a distinction between the two groups, given that we calculated the interaction between these groups and the repeated measure. For patient 1, the predicted score before the therapy becomes:

$$\text{Predicted value}_{\text{patient1 before}} = M_{\text{patient1}} + M_{11} - M_{1.}$$
$$= 30 + 34.5 - 28.5$$
$$= 36$$

This is the same as the observed value (36), and so the squared deviation for this cell is $(36 - 36)^2 = 0$.

In the same way, we can calculate the predicted score for patient 24, for instance, after the therapy, which is:

$$\text{Predicted value}_{\text{patient24 after}} = M_{\text{patient24}} + M_{22} - M_{2.}$$
$$= 22 + 18 - 22$$
$$= 18$$

This is one less than the observed value (19), and so the squared deviation between the observed and the predicted value for this cell is $(19 - 18)^2 = 1$. If we calculate the predicted values for all 48 cells and square the deviations between the observed and the predicted values, we get a total of 1117. Therefore,

$$SSerror_{\text{therapy}} = 1117$$

Now we have the error-related SS-values for all three F-statistics. The next step is to derive the **degrees of freedom**. The formulas are given in Table 13.11. In our example:

Number of participants = 24
Number of groups = 2 (young v. old)
Number of levels repeated measure = 2 (before v. after)

Table 13.11 Formulas to derive the degrees of freedom for an ANOVA with one between-samples variable and one repeated measure.

Effect between-groups Error between-groups	number of participant groups − 1 number of participants − number of groups
Effect repeated measure Error repeated measure	number of levels repeated measure − 1 (number of participants − number of groups) * (number of levels repeated measure − 1)
Effect interaction Error interaction	(number of groups − 1) * (number of levels repeated measure − 1) (number of participants − number of groups) * (number of levels repeated measure − 1)
SS total	number of observations − 1

13

Table 13.12 ANOVA table for the study of the efficacy of psychotherapy in younger and older patients. Age is a between-groups variable with two levels (young and old). Therapy is a repeated measures variable with two levels (before and after). There were 24 participants in the study (12 per group). Notice that the SS-values add up to SS_{Total}. The dfs also add up to df_{total}. The same error term is used to calculate the F-statistic for therapy (1200/50.77) and the interaction between therapy and age (48/50.77).

	SS	df	MS	F	p
Age	507	1	507.00	3.353	.081
Error (age)	3327	22	151.23		
Therapy	1200	1	1200.00	22.635	.000
Therapy * age	48	1	48.00	.945	.341
Error (therapy)	1117	22	50.77		
Total	6199	47			

We now have everything to make the ANOVA table for our split-plot design: the SS-values and the accompanying degrees of freedom. Table 13.10 shows the outcome.

Table 13.12 shows that the main effect of therapy was significant: for both groups the depression scores were lower after therapy than before. The main effect of age group failed to reach significance, meaning that either there was no genuine difference between the young and the old patients or that the groups were too small to find the difference. (Remember from Chapter 7 that you need many participants to find a medium-sized effect in a between-groups design.) Finally, there was no evidence for an interaction between age group and therapy effect, suggesting that the effects were the same for both age groups (or at least that any difference was too small to be picked up by our design).

13.3.2 Confidence intervals, effect sizes and likelihood ratios for a split-plot design

To calculate confidence intervals, the principles we used for the ANOVAs with a single independent variable can be generalised to the two-factor situation. It is important that you realise that the confidence intervals are different when you compare the means of the groups than when you compare the means of the repeated measure or the means involved in the interaction. Just as we used two different error terms for the F-statistics (Table 13.12), so we will use two different error terms to calculate the confidence intervals of the between-groups variable on the one hand and the repeated measure variable or the interaction between the two variables on the other hand.

To calculate the **confidence interval for the between-groups means**, we first must know the SE of the means. This is calculated with the following equation:

$$SE_{mean} = \sqrt{\frac{MSe_{between\ groups}}{N_{in\ cond} * N_{levels\ repeated\ measure}}} = \sqrt{\frac{151.23}{12 * 2}} = 2.51$$

in which $MSe_{between\ groups}$ is the error term used for the between-groups F-statistic, $N_{in\ cond}$ is the number of participants per group, and $N_{levels\ repeated\ measure}$ is the number of levels of the repeated measure. (An easier way to understand this may be to recall that each group mean was based on 24 observations and that this is the number you need in the denominator.)

To calculate the confidence interval, we further need to know the degrees of freedom in order to look up the critical t-value. The degrees of freedom are simply those associated with $MSe_{between\ groups}$, so the number of participants minus the number of groups, or $24-2=22$ in our example. The critical .05 t-value for $df=22$ is 2.074, giving us the following confidence intervals:

lower bound confidence interval around $M_{1.}$:
> $M_{1.} - $ critical t-value $* SE_{mean} = 28.5 - 2.074 * 2.51 = 23.29$

upper bound confidence interval around $M_{1.}$:
> $M_{1.} + $ critical t-value $* SE_{mean} = 28.5 + 2.074 * 2.51 = 33.71$

lower bound confidence interval around $M_{2.}$:
> $M_{2.} - $ critical t-value $* SE_{mean} = 22.0 - 2.074 * 2.51 = 16.79$

upper bound confidence interval around $M_{2.}$:
> $M_{2.} + $ critical t-value $* SE_{mean} = 22.0 + 2.074 * 2.51 = 27.21$

The considerable overlap of the two confidence intervals agrees with the finding that the difference between the groups failed to reach significance.

To calculate the **confidence interval for the repeated measure variable and the interaction**, we will calculate SE_{mean} on the basis of the error term related to these effects:

$$SE_{mean} = \sqrt{\frac{MSe_{repeated\ measure}}{N_{in\ cond} * N_{groups}}} = \sqrt{\frac{50.77}{12 * 2}} = 1.454$$

Notice that the denominator again refers to the number of observations on which each therapy mean is based (number of participants per condition times number of groups). This SE_{mean} not only applies to the comparison of the scores before and after the therapy, but also to the interaction. As before, the df corresponding to the $MSe_{repeated\ measure}$ is the df we need for the confidence interval. As can be seen in Table 13.12, this df is also 22 (as we had two groups and two levels of the repeated measure), giving us a critical .05 t-value of 2.074 as well.

Now we have everything to calculate the confidence intervals for both the therapy effect and the interaction.

Confidence intervals for the main effect of therapy:
lower bound confidence interval around $M_{.1}$:
> $M_{.1} - $ critical t-value $* SE_{mean} = 30.25 - 2.074 * 1.454 = 27.23$

upper bound confidence interval around $M_{.1}$:
> $M_{.1} + $ critical t-value $* SE_{mean} = 30.25 + 2.074 * 1.454 = 33.27$

lower bound confidence interval around $M_{.2}$:
> $M_{.2} - $ critical t-value $* SE_{mean} = 20.25 - 2.074 * 1.454 = 17.23$

upper bound confidence interval around $M_{.2}$:
> $M_{.2} + $ critical t-value $* SE_{mean} = 20.25 + 2.074 * 1.454 = 23.27$

The fact that the confidence intervals of the means do not overlap is in line with the highly significant main effect of therapy. We can draw the same whiskers (plus or minus $2.074 * 1.454$) around the four condition means to have an idea of the uncertainty intervals situated around these means. However, it is important for you to keep in mind that these confidence intervals are only related to the repeated measure and the interaction effect, NOT to the differences between the groups. For instance, if we calculate the confidence intervals around the four condition means, you see that it 'looks' as if there is a significant difference between the young and the old group (Figure 13.1), whereas we know from the ANOVA table and the confidence intervals around the group means that this is not the case. It is important to keep this peculiarity of split-plot design in mind when you look at a figure with confidence intervals included!

Confidence intervals for the interaction between group and therapy:
lower bound confidence interval around M_{11}:

M_{11} − critical t-value $* SE_{mean} = 34.5 - 2.074 * 1.454 = 31.48$

upper bound confidence interval around M_{11}:

M_{11} + critical t-value $* SE_{mean} = 34.5 + 2.074 * 1.454 = 37.52$

lower bound confidence interval around M_{12}:

M_{12} − critical t-value $* SE_{mean} = 22.5 - 2.074 * 1.454 = 19.48$

upper bound confidence interval around M_{12}:

M_{12} + critical t-value $* SE_{mean} = 22.5 + 2.074 * 1.454 = 25.52$

lower bound confidence interval around M_{21}:

M_{21} − critical t-value $* SE_{mean} = 26.0 - 2.074 * 1.454 = 22.98$

upper bound confidence interval around M_{21}:

M_{21} + critical t-value $* SE_{mean} = 26.0 + 2.074 * 1.454 = 29.02$

lower bound confidence interval around M_{21}:

M_{21} − critical t-value $* SE_{mean} = 18.0 - 2.074 * 1.454 = 14.98$

upper bound confidence interval around M_{21}:

M_{21} + critical t-value $* SE_{mean} = 18.0 + 2.074 * 1.454 = 21.02$

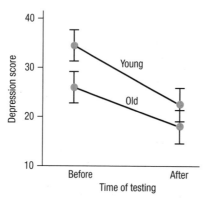

Figure 13.1 Confidence intervals for the interaction between age group and therapy effect in the example involving young and old patients. Notice that these confidence intervals are limited to the repeated measure (before v. after the therapy) and the interaction between the repeated measure and the between-groups variable. They provide misleading information about the between-groups variable (which was not significant). For the between-groups comparison you must draw other confidence intervals based on the within-groups variability.

To find the **effect sizes**, we will again make use of the ANOVA table (Table 13.10). Given that we have three effects, there are three effect sizes we can calculate. These are the equations we need:

$$\eta_{\text{between groups}}^2 = \frac{SS_{\text{between groups}}}{SS_{\text{between groups}} + SSerror_{\text{between groups}}}$$

$$= \frac{SS_{\text{age}}}{SS_{\text{age}} + SSerror_{\text{age}}}$$

$$= \frac{507}{507 + 3327} = .132$$

$$\eta_{\text{repeated measure}}^2 = \frac{SS_{\text{repeated measure}}}{SS_{\text{repeated measure}} + SSerror_{\text{repeated measure}}}$$

$$= \frac{SS_{\text{therapy}}}{SS_{\text{therapy}} + SSerror_{\text{therapy}}}$$

$$= \frac{1200}{1200 + 1117} = .518$$

$$\eta_{\text{interaction}}^2 = \frac{SS_{\text{interaction}}}{SS_{\text{interaction}} + SSError_{\text{repeated measure}}}$$

$$= \frac{48}{48 + 1117} = .041$$

The above equations show that 13.2% of the variance of the individual depression scores (averaged per patient over the before and after measurements) can be explained by age. More than half of the variance between the scores before and after the therapy (51.8%) is due to the fact that the patients received therapy, whereas only 4% can be explained by a divergent therapy effect for young and old patients.

Finally, we can calculate the likelihood ratios, telling us how much more likely each alternative hypothesis is than the null hypothesis. For this we use the following equations:

$$\text{Likelihood ratio}_{\text{between groups}} = \left(\frac{SS_{\text{between groups}} + SSerror_{\text{between groups}}}{SSerror_{\text{between groups}}} \right)^{(N_{\text{participants}}/2)}$$

in which $N_{\text{participants}}$ is the number of participants in the study.

Applied to the example this gives:

$$\text{Likelihood ratio}_{\text{between groups}} = \left(\frac{507 + 3327}{3327} \right)^{24/2} = 5.49$$

The likelihood ratio of 5 agrees with the finding that the effect is not significant in the ANOVA. (Remember that the alternative hypothesis must be 10 times more likely than the null hypothesis to be reliable.) For the main effect of therapy we have:

$$\text{Likelihood ratio}_{\text{repeated measure}}$$

$$= \left(\frac{SS_{\text{repeated measure}} + SSerror_{\text{repeated measure}}}{SSerror_{\text{repeated measure}}} \right)^{((N_{\text{levels repeated measure}} - 1) * N_{\text{participants}}/2)}$$

$$= \left(\frac{1200 + 1117}{1117} \right)^{(1*24)/2}$$

$$= 6346$$

The fact that the alternative hypothesis of a genuine therapeutic effect is more than 6000 times more likely than the null hypothesis of no effect is in line with the p-value obtained in the ANOVA table.

To find the likelihood ratio of the interaction, given the significant effect of therapy, it is best to compare a model that includes the interaction to a model that only includes the main effect of therapy. Given that the F-value of the interaction effect was very small ($F<1$), we expect the likelihood ratio of the interaction to be close to 1 (that is, the alternative hypothesis is as likely as the null hypothesis; see Chapter 7).

Likelihood ratio$_{\text{interaction}}$

$$= \left(\frac{SS_{\text{repeated measure}} + SS_{\text{interaction}} + SSerror_{\text{repeated measure}}}{SS_{\text{repeated measure}} + SSerror_{\text{repeated measure}}} \right)^{(N_{\text{levels repeated measure}} - 1)*N_{\text{participants}}/2}$$

$$= \left(\frac{1200 + 48 + 1117}{1200 + 1117} \right)^{(1*24)/2}$$

$$= 1.28$$

13.3.3 Doing the analysis with SPSS

By this time, I am sure that you are absolutely convinced that psychologists need computer programs to do the calculations for them! So you will be happy to hear that SPSS (or other programs available on the internet) gives you all you need, except for correct confidence intervals for the repeated measure and its interaction with the group.

Once again, I would refer you to Brace, Kemp and Snelgar's *SPSS for Psychologists* for further guidance on using SPSS: Chapter 8 covers the use of SPSS for ANOVA in detail.

First enter the data. You need three columns: one for the group membership (age group) and two for the repeated measure (before and after therapy). This is how your data file should look:

	Age_group	Before	After	var	var	var	var
1	Young	36	24				
2	Young	27	18				
3	Young	45	30				
4	Young	25	8				
5	Young	34	27				
6	Young	28	14				
7	Young	51	47				
8	Young	30	31				
9	Young	33	5				
10	Young	47	27				
11	Young	32	16				
12	Young	26	23				
13	Old	22	5				
14	Old	20	28				
15	Old	15	11				

Click on *Analyze*, *General Linear Model*, *Repeated Measures*.

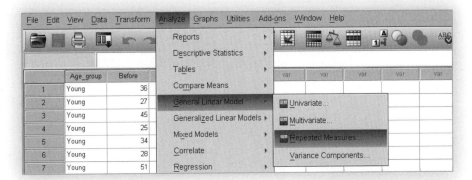

In the Repeated Measures panel name the variable Effect_therapy and indicate that it has two levels. Click on *Add* and *Define*.

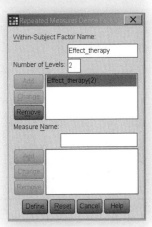

In the next dialogue box, define the levels of the Within-Subjects Variable (before v. after) ❶ and define Age-group as the Between-Subjects Factor ❷.

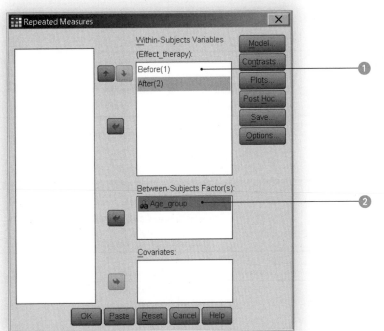

Click on Options to add information about the variables ❶ and the effect sizes ❷.

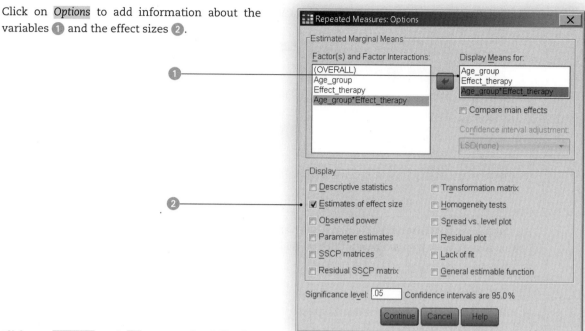

Click on Continue and OK to get the following output.

Tests of Within-Subjects Effects							
Measure: MEASURE_1							
Source		Type III Sum of Squares	df	Mean Square	F	Sig.	Partial Eta Squared
Effect_therapy	Sphericity assumed	1200.000	1	1200.000	23.635	.000	.518
	Greenhouse-Geisser	1200.000	1.000	1200.000	23.635	.000	.518
	Huynh-Feldt	1200.000	1.000	1200.000	23.635	.000	.518
	Lower-bound	1200.000	1.000	1200.000	23.635	.000	.518
Effect_therapy * Age_group	Sphericity assumed	48.000	1	48.000	.945	.341	.041
	Greenhouse-Geisser	48.000	1.000	48.000	.945	.341	.041
	Huynh-Feldt	48.000	1.000	48.000	.945	.341	.041
	Lower-bound	48.000	1.000	48.000	.945	.341	.041
Error (Effect_therapy)	Sphericity assumed	1117.000	22	50.773			
	Greenhouse-Geisser	1117.000	22.000	50.773			
	Huynh-Feldt	1117.000	22.000	50.773			
	Lower-bound	1117.000	22.000	50.773			

Tests of Between-Subjects Effects						
Measure: MEASURE_1						
Transfored Variable: Average						
Source	Type III Sum of Squares	df	Mean Square	F	Sig.	Partial Eta Squared
Intercept	30603.000	1	30603.000[a]	202.364	.000	.902
Age_group	507.000	1	507.000	3.353	.081	.132
Error	3327.000	22	3327.000			

Compare this output to Table 13.12. Can you find the relevant information and how it maps onto the computations we did? Also compare the Partial Eta Squared values to the η^2 values we computed.

Next, look at the output of Estimated Marginal Means.

1. Age_group

Measure: MEASURE_1

Age_group	Mean	Std. Error	95% Confidence Interval	
			Lower Bound	Upper Bound.
Old	22.000	2.510	16.794	27.206
Young	28.500	2.510	23.294	33.706

2. Effect_therapy

Measure: MEASURE_1

Effect_therapy	Mean	Std. Error	95% Confidence Interval	
			Lower Bound	Upper Bound.
1	30.250	1.791	26.536	33.964
2	20.250	2.283	15.516	24.984

3. Age_group * Effect_therapy

Measure: MEASURE_1

Age_group	Effect_therapy	Mean	Std. Error	95% Confidence Interval	
				Lower Bound	Upper Bound.
Old	1	26.000	2.532	20.748	31.252
	2	18.000	3.228	11.305	24.695
Young	1	34.500	2.532	29.248	39.752
	2	22.500	3.228	15.805	29.195

If you compare the confidence intervals to the ones we calculated, you see that only those of the between-subjects variable (Age_group) are correct. The others are too large, because they do not correct for the variance due to the individual differences. These you have to compute yourself on the basis of the SPSS output.

 ## 13.4 Answers to chapter questions

1 **When is analysis of variance (ANOVA) more interesting than t-tests?**

Analysis of variance is more interesting when you are dealing with more than two conditions, either because your independent variable has more than two levels or because your design includes more than one independent variable. When you only have two levels, the t-test provides you with the same information as the ANOVA.

13

2 **What is the core mechanism underlying analysis of variance and why is this rather difficult to understand?**

> The core mechanism is that the *differences* between the condition means are replaced by the *variance* in the condition means. This is rather difficult to understand, because many people do not know what variance is and because differences between conditions are closer to our intuitive understanding than variance of means.

3 **Which statistical test is used in analysis of variance and how does this relate to the t-test?**

> The statistical test used in analysis of variance is the F-test. It is a parametric test, just like the t-test (that is, it requires an interval/ratio scale and is based on the idea that the distributions of the variables are roughly normal). The F-test has two degrees of freedom, df_1 and df_2. df_1 is related to the number of conditions involved in the F-test; df_2 is related to the error term involved in the F-test. When there are only two conditions, then $df_1 = 1$ and the F-test is the same as the t-test, except that the t-value has been squared [i.e., $F(1, df_2) = t^2(df_2)$].

4 **What is a split-plot design?**

> A split-plot design is an experimental design that involves a between-groups variable and a repeated measure. In this design participants are tested several times (the levels of the repeated measure variable) and there are several groups of participants (the levels of the between-groups variable). The example used in this chapter was a design in which the effect of therapy (repeated measure with two levels: before v. after) was examined for two age groups (young v. old adults).

5 **When do you have interaction terms in an analysis of variance?**

> You have interaction terms in your analysis of variance when the analysis involves more than one independent variable. An interaction between two independent variables means that the effect of the variable (also called the main effect of the variable) is not the same for the different levels of the other variable. The example given in this chapter involved the effect of therapy in a group of young and old adults. If the interaction between therapy effect and age group is significant, this means that the therapy effect is different for the two groups. If the interaction is not significant, this suggests that the difference between the groups either does not exist or is not big enough to be picked up by the study (remember the power issue!).

Going further: more than two levels and multiple predictors

14

?

1 What are post-hoc tests and when do you need them?
2 What is a Bonferroni test?
3 What is a multiple regression analysis?

Chapter 13 nicely illustrated the take-home messages of this book. First, the principles underlying statistical analysis are not exceedingly difficult to grasp. Second, they give researchers many opportunities to test hypotheses, even in quite complex designs with multiple independent variables. At the same time (and this is the third message), the puzzle rapidly becomes too complex and error-prone for us humans. Therefore, the invention of computers and the development of statistical software packages have been a blessing for psychologists, students and researchers alike. Unless you have ambitions to become a computer programmer and develop statistical packages, we have more or less reached the point where the mathematical foundations of statistics stop for you. There is no point in delving deeper. From here, it is more important for you to learn how to use a computer package properly than to know exactly how the calculations are done and why. Brace et al.'s *SPSS for Psychologists* provides an excellent basis for more complex calculations using SPSS.

Two more issues relating to basic statistics are likely to interest you, however. The first concerns the questions: 'What happens when a variable has more than two levels?', 'What am I to do when I am comparing more than two groups of participants or when participants are tested under more than two conditions?' The second issue relates to the question, 'How can I predict a variable with more than a single predictor variable?' Remember from Chapters 11 and 12 that we use correlations and regression analysis to predict one variable on the basis of another. However, in many cases we have more than one predictor. For instance, to predict the height of a person we can make use of the mother's height, the father's height, the participant's sex, their birth order within the family, and so on. How do we determine which of these variables are important and which are not?

Both topics are on the limit of this book's scope. You can solve them by simply knowing the sequence of steps to follow in a software package. For regression analysis with multiple predictors this is by far the preferred option, unless you are willing to learn matrix algebra. On the other hand, ANOVAs with three or more levels are no more difficult to understand than ANOVAs with two levels. In case you want to know more about their foundations, a summary of the maths is given in Sections 14.1.1, 14.1.3, 14.2.1 and 14.2.3. If you are not interested, it is perfectly possible to skim through these parts and dive directly into the SPSS sections. The choice is up to you (or maybe your lecturer).

14.1 Analysing a study with three groups of participants

As indicated in Chapter 13, one of the interesting aspects of ANOVAs is that F-tests allow us to go beyond a situation in which two conditions are compared to each other. Although you are unlikely ever to calculate such a test by hand, the principles remain the same.

14.1.1 What happens to the calculations?

To illustrate the approach, let's see what happens if we add a third group of participants to the study of memory errors by young and old adult participants which we have been using throughout the book. Suppose we tested 10 primary school children and compared their results to those of the two groups of adults. Table 14.1 gives the data.

Table 14.1 Percentages of errors noticed by primary school children in addition to those noticed by young and old adults.

	Young adults	Old adults	Children
	71	72	74
	75	65	72
	81	70	59
	79	76	79
	75	72	77
	84	75	66
	74	68	68
	74	69	81
	71	71	74
	79	70	69
Mean	76.3	70.8	71.9
Variance	18.46	10.40	43.66

We start by calculating the sums of squares. Remember from Chapter 13 that we have three such sums in a design with a single between-groups variable: the total sum of squares, the sum of squares due to the treatment (or in this case the groups of participants), and the error sum of squares. Given that we have three groups, we use the following equations:

$$SS_{total} = \Sigma(X - M_{grand})^2$$

$$SS_{treatment} = N_{in\ cond} * \Sigma(M - M_{grand})^2$$

$$SS_{error} = \Sigma(X_1 - M_1)^2 + \Sigma(X_2 - M_2)^2 + \Sigma(X_3 - M_3)^2$$

We calculate SS_{total} by summing the squared deviations between each of the 30 observations (3 groups, 10 participants per group) and the grand mean. M_{grand} equals (76.3 + 70.8 + 71.9)/3 = 73, so:

$$SS_{total} = (71 - 73)^2 + (75 - 73)^2 + \ldots + (72 - 73)^2 + (65 - 73)^2 + \ldots$$
$$+ (74 - 73)^2 + (72 - 73)^2 + \ldots + (69 - 73)^2$$
$$= 822$$

$SS_{treatment}$ is the sum of the deviations between the condition means and the grand mean, multiplied by the number of participants per condition. So, this gives:

$$SS_{treatment} = 10 * \left[(76.3 - 73)^2 + (70.8 - 73)^2 + (71.9 - 73)^2\right]$$
$$= 10 * 16.94 = 169.4$$

14

SS_{error} is the sum of the squared differences between the observations and the condition means. So:

$$SS_{error} = \left[(71 - 76.3)^2 + \ldots + (79 - 76.3)^2\right] + \left[(72 - 70.8)^2 + \ldots + (70 - 70.8)^2\right] +$$
$$\left[(74 - 71.9)^2 + \ldots + (69 - 71.9)^2\right]$$
$$= 652.6$$

SS_{error} can also be obtained by simply subtracting $SS_{treatment}$ from SS_{total}:

$$SS_{error} = SS_{total} - SS_{treatment}$$
$$= 822 - 169.4$$
$$= 652.6$$

Next, we need the **degrees of freedom**. They are:

$$\text{df for } SS_{error} = N - 1$$
$$\text{df for } SS_{treatment} = N_{levels} - 1$$
$$\text{df for } SS_{error} = N - N_{levels}$$

In the above equations N is the total number of observations, and N_{levels} is the number of levels of the independent variable. Given that we are comparing three conditions (young adults, old adults, children), N_{levels} is 3. So, for our example:

$$\text{df for } SS_{error} = 30 - 1 = 29$$
$$\text{df for } SS_{treatment} = 3 - 1 = 2$$
$$\text{df for } SS_{error} = 30 - 3 = 27$$

The sums of squares and degrees of freedom allow us to calculate the **mean squares**:

$$MS_{treatment} = SS_{treatment}/df_{treatment}$$
$$= 169.4/2$$
$$= 84.7$$
$$MS_{error} = SS_{error}/df_{error}$$
$$= 652.6/27$$
$$= 24.17$$

The ratio of $MS_{treatment}$ to MS_{error} gives us the F-value: $84.7/24.17 = 3.504$. Because three conditions are compared, $df_1 = 3 - 1 = 2$. So, for the critical value we have to look at the column with $df_1 = 2$ in Table 13.5. According to the table, the critical .05 value for $F(2,27)$ is smaller than 3.49 (when $df_2 = 20$) and larger than 3.32 (when $df_2 = 30$). Given that 3.5 is higher than 3.49, we can be sure that the effect is significant at the .05 level. As a matter of fact, if we calculate the precise p-value, we get $p = .044$.

We now have all the information to make the **ANOVA table** (Table 14.2).

Table 14.2 ANOVA table for the data of Table 14.1

	SS	df	MS	F	p
Treatment	169.40	2	84.70	3.504	.044
Error	652.60	27	24.17		
Total	822.00	29			

From the ANOVA table we can conclude that the difference between the groups is still significant ($F(2,27) = 3.50$, $MSe = 24.17$, $p < .05$) after the children have been added to the study, but that the effect becomes less secure due to the addition of the new group with a mean that lies between the other two means and a rather large variability. Because three groups are compared, the F-test has two degrees of freedom in the numerator. At this point the ANOVA outgrows the more basic t-test, which can only compare two conditions.

The ANOVA table further provides us with the information we need to calculate the **confidence intervals** around the means. Fortunately, everything we learned in Chapter 13 can be applied without change. We again start by calculating SE_{mean} on the basis of MSe and by determining the critical t-value on the basis of the degrees of freedom of MSe:

$$SE_{mean} = \sqrt{\frac{MSe}{N_{in\ cond}}} = \sqrt{\frac{24.17}{10}} = 1.55$$

$df_{MSe} = 27$, so the critical .05 t-value is: $t(27) = 2.052$ (Appendix B)

Notice that SE_{mean} has increased relative to SE_{mean} in Chapter 13 (where it was 1.201; Table 13.7). This is because of the larger variability in the group of primary school children than in the groups of young and old adults. As a result, the confidence intervals of the young and old adults will be larger than in Chapter 13 because the confidence intervals are calculated on the basis of the pooled error term. These are the calculations we have to use:

lower bound confidence interval around M_1:
  $M_1 - \text{critical t-value} * SE_{mean} = 76.3 - 2.052 * 1.55 = 73.1$

upper bound confidence interval around M_1:
  $M_1 + \text{critical t-value} * SE_{mean} = 76.3 + 2.052 * 1.55 = 79.5$

lower bound confidence interval around M_2:
  $M_2 - \text{critical t-value} * SE_{mean} = 70.8 - 2.052 * 1.55 = 67.6$

upper bound confidence interval around M_2:
  $M_2 + \text{critical t-value} * SE_{mean} = 70.8 + 2.052 * 1.55 = 74.0$

lower bound confidence interval around M_3:
  $M_3 - \text{critical t-value} * SE_{mean} = 71.9 - 2.052 * 1.55 = 68.7$

upper bound confidence interval around M_3:
  $M_3 + \text{critical t-value} * SE_{mean} = 71.9 + 2.052 * 1.55 = 76.1$

Remember that the confidence intervals give us a good idea of which conditions differ significantly from each other. As we showed in Figure 7.4, differences between means are no longer significant when the overlap of the confidence intervals is larger than half a whisker. As can be seen in Figure 14.1, none of the differences are really clear (as we could expect from the p-value of .044). Even the difference between the young and the old adults now seems borderline. Below we will discuss how post-hoc tests can be used to obtain more precise information about the significance of the differences between the levels of a multi-level variable.

14

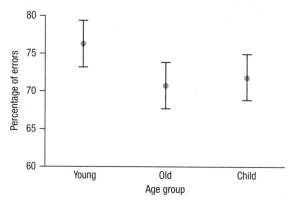

Figure 14.1 95% confidence intervals of the memory error experiment when the data from the primary school children are added.

To calculate the effect size and the likelihood ratio of a design with more than two conditions, we are confronted with a slight complication – an F-statistic with more than two degrees of freedom in the numerator has a less transparent relationship to $SS_{treatment}$ than the t-statistic or the F-statistic with $df_1 = 1$. To avoid this complication, we will work directly with the SS-values.

To calculate the **effect size**, Cohen's d-statistic is less interesting because it is limited to comparisons of two levels, which would require us to calculate three different d-measures (old v. young adults, old adults v. children, young adults v. children). However, the proportion of variance explained by the differences between the groups remains a valid index of the magnitude of the effect size. As we saw in Section 13.1.5, the proportion of variance explained in an ANOVA is called eta squared and given by the equation::

$$\eta^2 = \frac{SS_{treatment}}{SS_{total}}$$
$$= \frac{169.4}{822.0}$$
$$= .206$$

This means that 20.6% of the variance in the percentage of errors noticed by the participants (the dependent variable) is due to the differences between the three groups tested (the independent variable).

For the computation of the **likelihood ratio**, we have to go to the SS-values as well. An alternative definition of the likelihood ratio makes use of the variance explained:

$$\text{Likelihood ratio} = \sqrt{\left(\frac{\text{Variance unexplained by the null hypothesis}}{\text{Variance unexplained by the alternative hypothesis}}\right)^N}$$

in which N = the number of observations.

We can rewrite the equation as:

$$\text{Likelihood ratio} = \left(\frac{SS_{\text{total}}}{SS_{\text{error}}}\right)^{N/2}$$

$$= \left(\frac{822.0}{652.6}\right)^{30/2}$$

$$= 32.3$$

This means that the alternative hypothesis (of a genuine difference between the groups) is 32 times more likely than the null hypothesis of no reliable difference between the groups. Because the value is higher than 10, we can conclude that the alternative hypothesis is a better description of the situation than the null hypothesis (Chapter 7). Notice that the equation used here can also be applied to the situation in which only two conditions are compared with each other. (Verify this for the likelihood ratio of the old v. the young adults in the two-group analysis. Do you obtain 98, as we did in Section 13.1.5?)

14.1.2 Doing the analysis in SPSS

Running an ANOVA with three levels in SPSS is identical to the procedure in Chapter 13 for a design with two levels. SPSS automatically calculates the correct df_1 and df_2, and provides you with the required information.

We start by making a data file for the data listed in Table 14.1 (or by adding the childrens' data to those of the adults, if you still have that file on your computer). Remember that we define the Age_group in the first column. This can be done by using a label (young, old, child) or a number (1, 2, 3). The former notation is easier to understand; the latter allows you to run more types of analyses (and so you are likely to come to prefer it as you get more experience with SPSS). To retain the spirit of basic statistics, the label notation is used in this example. In the second column we enter the dependent variable (the percentage of errors noticed).

File	Edit	View	Data	Transform	Analyze

	Age_group	Errors	var
19	Old	71	
20	Old	70	
21	Child	74	
22	Child	72	
23	Child	59	
24	Child	79	
25	Child	77	
26	Child	66	
27	Child	68	
28	Child	81	
29	Child	74	
30	Child	69	
31			

14

Click on *Analyze*, *General Linear Model* and *Univariate* to start the between-groups ANOVA.

In the resulting dialogue box, put Errors in the *Dependent Variable* box ❶ and Age_group in the *Fixed Factor(s)* box ❷.

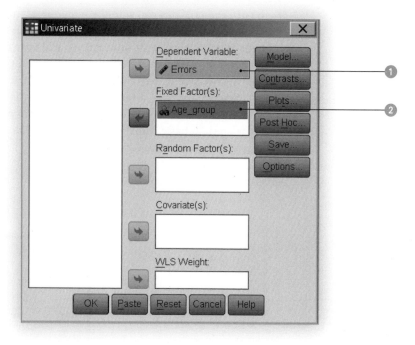

Also click on **Options** to get information about the means **1** and the effect size (partial eta squared) **2**.

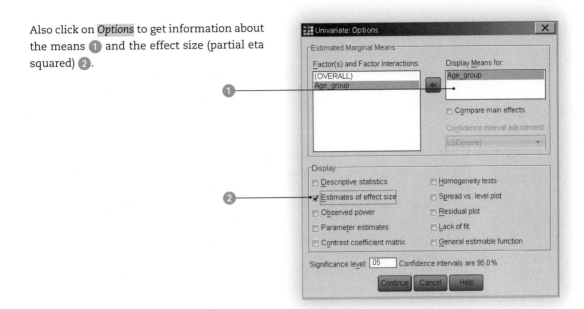

This gives you the following information, which you can easily relate to the ANOVA table and the further calculations we discussed.

Tests of Between-Subjects Effects						
Dependent Variable: Errors						
Source	Type III Sum of Squares	df	Mean Square	F	Sig.	Partial Eta Squared
Corrected Model	169.400ª	7	84.700	3.504	.044	.206
Intercept	159870.000	1	159870.000	6614.297	.000	.996
Age_group	169.400	2	84.700	3.504	.044	.206
Error	652.600	27	24.170			
Total	160692.000	30				
Corrected Total	822.000	29				
a. R Squared = .206 (Adjusted R Squared = .147)						

Age_group				
Dependent Variable: Errors				
Age_group			95% Confidence Interval	
	Mean	Std. Error	Lower Bound	Upper Bound
Child	71.900	1.555	68.710	76.090
Old	70.800	1.555	67.610	73.990
Young	76.300	1.555	73.110	79.490

The output tells us that the effect of age group is significant ($F(2,27) = 6.504$, $MSe = 24.17$, $p < .05$). It also gives us the 95% confidence intervals around the means.

14

14.1.3 Post-hoc tests for a between-groups design

A significant effect in a design with more than two levels immediately raises the question of which differences are significant and which are not. Given that we obtained $p < .05$ in our study with young and old adults and children, we want to know which conditions differ significantly from each other and which do not. We can assume that the biggest difference will be significant, namely that between young adults ($M = 76.3$) and old adults ($M = 70.8$), but will this also be the case for the difference between young adults and children ($M = 71.9$), and for the difference between old adults and children? We saw how the confidence intervals can help us to reach a decision in clear cases (Figure 14.1). Post-hoc tests are a more precise way to determine significance between pairs of means when the effects are borderline significant (as is the case for our example). An analysis of pairs of conditions is also called a **pairwise comparison**.

Intuitively, we may think that it is quite easy to compare two conditions. All we have to do is calculate a t-test for the difference between these two means. So, if we want to know whether the difference between the young and the old adults is significant, we simply run a t-test on these two conditions and see whether it is significant. To some extent, this is true but it is also cheating a bit. Suppose that, instead of comparing 3 groups, you compared hundreds of groups (10-year olds, 11-year olds, …, 100-year olds, males and females, tall and short people, people taking different degrees and so on). If you then calculated all t-tests between these groups (which would run into the tens of thousands) you are bound to find significant t-values even when at the population level there are no differences between the groups at all. Remember that, when we put $p < .05$, we accept a 5% chance that in reality (that is, at the population level) there is no difference, even though our t-statistic is significant. Now, if we run thousands of tests, we are bound to find many 'significant' values purely by chance.

Post-hoc tests correct for the fact that we have multiple t-tests. The simplest correction is the **Bonferroni test**. This test is based on the finding that if you divide the significance level by the number of tests you are running, the overall level of significance will never exceed the alpha value. Let's explain this with our example. In our study, three groups are compared to each other. This makes a total of three pairwise tests. If we now set the significance level of each test to $.05/3 = .0167$, then the p-level of the three tests together will never exceed $.05$. (As a matter of fact, it will usually be smaller.) Similarly, if we want to pairwise compare 100 levels of a variable (which would give us a total of 4950 tests), then setting the alpha-level of each individual test to $p < .05/4950$ or $p < .00001010$ ensures that overall we are not accepting erroneous 'significant' effects with a probability of more than 5% (i.e., overall $p < .05$). So, we create valid post-hoc tests by running t-tests and dividing the critical p-value (the alpha-level) by the number of comparison pairs.

However, most of the time the post-hoc tests in an ANOVA with independent groups of participants will not use the standard deviations of the individual conditions (as happens when we calculate the various t-tests), but will use the MSe of the ANOVA. In this way, post-hoc tests use all the information in the study to estimate the variability in the data. So, when we calculate the post-hoc test for the difference between the young and the old adults, we will not make use of the standard deviations of the young and the old adults, as we did for the t-test of independent samples (see Table 7.1). Instead, we will calculate the following test:

$$\text{Bonferroni young v. old adults} = \frac{M_{\text{young}} - M_{\text{old}}}{\sqrt{\frac{2 * MSe}{N_{\text{in cond}}}}}$$

$$= \frac{76.3 - 70.8}{\sqrt{\frac{2 * 24.17}{10}}} = 2.50$$

A t-value of 2.50 agrees with $p = .0187$ when df = 27 (that is, the degrees of freedom associated with MSe). This is slightly above the adjusted critical p-value we need for the Bonferroni test ($p = .0167$) so the difference between the young and the old adults will narrowly fail to reach significance.

Needless to say, the other two Bonferroni tests (between young adults and children, and between old adults and children) will also fail to reach significance. The respective values are:

$$\text{Bonferroni young adults v. children} = \frac{M_{\text{young}} - M_{\text{children}}}{\sqrt{\frac{2 * MSe}{N_{\text{in cond}}}}}$$

$$= \frac{76.3 - 71.9}{\sqrt{\frac{2 * 24.17}{10}}} = 2.00; \quad p = .0557 \text{ for } t(27)$$

$$\text{Bonferroni old adults v. children} = \frac{M_{\text{old}} - M_{\text{children}}}{\sqrt{\frac{2 * MSe}{N_{\text{in cond}}}}}$$

$$= \frac{70.8 - 71.9}{\sqrt{\frac{2 * 24.17}{10}}} = .50; \quad p = .621 \text{ for } t(27)$$

Statistical software packages such as SPSS use a simple trick to communicate the significance of a Bonferroni test more cogently to the users. They do not give information about the adjusted alpha-level and its implications for the post-hoc tests, they simply recalculate the p-values so that they have the same interpretation as the p-value of the F-statistic. This is done by multiplying the obtained p-value by the number of tests involved in the post-hoc comparisons. Indeed, another way of asserting that $p < .05/k$ for k tests is to make sure that $k * p < .05$ for each test. Applied to our example, SPSS will not inform the user that the value of the Bonferroni test of the difference between the young and the old adults is $t(27) = 2.50$, which is slightly below the critical value of 2.55 (the value of $t(27)$ for which $p = .0167$). Instead, SPSS will inform us that the significance value associated with the Bonferroni test is $p = .056$ (which is just short of significance). This value is obtained by first calculating p for $t(27) = 2.50$, which is .0187, and then multiplying this value by 3 (the number of tests). Indeed, $3 * .0187 = .056$.

Similarly, SPSS will inform the user that the p-value for the comparison of young adults v. children is .167. This value is obtained by calculating the p-value of $t(27) = 2.0$, which is .0557, and multiplying it by 3. Things go a bit pear-shaped for the comparison of the old adults and the children. Here $t(27) = .5$, with an associated p-value of .621. If we simply multiplied this probability by 3, we would get the impossible value of 1.863 (recall that the maximum value of p is 1.00). To circumvent this annoyance, SPSS informs the user that the probability cannot be estimated reliably and reaches the maximum of $p = 1.00$. (The p-values could be calculated more precisely but given that nobody is interested in p-values above .10, there is no incentive for SPSS to do so.) The advantage of recalculating the p-values is that the user can use the same criterion ($p < .05$) to interpret the outcome of post-hoc tests and the F-test.

The fact that none of the Bonferroni tests reaches significance in our example, despite the fact that the overall F-test narrowly made it ($p = .044$), may seem frustrating to you (as it usually is to researchers when confronted with such a situation!). How is it possible that the overall F-test is significant but none of the post-hoc tests are? The reason for this is that the Bonferroni test is slightly conservative. Remember we said that the overall significance level of k tests with a .05/k significance level cannot exceed .05, so that the overall p-level of the post-hoc tests will never be inflated, no matter how many tests are run. However, most of the time the overall p-level of k tests with .05/k significance level is lower than .05. Therefore, the Bonferroni test tends to underestimate the true p-value and requires slightly stronger evidence than is strictly necessary to reach statistical significance. As a result, it is very likely that no Bonferroni test will reach significance if the F-value just scrapes the significance threshold. The chances of such a situation increase as the number of conditions (and, hence, the number of comparisons) increase. This is one of the reasons why statisticians have come up with other, sharper, post-hoc tests (see the SPSS section below).

> **Tip** It is possible to find that no Bonferroni post-hoc test is significant in a design with more than two levels when the p-value of the F-statistic is slightly below .05. This is because the Bonferroni test is based on rather cautious assumptions. It illustrates that the difference between $p = .049$ and $p = .051$ should not be considered as a distinction between significant and non-significant, but as weak evidence in favour of the alternative hypothesis!

The 'contradiction' between the 'significant' F-value and the 'non-significant' Bonferroni tests once more reminds us that p-values in statistics are approximate values, which also have a confidence interval around them: $p = .049$ is not magically different from $p = .051$ because it crosses the .05-level! Both p-values suggest that there may be something at the population level, but that the evidence for it is rather weak. (In other words, you should be very careful about the conclusions you draw, as we saw in Chapter 7.) In this respect, the confidence intervals around the means (Figure 14.1) are more insightful because the confidence interval of $p = .051$ is only slightly larger than that of $p = .049$.

14.1.4 Doing the post-hoc tests in SPSS

The nice thing about SPSS is that you don't have to worry about the underlying reasoning. If you enter the right commands, you are guaranteed to get the desired outcome.

This example shows how to get the results of the Bonferroni post-hoc test in SPSS for our example. Start the commands to run a between-groups ANOVA:

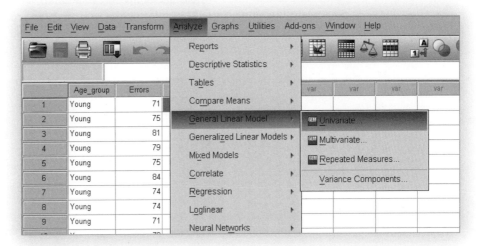

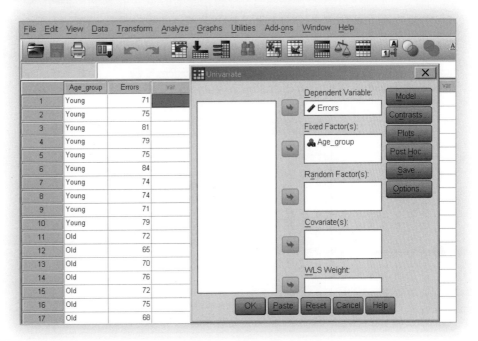

Click on *Post Hoc* to open the following panel:

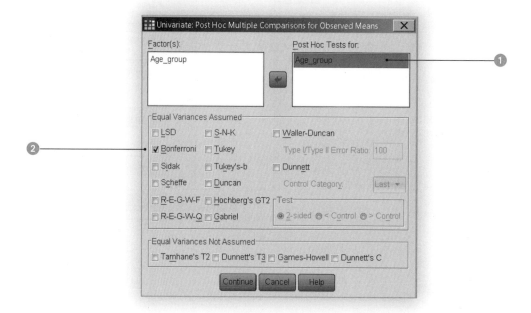

Use the central arrow to bring the Factor Age_group into the box entitled *Post Hoc Tests for* ①. This will activate the lower panels, from which you choose *Bonferroni* ②.
Click on *Continue* and *OK* to get the following output:

This outcome tells us that the difference between the young and the old adults narrowly failed

Multiple Comparisons							
Errors							
Bonferroni							
(I) Age_group	(J) Age_group	Mean Difference (I-J)	Std. Error	Sig.	95% Confidence Interval	
					Lower Bound	Upper Bound
Child	Old	1.10	2.199	1.000	-4.51	6.71
	Young	-4.40	2.199	.167	-10.01	1.21
Old	Child	-1.10	2.199	1.000	-6.71	4.51
	Young	-5.50	2.199	.056	-11.11	.11
Young	Child	4.40	2.199	.167	-1.21	10.01
	Old	5.50	2.199	.056	-.11	11.11

Based on observed means.
The error term is Mean Square(Error) = 24.170

to reach the .05 significance level ($p = .056$; see the column headed Sig). The output table further informs us that the difference between the young adults and the children was not significant either ($p = .167$), and that the difference between the old adults and the children was too small to be given a precise p-value (sig = 1.000). Underneath the table you notice that the statistics were based on mean square(error) as the error term, as we discussed in Section 14.1.3.

Learning check

SPSS contains many more *post-hoc* tests than the Bonferroni test. Try them to see which ones yield significance for the difference between young and old adults, and which ones do not.

14.2 Analysing a repeated measures study with more than two levels

An ANOVA also makes it possible to analyse repeated measures with more than two levels.

14.2.1 The calculations

To illustrate a repeated measure ANOVA with three levels, imagine that the therapy study we have been discussing throughout the book involved one more measurement one year later (that is, 1.5 years after the end of the therapy). Table 14.3 lists the data.

Table 14.3 Beck Depression Inventory scores of 12 patients before the onset of a therapy, 6 months after the end of the therapy, and 1 year later. Maximum score = 63. Any score above 30 is considered a sign of severe depression. A score between 5 and 9 indicates absence of depression.

	Before	6 months after	1 year later
patient 1	36	24	20
patient 2	27	18	19
patient 3	45	30	32
patient 4	25	8	7
patient 5	34	27	17
patient 6	28	14	15
patient 7	51	47	24
patient 8	30	31	29
patient 9	33	5	28
patient 10	47	27	20
patient 11	32	16	14
patient 12	26	23	3
	$M_1 = 34.5$	$M_2 = 22.5$	$M_3 = 19.0$

Although it is tempting to discuss the full calculations of the new design here, this is not really necessary. On the basis of the calculations given in Chapter 13 and what has been described in Section 14.1, it should not be overly difficult for you to do the mathematics yourself and to complete the ANOVA table. Try it! Do you obtain the results listed in Table 14.4? If not, have a look at our website (www.palgrave.com/pschology/brysbaert), where the procedure is explained step by step. Where did you go wrong?

Table 14.4 ANOVA table for the study of the efficacy of psychotherapy for depression when an extra measurement has been added 1 year later.

	SS	df	MS	F	p
Treatment	1586.0	2	793.00	17.814	.000025
Variability in treatment	979.3	22	44.52		
Differences between parts	2096.7	11	24.17		
Total	4662.00	35			

If we compare the results of this ANOVA to the one obtained in Chapter 13 (with two conditions only), we see that, although the F-value decreased because of the extra condition, the p-value is more 'significant'. This is mainly due to the higher degrees of freedom in the error term (22 instead of 11) as a result of the larger number of observations on which the effect is based.

The **degrees of freedom** are calculated as follows. For $SS_{treatment}$, $df = N_{levels} - 1$ (in which N_{levels} = number of levels of the independent variable). For $SS_{variability\ in\ treatment}$, $df = (N_{levels} - 1)(N_{in\ cond} - 1)$ (in which $N_{in\ cond}$ = number of observations in each condition or the number of participants). For $SS_{\text{differences between participants}}$, df remains the number of participants minus 1. Together the degrees of freedom add up to $N - 1$ (i.e., the number of observations minus 1).

To calculate the **confidence intervals**, we need SE_{mean} and the critical .05 t-value. The former is given by:

$$SE_{\text{mean}} = \sqrt{\frac{MSe}{N_{\text{in cond}}}}$$

$$= \sqrt{\frac{44.52}{12}} = 1.926$$

The critical .05 t-value depends on the df associated with the denominator of the F-test, i.e. df_2 or df_{error}. Given that $df_2 = 22$, $t(22, \alpha{=}.05) = 2.074$. This gives us:

lower limit confidence interval $M_1 = 34.5 - 2.074 * 1.926 = 30.51$
upper limit confidence interval $M_1 = 34.5 + 2.074 * 1.926 = 38.49$

lower limit confidence interval $M_2 = 22.5 - 2.074 * 1.926 = 18.51$
upper limit confidence interval $M_2 = 22.5 + 2.074 * 1.926 = 26.49$

lower limit confidence interval $M_3 = 19.0 - 2.074 * 1.926 = 15.01$
upper limit confidence interval $M_3 = 19.0 + 2.074 * 1.926 = 22.99$

These confidence intervals clearly indicate that the differences between the measurement before the therapy and the two measurements afterwards are significant, whereas there is no significant improvement between measurement 2 (after half a year) and measurement 3 (one year after measurement 2), as shown in Figure 14.2.

To calculate the **effect size**, there is no point in determining Cohen's d-statistic because this only compares two conditions. We have to make do with the proportion of variance explained, which is obtained by the following equation:

$$\eta^2 = \frac{SS_{\text{treatment}}}{SS_{\text{treatment}} + SS_{\text{error}}} = \frac{1586}{1586 + 979.3} = .618$$

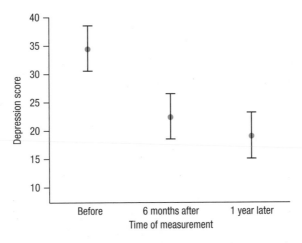

Figure 14.2 95% confidence intervals of the therapy study when the data from the later measurement are added.

The **likelihood ratio** is calculated as follows:

$$\text{Likelihood ratio} = \left(\frac{SS_{\text{treatment}} + SS_{\text{error term}}}{SS_{\text{error term}}}\right)^{(N_{\text{levels}}-1)*N_{\text{in cond}}/2}$$

in which N_{levels} = the number of levels of the independent variable or the number of conditions, and $N_{\text{in cond}}$ = the number of observations in each condition or the number of participants in the study. The reason we have to work with ($N_{\text{levels}} - 1$) is that, in a repeated measures design, we are actually looking at the deviation scores of the individuals rather than the raw scores. (For more information, see Bortolussi and Dixon (2003).) Recall that in a repeated t-test there is only one deviation score per participant (Table 9.2 and the accompanying discussion). Similarly, there are only two deviation scores per participant for three conditions or, in general ($N_{\text{levels}} - 1$) deviation scores for N_{levels} conditions. Applied to our example this gives:

$$\text{Likelihood ratio} = \left(\frac{1586 + 979.3}{979.3}\right)^{(3-1)*12/2}$$

$$= \left(\frac{1586 + 979.3}{979.3}\right)^{2*12/2}$$

$$= 104392$$

The very high value of the likelihood ratio agrees with the low p-value and shows that the significant effect becomes even more reliable due to the addition of an extra condition with a slightly larger difference relative to condition 1 (and a slightly lower standard deviation of the difference scores than in condition 2). Do not forget, however, that the hypothetical data presented in statistics books tend to idealise situations, so that you are unlikely ever to find something similar in real-life psychological research!

14.2.2 Doing the analysis in SPSS

Enter the data from Table 14.3 in SPSS.

| File | Edit | View | Data | Transform | Analyze | Graphs |

	Before	After	One_year	var
1	36	24	20	
2	27	18	19	
3	45	30	32	
4	25	8	7	
5	34	27	17	
6	28	14	15	
7	51	47	24	
8	30	31	29	
9	33	5	28	
10	47	27	20	
11	32	16	14	
12	26	23	3	

Start a repeated measures analysis by clicking on *Analyze*, *General Linear Model* and *Repeated Measures*.

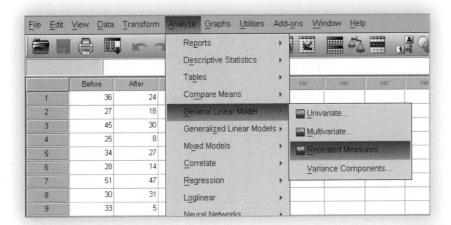

In the dialogue box, indicate that your are investigating the variable Effect_therapy with 3 levels.

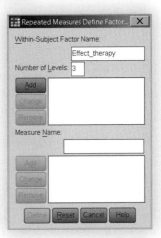

Click on *Add* and *Define* to get the following panel:

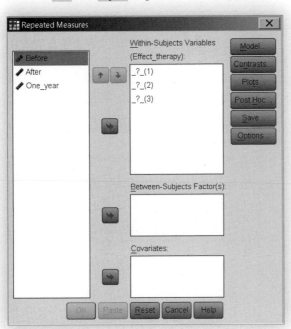

Enter the three levels in the panel *Within-Subjects Variables*.

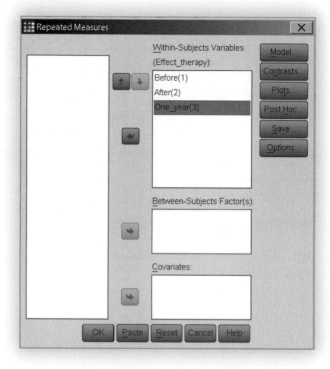

Click on Options to get information about the means and the effect size.

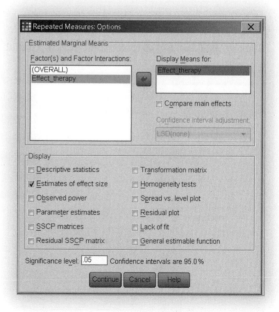

Click on Continue and OK to get the output.

Tests of Within-Subjects Effects

Measure: MEASURE_1

Source		Type III Sum of Squares	df	Mean Square	F	Sig.	Partial Eta Squared
Effect_therapy	Sphericity Assumed	1586.000	2	793.000	17.814	.000	.618
	Greenhouse-Geisser	1586.000	1.571	1009.467	17.814	.000	.618
	Huynh-Feldt	1586.000	1.787	887.304	17.814	.000	.618
	Lower-bound	1586.000	1.000	1586.000	17.814	.001	.618
Effect_therapy	Sphericity Assumed	979.333	22	44.515			
	Greenhouse-Geisser	979.333	17.282	56.667			
	Huynh-Feldt	979.333	19.662	49.809			
	Lower-bound	979.333	11.000	89.030			

Effect_therapy

Measure: MEASURE_1

Effect_therapy	Mean	Std. Error	95% Confidence Interval	
			Lower Bound	Upper Bound
1	34.500	2.509	28.978	40.022
2	22.500	3.283	15.273	29.727
3	19.000	2.495	13.508	24.492

This output tells us that the effect of the therapy was significant ($F(2,22) = 17.814$, $MSe = 44.515$, $p < .001$) with an effect size of $\eta^2 = .618$ (i.e., 62.8% of the variance is explained by the differences between the three conditions). We also get the mean values with confidence intervals. Unfortunately, these intervals in SPSS are wrong because they are the confidence intervals for a between-groups variable (see the previous section). You will have to calculate the confidence intervals by hand.

Be careful! Remember that the confidence intervals of the means in a repeated measures analysis are wrong in SPSS. The confidence intervals given are those of a between-groups design. In Section 14.2.1 we saw how you can use MSe to calculate the correct confidence intervals yourself.

14.2.3 Post-hoc tests for a repeated measures design

Confronted with a significant F-value for three or more levels, the first question we have, of course, is which levels differ significantly from each other. A pretty good idea of this can be obtained by looking at the confidence intervals, as shown in Figure 14.2. However, because the interpretation of confidence intervals tends to be rather crude, and because psychologists like to see p-values, it is always good to supplement your analyses with post-hoc tests.

As you may have become aware in Section 14.1.3, the exact calculation of the post-hoc test depends on the choices that have been made. Rather than discuss the various alternatives, we will try to discover the choices underlying SPSS, so that you have a better feeling of what is going on in this software package.

14

If we look at the SPSS output for the pairwise comparisons of the therapy example in Section 14.2.4, we get the following table:

Pairwise Comparisons

Measure: MEASURE_1

(I) Effect_therapy	(J) Effect_therapy	Mean Difference (I-J)	Std. Error	Sig.ª	95% Confidence Interval	
					Lower Bound	Upper Bound
1	2	12.000*	2.339	.001	5.405	18.595
	3	15.500*	2.344	.000	8.891	22.109
2	1	-12.000*	2.339	.001	-18.595	-5.405
	3	3.500	3.361	.960	-5.978	12.978
3	1	-15.500*	2.344	.000	-22.109	-8.891
	2	-3.500	3.361	.960	-12.978	5.978

Based on estimated marginal means.

*. The mean difference is significant at the .05 level.

a. Adjustment for multiple comparisons: Bonferroni.

This outcome shows that for a repeated measure, SPSS does not work with a pooled error term (such as MSe), but with different standard errors for each test. As a matter of fact, SPSS seems to simply calculate a repeated measures t-test for each pair of conditions and adjust the p-value according to the Bonferroni correction.

If we compute the various t-tests, we get:

Before v. after: $t(11) = 5.131, p = .000328$ (see Chapter 9)
Before v. one year later: $t(11) = 6.614, p = .000114$
After v. one year later: $t(11) = 1.041, p = .320216$

Multiplication of the p-values by 3 returns the 'Bonferroni adjusted' p-values of the SPSS output.

A review of the literature of multiple comparisons in a repeated measures design indicates that the choices made by SPSS are indeed good because the more traditional method of using the pooled variance tends to underestimate the p-values in repeated measures designs (that is, they will result in slightly more significances than warranted).

14.2.4 Post-hoc tests in SPSS

To do the post-hoc test in SPSS for a repeated measure design, we start by initiating the repeated measures analysis.

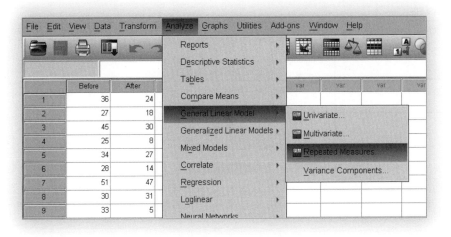

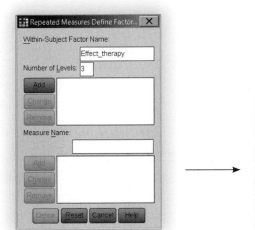

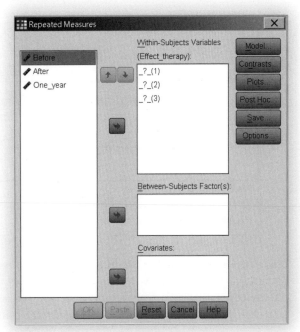

Surprisingly, if you click on *Post Hoc*, you will find out that it is impossible to check *Bonferroni*. This option only works for between-groups factors! Instead you have to click on *Options*.

To run a post-hoc test, you have to enter the repeated measure (Effect_therapy) in the *Display Means for* box ①. Then check the option *Compare main effect* ② and select *Bonferroni* in the pull-out panel ③.

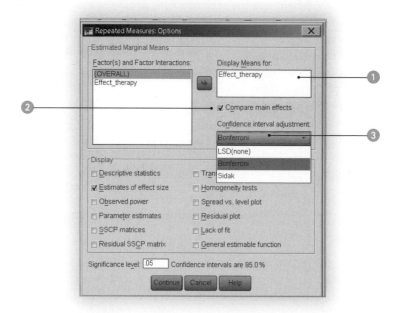

When this is done, click on *Continue* and *OK*, to get the following output.

Pairwise Comparisons

Measure: MEASURE_1

(I) Effect_therapy	(J) Effect_therapy	Mean Difference (I-J)	Std. Error	Sig.ᵃ	95% Confidence Interval	
					Lower Bound	Upper Bound
1	2	12.000*	2.339	.001	5.405	18.595
	3	15.500*	2.344	.000	8.891	22.109
2	1	-12.000*	2.339	.001	-18.595	-5.405
	3	3.500	3.361	.960	-5.978	12.978
3	1	-15.500*	2.344	.000	-22.109	-8.891
	2	-3.500	3.361	.960	-12.978	5.978

Based on estimated marginal means.

*. The mean difference is significant at the .05 level.

a. Adjustment for multiple comparisons: Bonferroni.

This panel informs you that the differences between before and after (level 1 v. 2) and between before and one year later (level 1 v. 3) are significant ($p = .001$ and $p \approx .000$ respectively), but that there is no difference between six months after the therapy and one year later (levels 2 v. 3; $p = .960$). This conclusion clearly agrees with the picture revealed by the confidence intervals (Figure 14.2).

14.3 Working with more than one predictor in a regression analysis

In Chapter 11 we saw how to calculate the Pearson product-moment correlation coefficient and the accompanying linear regression line that allowed us to predict one variable on the basis of the other. In many situations, however, we are confronted with more than one predictor variable. For instance, suppose we try to predict the heights of 20-year old students on the basis of their biological fathers and mothers. Several questions present themselves. First, is there a correlation between the height of the mother and the height of the student? Second, is there a correlation between the height of the father and the height of the student? But also, is there a correlation between the heights of the fathers and the mothers? Is the prediction of the student's height better when you know both the height of the father and the mother than if you know only one of them? And, finally, how do we calculate the resulting regression line? These are all questions within the realm of **multiple regression analysis**.

14.3.1 An example: predicting the height of a student on the basis of the heights of the father and the mother

Because the questions raised at the end of the previous paragraph are easier to handle when we have a hands-on example, Table 14.5 presents the data of 12 student-mother-father triplets.

Although it is tempting to do the full calculations here in order to determine the correlations between students, mothers and fathers, for the sake of brevity we will make use of the SPSS outcome.

Table 14.5 Heights of students and their mothers and fathers (in cm).

Student	Mother	Father
175	163	176
180	170	185
164	160	162
167	157	174
186	168	183
178	162	179
169	159	168
177	170	171
169	166	180
161	160	175
182	168	179
180	171	180

14

First, we enter the data:

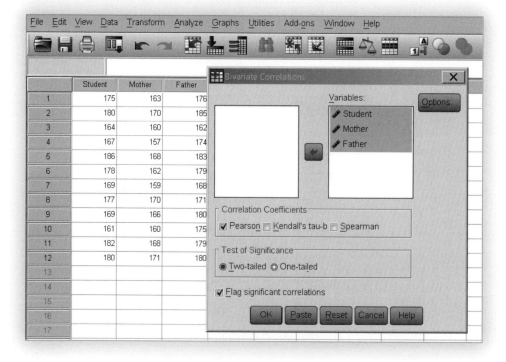

Then we calculate the correlations between the three variables. First, we click on *Analyze*, then on *Correlate* and *Bivariate*. We enter the three variables as follows:

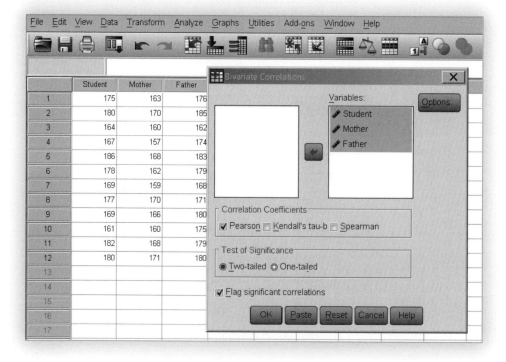

After clicking on OK, we get the following output table:

Correlations		Student	Mother	Father
Source				
Student	Pearson Correlation	1	.764**	.657*
	Sig. (2-tailed)		.004	.020
	N	12	12	12
Mother	Pearson Correlation	.764**	1	.589*
	Sig. (2-tailed)	.004		.044
	N	12	12	12
Father	Pearson Correlation	.657*	.589*	1
	Sig. (2-tailed)	.020	.044	
	N	12	12	12

**. Correlation is significant at the 0.01 level (2-tailed)
*. Correlation is significant at the 0.05 level (2-tailed).

If we first look at the correlation between the heights of the students and their mothers, we see that $r = .764$ ($N = 12$, $p = .004$). To find the regression line, we use the options Analyze, Regression, Linear and enter the dependent ① and independent variables ② as follows:

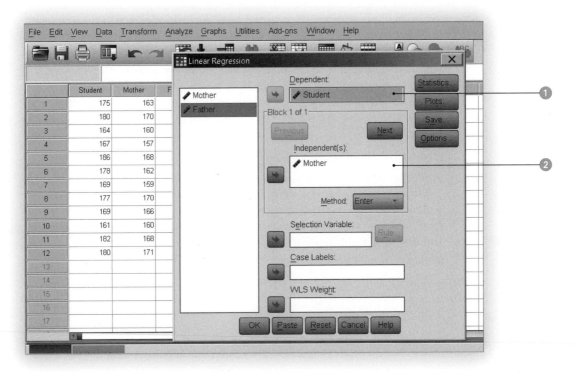

Clicking on OK, gives us the following output:

Model Summary

Model	R	R Square	Adjusted R Square	Std. Error of the Estimate
1	.764[a]	.584	.543	5.294

a. Predictors: (Constant), Mother

Coefficients[a]

Model		Unstandardized Coefficients		Standardized Coefficients	t	Sig.
		B	Std. Error	Beta		
1	(Constant)	-26.504	53.522		-.495	.631
	Mother	1.219	.325	.764	3.748	.004

a. Dependent Variable: Student.

The output allows us to write the regression line:

Predicted height of student = -26.504 + 1.219 ∗ height of mother

For instance, the predicted height of the first student (actual height = 175 cm) is −26.504 + 1.219 ∗ 163 = 172.2 cm. The percentage of variance explained by the regression line is R^2 = .584 (see the Model Summary panel), which equals the correlation squared ($.764^2$).

The correlation between the heights of the students and their fathers was also significant (r = .657, N = 12, p = .020, R^2 = .432). If we calculate the regression line, we find that:

Predicted height of student = 35.447 + .787 ∗ height of father

So, the predicted height of the first student is 35.447 + .787 ∗ 176 = 174.0 cm.

The two positive correlations indicate that tall students tend to have tall mothers and fathers, whereas short students tend to have short parents. At the same time, there seems to be an association between the heights of the mothers and the fathers: tall women tend to have tall partners (r = .589, N = 12, p = .044; see the screenshot with the outcome of the correlational analysis).

Given this constellation of data, we can ask ourselves whether the students' heights are predicted better when we combine the information on the mothers and the fathers. This is done by opening *Analyze*, *Regression*, *Linear* and entering both the independent variables Mother ❶ and Father ❷, as shown here:

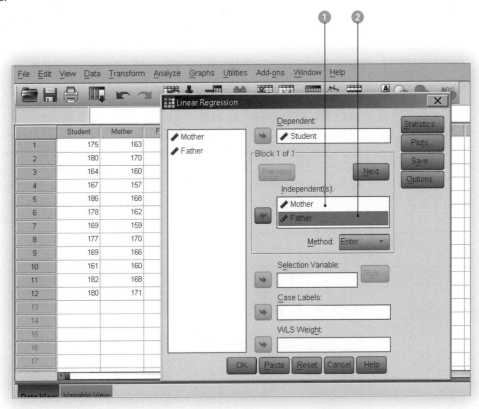

The outcome of this analysis (click on OK) is the following:

Model Summary

Model	R	R Square	Adjusted R Square	Std. Error of the Estimate
1	.806ᵃ	.650	.572	5.122

a. Predictors: (Constant), Father, Mother

Coefficientsᵃ

Model		Unstandardized Coefficients		Standardized Coefficients	t	Sig.
		B	Std. Error	Beta		
1	(Constant)	-44.306	53.560		-.827	.429
	Mother	.921	.389	.577	2.364	.042
	Father	.380	.292	.317	1.299	.226

a. Dependent Variable: Student.

From these tables, we see that no significant information is added when we know the height of the father in addition to that of the mother. The percentage of variance only increases from .584 to .650 (see the Model Summary panel), and the regression weight of the father's height is not significant ($p = .226$). This means that we can work with the regression line on the basis of the mothers alone. If the coefficient of the father had been significant, the regression equation would have become:

Predicted height of student $= -44.306 + .921 *$ height of mother
$+ .380 *$ height of father

which for the first student would have given a predicted height of:

$-44.306 + .921 * 163 + .380 * 176 = 172.7$

This example illustrates the basic approach of multiple regression analysis. It can easily be extended to more than two predictors. For instance, you might have spotted that an important variable in Table 14.5 has been overlooked. Given that males in general are taller than females, you would want to know the sex of the students and see whether the correlations still hold when this variable is entered, as shown in the following screenshot (1 = female, 2 = male for the variable Sex):

	Student	Mother	Father	Sex	var
1	175	163	176	1	
2	180	170	185	2	
3	164	160	162	1	
4	167	157	174	1	
5	186	168	183	2	
6	178	162	179	2	
7	169	159	168	2	
8	177	170	171	1	
9	169	166	180	1	
10	161	160	175	1	
11	182	168	179	2	
12	180	171	180	2	
13					

Now there are three possible predictors, which all correlate with the students' heights, as can be seen in the SPSS table.

Correlations					
Source		Student	Mother	Father	Sex
Student	Pearson Correlation	1	.764**	.657*	.689*
	Sig. (2-tailed)		.004	.020	.013
	N	12	12	12	12
Mother	Pearson Correlation	.764**	1	.589*	.390
	Sig. (2-tailed)	.004		.044	.210
	N	12	12	12	12
Father	Pearson Correlation	.657*	.589*	1	.479
	Sig. (2-tailed)	.020	.044		.115
	N	12	12	12	12
Sex	Pearson Correlation	.689*	.390	.479	1
	Sig. (2-tailed)	.013	.210	.115	
	N	12	12	12	12

**. Correlation is significant at the 0.01 level (2-tailed)

*. Correlation is significant at the 0.05 level (2-tailed).

When all three predictors are entered in the regression we see that R^2 increases to .779, but that only the mother's height reaches significance.

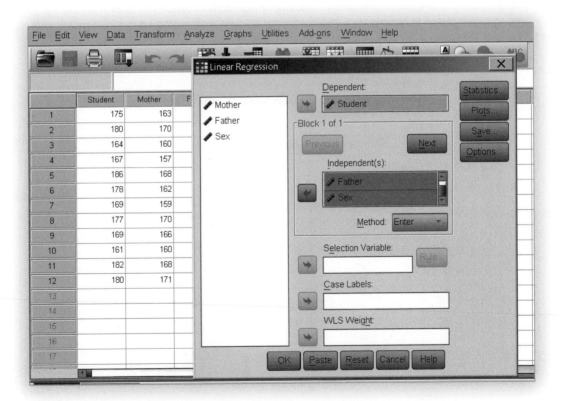

14

Model Summary

Model	R	R Square	Adjusted R Square	Std. Error of the Estimate
1	.883[a]	.779	.696	4.313

a. Predictors: (Constant), Sex, Mother, Father

Coefficients[a]

Model		Unstandardized Coefficients		Standardized Coefficients	t	Sig.
		B	Std. Error	Beta		
1	(Constant)	-2.275	49.099		-.046	.964
	Mother	.812	.332	.509	2.447	.040
	Father	.190	.261	.159	.726	.488
	Sex	6.218	2.871	.415	2.166	.062

a. Dependent Variable: Student.

One explanation may be that the father's height, due to its intercorrelation with the other variables, masks these variables. Given that this variable does not reach significance, it has to be ejected from the regression analysis anyway. Below, you see the outcome of the analysis when the predictors are limited to the student's sex and their mother's height. We see that R^2 remains very much the same (.765) and that now the two remaining predictors are significant.

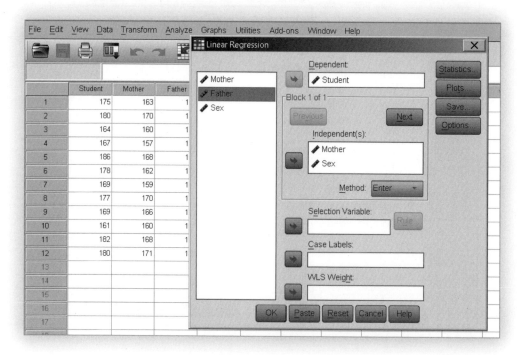

Model Summary

Model	R	R Square	Adjusted R Square	Std. Error of the Estimate
1	.874[a]	.765	.712	4.198

a. Predictors: (Constant), Sex, Mother

Coefficients[a]

Model		Unstandardized Coefficients		Standardized Coefficients	t	Sig.
		B	Std. Error	Beta		
1	(Constant)	10.352	44.698		.232	.822
	Mother	.932	.280	.584	3.327	.009
	Sex	6.917	2.632	.461	2.628	.027

a. Dependent Variable: Student.

The resulting regression equation is:

$$\text{Predicted height of student} = 10.352 + .932 * \text{height of mother} + 6.917 * \text{sex of student}$$

For the first student, this gives a predicted height of

$$10.352 + .932 * 163 + 1 * 6.917 = 169.2$$

(Notice that the prediction for this particular student seems to be worse than in the previous regressions because she is the second tallest girl.)

To know which variables to include in a regression analysis and which to exclude, it is best if you can start from a theory. For instance, on the basis of biological findings you might know that the height of a child in general correlates more with the mother's height than with the father's height; it then makes sense to enter the mother's height in the regression before the father's. If there is no theory, you can also look at the correlations and start with the variable that has the highest correlation with the dependent variable. (SPSS even has a procedure, STEPWISE, that does this automatically for you; see Brace et al.) A shortcoming of this technique is that sampling error may accidentally make a secondary predictor the most important in the results you collected. For instance, it could very well be that the fathers' heights correlate best with the students' in the data sample you collected, although in most other samples you would find that the mothers' heights are more informative. Then simply using the predictor with the highest correlation in your sample without further checking it on new data would give you the wrong impression of the relative importance of the predictor variables.

However, these are issues that are best left for a course dealing more extensively with mulitple regression analysis and other advanced statistics. For the moment, I think you've digested enough and it is time for us to go our separate ways. All the best with the rest of your career!

14

❓ 14.4 Answers to chapter questions

1 **What are post-hoc tests and when do you need them?**

Post-hoc tests are procedures to determine which levels of an independent variable differ significantly from each other. They correct for the fact that if you do multiple tests with a significance level of $p = .05$, you are too likely to find significance when in reality (i.e., at the population level) there is no difference. You need post-hoc tests when one of your independent variables contains more than two levels and has a significant main effect.

2 **What is a Bonferroni test?**

The Bonferroni test is one of the most often used post-hoc tests. It allows the researcher to assess the significance of pairs of conditions of a multilevel variable. This test is one of the simplest post-hoc tests and tends to be slightly conservative (that is, the resulting p-value is slightly higher than theoretically possible). When you find significance with the Bonferroni test, you can safely interpret the effect; when you narrowly fail to find significance, it may be interesting to try out another, more precise post-hoc test.

3 **What is a multiple regression analysis?**

A multiple regression analysis is a correlation analysis in which the dependent variable is predicted on the basis of one or more predictor variables. It is an extension of the Pearson correlation. The technique allows researchers to determine which predictors are significant and which not, and to find their regression weights. The analysis only works well if there is a linear relationship between the predictors and the dependent variable (see Chapters 11 and 12).

References

Anderson, C.A. et al. (2003) The influence of media violence on youth. *Psychological Science*, 81–110. Supplement S.

Belmont, L. and Marolla, E.A. (1973) Birth order, family size, and intelligence. *Science*, 182, 1096–1101.

Bertolussi, M. and Dixon, P. (2003). *Psychonarratology: Foundations for the empirical study of literary response.* Cambridge: Cambridge University Press.

Brace, N., Kemp, R. and Snelgar, R. (2009) *SPSS for Psychologists* (4th edn). Basingstoke: Palgrave Macmillan.

Cohen, J. (1988) *Statistical Power Analysis for the Behavioral Sciences.* Hillsdale, NJ: Lawrence Erlbaum.

Corkin, S. (2002) What's new with the amnesic patient H.M.? *Nature Reviews Neuroscience*, 3, 153–160.

Craggs, A. (ed.) (2004) *Family Spending: A Report on the 2002–2003 Expenditure and Food Survey.* Norwich: National Statistics.

Cumming, G. and Finch, S. (2005) Inference by eye: confidence intervals and how to read pictures of data. *American Psychologist*, 60, 170–180.

Dixon, P. (2003) The *p*-value fallacy and how to avoid it. *Canadian Journal of Experimental Psychology*, 57, 189–202.

Doll, R., Peto, R., Boreham, J. and Sutherland, I. (2004) Mortality in relation to smoking: 50 years' observations on male British doctors. *British Medical Journal*, 328, 1519–1528.

Dougherty, T.W., Turban, D.B. and Callender, J.C. (1994) Confirming first impressions in the employment interview: a field-study of interviewer behavior. *Journal of Applied Psychology*, 79, 659–665.

Durex (2003) *Global Sex Survey.* Retrieved 3 October 2003 from www.durex.co.uk.

Ekman, P. (1998) Epilogue, in C. Darwin, *The Expression of the Emotions in Man and Animals*, 3rd edn. New York: HarperCollins.

Galton, F. (1894) *Natural Inheritance.* London: Macmillan.

Glorieux, I., Coppens, K., Koelet, S., Moens, M. and Vandeweyer, J. (2002) *Vlaanderen in uren en minuten* [*Flanders in hours and minutes*]. Brussels: VUBPress (CD-rom).

Goho, J. and Blackman, A. (2006) The effectiveness of academic admission interviews: an exploratory meta-analysis. *Medical Teacher*, 28, 335–340.

Herrmann, J.A., Matyas, T. and Pratt, C. (2006) Meta-analysis of the nonword reading deficit in specific reading disorder. *Dyslexia*, 12, 195–221.

Hittner, J.B. and Swickert, R. (2006) Sensation seeking and alcohol use: a meta-analytic review. *Addictive Behaviors*, 31, 1383–1401.

Hyde, J.S. (2005) The gender similarities hypothesis. *American Psychologist*, 60, 581–592.

Kinsey, A.C., Pomeroy, W.B. and Martin, C.E. (1948) *Sexual behavior in the human male.* Philadelphia: Saunders.

Kinsey, A.C., Pomeroy, W.B., Martin, C.E. and Gebhard, P.H. (1953) *Sexual behavior in the human female.* Philadelphia: Saunders.

Kobayashi, K. (2006) Conditional effects of interventions in note-taking procedures on learning: a meta-analysis. *Japanese Psychological Research*, 48, 109–114.

Leaseplan (2002) *A survey of drivers' attitudes worldwide: global report 2002.* Leaseplan Corporation N.V.

Masson, M.E.J. and Loftus, G.R. (2003) Using confidence intervals for graphically based data interpretation. *Canadian Journal of Experimental Psychology*, 57, 203–220.

Meyer, G.J. et al. (2001). Psychological testing and psychological assessment: a review of evidence and issues. *American Psychologist*, 56, 128–165.

Noar, S.M., Carlyle, K. and Cole, C. (2006) Why communication is crucial: meta-analysis of the relationship between safer sexual communication and condom use. *Journal of Health Communication*, 11, 365–390.

Rabbitt, P. (2002) Consciousness is slower than you think. *Quarterly Journal of Experimental Psychology*, 55A, 1080–1092.

Salsburg, D. (2001) *The Lady Tasting Tea: How Statistics Revolutionized Science in the Twentieth Century.* W.H. Freeman and Company.

Singer, G.H.S. (2006) Meta-analysis of comparative studies of depression in mothers of children with and without developmental disabilities. *American Journal on Mental Retardation*, 111, 155–169.

Sitzer, D.I., Twamley, E.W. and Jeste, D.V. (2006) Cognitive training in Alzheimer's disease: a meta-analysis of the literature. *Acta Psychiatrica Scandinavica*, 114, 75–90.

Smeeth, L. et al. (2004) MMR vaccination and pervasive developmental disorders: a case-control study. *The Lancet,* 364, 963-969.

Stanton, J.M. (2001) Galton, Pearson, and the Peas: A brief history of linear regression for statistics instructors. *Journal of Statistics Education*, 9 (3). Retrieved 16 May 2007 from www.amstat.org/publications/jse/.

Thornton, A.E., Van Snellenberg, J.X., Sepehry, A.A. and Honer, W.G. (2006) The impact of atypical antipsychotic medications on long-term memory dysfunction in schizophrenia spectrum disorder:

a quantitative review. *Journal of Psychopharmacology,* 20, 335–346.

Torgerson, C.J., Brooks, G. and Hall, J. (2006) *A Systematic Review of the Research Literature on the Use of Phonics in the Teaching of Reading and Spelling.* Department of Education and Skills: Research Report RR711.

Twenge, J.M., Campbell, W.K. and Foster, C.A. (2003) Parenthood and marital satisfaction: a meta-analytic review. *Journal of Marriage and the Family*, 65, 574–583.

Vermeer, H.J. and van IJzendoorn, M.H. (2006). Children's elevated cortisol levels at daycare: a review and meta-analysis. *Early Childhood Research Quarterly*, 21, 390-401. meta-analysis. *Early Childhood Research Quarterly*, 21, 390–401.

Probabilities associated with the standard normal distribution

In each row, you first see the z-value, then the probability of a lower z-value and the probability of a higher z-value. For instance, for $z = -1.17$, $p(\text{lower}) = .1210$ and $p(\text{higher}) = .8790$.

If you want to calculate the two-tailed probability associated with a z-value (see Chapters 8 and 10), you have to take twice the smaller probability for that value. For instance, the two-tailed p-value for $z = -1.17$ equals $p = 2 * .1210 = .2420$. This is the probability of a z-value lower than -1.17 and higher than $+1.17$ (see Figure 7.6 and the associated discussion)

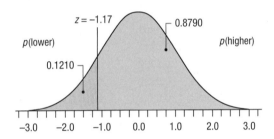

z	p(lower)	p(higher)	z	p(lower)	p(higher)	z	p(lower)	p(higher)
−3.00	0.0013	0.9987	−2.84	0.0023	0.9977	−2.68	0.0037	0.9963
−2.99	0.0014	0.9986	−2.83	0.0023	0.9977	−2.67	0.0038	0.9962
−2.98	0.0014	0.9986	−2.82	0.0024	0.9976	−2.66	0.0039	0.9961
−2.97	0.0015	0.9985	−2.81	0.0025	0.9975	−2.65	0.0040	0.9960
−2.96	0.0015	0.9985	−2.80	0.0026	0.9974	−2.64	0.0041	0.9959
−2.95	0.0016	0.9984	−2.79	0.0026	0.9974	−2.63	0.0043	0.9957
−2.94	0.0016	0.9984	−2.78	0.0027	0.9973	−2.62	0.0044	0.9956
−2.93	0.0017	0.9983	−2.77	0.0028	0.9972	−2.61	0.0045	0.9955
−2.92	0.0018	0.9982	−2.76	0.0029	0.9971	−2.60	0.0047	0.9953
−2.91	0.0018	0.9982	−2.75	0.0030	0.9970	−2.59	0.0048	0.9952
−2.90	0.0019	0.9981	−2.74	0.0031	0.9969	−2.58	0.0049	0.9951
−2.89	0.0019	0.9981	−2.73	0.0032	0.9968	−2.57	0.0051	0.9949
−2.88	0.0020	0.9980	−2.72	0.0033	0.9967	−2.56	0.0052	0.9948
−2.87	0.0021	0.9979	−2.71	0.0034	0.9966	−2.55	0.0054	0.9946
−2.86	0.0021	0.9979	−2.70	0.0035	0.9965	−2.54	0.0055	0.9945
−2.85	0.0022	0.9978	−2.69	0.0036	0.9964	−2.53	0.0057	0.9943

z	p(lower)	p(higher)	z	p(lower)	p(higher)	z	p(lower)	p(higher)
−2.52	0.0059	0.9941	−2.07	0.0192	0.9808	−1.62	0.0526	0.9474
−2.51	0.0060	0.9940	−2.06	0.0197	0.9803	−1.61	0.0537	0.9463
−2.50	0.0062	0.9938	−2.05	0.0202	0.9798	−1.60	0.0548	0.9452
−2.49	0.0064	0.9936	−2.04	0.0207	0.9793	−1.59	0.0559	0.9441
−2.48	0.0066	0.9934	−2.03	0.0212	0.9788	−1.58	0.0571	0.9429
−2.47	0.0068	0.9932	−2.02	0.0217	0.9783	−1.57	0.0582	0.9418
−2.46	0.0069	0.9931	−2.01	0.0222	0.9778	−1.56	0.0594	0.9406
−2.45	0.0071	0.9929	−2.00	0.0228	0.9772	−1.55	0.0606	0.9394
−2.44	0.0073	0.9927	−1.99	0.0233	0.9767	−1.54	0.0618	0.9382
−2.43	0.0075	0.9925	−1.98	0.0239	0.9761	−1.53	0.0630	0.9370
−2.42	0.0078	0.9922	−1.97	0.0244	0.9756	−1.52	0.0643	0.9357
−2.41	0.0080	0.9920	−1.96	0.0250	0.9750	−1.51	0.0655	0.9345
−2.40	0.0082	0.9918	−1.95	0.0256	0.9744	−1.50	0.0668	0.9332
−2.39	0.0084	0.9916	−1.94	0.0262	0.9738	−1.49	0.0681	0.9319
−2.38	0.0087	0.9913	−1.93	0.0268	0.9732	−1.48	0.0694	0.9306
−2.37	0.0089	0.9911	−1.92	0.0274	0.9726	−1.47	0.0708	0.9292
−2.36	0.0091	0.9909	−1.91	0.0281	0.9719	−1.46	0.0721	0.9279
−2.35	0.0094	0.9906	−1.90	0.0287	0.9713	−1.45	0.0735	0.9265
−2.34	0.0096	0.9904	−1.89	0.0294	0.9706	−1.44	0.0749	0.9251
−2.33	0.0099	0.9901	−1.88	0.0301	0.9699	−1.43	0.0764	0.9236
−2.32	0.0102	0.9898	−1.87	0.0307	0.9693	−1.42	0.0778	0.9222
−2.31	0.0104	0.9896	−1.86	0.0314	0.9686	−1.41	0.0793	0.9207
−2.30	0.0107	0.9893	−1.85	0.0322	0.9678	−1.40	0.0808	0.9192
−2.29	0.0110	0.9890	−1.84	0.0329	0.9671	−1.39	0.0823	0.9177
−2.28	0.0113	0.9887	−1.83	0.0336	0.9664	−1.38	0.0838	0.9162
−2.27	0.0116	0.9884	−1.82	0.0344	0.9656	−1.37	0.0853	0.9147
−2.26	0.0119	0.9881	−1.81	0.0351	0.9649	−1.36	0.0869	0.9131
−2.25	0.0122	0.9878	−1.80	0.0359	0.9641	−1.35	0.0885	0.9115
−2.24	0.0125	0.9875	−1.79	0.0367	0.9633	−1.34	0.0901	0.9099
−2.23	0.0129	0.9871	−1.78	0.0375	0.9625	−1.33	0.0918	0.9082
−2.22	0.0132	0.9868	−1.77	0.0384	0.9616	−1.32	0.0934	0.9066
−2.21	0.0136	0.9864	−1.76	0.0392	0.9608	−1.31	0.0951	0.9049
−2.20	0.0139	0.9861	−1.75	0.0401	0.9599	−1.30	0.0968	0.9032
−2.19	0.0143	0.9857	−1.74	0.0409	0.9591	−1.29	0.0985	0.9015
−2.18	0.0146	0.9854	−1.73	0.0418	0.9582	−1.28	0.1003	0.8997
−2.17	0.0150	0.9850	−1.72	0.0427	0.9573	−1.27	0.1020	0.8980
−2.16	0.0154	0.9846	−1.71	0.0436	0.9564	−1.26	0.1038	0.8962
−2.15	0.0158	0.9842	−1.70	0.0446	0.9554	−1.25	0.1056	0.8944
−2.14	0.0162	0.9838	−1.69	0.0455	0.9545	−1.24	0.1075	0.8925
−2.13	0.0166	0.9834	−1.68	0.0465	0.9535	−1.23	0.1093	0.8907
−2.12	0.0170	0.9830	−1.67	0.0475	0.9525	−1.22	0.1112	0.8888
−2.11	0.0174	0.9826	−1.66	0.0485	0.9515	−1.21	0.1131	0.8869
−2.10	0.0179	0.9821	−1.65	0.0495	0.9505	−1.20	0.1151	0.8849
−2.09	0.0183	0.9817	−1.64	0.0505	0.9495	−1.19	0.1170	0.8830
−2.08	0.0188	0.9812	−1.63	0.0516	0.9484	−1.18	0.1190	0.8810

z	p(lower)	p(higher)	z	p(lower)	p(higher)	z	p(lower)	p(higher)
−1.17	0.1210	0.8790	−0.72	0.2358	0.7642	−0.27	0.3936	0.6064
−1.16	0.1230	0.8770	−0.71	0.2389	0.7611	−0.26	0.3974	0.6026
−1.15	0.1251	0.8749	−0.70	0.2420	0.7580	−0.25	0.4013	0.5987
−1.14	0.1271	0.8729	−0.69	0.2451	0.7549	−0.24	0.4052	0.5948
−1.13	0.1292	0.8708	−0.68	0.2483	0.7517	−0.23	0.4090	0.5910
−1.12	0.1314	0.8686	−0.67	0.2514	0.7486	−0.22	0.4129	0.5871
−1.11	0.1335	0.8665	−0.66	0.2546	0.7454	−0.21	0.4168	0.5832
−1.10	0.1357	0.8643	−0.65	0.2578	0.7422	−0.20	0.4207	0.5793
−1.09	0.1379	0.8621	−0.64	0.2611	0.7389	−0.19	0.4247	0.5753
−1.08	0.1401	0.8599	−0.63	0.2643	0.7357	−0.18	0.4286	0.5714
−1.07	0.1423	0.8577	−0.62	0.2676	0.7324	−0.17	0.4325	0.5675
−1.06	0.1446	0.8554	−0.61	0.2709	0.7291	−0.16	0.4364	0.5636
−1.05	0.1469	0.8531	−0.60	0.2743	0.7257	−0.15	0.4404	0.5596
−1.04	0.1492	0.8508	−0.59	0.2776	0.7224	−0.14	0.4443	0.5557
−1.03	0.1515	0.8485	−0.58	0.2810	0.7190	−0.13	0.4483	0.5517
−1.02	0.1539	0.8461	−0.57	0.2843	0.7157	−0.12	0.4522	0.5478
−1.01	0.1562	0.8438	−0.56	0.2877	0.7123	−0.11	0.4562	0.5438
−1.00	0.1587	0.8413	−0.55	0.2912	0.7088	−0.10	0.4602	0.5398
−0.99	0.1611	0.8389	−0.54	0.2946	0.7054	−0.09	0.4641	0.5359
−0.98	0.1635	0.8365	−0.53	0.2981	0.7019	−0.08	0.4681	0.5319
−0.97	0.1660	0.8340	−0.52	0.3015	0.6985	−0.07	0.4721	0.5279
−0.96	0.1685	0.8315	−0.51	0.3050	0.6950	−0.06	0.4761	0.5239
−0.95	0.1711	0.8289	−0.50	0.3085	0.6915	−0.05	0.4801	0.5199
−0.94	0.1736	0.8264	−0.49	0.3121	0.6879	−0.04	0.4840	0.5160
−0.93	0.1762	0.8238	−0.48	0.3156	0.6844	−0.03	0.4880	0.5120
−0.92	0.1788	0.8212	−0.47	0.3192	0.6808	−0.02	0.4920	0.5080
−0.91	0.1814	0.8186	−0.46	0.3228	0.6772	−0.01	0.4960	0.5040
−0.90	0.1841	0.8159	−0.45	0.3264	0.6736	0.00	0.5000	0.5000
−0.89	0.1867	0.8133	−0.44	0.3300	0.6700	0.01	0.5040	0.4960
−0.88	0.1894	0.8106	−0.43	0.3336	0.6664	0.02	0.5080	0.4920
−0.87	0.1922	0.8078	−0.42	0.3372	0.6628	0.03	0.5120	0.4880
−0.86	0.1949	0.8051	−0.41	0.3409	0.6591	0.04	0.5160	0.4840
−0.85	0.1977	0.8023	−0.40	0.3446	0.6554	0.05	0.5199	0.4801
−0.84	0.2005	0.7995	−0.39	0.3483	0.6517	0.06	0.5239	0.4761
−0.83	0.2033	0.7967	−0.38	0.3520	0.6480	0.07	0.5279	0.4721
−0.82	0.2061	0.7939	−0.37	0.3557	0.6443	0.08	0.5319	0.4681
−0.81	0.2090	0.7910	−0.36	0.3594	0.6406	0.09	0.5359	0.4641
−0.80	0.2119	0.7881	−0.35	0.3632	0.6368	0.10	0.5398	0.4602
−0.79	0.2148	0.7852	−0.34	0.3669	0.6331	0.11	0.5438	0.4562
−0.78	0.2177	0.7823	−0.33	0.3707	0.6293	0.12	0.5478	0.4522
−0.77	0.2206	0.7794	−0.32	0.3745	0.6255	0.13	0.5517	0.4483
−0.76	0.2236	0.7764	−0.31	0.3783	0.6217	0.14	0.5557	0.4443
−0.75	0.2266	0.7734	−0.30	0.3821	0.6179	0.15	0.5596	0.4404
−0.74	0.2296	0.7704	−0.29	0.3859	0.6141	0.16	0.5636	0.4364
−0.73	0.2327	0.7673	−0.28	0.3897	0.6103	0.17	0.5675	0.4325

z	p(lower)	p(higher)	z	p(lower)	p(higher)	z	p(lower)	p(higher)
0.18	0.5714	0.4286	0.63	0.7357	0.2643	1.08	0.8599	0.1401
0.19	0.5753	0.4247	0.64	0.7389	0.2611	1.09	0.8621	0.1379
0.20	0.5793	0.4207	0.65	0.7422	0.2578	1.10	0.8643	0.1357
0.21	0.5832	0.4168	0.66	0.7454	0.2546	1.11	0.8665	0.1335
0.22	0.5871	0.4129	0.67	0.7486	0.2514	1.12	0.8686	0.1314
0.23	0.5910	0.4090	0.68	0.7517	0.2483	1.13	0.8708	0.1292
0.24	0.5948	0.4052	0.69	0.7549	0.2451	1.14	0.8729	0.1271
0.25	0.5987	0.4013	0.70	0.7580	0.2420	1.15	0.8749	0.1251
0.26	0.6026	0.3974	0.71	0.7611	0.2389	1.16	0.8770	0.1230
0.27	0.6064	0.3936	0.72	0.7642	0.2358	1.17	0.8790	0.1210
0.28	0.6103	0.3897	0.73	0.7673	0.2327	1.18	0.8810	0.1190
0.29	0.6141	0.3859	0.74	0.7704	0.2296	1.19	0.8830	0.1170
0.30	0.6179	0.3821	0.75	0.7734	0.2266	1.20	0.8849	0.1151
0.31	0.6217	0.3783	0.76	0.7764	0.2236	1.21	0.8869	0.1131
0.32	0.6255	0.3745	0.77	0.7794	0.2206	1.22	0.8888	0.1112
0.33	0.6293	0.3707	0.78	0.7823	0.2177	1.23	0.8907	0.1093
0.34	0.6331	0.3669	0.79	0.7852	0.2148	1.24	0.8925	0.1075
0.35	0.6368	0.3632	0.80	0.7881	0.2119	1.25	0.8944	0.1056
0.36	0.6406	0.3594	0.81	0.7910	0.2090	1.26	0.8962	0.1038
0.37	0.6443	0.3557	0.82	0.7939	0.2061	1.27	0.8980	0.1020
0.38	0.6480	0.3520	0.83	0.7967	0.2033	1.28	0.8997	0.1003
0.39	0.6517	0.3483	0.84	0.7995	0.2005	1.29	0.9015	0.0985
0.40	0.6554	0.3446	0.85	0.8023	0.1977	1.30	0.9032	0.0968
0.41	0.6591	0.3409	0.86	0.8051	0.1949	1.31	0.9049	0.0951
0.42	0.6628	0.3372	0.87	0.8078	0.1922	1.32	0.9066	0.0934
0.43	0.6664	0.3336	0.88	0.8106	0.1894	1.33	0.9082	0.0918
0.44	0.6700	0.3300	0.89	0.8133	0.1867	1.34	0.9099	0.0901
0.45	0.6736	0.3264	0.90	0.8159	0.1841	1.35	0.9115	0.0885
0.46	0.6772	0.3228	0.91	0.8186	0.1814	1.36	0.9131	0.0869
0.47	0.6808	0.3192	0.92	0.8212	0.1788	1.37	0.9147	0.0853
0.48	0.6844	0.3156	0.93	0.8238	0.1762	1.38	0.9162	0.0838
0.49	0.6879	0.3121	0.94	0.8264	0.1736	1.39	0.9177	0.0823
0.50	0.6915	0.3085	0.95	0.8289	0.1711	1.40	0.9192	0.0808
0.51	0.6950	0.3050	0.96	0.8315	0.1685	1.41	0.9207	0.0793
0.52	0.6985	0.3015	0.97	0.8340	0.1660	1.42	0.9222	0.0778
0.53	0.7019	0.2981	0.98	0.8365	0.1635	1.43	0.9236	0.0764
0.54	0.7054	0.2946	0.99	0.8389	0.1611	1.44	0.9251	0.0749
0.55	0.7088	0.2912	1.00	0.8413	0.1587	1.45	0.9265	0.0735
0.56	0.7123	0.2877	1.01	0.8438	0.1562	1.46	0.9279	0.0721
0.57	0.7157	0.2843	1.02	0.8461	0.1539	1.47	0.9292	0.0708
0.58	0.7190	0.2810	1.03	0.8485	0.1515	1.48	0.9306	0.0694
0.59	0.7224	0.2776	1.04	0.8508	0.1492	1.49	0.9319	0.0681
0.60	0.7257	0.2743	1.05	0.8531	0.1469	1.50	0.9332	0.0668
0.61	0.7291	0.2709	1.06	0.8554	0.1446	1.51	0.9345	0.0655
0.62	0.7324	0.2676	1.07	0.8577	0.1423	1.52	0.9357	0.0643

z	p(lower)	p(higher)	z	p(lower)	p(higher)	z	p(lower)	p(higher)
1.53	0.9370	0.0630	1.98	0.9761	0.0239	2.43	0.9925	0.0075
1.54	0.9382	0.0618	1.99	0.9767	0.0233	2.44	0.9927	0.0073
1.55	0.9394	0.0606	2.00	0.9772	0.0228	2.45	0.9929	0.0071
1.56	0.9406	0.0594	2.01	0.9778	0.0222	2.46	0.9931	0.0069
1.57	0.9418	0.0582	2.02	0.9783	0.0217	2.47	0.9932	0.0068
1.58	0.9429	0.0571	2.03	0.9788	0.0212	2.48	0.9934	0.0066
1.59	0.9441	0.0559	2.04	0.9793	0.0207	2.49	0.9936	0.0064
1.60	0.9452	0.0548	2.05	0.9798	0.0202	2.50	0.9938	0.0062
1.61	0.9463	0.0537	2.06	0.9803	0.0197	2.51	0.9940	0.0060
1.62	0.9474	0.0526	2.07	0.9808	0.0192	2.52	0.9941	0.0059
1.63	0.9484	0.0516	2.08	0.9812	0.0188	2.53	0.9943	0.0057
1.64	0.9495	0.0505	2.09	0.9817	0.0183	2.54	0.9945	0.0055
1.65	0.9505	0.0495	2.10	0.9821	0.0179	2.55	0.9946	0.0054
1.66	0.9515	0.0485	2.11	0.9826	0.0174	2.56	0.9948	0.0052
1.67	0.9525	0.0475	2.12	0.9830	0.0170	2.57	0.9949	0.0051
1.68	0.9535	0.0465	2.13	0.9834	0.0166	2.58	0.9951	0.0049
1.69	0.9545	0.0455	2.14	0.9838	0.0162	2.59	0.9952	0.0048
1.70	0.9554	0.0446	2.15	0.9842	0.0158	2.60	0.9953	0.0047
1.71	0.9564	0.0436	2.16	0.9846	0.0154	2.61	0.9955	0.0045
1.72	0.9573	0.0427	2.17	0.9850	0.0150	2.62	0.9956	0.0044
1.73	0.9582	0.0418	2.18	0.9854	0.0146	2.63	0.9957	0.0043
1.74	0.9591	0.0409	2.19	0.9857	0.0143	2.64	0.9959	0.0041
1.75	0.9599	0.0401	2.20	0.9861	0.0139	2.65	0.9960	0.0040
1.76	0.9608	0.0392	2.21	0.9864	0.0136	2.66	0.9961	0.0039
1.77	0.9616	0.0384	2.22	0.9868	0.0132	2.67	0.9962	0.0038
1.78	0.9625	0.0375	2.23	0.9871	0.0129	2.68	0.9963	0.0037
1.79	0.9633	0.0367	2.24	0.9875	0.0125	2.69	0.9964	0.0036
1.80	0.9641	0.0359	2.25	0.9878	0.0122	2.70	0.9965	0.0035
1.81	0.9649	0.0351	2.26	0.9881	0.0119	2.71	0.9966	0.0034
1.82	0.9656	0.0344	2.27	0.9884	0.0116	2.72	0.9967	0.0033
1.83	0.9664	0.0336	2.28	0.9887	0.0113	2.73	0.9968	0.0032
1.84	0.9671	0.0329	2.29	0.9890	0.0110	2.74	0.9969	0.0031
1.85	0.9678	0.0322	2.30	0.9893	0.0107	2.75	0.9970	0.0030
1.86	0.9686	0.0314	2.31	0.9896	0.0104	2.76	0.9971	0.0029
1.87	0.9693	0.0307	2.32	0.9898	0.0102	2.77	0.9972	0.0028
1.88	0.9699	0.0301	2.33	0.9901	0.0099	2.78	0.9973	0.0027
1.89	0.9706	0.0294	2.34	0.9904	0.0096	2.79	0.9974	0.0026
1.90	0.9713	0.0287	2.35	0.9906	0.0094	2.80	0.9974	0.0026
1.91	0.9719	0.0281	2.36	0.9909	0.0091	2.81	0.9975	0.0025
1.92	0.9726	0.0274	2.37	0.9911	0.0089	2.82	0.9976	0.0024
1.93	0.9732	0.0268	2.38	0.9913	0.0087	2.83	0.9977	0.0023
1.94	0.9738	0.0262	2.39	0.9916	0.0084	2.84	0.9977	0.0023
1.95	0.9744	0.0256	2.40	0.9918	0.0082	2.85	0.9978	0.0022
1.96	0.9750	0.0250	2.41	0.9920	0.0080	2.86	0.9979	0.0021
1.97	0.9756	0.0244	2.42	0.9922	0.0078	2.87	0.9979	0.0021

z	p(lower)	p(higher)	z	p(lower)	p(higher)	z	p(lower)	p(higher)
2.88	0.9980	0.0020	2.93	0.9983	0.0017	2.98	0.9986	0.0014
2.89	0.9981	0.0019	2.94	0.9984	0.0016	2.99	0.9986	0.0014
2.90	0.9981	0.0019	2.95	0.9984	0.0016	3.00	0.9987	0.0013
2.91	0.9982	0.0018	2.96	0.9985	0.0015			
2.92	0.9982	0.0018	2.97	0.9985	0.0015			

Critical values for the *t*-test

This table includes the critical *t*-values for $p < .05$ and $p < .01$ (both two-tailed) for different degrees of freedom. If $t_{obs} \leq -t_{crit}$ or $t_{obs} \geq t_{crit}$ then the *t*-test is significant. Otherwise, the observed t-statistic does not deviate enough from 0 to reach significance. For instance, when df = 1, both $t_{obs} = -15$ and $t_{obs} = +15$ are significant at $\alpha = .05$, but $t_{obs} = -10$ and $t_{obs} = +10$ are not significant.

df	$t_{.05crit}$	$t_{.01crit}$	df	$t_{.05crit}$	$t_{.01crit}$	df	$t_{.05crit}$	$t_{.01crit}$
1	12.706	63.657	28	2.048	2.763	55	2.004	2.668
2	4.303	9.925	29	2.045	2.756	56	2.003	2.667
3	3.182	5.841	30	2.042	2.750	57	2.002	2.665
4	2.776	4.604	31	2.040	2.744	58	2.002	2.663
5	2.571	4.032	32	2.037	2.738	59	2.001	2.662
6	2.447	3.707	33	2.035	2.733	60	2.000	2.660
7	2.365	3.499	34	2.032	2.728	61	2.000	2.659
8	2.306	3.355	35	2.030	2.724	62	1.999	2.657
9	2.262	3.250	36	2.028	2.719	63	1.998	2.656
10	2.228	3.169	37	2.026	2.715	64	1.998	2.655
11	2.201	3.106	38	2.024	2.712	65	1.997	2.654
12	2.179	3.055	39	2.023	2.708	66	1.997	2.652
13	2.160	3.012	40	2.021	2.704	67	1.996	2.651
14	2.145	2.977	41	2.020	2.701	68	1.995	2.650
15	2.131	2.947	42	2.018	2.698	69	1.995	2.649
16	2.120	2.921	43	2.017	2.695	70	1.994	2.648
17	2.110	2.898	44	2.015	2.692	71	1.994	2.647
18	2.101	2.878	45	2.014	2.690	72	1.993	2.646
19	2.093	2.861	46	2.013	2.687	73	1.993	2.645
20	2.086	2.845	47	2.012	2.685	74	1.993	2.644
21	2.080	2.831	48	2.011	2.682	75	1.992	2.643
22	2.074	2.819	49	2.010	2.680	76	1.992	2.642
23	2.069	2.807	50	2.009	2.678	77	1.991	2.641
24	2.064	2.797	51	2.008	2.676	78	1.991	2.640
25	2.060	2.787	52	2.007	2.674	79	1.990	2.640
26	2.056	2.779	53	2.006	2.672	80	1.990	2.639
27	2.052	2.771	54	2.005	2.670	81	1.990	2.638

df	$t_{.05crit}$	$t_{.01crit}$	df	$t_{.05crit}$	$t_{.01crit}$	df	$t_{.05crit}$	$t_{.01crit}$
82	1.989	2.637	89	1.987	2.632	96	1.985	2.628
83	1.989	2.636	90	1.987	2.632	97	1.985	2.627
84	1.989	2.636	91	1.986	2.631	98	1.984	2.627
85	1.988	2.635	92	1.986	2.630	99	1.984	2.626
86	1.988	2.634	93	1.986	2.630	100	1.984	2.626
87	1.988	2.634	94	1.986	2.629			
88	1.987	2.633	95	1.985	2.629			

Appendix C

Critical values for the Mann–Whitney U-test

This table includes the critical U-values for $p < .05$ (two-tailed) for different values of N_S and N_L (in which N_S = the number of participants in the condition with the least participants and N_L = the number of participants in the condition with the most participants). Be careful: U_{obs} has to be equal to or smaller than U_{crit} to be significant! So $U_{obs} = 0$ is significant at $\alpha = .05$ for $N_S = 3$ and $N_L = 6$, whereas $U_{obs} = 2$ is not.

N_1	N_2	$U_{.05crit}$	N_1	N_2	$U_{.05crit}$	N_1	N_2	$U_{.05crit}$
3	3	–	4	12	7	6	7	6
3	4	–	4	13	8	6	8	8
3	5	0	4	14	9	6	9	10
3	6	1	4	15	10	6	10	11
3	7	1	4	16	11	6	11	13
3	8	2	4	17	11	6	12	14
3	9	2	4	18	12	6	13	16
3	10	3	4	19	13	6	14	17
3	11	3	4	20	13	6	15	19
3	12	4	5	5	2	6	16	21
3	13	4	5	6	3	6	17	22
3	14	5	5	7	5	6	18	24
3	15	5	5	8	6	6	19	25
3	16	6	5	9	7	6	20	27
3	17	6	5	10	8	7	7	8
3	18	7	5	11	9	7	8	10
3	19	7	5	12	11	7	9	12
3	20	8	5	13	12	7	10	14
4	4	0	5	14	13	7	11	16
4	5	1	5	15	14	7	12	18
4	6	2	5	16	15	7	13	20
4	7	3	5	17	17	7	14	22
4	8	4	5	18	18	7	15	24
4	9	4	5	19	19	7	16	26
4	10	5	5	20	20	7	17	28
4	11	6	6	6	5	7	18	30

N_1	N_2	$U_{.05crit}$	N_1	N_2	$U_{.05crit}$	N_1	N_2	$U_{.05crit}$
7	19	32	10	14	36	13	18	67
7	20	34	10	15	39	13	19	72
8	8	13	10	16	42	13	20	76
8	9	15	10	17	45	14	14	55
8	10	17	10	18	48	14	15	59
8	11	19	10	19	52	14	16	64
8	12	22	10	20	55	14	17	67
8	13	24	11	11	30	14	18	74
8	14	26	11	12	33	14	19	78
8	15	29	11	13	37	14	20	83
8	16	31	11	14	40	15	15	64
8	17	34	11	15	44	15	16	70
8	18	36	11	16	47	15	17	75
8	19	38	11	17	51	15	18	80
8	20	41	11	18	55	15	19	85
9	9	17	11	19	58	15	20	90
9	10	20	11	20	62	16	16	75
9	11	23	12	12	37	16	17	81
9	12	26	12	13	41	16	18	86
9	13	28	12	14	45	16	19	92
9	14	31	12	15	49	16	20	98
9	15	34	12	16	53	17	17	87
9	16	37	12	17	57	17	18	93
9	17	39	12	18	61	17	19	99
9	18	42	12	19	65	17	20	105
9	19	45	12	20	69	18	18	99
9	20	48	13	13	45	18	19	106
10	10	23	13	14	50	18	20	112
10	11	26	13	15	54	19	19	113
10	12	29	13	16	59	19	20	119
10	13	33	13	17	63	20	20	127

Critical values for the Wilcoxon signed-ranks test

This table includes the critical W-values for $p < .05$ (two-tailed) for different values of N. Be careful: W_{obs} has to be equal to or smaller than W_{crit} to be significant! So $W_{obs} = 1$ is significant at $\alpha = .05$ for N = 7, whereas $W_{obs} = 3$ is not.

N	$U_{.05crit}$		N	$U_{.05crit}$		N	$U_{.05crit}$
6	0		21	58		36	208
7	2		22	65		37	221
8	3		23	73		38	235
9	5		24	81		39	249
10	8		25	89		40	264
11	10		26	98		41	279
12	13		27	107		42	294
13	17		28	116		43	310
14	21		29	126		44	327
15	25		30	137		45	343
16	29		31	147		46	361
17	34		32	159		47	378
18	40		33	170		48	396
19	46		34	182		49	415
20	52		35	195		50	434

Critical values for the Pearson and Spearman correlations

This table includes the critical correlations for $p < .05$ and $p < .01$ (both two-tailed) for different numbers of data pairs. If $r_{obs} \le -r_{crit}$ or $r_{obs} \ge r_{crit}$ then the correlation is significant. Otherwise, the observed correlation does not deviate enough from 0 to reach significance. For instance, when $N = 10$, both $r_{obs} = -.635$ and $r_{obs} = +.635$ are significant at $\alpha = .05$, but $r_{obs} = -.525$ and $r_{obs} = +.525$ are not significant.

Number of data pairs	$r_{.05crit}$ ($\alpha = .05$)	$r_{.01crit}$ ($\alpha = .01$)	Number of data pairs	$r_{.05crit}$ ($\alpha = .05$)	$r_{.01crit}$ ($\alpha = .01$)
1	—	—	30	.361	.463
2	—	—	35	.334	.430
3	.997	.9999	40	.312	.403
4	.950	.990	45	.294	.380
5	.878	.959	50	.279	.361
6	.811	.917	60	.254	.330
7	.754	.874	70	.235	.306
8	.707	.834	80	.220	.286
9	.666	.798	90	.207	.270
10	.632	.765	100	.197	.256
12	.576	.708	200	.139	.182
14	.532	.661	300	.113	.149
16	.497	.623	400	.098	.129
18	.468	.590	500	.088	.115
20	.444	.561	1000	.062	.081
25	.396	.505			

Appendix F

Critical values for the chi-square test

This table includes the critical χ^2-values for $p < .05$ and $p < .01$ (both two-tailed) for different degrees of freedom. If $\chi^2_{obs} \geq \chi^2 crit$ then the test is significant, else the differences between the observed and expected frequencies do not deviate enough to reach significance. For instance, when df = 4, $\chi^2 = 10$ is significant at the .05 level, but $\chi^2 = 9$ is not.

df	$\chi^2_{.05crit}$	$\chi^2_{.01crit}$	df	$\chi^2_{.05crit}$	$\chi^2_{.01crit}$	df	$\chi^2_{.05crit}$	$\chi^2_{.01crit}$
1	3.84	6.63	10	18.31	23.21	19	30.14	36.19
2	5.99	9.21	11	19.68	24.72	20	31.41	37.57
3	7.81	11.34	12	21.03	26.22	21	32.67	38.93
4	9.49	13.28	13	22.36	27.69	22	33.92	40.29
5	11.07	15.09	14	23.68	29.14	23	35.17	41.64
6	12.59	16.81	15	25.00	30.58	24	36.42	42.98
7	14.07	18.48	16	26.30	32.00	25	37.65	44.31
8	15.51	20.09	17	27.59	33.41			
9	16.92	21.67	18	28.87	34.81			

Appendix G

Critical .05 values for the *F*-test

The columns indicate the degrees of freedom in the numerator (df1, related to the treatment variable); the rows indicate the degrees of freedom in the denominator (df2, related to the error variance).

	1	2	3	4	5	6
1	161.45	199.50	215.71	224.58	230.16	233.99
2	18.51	19.00	19.16	19.25	19.30	19.33
3	10.13	9.55	9.28	9.12	9.01	8.94
4	7.71	6.94	6.59	6.39	6.26	6.16
5	6.61	5.79	5.41	5.19	5.05	4.95
6	5.99	5.14	4.76	4.53	4.39	4.28
7	5.59	4.74	4.35	4.12	3.97	3.87
8	5.32	4.46	4.07	3.84	3.69	3.58
9	5.12	4.26	3.86	3.63	3.48	3.37
10	4.96	4.10	3.71	3.48	3.33	3.22
11	4.84	3.98	3.59	3.36	3.20	3.09
12	4.75	3.89	3.49	3.26	3.11	3.00
13	4.67	3.81	3.41	3.18	3.03	2.92
14	4.60	3.74	3.34	3.11	2.96	2.85
15	4.54	3.68	3.29	3.06	2.90	2.79
16	4.49	3.63	3.24	3.01	2.85	2.74
17	4.45	3.59	3.20	2.96	2.81	2.70
18	4.41	3.55	3.16	2.93	2.77	2.66
19	4.38	3.52	3.13	2.90	2.74	2.63
20	4.35	3.49	3.10	2.87	2.71	2.60
30	4.17	3.32	2.92	2.69	2.53	2.42
40	4.08	3.23	2.84	2.61	2.45	2.34
50	4.03	3.18	2.79	2.56	2.40	2.29
60	4.00	3.15	2.76	2.53	2.37	2.25
70	3.98	3.13	2.74	2.50	2.35	2.23
80	3.96	3.11	2.72	2.49	2.33	2.21
90	3.95	3.10	2.71	2.47	2.32	2.20
100	3.94	3.09	2.70	2.46	2.31	2.19
200	3.89	3.04	2.65	2.42	2.26	2.14
500	3.86	3.01	2.62	2.39	2.23	2.12
1000	3.85	3.00	2.61	2.38	2.22	2.11

Index